£15.95

SELECTED LETTERS OF
E. M. FORSTER

SELECTED LETTERS OF

E. M. Forster

VOLUME ONE
1879-1920

EDITED BY

MARY LAGO AND P. N. FURBANK

COLLINS
8 Grafton Street, London W1
1983

William Collins Sons and Co. Ltd
London · Glasgow · Sydney · Auckland
Toronto · Johannesburg

Forster, E. M.
Selected letters of E. M. Forster.
vol. 1: 1879–1920
1. Forster, E. M.—Biography
2. Novelists, England—20th century—Biography
I. Title   II. Lago, Mary
III. Furbank, P. N.
823'.912   PR6011.O582/

ISBN 0 00 216718 2

First published 1983
Letters of E. M. Forster
© The Provost and Scholars of King's College, Cambridge 1983
Selection and editorial matter
© Mary Lago and P. N. Furbank 1983

Set in Garamond

Made and Printed in Great Britain by
William Collins Sons & Co. Ltd Glasgow

CONTENTS

Introduction   *page vii*
Editorial note   *xx*
Acknowledgements   *xxi*
Abbreviations   *xxiii*

BOYHOOD, 1879–97
Preface   1
Letters: [1883]–[1896?]   2

CAMBRIDGE, 1897–1901
Preface   15
Letters: [late November 1897]–[2 March 1900]   16

THE FIRST NOVELS, 1901–12
Preface   41
Letters: [2 March 1901]–19 June 1912   43

INDIA, 1912–13
Preface   137
Letters: 26 August 1912–13 April 1913   138

THE FIRST WAR, 1913–20
Preface   205
Letters: 4 October 1913–10 November 1920   206

Index   321

INTRODUCTION

The biography of writers, according to Proust in *Contre Sainte-Beuve*, is irrelevant to their works, because the works are created by a different person, and 'a book is the product of an other *me* than the one we display in our habits, in society, and in our vices'.[1] E. M. Forster held a view surprisingly close to this. According to his experience, the person or personality who sat writing his own novels was a quite distinct one. There was no call for awe or superstition about him; nevertheless he ceased to exist the moment someone entered the room. Thus there was not much profit in interrogating the person who replaced him, the one who confronted the intruder, about the 'sources' of his art. He once remarked to some interviewers: 'What was it Mahler said? "Anyone will sufficiently understand me who will trace my development through my nine symphonies"? This seems odd to me; I couldn't imagine myself making such a remark.' He added: 'It seems too uncasual.'[2]

We must not expect, then, when reading Forster's letters, any more than from reading his biography, to trace the creator to his lair, or to find 'explanations' of his novels. What we must look for, and certainly will find, is a man, and the man extends a long way on either side of the work. For one thing, his novels were written in aid of a philosophy, one which it might still be possible to live by—a coherent system, the heart of which was the saying fathered by Forster on Michelangelo: 'Death destroys a man: the idea of Death saves him.'[3] For another, he was a person of much fascination. By no means was he congenial to everyone: some found him unpatriotic, some found him drab and mousy, some found him spiky, some sentimental, some governessy. His friends, however, regarded him as quite special—most charming, and absorbingly interesting. They found him a very strong character in certain respects, and one whom if need be they could lean on; and to the end of his life he was capable of taking them by surprise.

He was very successful in the art of friendship—a fact he was conscious of himself. 'I was always determined to get to know you,' he wrote to Siegfried Sassoon (12 June 1922), 'and when I am determined I always succeed.' (We may see here a rebuttal of the view, trite and rather mistaken, that he was shy.) Again, in 1935, when he was due to have an operation on the prostate and thought he might very likely die, he wrote to R. C. Trevelyan's wife Bessie (9 December 1935) that all that worried him was leaving bits of his work unfinished, 'Odd in one who has always taken work so unconscientiously, but I fancy what has happened is that I have been so out-of-the-way happy in my friends, particularly of late years, and am never feeling that I have "missed" private relationships, which is what so many people of our age seem to feel.'

As a novelist he 'found' himself very early on—indeed one can date the event fairly precisely to the moment in 1902 when, at Ravello in Italy, he wrote 'The Story of a Panic'. He had known already that he had certain definite talents for observation and expression. Also he had created for himself an original *persona*— odd, demure and whimsical—which served him well in writing as in everyday life. What he now gained was assurance that his gift, or as he called it his 'equipment', *mattered*. The 'mattering' was in a sense philosophical. He had been born into a period when, under the influence of Flaubert and Zola, serious literature seemed committed to pessimism and to a mask of 'coldness'. For himself, by contrast, he realised that the impulse to write was bound up with optimism. That the universe was good, that life was worth living: these seemed the only messages that justified the effort of writing. Accordingly, during his early career, much of his thinking turned upon 'warmth'. The Keats of the *Letters* became a hero to him for this reason (was he, Forster wondered, almost the best person who had ever lived?). Similarly, he formed a critique of Walter Pater and Matthew Arnold that was based on their lack of warmth: 'dead and wounded flesh gives Pater the thrill he can never get from healthiness,' he remarked in his diary (2 May 1905); and in a letter to Malcolm Darling (12 August 1910) he defined the central weakness of Arnold as 'prudishness': 'I don't use the word in its narrow sense, but as implying a general dislike to all warmth. He thinks warmth either vulgar or hysterical.' In much the same spirit he pondered 'the sentimental' and decided to take his stand by it. 'What I want, I think, is the sentimental,' he wrote to R. C. Trevelyan (28 October 1905), 'but the sentimental reached by no easy beaten track . . . .' Early on in his life a quotation from Pindar's Eighth Pythian Ode became a sort of charm or talisman to him, and it catches the flavour of his optimism:

Man's life is a day. What is he, what is he not?
Man is the dream of a shadow. But when the god-given
    brightness comes
A bright light is among men, and an age that is gentle comes
    to birth.

(In his old age he kept a scrap of paper bearing this quotation tucked

into his barometer.) An entry in his *Commonplace Book* (p. 64)
brings the issue about optimism close to his novels: 'Two people
pulling each other into salvation is the only theme I find worth
while.' It is worth noting that in later years he grew rather sceptical
about this theme of mutual salvation. Thus it was an excitement to
him when, near the end of his life, he found himself writing a
powerful story ('The Other Boat') on the opposite theme, that of
mutual destruction.

In the stories 'The Road from Colonus' and 'The Story of a
Panic', written in the following year, his literary personality is, one
might say, already more or less defined and complete. The novel
Where Angels Fear to Tread, which followed in 1905, seems entirely
assured and wholly characteristic; and though the succeeding three
novels did not exactly come easily, for he revised copiously and
painstakingly, they came pleasurably—so that he said later in life
that he had never experienced 'the pains of writing'. Allowing for
modesty, his self-assessment was confident, and also very accurate.
He writes to R. C. Trevelyan (28 October 1905) that 'my equipment
is frightfully limited, but so good in parts that I want to do with it
what I can.' Many are the complaints and self-doubts that he
expresses to friends while writing *A Room with a View* and
Howards End, but, as we can sense, they are in no way agonised and
are no more than one would expect from an intensely self-critical
man.

It follows that these early and extremely productive years from
1902 to 1910 can, on the whole, be termed very happy ones. He had
chosen to remain tied to his mother and to his family circle, no
doubt somewhat in the spirit that, in a diary entry (20 July 1905) he
attributed to Keats: 'He is contented with his stuffy set, as he would
have been contented with anyone he knew long enough.' Moreover,
he and his mother had a great deal in common; she was a sharp
observer of people, with a witty and malicious turn of phrase, and
they shared innumerable private jokes. Nevertheless, it also meant
tying himself to that narrow Surrey *milieu* whose petty snobberies
and futilities his novels explore and castigate. Since Cambridge,
however, he had not felt a prisoner of this *milieu*. For one thing, he
had a talent for adapting himself to circumstances and making the
best of them. We observe it in his success, against all probability, in
the role of tutor to the young daughters of Elizabeth von Arnim.
These few months in Germany were intensely happy ones—in
which, incidentally, he quite got the upper hand over the
obstreperous 'Elizabeth'. The talent would reveal itself again, to
larger effect, in 1921 when, equally improbably, he became private
secretary to the Maharaja of Dewas.

That his happiness in the way of life just described would have
continued one may perhaps doubt. At all events, the happiness came

to an end rather suddenly and in a curious manner—to a considerable extent, because of the great public success of *Howards End*. The success seems to have paralysed him. Perhaps this puts it too strongly; nevertheless, almost immediately afterwards, he became convinced that he was 'dried up' as a writer. Soon the problem became intertwined with trouble with his mother. Her own mother had died early in 1911, and her grief and irrational remorse at this event—so at least Forster came to think—caused a permanent embittering of her temper. Before long he was fretting acutely at her attitude to him: her implied criticisms, her indifference to his writing, and her way of treating him as if he were still a child. 'I live the life of a little girl,' he complained to himself. However, he could see no immediate chance of escape—nor did his trip to India in 1912–13, fruitful as it was in all sorts of ways, provide one. He began an Indian novel but before long came to a halt, unable to believe in what he was doing.

It is from this moment, perhaps, that we should date that 'cramp' that many observers, among them D. H. Lawrence and Virginia Woolf, perceived in him. An important element in it, of course, was his growing sense of sexual frustration. Thus the leading events of his next few years may be said to have been, first, his encounter with Edward Carpenter and its sequel, the writing of his homosexual novel *Maurice*—a gesture that for a moment, but only a moment, seemed to spell liberation. Secondly, the coming of the war, which, or so he decided, made creation impossible for him. And thirdly, his achievement in war-time Egypt of a physical love-affair, with the young Egyptian Mohammed el Adl. Even this was not the emancipation that, at the time, he imagined it. Nevertheless, this affair and the war and the Amritsar Massacre of 1919 were decisive steps in his experience, so that when he resumed his pre-war Indian novel, it became a different and darker affair, also a more complex and powerful one, than as originally conceived.

It is interesting, in the Letters, to observe the development of Forster's attitude to the war. It was a war for which, like many of his Bloomsbury friends, he refused, as it were, to take responsibility, for he felt that it would bring out all that he most loathed—the conformism and hysteria—in English society. Thus, at its outbreak, it filled him with despair—but also with self-contempt, for he could sense his own attitude to be inadequate. Characteristically, he did not shelve the issue, nor did he attempt to shut his mind and imagination to the horror surrounding him. It haunted him, as one can perceive from the heartfelt and eloquent letters he wrote at this time, to Dickinson in particular. And eventually, by persistent reflection, he was led to a settled and thought-out position, *viz.* that the sole acceptable stance was an 'Alexandrian' philosophy of epicureanism and *fainéantisme*. 'For what, in that world of gigantic horror, was tolerable except the slighter gestures of dissent?' These were words he used in writing later of Eliot's 'Prufrock', a poem that he came upon with delight in 1917.[4] It was, for him, an 'Alexandrian' poem. And even more Alexandrian and more suited to his mood was, of course, the work of C. P. Cavafy. It makes a satisfying pattern in Forster's career that he should have discovered Cavafy at this moment; it was, too, an event of importance for literature. One of the things Forster was proudest of in his life was that, by his efforts, he got Cavafy's reputation launched in the English-speaking world. His letters addressed to Cavafy, or written on his behalf, show Forster in a most attractive light.

That quality in Forster of consistency, or persistency, is a feature of his letters generally. There were certain topics which, throughout his life, he strove to clear his mind upon, and in his letters he keeps coming back to them. For instance the question of how he should rate Henry James—so 'precious' and fatuous as James usually appeared to him, yet occasionally so astonishingly powerful. (He never finally settled this problem to his own satisfaction.) Again, what should he think of *asceticism*? He knew, or at any rate believed, that he was not an ascetic himself nor ever would be; but could asceticism not, all the same, be a viable way of life? He wrote to Siegfried Sassoon (11 October 1920): 'Point being that it can get things the other line of conduct can't, though it has to drop things as well. Which is "better" is to my mind a most uninteresting question: what I want is a survey of the two respective fields. Science can't give it because she stumbles off into sublimations and repressions, and misses the quality and intensity of the emotion, which (however produced) is the real index of a man's worth. Ascetics ~~have~~ live by emotion just as much as do their opponents.' He returns to the theme, or rather to the related one of self-abnegation, in a letter to William Plomer (19 January 1933), and in the same tone of enlightened curiosity, writing, 'To be humble and not self-seeking is difficult and I am not sure about it. I have a feeling that there are two ways of enforcing one's will, a good and a bad, as well as the way of abnegation. This last may be the best, but I cannot distinguish it from death.'

We spoke earlier of Forster's 'literary personality', but in fact he had a variety of literary personalities. The nimble and teasing essayist does not quite prepare us for the gravity or passion of some pages in the novels, nor does the severe truth-telling in his diaries fit very obviously with the fooling and chattiness common in his letters. Within the letters themselves there is enormous variety too. It was basic to Forster's attitude to letter-writing that he should write *for* the particular recipient and with that particular relationship in mind. Thus the letters from India (those at least that are printed in *The Hill of Devi*) were written very specifically for his mother and aunts (and to be handed round among them); they are coloured by this through and through. He in fact expressed some regret about this later. 'I was writing to people of whom I was fond and whom I wanted to amuse,' he noted in the preface to *The Hill of Devi*, 'with the result that I became too humorous and conciliatory, and too prone to turn remote and rare matters into suburban jokes.' The 'amusingness' was an ingrained habit. 'Someone told me, many years ago, that I was amusing, and I have never quite recovered from the effects,' he wrote to R. C. Trevelyan (5 July 1904). Many years later he wrote to G. L. Dickinson (26 February 1932) that 'it's now only in letters I write what I feel, not in literature any more, and I seldom say it, because I keep trying to be amusing.' None the less, as I have said, no two of his correspondences are alike. His business letters can be remarkably formal, even severe. His letters to Lowes Dickinson are generally serious, earnest, and high-minded, tackling the large ethical issues of which Dickinson was fond. Those to Forrest Reid are long 'literary' letters, such as he guessed Reid, who lived for writing and felt isolated, would find a support. Those to T. E. Lawrence have the enthusiastic and heated quality Lawrence's personality seemed to demand; and those to Sebastian Sprott are, almost invariably, in a vein of guileless 'camp' frivolity.

Forster was an indefatigable letter-writer. One is tempted to say a compulsive one, but that would not really be just. For his life was avowedly based on the assumption that friendship and personal relationships were, by far, the most important thing in life. It was based, further, on the belief that exclusive and possessive friendships were a bad thing—the aim should be to enjoy, and to keep up, very many friendships, of many different grades and intensities. How else, then, than by letters, for one not brought up to use the telephone, was such a life-pattern to be maintained?

Not all his letter-writing, naturally, was prompted by simple friendship. He was a keen writer to the press, especially on civil-liberty matters. For most of his life he used no literary agent; therefore, he conducted his own business correspondence. He took the duty of professional man of letters very seriously and would write fan letters to authors he admired—thereby, of course, often beginning a permanent friendship. (Not, however, in the case of A. E. Housman, whose reply to a fan letter was so fearful that Forster hurriedly threw it on the fire.) Again, friends might engage his interest on behalf of some unknown or unpublished writer, and then very likely he would write him or her letters, many pages long, of detailed criticism on the work. His campaign to launch Cavafy's reputation in Britain was a similar self-imposed labour, and that too involved a great deal of letter-writing. Every so often, out of the blue, he would feel obliged to write to some acquaintance a letter reproving some bit of behaviour. Nor was he above writing anonymous letters.

Certain traits in his letter-writing are instructive. For one who often wrote half-a-dozen letters of friendship a day, it was rare for him to repeat himself exactly, and the same idea or joke will be given a different twist according to the particular correspondent. Similarly, he will always notice and apologise, or in any case draw attention to the fact, if he happens to repeat a word or phrase in the same letter. Again, if he erases a word or phrase, he will usually (evidently on some truth-telling principle) deliberately leave the cancelled words legible.

In his letters, too, as much as in his novels and his essays, we are made aware of basic features of his prose style. One of these is that he possessed—that is to say made daily use of—an enormous vocabulary. The fact can be missed, for the point is not that he dallies with *recherché* words or loves bizarre constructions: it is that he is master, to an exceptional degree, of the middle range of words and expressions. He habitually employs precise words like 'vex, 'abased', 'fend', which could not be called old-fashioned or obsolescent, yet which lie rather on the margins of most people's vocabulary. He loved the *mot juste*, the standard-English word that is exactly, and not just nearly, the appropriate one; and sometimes in letters, for instance when trying to define his own state of mind or feelings, he will run through a series of words in quest of the right one.

Equally, he commanded an exceptionally wide range of common phrases and expressions. Here we approach a feature of especial importance to his prose style, as indeed to his conversation, namely a peculiar alertness to the words and expressions he is using. He did not deliberately avoid stock phrases but had a habit of catching sight of them, as it were, out of the corner of his eye, in the very act of using them, and of following out their literal implications, for comic or other effect. It was this habit that gave its special colour to his conversation, which presented a continual series of tiny verbal surprises: they were quite definite surprises, but so unobtrusive and fleeting as to be hard to remember or record. One meets with the same characteristic in his letters. For instance, he begins a letter to R. C. Trevelyan (5 July 1904): 'I'm very glad you like the story better than I expected: I think you do.' As we read this, we register a faint logical shock, too elusive to pin down. Such effects are very common in his letters, and one senses a connection with his habit, or principle, of being always faithful to his own metaphors, however apparently 'dead'—following them through as literally as possible, often ironically, and sometimes to profound imaginative effect. Thus, when writing to E. J. Dent (19 October 1908) about Lucy Honeychurch and Cecil in *A Room with a View*, he says: 'She may only be a peg to hang his artistic sensations on, but she is a peg he can't reach easily.' And again, writing to Florence Barger (18 March 1920) about a post in the Foreign Office recently offered to him, he tells her: 'It is, from the worldly aspect, a tremendous but a cavernous opening.' This habit represents one of his ways of finding new resources in the common stock of language, and his more explicit witticisms often derive from a similar source. They work by a mischievous looking-afresh at a trite or common word or phrase; for instance, when he remarks that 'Belfast stands at the head of Belfast Lough, and for no nonsense,' or re-defines white, in its racial sense, as 'pinko-grey'. How characteristic, too, that at some stage in his life he should have scrutinised the expression 'P.T.O.' and decided to drop the 'P' from it, finding it too absurd to say 'Please' to a close friend.[5]

A further tiny thing noticeable in his letters, again perhaps not quite without significance, is his habit of dividing up compound words, writing 'to morrow' or 'every body' for 'tomorrow' and for 'everybody'. It makes a striking contrast to Joyce, who had an equal passion for welding and combining words into elaborate Germanic compounds. We shall not offer to explain this trait of Joyce's, but as for Forster's, it may be thought connected with his tendency to separate and discriminate. He had quite a mania for discrimination and was deeply suspicious of wholes, or at least refused to have wholes imposed on him, for blanket approval. It was in this fashion that, on 'great' occasions, he would find his attention fatally caught by some trivial detail and puzzle over it, when he should have been receiving the classic impression. The same trait was the strength, and occasionally also the weakness, of his literary criticism.

P. N. Furbank

The project of editing E. M. Forster's letters was initiated in 1978. Since then, along with the usual conversational openers about work in progress, the same questions have been asked repeatedly, by specialists in literary and other areas of scholarship as well as by well-informed general readers. How did we locate Forster's letters? How many are there? How did we select those for inclusion here? Is his handwriting legible? And, finally, how did we divide the work between us?

We are grateful for such questions, for they indicate an interest in E. M. Forster (and in us), as well as a pleasing curiosity about procedures seldom described for readers, to many of whom lists of formal acknowledgements convey little idea of the problems—and the satisfactions—that letters bestow upon their editors. In fact, many of those procedures will be immediately recognisable to devotees of the detective story: the satisfactions for a mystery-solver are often the same as those for the editor who successfully transcribes and annotates a puzzling letter.

How did we find the letters? We began with the several thousands located by PNF in the course of writing *E. M. Forster: A Life*.[6] Many, such as those deposited in King's College Library, Cambridge, required no widespread search. Finding other letters to Forster's close friends and associates was a matter of contacting them or their heirs; with few exceptions the letters had been treasured and preserved with care. General requests published in newspapers and literary journals brought us letters to persons with whom we had not known Forster to have had contacts, or they brought us letters to known correspondents whose whereabouts had been unknown to us. Beyond these, detective work commenced. It comprised a search for missing persons and the piecing together of the most disparate bits of evidence. Information about recipients was assembled from oblique allusions in Forster's own correspondence, or in that of his friends; from newspaper archives; from telephone, business, and university directories; probated wills and property records, encyclopedias and dictionaries of every description; daily diaries, address books, journals; exhibition and auction catalogues; book reviews and fortuitous footnotes; and, above all, from a great deal of help by librarians and archivists, by our students and our colleagues. Sometimes an enquiry sent out like a dove upon the waters, to an address that seemed hopelessly obsolete, brought back unhoped-for results; one of the most touching of these is a 1948 letter from Forster to Herr Steinweg, his fellow tutor at Nassenheide in 1905. Herr Steinweg died more than two decades ago, but first his widow and then his daughter had cherished this earnest of good will after the terrible war years.

In fact there is—literally—a world of difference between Morgan Forster as correspondent and the notion of him as a mousy and rather old-fashioned gentleman shut away from the realities of the world, first in the suburbs of Hertfordshire and Surrey, then in his rooms at King's College. His own letters came back to England from the most far-flung locations: Egypt and India, Romania and Scandinavia, South Africa and the United States, and from every point of the Continental compass. The envelopes would have been a stamp-collector's delight. Everywhere he went, he struck up new correspondences, and some of these lasted for a lifetime. As his fame increased, and more and more of his works were translated into a considerable variety of foreign languages, increasing numbers of letters came from students and other interested readers, until, in his last years, the burden of writing answers (he seldom used a typewriter, and then not very well) became too much for him.

Recent years have seen a kind of diaspora of his letters, as many in private hands have passed into ownership by dealers, collectors, and research libraries. We have followed their paths as best we could, and at times it seemed that for every letter of Forster's traced to a new owner, we had written a dozen letters ourselves. This dispersal will continue; however, we have indicated the present owners of letters reproduced here, and the resourceful scholar will know how to trace them further.

How many letters did we find, and how did we make this selection? We certainly cannot claim yet to have found them all, but the total number, estimated here (and enumerated, as of its publication date, in *A Calendar of the Letters of E. M. Forster*) is in the neighbourhood of 15,000—an extraordinary production, even from a man whose time was his own, and for whom letter-writing was a principal channel of communication.[7] Sheer bulk ruled out, at the present time, a comprehensive edition, not only because of production costs that would make the price prohibitive for many readers and for smaller libraries, but because we wished, in this first extensive presentation of Forster as letter-writer, to avoid obscuring the outlines of his self-portrait with dinner-invitation and train-arrival notes. (Actually, the proportion of these, in so large an epistolary canon, is not excessive.)

We have tried, therefore, to choose letters for the numbered sequence according to quite specific criteria. In general, they should parallel the biographical outline, complementing and amplifying it. They should be representative of the various—and varied—circles of his friends and of the wide spectrum of his interests. They should reflect characteristic shifts of mood and the waxing and waning, or the enduring nature, of friendships. They should create for the reader a sense of the personal and the historical atmosphere in which Forster wrote his letters. They should also convey that special quality of wit and turn of phrase that gave uniqueness to his conversation and still brighten his letters, his fiction, and his essays. We hoped that our selection might help to trace the progress of his works, and in fact it is so faithfully reflected in his correspondence of most substance, that finding letters of the kind that will delight the literary historian and critic presented no problems at all: the problem was the reverse of difficult, for his letters often are in fact long-distance editorial conferences with literary friends—not only about his own work, but about theirs as well. Above all, the letters must make the reader feel the intensity of the convictions that motivated Forster as a professional and spiritual being: the importance of friendship, the evil of restrictions (such as censorship) on the free exchange of ideas, and the importance of all the arts as a bulwark for the desperate fragility of civilisation.

Here a word should be said about letters *to* Forster. He was, alas, not usually a letter-saver. This made our task easier with respect to quantity, for it reduced by half the amount of reading and sorting to be done. On the other hand, it deprived readers of that detached and pleasant experience of listening in on a perfectly candid conversation in which the speakers reveal their selves as in no other way—a legitimate eavesdropping, as it were, by the reader. Editions of letters that provide both sides of a correspondence make it possible to appreciate the points and counterpoint of exchanges for which no amount of annotation can be a perfect substitute.

For editors, the lack of complementary texts can be frustrating. Cross-correspondence among Forster's friends sometimes enabled us to piece together the facts of a situation. Sometimes the tone of his letter is a fairly safe indication of the nature of that received. For example, a full and genial response to queries about his works— their sources, structure, symbolism, and the like—probably means that the writer had asked questions that Forster considered intelligent and perceptive. An answer that is brief and brusque plainly implies that the petitioner has not done enough homework. Conjecturing the contents of a non-existent letter on the basis of a letter at hand, however, can leave editors at the end of a long limb too likely to be sawed off by critical hands. We have tried to avoid this peril, and we have not been altogether without supporting evidence, for he kept some letters that had special personal or professional importance for him (now in King's College Library), but these are, relatively speaking, only a handful in comparison with what we know to have existed. In letters and in diaries he mentions from time to time a fit of sorting and burning of old letters. One of the most extensive and most painful of these housecleanings occurred when he had to move out of West Hackhurst. He was not trying to cut himself off from the past. He was a man who lived in the present, but he liked to meditate on the past, and he kept many sentimental souvenirs of it. Obviously, in his room at King's he could not accommodate his mother's and his aunt's huge accumulations of family papers, but it is more likely that a principal reason for destroying so many letters was simple discretion. Many Edwardians felt that it was *wrong* to preserve friends' letters for posterity; G. M. Trevelyan, for example, certainly thought so. Letters were regarded as conversation, not as writing, to be read and then destroyed. (Is it possible that we now make such efforts to collect and preserve their surviving letters because they speak to us, in the age of telephone and telex, of a time when people *did* converse by letter, and the distinctive mark of a friend's hand upon the envelope was literally a personal touch?)

Are the letters legible? On the whole, yes, once one becomes accustomed to idiosyncrasies such as the final -*ly* that often seems only a vague downward flourish. In only a very few instances was it necessary to leave a word queried. Several characteristic spellings have been preserved because they are so consistent as to become hallmarks of his style. He used the archaic *ancle*, and the word appears frequently because his ankles were notoriously weak. Baedeker was written usually with the *æ* diphthong, and to the very end he wrote *aimiable* for amiable. His handwriting evolved early from a schoolboys' copybook hand to that which became uniquely his as an adult (facsimiles, pp. 20 and 50). Even as a boy he would put a firm full-stop (a period) after his signature. Later, he had a habit of running together initials and family name as EMForster. In the transcriptions, we have preserved these small but interesting characteristics, as also his childhood spellings.

How did we divide the work between us? Since PNF was in London, and ML was in Missouri for most of the year, we could not spurn modern technology altogether, no matter how much we wished to enter the mood of Edwardian letter-writers. We began by collecting duplicate sets of photocopies of all the letters that came to hand. We then read each sequence, independent of each other, choosing letters for possible inclusion. Almost invariably, we made the same choices. PNF then sent ML lists of 'rough-editing', biographical facts and suggestions of sources, while both of us continued to pursue elusive facts and oblique allusions. ML transcribed the letters and wrote drafts of the annotations. That much was managed under trans-Atlantic restrictions, with ML spending summers in England. A year's research leave from the University of Missouri then made possible the final work that had to be done together: proof-reading the transcriptions, revising the annotations, choosing illustrations, writing the biographical-critical and editorial Introductions. PNF wrote the sectional biographical prefaces and the extended biographical sketches in the annotations; ML compiled the Bibliography (Volume 2) and the Indexes (Volumes 1 and 2).

We are sorry that we could not include at least a sample of every one of Forster's correspondences. Many splendid letters had to be omitted because of an embarrassment of such riches. Some passages from those have been included, as appropriate, in the annotations. Sometimes a perfectly routine letter or note is illuminated by a sparkling sentence or two, and we have included some of these as well. We hope, finally, that we have presented Forster's self-portrait, if not literally in full, at least in eloquent outline and in full light.

Mary Lago

[1] Marcel Proust, *Contre Sainte-Beuve*, p. 157.

[2] 'The Art of Fiction I: E. M. Forster,' interview by P. N. Furbank and F. J. H. Haskell, *The Paris Review*, 1 (1953), 40.

[3] See note by Oliver Stallybrass in *Howards End* (Abinger Edition), p. 362: ' "Death destroys a man; the idea of Death saves him." This is adapted from Michelangelo, apparently via John Addington Symonds; see George H. Thomson, *The Fiction of E. M. Forster* (Detroit, Wayne State University Press, 1967), p. 286.'

[4] Forster, 'Some of Our Difficulties', *The New York Herald Tribune*, 12 May 1929, Section II, Books, pp. 1, 6; reprinted as 'T. S. Eliot,' *Abinger Harvest*, p. 278–81.

[5] A convention of British letter-writers: 'Please Turn Over.'

[6] P. N. Furbank, *E. M. Forster: A Life* (1977–8).

[7] Mary Lago, compiler, *A Calendar of the Letters of E. M. Forster*. Publication late 1984.

EDITORIAL NOTE

The letters in the numbered sequence are published uncut. In these and in the notes, letter-writers' own ellipses are indicated by unspaced points, as: ... ; editorial ellipses in the notes are indicated by spaced points, as: . . . . All material quoted has been taken, if not from original material, from photocopies or from microfilms. Where transcripts only were available, we have indicated that fact, with the source of the transcript.

Punctuation is Forster's own, except where meaning was in doubt; in such cases we have supplied missing punctuation in square brackets. We have kept idiosyncratic punctuation that does not affect meaning, such as the period outside the parenthesis after a parenthetical sentence. Square brackets always indicate editorial insertions. Where Forster himself used square brackets, we have substituted angle brackets. We have retained Forster's deletions where they plainly indicate value judgements or marked changes in the direction of his thought.

Our only liberty in transcription is the standardisation of date lines, in order to avoid confusion between British numerical usage, which places day before month, and American usage, which places the month first. Forster used a variety of forms. We have therefore used the British form and in all cases have written out the name of the month.

Many of Forster's essays, reviews, and fiction have appeared in collections or in translation. We have not attempted to list these in full in the notes; details are to be found in B. J. Kirkpatrick, *A Bibliography of E. M. Forster*. Reviews of Forster's writings are the subject of *E. M. Forster: The Critical Heritage*, edited by Philip Gardner, and in *E. M. Forster: An Annotated Bibliography of Writings about Him*, compiled and edited by Frederick McDowell.

ACKNOWLEDGEMENTS

This edition of E. M. Forster's letters was undertaken at the invitation of the Provost and Fellows of King's College, Cambridge, Executors of the Forster Estate. We wish to thank them for their helpful co-operation.

So many librarians and archivists in universities, libraries, and research institutions have given us so much generous assistance that restrictions upon space forbid our listing all of them by name here. However, we must mention Peter Croft and Michael Halls, at the Library of King's College, Cambridge; Jeaneice Brewer, at the University of Missouri-Columbia; Ellen Dunlap, at the Humanities Research Center, University of Texas at Austin; Mary Thatcher, at the Centre for South Asian Studies, Cambridge University; Lola Szladits, at the Berg Collection, New York Public Library; Elizabeth Inglis, University of Sussex; Roma Woodnutt, of The Society of Authors; Ian H. C. Fraser, at the University of Keele; Richard Bingle, at the India Office Library, London; David Burnett, at Durham University; Charles Mann and Sandy Stelts at Pennsylvania State University; and C. H. Knott, Registrar of Tonbridge School.

We are deeply indebted to others whose work on E. M. Forster, and whose willingness to answer our questions, have immensely facilitated our own work: to the late Oliver Stallybrass and to Elizabeth Heine, editors of the Abinger Editions of Forster's works; Philip Gardner, editor of the Critical Heritage volume on Forster; B. J. Kirkpatrick, compiler of the bibliography of his works; and Frederick McDowell, compiler and editor of the annotated bibliography of Forster criticism. Two books on Forster's India have also been invaluable: *E. M. Forster's India*, by G. K. Das, and *E. M. Forster's Passages to India*, by Robin Jared Lewis.

Answers to our questions and generous suggestions of specific sources have come to us from every part of the globe. We wish particularly to thank Mollie Barger, Dinah Barsham, Quentin and Olivia Bell, Alex Cain, Hugh Carey, Hilary Corke and the Hon. Shirley Corke, April Darling, Sir Rupert Hart-Davis, Lord Kennet, Jalil Ahmad Kidwai, Paul Levy, Russell Maylone, Masanari Morito,

Lucy Norton, Donald Parry, Jan Reynolds, William Rutherford, George Savidis, George Sassoon, George Spater, Brian Taylor, George Thomson, Julian Trevelyan, Philip Whichelo.

For permission to quote from unpublished materials other than E. M. Forster's letters, we wish to thank April Darling (Malcolm Darling), Lord Kennet (Hilton Young, Lord Kennet of the Dene), George Sassoon (Siegfried Sassoon), Julian Trevelyan (Robert C. Trevelyan), University Library, Cambridge (A. C. Benson), Gordon Spry (Edward Carpenter), Jane Wedmore (D. H. Collingham).

We wish to thank these owners of Forster's letters for their co-operation in making them available to us: Library of King's College, Cambridge; University Library, Cambridge; Trinity College, Cambridge; Berg Collection, Astor and Tilden Foundations, The New York Public Library; Fawcett Collection of the City of London Polytechnic and Learning Resources Service; Special Collections Department, Hofstra University Library; Humanities Research Center, University of Texas at Austin; The Beinecke Library, Yale University; Hugo Cole, Stephen Gilbert, Ashley W. Olmstead, George Sassoon, and George Savidis. For material supplied in the form of typewritten transcripts, we wish to thank Mollie Barger, Sir Rupert Hart-Davis, J. A. Kidwai, and the late Akbar Masood.

We wish to thank the Open University for financial assistance to PNF for purposes of photocopying, and the Research Council of the University of Missouri-Columbia for a travel grant to ML in 1979 and a Summer Research Fellowship in 1980. The English Department of that University provided the part-time services of two student assistants for most of one year: Orna Raz and Susanna Bullock delved tirelessly in the library, and the most tedious assignment never discouraged them. Finally, we wish to thank the University of Missouri-Columbia for ML's Research Leave in 1982–3, and St Edmund's House, Cambridge University, for her appointment as a Visiting Fellow, both of which helped us to complete this edition.

Mary Lago   P. N. Furbank

Cambridge and London
November 1982

ABBREVIATIONS

AH	E. M. Forster, *Abinger Harvest* (1936)
ALS	autograph letter, signed
ALU	autograph letter, unsigned
AMS	autograph manuscript
APC	autograph postcard
ASOF	E. M. Forster, *Arctic Summer and other fiction* (Abinger Edition, 1980)
ATr	autograph transcript
Berg	Berg Collection, New York Public Library
CB	E. M. Forster, *Commonplace Book* (Facsimile Edition, 1979)
COOS	E. M. Forster, *The Celestial Omnibus and Other Stories* (1911)
CSAS	Centre of South Asian Studies, Cambridge University
DNB	*Dictionary of National Biography*
EMF	P. N. Furbank, *E. M. Forster: A Life* (1968–69)
EMOS	E. M. Forster, *The Eternal Moment and Other Stories* (1928)
GLD	E. M. Forster, *Goldsworthy Lowes Dickinson* (Abinger Edition, 1973)
HD	E. M. Forster, *The Hill of Devi* (Abinger Edition, 1983)
HE	E. M. Forster, *Howards End* (Abinger Edition, 1973)
HRC	Humanities Research Center, University of Texas at Austin
IE	*Imperfect Encounter: Letters of William Rothenstein and Rabindranath Tagore, 1911–1941* (1972)
KCC	Library of King's College, Cambridge
Kirkpatrick	B. J. Kirkpatrick, *A Bibliography of E. M. Forster* (2nd ed., revised, 1968)
LJ	E. M. Forster, *The Longest Journey* (1907)
LTC	E. M. Forster, *The Life to Come & Other Stories* (Abinger Edition, 1972)

MM	William Rothenstein, *Men and Memories* (abridged edition, 1978)
MS	manuscript
[N.d.]	no date
[N.p.]	no place
PI	E. M. Forster, *A Passage to India* (Abinger Edition, 1978)
RV	E. M. Forster, *A Room with a View* (Abinger Edition, 1977)
TCC	Library of Trinity College, Cambridge
TCD	E. M. Forster, *Two Cheers for Democracy* (Abinger Edition, 1972)
TLS	*The Times Literary Supplement* (London)
TLS	typewritten letter, signed
TLTS	typewritten letter, typewritten signature
TS	typescript
TTr	typewritten transcript
WAFT	E. M. Forster, *Where Angels Fear to Tread* (Abinger Edition, 1975)

BOYHOOD, 1879–97

Edward Morgan Forster was born on 1 January 1879. His father, Edward Morgan Llewellyn Forster (1847–80), an architect, was the son of an Irish clergyman, Charles Forster (1789–1871), Rector of Stisted in Essex, and of Laura Thornton (1808–69), wealthy daughter of Henry Thornton of Clapham Sect fame. His mother, Alice Clara ('Lily') Whichelo (1855–1945), was one of the ten children of the artist and art-master Henry Mayle Whichelo and Louisa Graham. Lily Whichelo became a protégée of Laura's unmarried elder sister Marianne (1797–1887), who still lived at Clapham. Through her influence and that of the novelist's aunt Laura Mary Forster, Lily obtained a post as governess in the household of the first Lord Farrer in Abinger Hammer, Surrey. It was here that she met Edward Forster, and they were married in 1877.

Edward died of consumption in 1880, and Lily, after sojourning at the houses of various friends, moved in March 1883 to 'Rooksnest' in Stevenage, a house much loved by E. M. Forster and the model for 'Howards End' in the novel of that name. He was an adored only child and spent his boyhood, he said later, in 'a haze of old ladies'. There were his Whichelo aunts Georgiana (Georgie), Mary Eleanor (Nellie), and Rosalie (Rosie—who was his favourite); his grandmother Louisa, to whom he was greatly attached; his mother's great friend Mary ('Maimie') Aylward, who was a Thornton connection by her first marriage; Maimie's sister Kate and half-sister Maggie Preston, who lived in the Isle of Wight; his aunt Laura Mary Forster, in whose house at Abinger Hammer, 'West Hackhurst' (designed by his father), the future novelist and his mother often stayed; and his great-aunt Marianne Thornton, with whom they also sometimes stayed, and who at her death in 1887 left him £8,000—a legacy that, he was to say, represented his 'financial salvation' and enabled him to travel and write. His biography of her, *Marianne Thornton*, published in 1956, was an acknowledgement of this debt to her.

His education began under an Irish tutor named Augustus Hervey; then in 1890 he was sent to the preparatory school, Kent House, in Eastbourne; and in 1893, after a brief and ignominious spell at a Stevenage school called 'The Grange', he was sent to Tonbridge School. His mother, fearing that he would be unhappy as a boarder, moved to Tonbridge so that he could attend as a day boy. He disliked his schooldays but achieved a certain amount of academic success and secured a place at King's College, Cambridge, to which he went in October 1897.

1   To Alice Clara Forster

[1883. West Hackhurst, Abinger Hammer]

My dear mamma—I've a garden of roses and all sorts of things and ivy and marguerites and red lobelia and geraniums like that———— that's my wheelbarrow——that's a weed. I pull it up first and put it in the wheelbarrow. Aunt Laura and me went in the wood behind the hammock—that we swing in.[2] Mr Farrer rolled down the steps with me and I rolled down.[3]

Baby

ALS/ATr by EMF:[1] KCC

[1] EMF transcribed this, his first letter, as conclusion (f. 57) to his manuscript memoir, 'West Hackhurst: A Surrey Ramble', ([c. 1947] KCC). 'It [the letter] is not in my handwriting,' he explained, 'for my age was three and a half at the time. My aunt took it down at my dictation to send to my mother, and she has illustrated it with some little sketches.'

[2] Laura Mary Forster (1839–1924) was EMF's paternal aunt. She became friendly in childhood with Katherine Euphemia ('Effy') Wedgwood (1839–1931) of the family of master-potters. After nursing several of her own brothers and sisters while they were dying of consumption, Laura moved to Abinger Hammer in Surrey, to be near Effy, now married to the first Lord Farrer and living in Abinger Hall. Laura built a house, 'West Hackhurst', designed by Forster's father, on land leased from the Farrers. From his childhood onward, Morgan and his mother were frequent visitors there. Laura liked to 'use her influence' on behalf of his career, although he was of the opinion that she exaggerated the extent of that influence. About 1900, she took permanently to her bed, probably more for psychological than for physical reasons, but from that position of vantage she continued a vigorous conduct of her affairs. She was a beaky-nosed, autocratic woman, whom Forster respected but did not love. His mother too was kept on the defensive with her, since Laura had opposed her marriage, but at the very end of Laura's life they had a curious reconciliation.

[3] This was Thomas Cecil Farrer, 2nd Baron Farrer (1859–1940).

2   To Louisa Whichelo[1]

Rooks' nest [Stevenage, Hertfordshire]
March 1886

My dear grandmamma
    I have finished the copybook I was writing when you were here
    We have a peacock butterfly alive. it feeds on a pink hyacinth.
    I have had your letter.
    puppy's malady is better. that is a rhyme
    I am glad Tim Tot is not gone as I should like to see him

We have made a lot of flags to stick in the garden.[2] I am your dear

Morgan

ALS: KCC

[1] Louisa Whichelo (née Graham) (1827–1911), EMF's maternal grandmother, married Henry Mayle Whichelo (1826–67). After being widowed, she brought up her large family in straitened circumstances and therefore welcomed the adoption of EMF's mother, 'Lily', by their wealthy Clapham neighbour Marianne Thornton. From the 1890s onward, Louisa lived with her daughters Rosie, Nellie, and Georgie in Werter Road, Putney. She was a genial, downright, and amusing woman, and EMF, who adored her (as she did him), based Mrs Honeychurch in *A Room with a View* on her.
[2] The flags in the garden are unexplained.

3 To Mary Aylward[1]

Rooks' nest [Stevenage, Hertfordshire]
18 June 1886

Dear Mamie

Thank you for the strawberries and do you know we have an aquarium and some tadpoles and water-snails in it. Aunt Laura has been here. Emma and I went for a walk and found a most lovely pond, the trees drooped over it. How does your garden look, and how is Many?[2]

I am
your dear
Morgan.

ALS: KCC

[1] Mary Maria ('Maimie') Aylward, née Preston (d. 1917) was the daughter of an Indian Army Surgeon-General, James Blair Preston. She and her sister Catherine ('Kate') (1837–1927) were sent home as girls and put in the care of two Misses Wilson at Brighstone in the Isle of Wight. They were joined there by Margaret ('Maggie') (1846–1927), their father's daughter by a second marriage, and all three formed a constant element in EMF's life. Kate and Maggie remained at Brighstone for the rest of their long lives, but about 1859 Maimie married Marianne Thornton's nephew Inglis Synnot. After his early death Maimie lived for some years in Clapham, under the sway of Marianne Thornton, and in due course she became Lily Forster's friend and was her chief comforter when EMF's father died. In 1884, to the great scandal of the Thornton-Forster clan, she married William Price Aylward (1810–90), an elderly widower who had retired as proprietor of a music shop in Salisbury and was something of a local figure. He was a Town Councillor, Mayor in 1868, and member of the Commission of the Peace. He conducted the Sarum Choral Society and had arranged visits to Salisbury of such musical luminaries as Jenny Lind and Adelina Patti. EMF loved Maimie fondly, and he visited her repeatedly in Salisbury (as he and Lily visited Kate and Maggie in Brighstone). Maimie was an intensely innocent, pious, and simple-minded woman, with a retinue of charity dependents.
[2] Emma: a maid. Many: spelling is distinct, but meaning is not.

4 To Mary Aylward

Rooks Nest, Stevenage, Herts.
January 1888

Dear Maimie,

Thank you so much for the books, and Reversi.[1] At Xmas Mamma gave me a Stamp Album; and Alice has sent me stamps for it.[2] We have a rabbit—it is very fat.

Uncle Harry has made it a hutch.[3] On wednesday Mamma went to see Grandmamma. Have you had much snow? Has the Cathedral fallen down? I hope you, Mr Aleward, and Harriet are quite well.[4]

I am your dear

Morgan

ALS: KCC

[1] Reversi: game played with draught-board and counters.
[2] Perhaps Alice Greenwood, one of Lily's godparents, from whom she undoubtedly received her first name. The Greenwoods were old family friends of the Whichelos.
[3] Harry Whichelo (1867–1904), Lily's youngest brother, whom EMF as a boy hero-worshipped, joined the Bechuanaland police.
[4] Harriet: perhaps Maimie's maid.

5 To Louisa Whichelo

Rooksnest, Stevenage
22 December 1888

Dear "Grandma"

I hope you are quite well and enjoying your visit to Unkle Frank and Aunt Eliza; are they quite well?[1]

Mamma is going to give to Hide and Mary each, a muff, and to Ansel a silver chain.[2] I hope you will have a happy Xmas; Hide and I are going to make a "Xmas Banner." I am going to give Mamma a book called "Scenes of Clerical Life."[3] On Dec. 12th Mamma and I went to a play acted by the boys at Mr Seager's school.[4] It was in two parts. The 1st part consisted of Tableaux Vivants called the Queen of Hearts. The dresses were very pretty and the Queen was so beautifully got up that nobody could tell who she was. A friend of mine Jack Fry was acting as one of the king's children and had to eat one of the tarts on the stage. The next part was a fairy tale called Fritz; it was very funny. One scene was very pretty. The little princess who was supposed to be learning her lessons was fast asleep; then a maid came in and sang a song (this was my friend Stephen Fry) dusting the room all the time.

With love to all

I remain
Your dear
Morgan.

ALS: KCC

[1] Frank (d. 1905) and Eliza Fowler (1840–1931) were EMF's maternal great-uncle and great-aunt. They lived in Plymouth, and Frank worked on the railways. Eliza, née Graham, younger sister of Louisa Whichelo, was an extremely loquacious and opinionated woman.
[2] Hide, Mary: probably servants. Ansell: one of a succession of 'garden boys' at Rooksnest; he and EMF became great friends.
[3] By George Eliot, published in 1858.

⁴ The Rev. John Osbourne Seager (1807–89) founded 'The Grange' in 1852, a school on Arnoldian lines at the Swan Inn, in the High Street, Stevenage. EMF was an unhappy boarder there in 1893; see *EMF*, I, 39–40.

6 To Laura Mary Forster

[Kent House, Eastbourne.¹ September 1890?]

Dear Aunt Laura

Thank you for your nice long letter it was the first I had this term. What a pity I just missed Maitie.² I cant write very well as boys are looking over the letter while I write. They have stopped now, so I can write in comfort. Have you heard anything more about Christopher Herringham Is he better?³ Directly I arrived here Hughes accosted me with a very muddled speech which ran something like this; Oh Forster will you do you think you can may you come before you go home not at your aunt's by the other train to sleep the night but of course we will do the writing and all that and go on in the morning. See what you can make of that I think it means will I come and spend the night, not when I am staying with you, but go back with him by the later train from Eastbourne which stops at Red Hill, where he changes for Reigate. How are all the animals? What a success the new brougham seems. I have been to the baths one day, and rather liked it. I find the work rather hard after seven weeks holiday. I am learning drawing, and got highest marks. How are King and Clara?⁴

I remain
Your loving
Morgan

ALS: KCC

¹ This school was founded about 1887. A 1902 description reads: 'The Rev. C. P. Hutchinson, MA, late scholar of Gonville & Caius College, Cambridge, receives about 30 young boys to prepare for entrance and scholarships at the public schools and for the Royal Navy.... Particular attention is paid to neatness in all school work, and special care is taken in handwriting and in all elementary English subjects.' (*Paton's List of Schools & Tutors*, 5th ed., 1902.)
² Maitie: unidentified.
³ Dr Wilmot (1855–1936) and Christiana Jane Herringham (1853–1929) were friends of Laura Forster. Their nine-year-old son Christopher, who at the time of this letter had been taken to Egypt to recover from meningitis, died soon afterwards.
⁴ The King family were builders in Abinger Hammer. EMF was friendly with the younger Willie King.

7 To Alice Clara Forster

Kent House [Eastbourne]
Sunday [late September 1890]

Dear Mamma,

I have been on the beach yesterday, and found some limpets and lots of crabs. When the tide goes out a long way it uncovers rocks, shingle, and sand. I put some crabs on the sand and saw them burrow. Mr Bailey [Baillie], the music master, wants me to play in a trio which they are going to have in the concert in the middle of the term. I have been to the baths once and did not like or dislike them. When I got in a little way I could not get my breath. After a few seconds I did. Then they made me dip my head, which I did not like, and then a gentleman, not a swimming master, belonging to the baths, took me by one hand, and led me along the baths. I think I will tell you I am not happy. What with the moving and other things it makes me feel bad. I was not well yesterday (Sunday), so I had to finish my letter to-day. Please send another bible. Take care of kitty

Morgan

ALS: KCC

8   To Alice Clara Forster

Kent House [Eastbourne]
Sunday [18 October 1890][1]

Ma bonne mère que je toute aime

I had the extra blanket, the thick combinations, and the cofee, and liked them all very much. There is very little to tell you, except that I am happier than ever since you have come to see me. Of course I have forgotten to ask you for the stamp Gran gave me. Mr Bailey says that I know my part in the trio, but that the other two do not.[2] I am going to be kind to Henson; we are going for a walk this afternoon, so it will be a good time to begin. I shall write to Emma soon.

I am
Your happy son
Morgan.

ALS: KCC

[1] Inscribed by Lily, 'Oct. 18th After my visit.'
[2] On 26 November EMF took part in a concert at the school, playing triangle in 'Toy Symphony in C' by Gurlitt, and playing in 'Piano Trio' by H. Stanislaus.

9   To Alice Clara Forster

Kent House [Eastbourne. Late October 1890]

Dear Mamma,

I have a good deal to tell you. Yesterday, as it was wet, we went to the theatre. I enjoyed going, but did not care for the piece. It was a

Louisa Whichelo, EMF's grandmother. *Below* The four Whichelo sisters. *Left to right:* Rosalie (Rosie; EMF's favourite aunt); Alice Clara (Lily; EMF's mother); Mary Eleanor (Nellie); and Georgiana (Georgie).

EMF with his mother in 1882.
Right Maimie Aylward, Lily
Forster's closest friend. *Below*
EMF with his mother in 1889.

grown-up one, not at all suitable for us to go to, I should have thought. On Wednesday we played another match, and we won.

I received your letter. I was very surprised to hear you are looking at flats. I hope you are looking at them only to live in them till you find a house in the country for I know you would not like London and I should hate it.

The trio is getting on very well; I hope you are coming for it. We had such a nice sermon this morning, Mr Hervey ought to have heard it, it was about *society*, and the ways it led people astray.[1] The sermons we have in that church are generally too difficult for me. Mrs H[utchinson] tells me to tell you that she has asked about the wooly waistcoats and finds that they are only made with sleeves, that they can be made specially without them, but, as that it [*sic*] would take nearly a month to do so, she thinks it would be best to leave them to you. We now are only talking about fireworks. We did not know if it would be better to have big ones from Brocks, or little ones to let off ourselves.[2] We shall have both.

I am your loving son

Morgan

ALS: KCC

[1] Augustus Hervey, EMF's pre-school tutor who had been a master at The Grange, was not a favourite; see *EMF*, I, 29–30, 31.
[2] Brocks: famous fireworks manufacturers.

10   To Alice Clara Forster

Kent House [Eastbourne]
Sunday [5 November? 1890]

Dear Mamma,

I have a lot to tell you. I am kind to Henson, and I think he is much happier.[1] The others are kinder to him now. I *did* run in the paper-chase after all, for when I told Mr H[utchinson] that you said I had better not run, he said, never mind I will see to that. Now I must tell you all about it. We had it on Thursday. We finished breakfast at 8.30., and then went on tearing up paper. I tore for some time, and then changed. I left on the jaegers of course, and was immediately told by everybody that I should be so hot. But afterwards Mr H. came down and made everyone put on vests. We had on our foot-ball things of course. Then each took a large bun for his luncheon. It was now about 10.30. The hares, Mr H. and some of the boys who could not run, me among them, were to go to a place called Paridise, about half a mile from here.[2] Then we took one large bag and walked over the downs some way with the hares, who then gradually edged away from us, and quickened their pace. We afterwards met them at a place called Jerrytown, about 5½ from Eastbourne, and gave them the bag of paper.[3] They were not caught, but came in about a mile before the hounds We came home when we reached Jerrytown.[3] In the evening we had the fireworks.

Morgan

ALS: KCC

[1] Henson, who is unidentified, appears in the correspondence only as the object of EMF's benevolence.
[2] Paradise Wood, which contains a reservoir, about one mile west of Eastbourne.
[3] Perhaps Jevington, northwest of Eastbourne.

11   To Alice Clara Forster

Kent House [School, Eastbourne]
[Before 26 November 1890]

Dear Mother,

I will not neglect you again and promise to write twice in the week. I have letters pouring in from every side. One from Gran yesterday which I was very pleased to get, and one from Miss Lo[c]ke King, Miss Eleanor of course, with a long account about everything. She is now staying with Aunt Laura. A long description about the animals. Aunt Laura is better. Miss Eleanor has been staying with the Caliphrandses.[1] Mr. Head saw my arm on Friday and began working it up and down which hurt rather, but not so much as when Miss Wells does it. You and Gran will be enraged to hear that Mr Hatch has hurt my arm.[2] I was lying in bed this morning waiting for my breakfast and he came in and tried to be funny, pinching me under the bedclothes, and he gave me my book and dropped it to be funny on me and the corners went on my arm. It did hurt but is all right now. The swelling and bruise have gone down very much. Tell Gran that my arm does not pain much.

Love to Gran and thank her for her letter also to everyone else.

Morgan

Excuse dirty smudge at end. It is Hensons dirty fingers

ALS: KCC

[1] Eleanor Locke King was a neighbour and friend of Laura Mary Forster. The Caliphrandses are unidentified.
[2] Mr W. S. Hatch, one of the masters, is otherwise unidentified.

12   To Alice Clara Forster

Kent House [Eastbourne]
[December 1890]

Dear Mamma,

I received your letter on Monday, and your card Tuesday. We come home on Sat. 20th, am I to go to London Bridge or Victoria

from here? I should think Victoria, write and tell me, I shall also
expect a letter soon, telling me where I am to come for the holidays.
How did you like trotting the German girl about?[1] I am not quite
sure when the train we are going in starts. I think it is 9.55. a.m. My
cold is better I think, and so is my cougth. I have now heard that we
go at all times of the day, according to the distance we have to go; do
let me come by an early one, although I have not far to go, I shall
only get tired and worrying by not coming sooner and seeing you,
the early train starts at about 8.30., the other as I told you at 9.55.,
mind you meet me at Victoria, for I shall be in a terrible state of mind
if I get there and find you not on the platform; perhaps you are not
able to come on the platform like at Charing X, if so I shall go to
where they collect the tickets, and I shall expect to see you there, if
not, I shall wait in the station for about half-an-hour, and if you do
not appear I shall go to Alfords at Edinburgh Mansions, I know the
way and leave the luggage in the cloak-room, and ask them, the
Alfords, I mean, what I had better do.[2] I have since heard that the
boys all go home by the 9.55. train. Again I say take care you meet
me. My cold is much better, nearly well, so is my cough[?]. Write me
a nice long letter, it is so nice to have them. You must think me rather
odd to write about meeting me, but I feel so very nervous somehow.
I don't know why it is but perhaps it is excitement, but lately I have
always been taking the dark side of things. I have never been like it
before, but it is not at all nice. It is very much like despondency; I am
afraid I shall miss the train in the morning, afraid you will not meet
me, afraid I shall lose my tickets; those are instances of the kind of
state of mind I am in; it is not so bad in the day-time as at night, then
I cry a lot. I also have also a kind of forboding that something
dreadful will happen before the holidays. I have not told you that in
a grumbling mood, but because I think you could write a nice long
comforting letter, you can always comfort me when I am at home so
why could you not comfort me with a letter. The worst of school is
that you have nothing and nobody to love, if I only had only
somebody; I shall be much happier. To stop at Rooksnest for the
holidays for though they would be very pleasant anyway, they
would not be nearly so nice if you were always looking after
furniture, and settling tradesmen, and Chick; they would hardly be
holidays at all.[3] There has been a row. Mr Hatch when they were out
for a walk told a boy who had been naughty to walk in front alone.
The boy did so and said "it does not make much difference to me",
and Mr Hatch hit him with a stick, and he began to cry and went
home and told M^r H[utchinson].

Morgan

ALS: KCC

[1] German girl: unidentified.
[2] Robert Alford (1838–1923), a prosperous carriage-maker, in 1860 had married Georgiana

Greenwood, sister of Lily's godmother Alice Greenwood. In 1906, as a middle-aged widower, he married EMF's aunt Rosalie Whichelo (1866–1957).
   ³ Furniture . . . Chick: perhaps related to Lily's thoughts of moving to a London flat; see Letter 9.

13   To Alice Clara Forster

Kent House [Eastbourne]
Sunday [Winter 1891]

Dear Mamma,
   I have written a post-card to Aunt Laura thanking her for the pin. I have got a very bad lip. I have heardly ever had such a bad one. Not content with distorting my lower lip I have one on my upper also. The colours of my lip are various:—black, grey, white, red, pink and pale yellow. We now have hot water in the morning, at least some do, but in the cubicles the big boys take all the hot water and we have none.
   Don't you think I had better complain to Mrs Sawyer? If that does not do, I can wash in the evening with hot water. We have been having winter with a vengeance the last few days. Snow and ice; in the morning windows are covered with ice, and cannot see through them. I am pretty warm in spite of the cold. At night I spread my dressing-gown over the bed, and with that and 3 blankets, and a quilt I am pretty warm. They take great care of me, indeed I am afraid they have coddled me almost to much. The boys all went out for a snowball fight a few days ago: I wanted to go but they did not let me, so I was allowed to [go] up stairs to Totsey and Tom.¹

Je demeure
Votre aimant fils
Morgan

P.S.   Send the shoes

ALS: KCC

   ¹ Mr Hutchinson's sons. In 1935 EMF visited Hilton Hutchinson ('Totsey'?), who had been a diplomat and businessman, at Eastbourne, a melancholy and inconsequential weekend described in CB, p. 104.

14   To Alice Clara Forster

Kent House [Eastbourne]
Good Friday [27 March 1891]¹

Dear Mamma,
   I am glad you liked the flowers, I wish there had been more of them. I have got rather a bad cold and cough, but do not worry, for I am taken great care of. They all went to church this morning except

me and Henson. I thought it rather a good opportunaty to talk to
Henson about Good Friday. I asked him if he knew why they went
to church. He did *not* Then I explained why, and told him about
Easter and Ascension day. I was so shocked. He did not know
anything about Christ. He did not understand He would say that
Jesus could not have lived before if he had been born on earth at
Xmas.

I was quite shocked

Morgan

ALS: KCC
[1] EMF later inscribed this letter: 'Instructing Henson (*c.* 1891) Keep.'

15   To Alice Clara Forster

Sylfield House, Cambridge[1]
Friday [1896?]

Dear Mother,

I have been wanting to write to you, but my time has been
crammed with every kind of amusement, & I deserve the censure of
"going from one dissipation to another". To begin. I arrived unable
to shake hands, as I tried to open the cab door, which was coated
with wet mud. Next morning I had a letter from Miss Darwin asking
me to go to luncheon that same day, which I did, in my best clothes.
I saw M^rs D who was lying down, but I thought looked well.[2] The
rest of the day I looked superficially at the town & colleges.
Yesterday we went to the museum in the morning, & walked about
in the afternoon. In the evening we went to a dance. Of course I only
expected to dance once or twice, but I danced nearly the whole time,
& enjoyed myself immensely. This morning we spent at Ely, which I
admire very much indeed. This evening we are going to a dance at
the Masonic Hall. Tomorrow there is a little dance here. I have got
the Virgil. Not very cheap—5/6 (published at 12/–) but I think it is
worthwhile. It is very clean. The Aristophanes is only 2/11 new, & if
I cannot get 2nd hand I will buy it. My teeth are very comfortable. I
have written to Gran, Aunt Laura & Aunt Lucy.[3] What ought I to
give the maid when I leave? Thank you for your letter. Please give
my love to Mrs Snell.[4] I hope you are enjoying yourself as much as I
am.

I remain
Your loving
Morgan.

ALS: KCC
[1] EMF was visiting Francis Woodbury Fulford (1879–1941), a Tonbridge school-fellow, and
son of the Rev. W. H. Fulford, Dean of Clare College, Cambridge. Francis entered Jesus
College in October 1898, became a clergyman, and published books on Kierkegaarde and on
the Cambridge Platonists.
[2] Miss Darwin: perhaps Ruth (1883–1968), elder daughter of Sir Horace Darwin

(1851–1928), who was a son of Charles Darwin and a founder of the Cambridge Scientific Instrument Company. The Darwins' house, in the Huntingdon Road, was called 'The Orchard'. Mrs Darwin was the Hon. Emma Cecilia ('Ida') Farrer (1854–1946), daughter of the 1st Lord Farrer by his first marriage; Ida had been briefly in Lily's charge during her career as a governess at Abinger Hall. She was the wife of Sir Horace Darwin.

[3] EMF's aunt Lucy Forster (d. 1917).

[4] Mrs Snell: unidentified.

CAMBRIDGE, 1897–1901

Forster went up to King's College, Cambridge, in October 1897. He had chosen to read Classics and studied under the King's dons John Edwin Nixon and Nathaniel Wedd. In due course Forster became very friendly with Wedd; indeed, it was to some extent because of a remark of his that, during his Cambridge years, Forster began to consider writing as a career. He was also shown hospitality by the famous Oscar Browning, who invited him to lunch and to play piano duets, regaling him the while with many anecdotes of friendships with princes.

During his first year Forster felt a little out of things, partly as a result of being in lodgings rather than in College, and he tended to keep to the company of old school-friends, in particular Sydney Worters and Howard MacMunn. By his second year, however, he had warmed to the place and (being now in College) found himself living a most enjoyable, sociable and intellectually stimulating existence. The most significant event of this year was his growing acquaintance with Hugh Owen Meredith, a fellow-Kingsman who for some years had great influence over him, and with whom he fell in love. (Their friendship forms the basis of much in the novel *Maurice*.) Through Meredith's influence at this time, Forster gave up, fairly painlessly, his Christian beliefs. Another important friendship begun then, although much slower to develop, was that with Goldsworthy Lowes Dickinson, King's don and author of *The Greek View of Life*, and a dominant figure in the College during that period.

By his third year, Forster was acquiring a minor reputation in Cambridge through his whimsical articles in the college magazine *Basileona*, and then, or a little later, he embarked on a novel, the uncompleted fragment of which (since his death known as 'Nottingham Lace') has survived. The College thought highly enough of him, despite his undistinguished academic record, to allow him to stay on for a fourth year to study history. During this extra year he was elected to the Apostles, then enjoying a brilliant period under the domination of G. E. Moore. Through 'the Society' (whose meetings he evoked in the opening chapter of *The Longest Journey*) he came to know Lytton Strachey, Maynard Keynes, and other Bloomsbury figures, and he remained faithful to it for the remainder of his life.

16   To Alice Clara Forster

[King's College, Cambridge]
Sunday [late November 1897]

Dear Mother

Thank you for your letters. I have very little news to tell. Today I went to lunch at the Horts, & saw lots of Italian photographs.[1] Tuesday I go to Ely with MacMunn, & while he is calling on some friends I shall go, as you suggested, to Lady A. C.[2] It seems a good opportunity. I will make an appointment for the phot[ograph] tomorrow. As I have my cap on I don't think my hair will matter. I am not doing very much work. Among other things Howley does interrupt so—comes in & sits boring for hours.[3] He says people have all run to muscle at Cambridge; it is such a comfort to find someone with whom one can converse intelligently. Poor boy; he really means that no one else will listen to his drivel. I am trying to get some friends, but it is uphill work. One never seems to get to know the nice people, though there are plenty of them. However I am very happy in the present; it is only the future I sometimes feel anxious about. I could not go to the O[ld] T[onbridgian] dinner as I had refused about a month before. However several others did not go, so I was not peculiar. I met Hilary & Toddie in the town.[4] They congratulated me, & said they would tell you they had seen me. Worters bothered me to go [to] the Geisha yesterday, but I would not, & spent a pleasant afternoon with Mollison.[5] Now he (W) has asked me to tea, & I cannot get out of it. Fancy Fulford's speech. I hope there are not a pair of them. W. plagues Mollison as much as me; always coming in. All this struggling for friends is very unbecoming, but I suppose all go through it. I often think of your ~~manifold~~ precepts 'don't rush into everybody's arms, but be very pleasant to all'. Aunt L[aura] has paid the 2/– & enjoyed the play. I enjoyed the concert very much. Oh such a splendid Beethoven Op. 5 n° 2 if you are the wiser, which I wasn't.[6] I am looking forward to the holidays. Shan't we talk. And I looking forward to playing the piano too. I want to find out how soon I can come home.

In return for your varied advice in the letter I will give you one piece. Do not underline your words. It is a proof of a 'female mind'. You did it 29 times. 'Oh the rising generation, you will say'.

My schol[arship] is deducted off the college account each term[7] I do hope Nic[holas] will be successful.[8]

ALU: KCC

[1] Presumably the relations of the Rev. Fenton John Anthony Hort (1828–92), who was Hulsean Professor of Divinity, 1878–87.

[2] Howard Fletcher MacMunn (1878–1947), Tonbridge School friend, took a BA degree from Emmanuel College, Cambridge, in 1900, then entered Ely Theological College. He became an Honorary Canon of Durham Cathedral in 1933. Lady A. C.: unidentified.
[3] James Henry Edward Howley, son of an Irish barrister, entered King's in 1897. He died in August 1898.
[4] Hilary and Toddie: apparently Tonbridge School acquaintances.
[5] Sydney Robert Worters (1879–1959) also became a clergyman, after taking a degree from Trinity College; and William Mayhew Mollison (1878–1967), son of the Master of Clare College, became a distinguished otolaryngologist. EMF and Mollison lived on the same staircase at King's, and EMF thought him intelligent but worldly and 'not very profound'. The Geisha: A Story of a Tea-House, by Sidney Jones, with libretto by Owen Hall (pseudonym of James Davie), and lyrics by Harry Greenbank, was performed at the New Theatre, Cambridge, 25–27 November 1897.
[6] This was Beethoven's violoncello sonata, Op. 5, No. 2 (1796).
[7] In November 1897 EMF was awarded an Exhibition (a College grant toward fees based on performance in examinations) for £40 for two years.
[8] This friend, perhaps from Tonbridge School, remains unidentified.

17   To Alice Clara Forster

[King's College, Cambridge]
Sunday [13 February 1898]

Dear Mother,

I am so glad you think you are better; you see how really ill you have been; it must be influenza, aren't you glad after all that I knew, when Mr Cardell told you to go to bed. Now don't be rash, for you will be weak for a long time, & do take care that the cough does not settle on your chest. My breakfast party today was rather a fiasco, owing to tiresome Mollison. I was going to have him alone, when he very stupidly said before Worters & MacMunn that it would be much better if all three came to him instead. Of course I had to persist, & include them in the invitation though I didn't want them & had no occasion to ask them. That was bad enough but if you please the next thing is that Mollison can't come, because he has an invitation from the dean whom he has so often refused that he doesn't like to do it again. I felt very cross, but being "such a lady" behaved in an exemplary manner, being left with the two I didn't want, and without the one I did. Tomorrow I breakfast with Millner, who is much pleased with the wine.[1] O such fun on Friday night! all the undergraduates ran up & down the streets yelling at the tops of their voices. Very foolish, but I much enjoyed it, for I saw it from my window beautifully. After a season there were cries of "Fluffy" & Mr Fulford appeared in his proctorial robes. He advanced with great intrepidity, tell Fulford, but was compelled to retreat by an unexpected charge straight in his direction. I think he reaped a rich harvest of fines.[2] Have you read Crockett's new book, the Adventures of Sir Toady Lion?[3] It is splendid: a child's story, & reminds me of the times I used to have with Ansell & Frankie.[4] My golf is slowly improving; I am down to 103. Last night we had a very wearisome whist party at Worter's. Mind you get hold of Begbie's poem.[5] It is simply splendid. He meditates coming to see you when you are better. I endeavoured to go to a lecture on painting last Wednesday, but could not.[6] Yesterday I went to tea with the Grant's, who are very nice.[7] We talked about Mont St Michel. Love to Rosy & thank her again for cushion. Why Monday is St Valentine's day! I ought to have written you a poem "To Cynthia on recovering from sickness" or something like that.

Your loving
Morgan

Any news about Mrs Mawe's money?[8]

ALS: KCC

[1] Millner: unidentified.

[2] On Friday, 11 February, occurred what the *Granta* (19 February 1898, p. 196) called 'the makings of a very healthy riot' round about the Market Place. It began with a scuffle in a Cycle Show, led to the wrecking of some booths erected for the Saturday market, and ended with the arrival of proctors who imposed fines right and left.

[3] Samuel Rutherford Crockett (1860–1914), popular Scottish novelist who wrote sentimental stories of rural Scottish life. *The Surprising Adventures of Sir Toady Lion* (1897) is one of a series about imaginary adventures.

[4] The Franklyn family were the neighbouring farmers to Rooksnest.

[5] Lionel Frank Begbie (1877–1911), another Tonbridge School friend, wrote whimsical verse collected as *Boshtan Ballads: Flotsam from the Isis and Other Verses* (1901).

[6] The lecture was by Charles Waldstein (later Walston) (1856–1921), American-born Director of the Fitzwilliam Museum, 1882–89; Slade Professor of Fine Art, 1895–1901 and 1904–12; and a Fellow of King's from 1894 until his death.

[7] These Grants were probably descended from Charles Grant (1764–1823), of the East India Company and a leading figure with Henry Thornton in the Clapham Sect. EMF was friendly with Frank Grant, who was with the Public Works Department in India, 1885–91. In 1897 he entered Queen's College, Cambridge, and afterwards was a private tutor and demonstrator in engineering at Cambridge, where he is known to have lived until 1956, when he moved to London.

[8] Mrs Cecilia Mawe (d. 1942) was a Tonbridge friend of Lily.

18   To Alice Clara Forster

[King's College, Cambridge]
Sunday [30 October 1898]

Dear Mother

Very little news to tell you. There has evidently been some juggling over the chest of drawers, for the latest is that the owner, Cornish, has given them to his old bedmaker, who had them removed but would be 'willing to let me have them'. I am given to understand that she wrote to him and said I might be willing to have them: it seems odd that he should 'never mention it at all' in his answer, but give them to her. 15/– or 17/– you said would be a fair price, did you not, if I had them? I have been out to luncheon, & then for a walk, and then to see Bubble, who had called on me. Friday I went to a bazaar—'mission to deep sea fishes' we call it—which Mrs Fulford had made us all come to. I bought something at her stall; she gave me rather a shock; she was so sharp; one might

The mantelpiece in the
Rooksnest drawing-room was
designed by EMF's father and
accompanied the family from
home to home. *Below* EMF and
his mother (standing) in the
garden at Rooksnest, with
Charles Poston and Alice
Alford (seated in hammock)
and Rosalie Whichelo (seated
on ground).

Sylfield House.
Cambridge.

Friday

Dear Mother,

I have been wanting to write to you, but my time has been crammed with every kind of amusement, & I deserve the censure of "going from one dissipation to another". To begin. I arrived unable to shake hands, as I tried to open the cab door, which was coated with wet mud. Next morning I had a letter from Miss Darwin asking me to go to luncheon that same day, which I did, in my best clothes. I saw Mrs D. who was lying down, but I thought looked well. The rest of the day I looked superficially at the town & colledges. Yesterday we went to the museum in the morning, & walked about in the after-noon. In the evening we went to a dance. Of course I only expected to dance once or twice, but I danced nearly the whole time, & enjoyed myself immensely. This morning we spent at Ely, which I admire very much indeed. This evening we are going to a dance at the Masonic Hall. Tomorrow there is a little dance here. I have got the Virgil. Not very cheap — 5/6 (published at 12/-) but I think it is worthwhile. It is very clean. The Aristophanes is only 2/11 new, & if I cannot get 2nd hand I will buy it. My teeth are very comfortable. I have written to Gran, Aunt Laura & Aunt Lucy. What ought I to give the maid when I leave! Thank you for your letter. Please give my love to Mrs Snell. I hope you are enjoying yourself as much as I am.

I remain
  Your loving Morgan.

A letter from EMF to his mother, written whilst staying with Francis Fulford (see Letter 15 in text).

say dishonest. I will tell you about [it] when we meet; it is too long to write. I took 2/6 in my pocket, & refused to spend any more, so was not ruined, though the others were. I think it is most scandalous trying to make "youths" like us spend all our money. I had one man to breakfast, & went to lunch with another. The old English Essay is a great nuisance, I feel I ought to send it in to the University, and yet I shall hardly get a 2nd class for my King's one, as I have heard bits of other people's and they are much better.[1] I took Fulford to the Club Concert yesterday.[2] He is rowing, and—to speak vulgarly—has to seat himself with great deliberation. I believe he is going to write to you; he thinks my behaviour is decidedly rowdy, and you ought to know. He is decidedly virtuous "There is no reason" clasping his hands, "why we should not always wear our caps and gowns at all seasons that the University appoints, not merely at those hours when the proctors are on their rounds." Mollison is enraged with Fulford's Ecclesiastical talk. F. said: "The Master of Jesus is glad I am going to be a clergyman. He says there is a great need for clever men in the church.[3] High church men are apt to be either foolishly ritualistic, or else too full of worldly ambition." "And which are you going to be?" said M. viciously. We had a tea party of guava jelly. I must write to Mrs Walker about it.[4] The bed maker does not steal my things, & is very agreeable, but I am having trouble with the laundress who has lost a sock and—I think—a pair of pygamas. How many of the latter ought I to have? It is very kind of you about Rome, but I don't see how it could be managed, & it seems rather wasteful, as they are only going for about 10 days.[5] I had much rather wait a little longer and go to Venice with you. I am getting to know some nice people, chiefly through the Musical Club. Your loving

Morgan

I notice that you persistently refuse to answer questions about your health. How are you??

ALS: KCC

[1] A typescript survives (probably 1897. KCC): 'English Essay. The Relation of Dryden to Milton and Pope', signed 'Peer-Gynt' (EMF's pseudonym as undergraduate).
[2] Presumably at the Cambridge University Musical Club.
[3] The Rev. Henry Arthur Morgan (1830–1912) had been Master of Jesus College since 1885.
[4] Mrs Walker: unidentified.
[5] An expedition to Rome, organised in the University.

19   To Alice Clara Forster

King's [College, Cambridge]
Thursday. [24 November 1898]

Dear Mother,

Your letter just arrived. How funny about Jolley's bill: I was sure

I had put it in. I have had a very exciting day. I could not get a ticket for the Senate House but stood outside in a place Mr Cooke told me of, between King's Chapel and the Senate House where I hung like a bear on a railing and saw beautifully without the slightest crowd.[1] The Sirdar passed so close that I could have almost have touched him through the bars.[2] Just as he drove up King's Parade, the weight of the people pulling against the high iron fence that runs along by the Senate House Green opposite the University Church wrenched it out of its fastenings, and for the length of about 50 feet fell backwards into the crowd. It is a very great miracle that no one was killed, as they were all flung down with the heavy iron on top of them. As it was, only about six were at all hurt, one having his leg broken. I write this today, in case you may see anything in Friday's paper, and think I or anyone you know was hurt. The Sirdar walked with a long procession into the Senate House. He wore his red doctor's gown over his uniform and had his helmet on so he looked very ridiculous. As soon as he was in I ran to the Union to find all the passages crammed. At 2.30 the doors of the debating hall were opened and we squeezed in and waited for an hour and a quarter. It reminded me of the school concerts; there were violent cheers when the electric light was turned on. At last the Sirdar appeared looking rather a chaw-bacon in a grey suit which even I knew was not a proper fit.[3] He was proposed and seconded, and then made a little speech. This evening there was a grand bonfire in the market place. Mollison fetched me, and we stayed quite a long time. I have never seen such a night; they pulled up all the goal-posts and railings and posts from the backs to feed the fire. It began in the middle of the square, but gradually worked its away [sic] across till it embraced a gas lamp, which sent out a spout of flame, and there were quantities of squibs & crackers & roman candles which were thrown in at the windows. We all said How foolish, but enjoyed it very much. The chapel & senate house looked marvellous with the red light. I should very much like the Hall Carpet for my bedroom; how is it you do not want it. I almost think it would be better if I brought the big picture of Aunt Monie back with me and put [it] in the upstairs sitting-room, as the small one looks so very nice beside the photograph of my great-grandmother's, and it would seem a pity to put the big one in my bedroom.[4] Mr Cooke is really a most extraordinary man; I told him that I thought he knew my uncle at Hinxton; he said he did and added 'you know, in his last years I do not think he was right in his head; in fact he had to be kept under restraint.'[5] Perhaps such conversation is the fashion, as Mr Forster did much the same to you.[6] I am glad to hear that Aunt Laura is better.

Your loving
Morgan

ALS: KCC

[1] Alfred Hands Cooke (1854–1937), zoologist; King's College Lecturer, 1879–1900; Dean, 1889–93; and Tutor, 1893–1900.

[2] Horatio Herbert Kitchener, 1st Earl Kitchener of Khartoum (1850–1916) became Governor of British Red Sea Territories in 1886, and eventually of Egypt; and, in 1890, Sirdar (Commander-in-Chief) of the Egyptian Army. EMF describes above the occasion of Kitchener's receiving an honorary degree. The *Granta* editorialised: 'There is no one in England at present who could raise such enthusiasm amongst undergraduates as Lord Kitchener. For there is nothing that a healthy youth admires so much as strength, whether strength of body or character. . . . Houses and roofs around were black with spectators. . . . The wit of the gallery scintillated uninterruptedly.' See 'Cambridge and the Sirdar,' 12 (1898), 97–98.

[3] Chaw-bacon: yokel.

[4] Perhaps an engraving after George Richmond's drawing of Marianne Thornton (1873), frontispiece to EMF's *Marianne Thornton*. The smaller picture is unidentified. 'Photograph . . . great-grandmother': Marianne Sykes, by Sir George Chalmers (1777); see *ibid*., facing p. 26. The original, an oil, hung above EMF's mantelpiece at King's, in his last years.

[5] Uncle at Hinxton: the Rev. Charles Thornton Forster (1836–91), sometime Fellow of Jesus College, Cambridge, and Vicar of Hinxton, Cambridgeshire. His wife was EMF's Aunt Lucy (Letter 15).

[6] This Mr Forster is unidentified.

20   To Alice Clara Forster

University Musical Club [Cambridge]
Saturday [18 February 1899]

Dear Mother

I am so glad that Agatha's wedding has gone off successfully, and that Birdie was bridesmaid.[1] You do not mention your rheumatism in your last letter, but I hope it is all right. My chief bit of amusing news is that I have been for a walk with O. B.[2] He met me going to the University library to look at editions of Jane Austen, and told me to come to his room as he had far nicer.[3] He hadn't but I didn't say so, and then he suddenly said 'Are you fond of chickens?' I felt rather dazed, but said I was, and he then said 'Come a little stroll with me and see mine; I have such beauties.' On the way he 'drew me out'. 'Did I like Sophocles?' 'No.' 'A great mistake!' 'Pindar?' 'Yes very much' 'For his part he never could stand him.' And so on till we reached a small house in the back yard of which were six disconsolate hens. When I had sufficiently admired we gathered up the eggs they had laid and started back. Progress was slow, for we met heaps of his acquaintances, among them Frank Darwin.[4] 'Dear me, do you know him,' said O. B., 'how is that?' I explained, and his interest in me rose visibly. I strengthened my position by saying I had met Mr Grissel. 'A man of great importance in Rome: English secretary to the Pope.'[5]

King's is going to do so badly in the Lents.[6] We hoped to go up two places and shall probably go down four. The first boat got wrong in some mysterious way about a week ago and the races begin on Thursday. To be patriotic I rode with them on my bicycle today, with the result that I cannoned into another bicyclist—or he into me—and we both hastily dismounted. My front wheel buckled, but being good material mercifully hopped [popped?] back into shape & was none the worse. Yesterday I went to tea with Fulford. Sewell was there, and seemed an utter ass; and kept explaining why it was he hadn't been to see me.[7] it was

ALU, incomplete: KCC

[1] Agatha: unidentified. Birdie: nickname of Elaine Mawe (1888–1965), daughter of Lily's friend Mrs Mawe. Elaine married Clifford White, an obstetrical surgeon.

[2] O. B.: the famous Oscar Browning (1837–1923), a controversial Assistant Master at Eton, 1860–75; Fellow of King's, from 1859; and writer on Italian history. See H. E. Wortham, *Oscar Browning*; and, for a less sympathetic view, David Newsome, *On the Edge of Paradise: A. C. Benson: The Diarist*, pp. 134–35, 192–94.

[3] Editions . . . Austen: he meant to buy them with his college prize-money.

[4] Sir Francis Darwin (1848–1925), third son of Charles Darwin; botanist, and biographer of his father. On EMF's various lines of connection with the Darwins, by family friendship and by marriage, see Letter 15.

[5] Hartwell de la Garde Grissel (1839–1907) was Chamberlain of Honour to the Pope, from 1869.

[6] Lents: Lent term boat-races.

[7] Perhaps the zoologist Robert B. S. Sewell (1880–1964), who was at Christ's College as an exhibitioner, but there is no suggestion of further acquaintance.

21   To Laura Mary Forster

King's College, Cambridge
Friday [3 March 1899]

Dear Aunt Laura,

I have been intending to write to you for a long time. I have quite a lot of news to tell. In the first place I will tell how I spent my prize money. I got Browning's Poems in two volumes, two volumes of Jebb's Sophocles, Kugler's History of Italian Painting in two volumes, and last but not least Jane Austen in 10 volumes.[1] It is such a lovely edition, in green cloth with beautiful print and paper, and each volume is very light to hold. I must bring some of them to visit you; I know you will like them. Each novel goes into two volumes, except Persuasion & Northanger Abbey, who only take one. I am reading the latter again, & I am more delighted with it than ever. I have still £1 of my money to spend: what do you advise me to do with it? I hope you are pretty well now. I heard from Mother that you were at Leith Hill, but I have since heard that you were driven away by an outbreak of influenza: I do hope you did not catch it.[2] I was at lunch at Miss Darwin's last Sunday.[3] I have just read a paper to the Classical Society on 'The Greek feeling for Nature'; everyone sat upon it very much, and disagreed with everything I said.[4] I am just going to a concert, and will leave this letter till I come back.

We had a very nice concert. I am in the midst of a very unpleasant time—the dentist. I thought I would not wait for Carling Hope as there is a very good dentist here and one of my teeth began to ache a little. I have an examination at the end of this term and wanted to be comfortable during it, so I was courageous enough to write to the dentist. He did not hurt me at all today, but I am going again on Tuesday. I am otherwise having a very pleasant time this term; I go for a ride or a walk with someone every afternoon, and have got to know some of the dons a great deal better. Thank you for all the Punches. We enjoy them very much. What is the end of the Woking waterworks scheme? I agree with you that no amount of compensation could make up to you for your 'amænities'

Yours very affect^{ly}
E. M. Forster.

ALS: KCC

[1] Sir Richard Claverhouse Jebb (1841–1905) translated and edited *Sophocles: The Plays and Fragments with Critical Notes*, 7 vols. (1892–1900). Franz Theodor Kugler, *Handbook of Painting: The Italian Schools* (1855). The prize money was a half-share of a College prize for Latin verse.
[2] Leith Hill Place: i.e. with the Vaughan Williams family.
[3] Miss Darwin: see Letter 15.
[4] This paper has not survived.

22   To Alice Clara Forster

[King's College, Cambridge]
Sunday [postmark 23 April 1899]

Dear Mother

I know how your letter will go 'Ow Morgan, you've never sent the scissors'. I will put them in here, or send them in my next. I have been to Mr Wedd.[1] He was as extenuating as even you, but did not comfort me much. He thinks I might come up in the Long [Vacation] to coach, but does not think I have any chance of a 1st at all, unless I make very great improvement. We talked about the system of education at Tonbridge, and agreed that much of my backwardness was due to the time wasted on repetition. He was horrified at the amount learnt, and always thought that D^r W[ood] was a stupid narrow minded man with regard to teaching.[2] He advises me to think of journalistic work as one of the things I might do. I certainly should like it, but it is rather a pit to attempt without influence and I don't think I should be good enough. However "there is no occasion to talk about that now." I and Meredith had eggs & ham in company and went for a walk.[3] The Rome people have brought back an astonishing amount of photographs which I have much enjoyed looking at.[4] Collingham & I have had another 'discussion', to use an elegant word, about Kensit.[5] Nothing much was effected, and we both came out victorious. "He is so unjust" and narrowminded, and I will not give in, for Kensit was quite illegal in going into the church & disturbing the services, however wrong

they were. How are you two ladies? What about a housemaid?
Meredith's people are in the same plight. They only keep their
servants by giving them hot roast pork—like Mrs Platt. I said you
used stout.[6]

Your loving Morgan.

ALS: KCC

[1] EMF's results in the first part of his Tripos examinations were not very good. His tutor,
Nathaniel Wedd (1864–1940), was Lecturer in Classics and in Ancient History. He was a
warm-hearted, pugnacious, and hard-swearing agnostic; a militant humanist and anticleric; at
that time a Fabian and a radical in politics, and a determined enemy of *fin-de-siècle*
aestheticism and of exclusiveness in general.

[2] The Rev. Joseph Wood (1842–1923), Headmaster of Tonbridge School, 1890–98, and of
Harrow, 1898–1910. As a teacher of classics, he made a fetish of the memorising of passages;
his *Ediscenda* (1893) was a volume of extracts for that purpose.

[3] Hugh Owen Meredith (1873–1963) was the son of a struggling Irish legal shorthand-writer
who lived in Wimbledon. The father was socially ambitious and sent Hugh to good schools:
first to Mr Seager's in Stevenage, then to Shrewsbury, whence he came to Cambridge with a
great reputation for brilliance, a reputation maintained (at least among his friends) at King's,
where he spent his days in endless philosophical debate. His good looks and intellectual
confidence impressed EMF, who was to become romantically attached to him. Through his
influence EMF became de-converted from Christianity, and under his auspices was elected to
the Apostles. Meredith married Christabel Iles in 1906, and from 1911 was Professor of
Economics at Queen's University, Belfast.

[4] Rome people: see Letter 18.

[5] John Kensit (1853–1902) founded the Protestant Truth Society in 1890; it specialised in
breaking up ritualistic church services.

[6] Mrs Platt: unidentified.

23   To Laura Mary Forster

King's College, Cambridge
Sunday [7 May 1899]

Dear Aunt Laura,

Thank you very much for your letter: also for the Punches &
Antiquaries which I much enjoy. I see from 'Nature Notes' that
yesterday a party were going for a ramble and then coming to tea
with you.[1] I hope it was a success—the day at least was perfect—and
that you were well enough to see something of it. I do hope the
beautiful spring weather now beginning will set you up: I have not
much faith in summer after the hot dusty leaves that were such
trouble to you last year. I have been very well—except yesterday
when I kept in bed all the morning believing I had the influenza.
Mollison solemnly felt my pulse & said it was high, but by the
evening I could go to hall, and this morning am perfectly well except
for a little relaxed throat, so it was not anything serious. I have spent
my remaining money on a handbook to Greek Sculpture and
Hallam's Life of Tennyson—a smaller edition that has lately come
out. I debated long between the latter and Gibbon's Autobiography
which you suggested. The Vicar of Wakefield, the other book you
proposed, we have already got.[2] Mother has told you about my

examinations. I did very badly and am quite certain to lose my exhibition. Mr Wedd, the Tutor with whom I have most to do, has tried to console me. He does not think I have any chance for a first and it would be no good trying for the Home Civil [Service], as I work slowly and cannot cram. He suggests that I should think of journalism among other things. It is certainly the kind of thing I should like, if only I could get work, and subjects to suit me: but that is so difficult. I am enjoying the spring here very much. I don't feel ever to have been in the country so much before. I can count over 49 rooks' nests from the sitting room window, and all the trees are coming out in different shades of pale green.³ On Thursday MacMunn and I went for a ride and got some cowslips, and coming back we met Mrs Frank Darwin who told us of a field where we could find quantities. On Friday the Grants came to tea—Sybil Grant also, who was stopping with them.⁴ They all wish to be remembered to you. Mother and my grandmother are perhaps coming to see ~~us~~ me this term, but it is a little uncertain as the housemaid we like so much has left to nurse her sick sister and leaves us in difficulties. I suppose there is no chance of you coming up this term so soon after your illness. I may be here in the long [vacation], during July: could you come then? I was so sorry I could not see you last holidays.

Yours affectly
E. M. Forster.

ALS: KCC

¹ *The Antiquary: A Magazine Devoted to the Study of the Past* was published from 1880 to 1915. *Nature Notes*, published from 1890 by The Selborne Society for the Protection of Birds, Plants and Places, later became *The Selborne Society's Magazine*.
² This was Hallam Tennyson's biography, *Alfred Lord Tennyson: A Memoir, by His Son*, first published (2 vols.) in 1897. EMF was to keep a lasting admiration for *The Autobiographies of Edward Gibbon* (1796), and *The Vicar of Wakefield*, by Oliver Goldsmith, published 1766.
³ His room (W.7) in Bodley's Building at King's overlooked the river and the 'Backs'.
⁴ Frank Grant's family: see Letter 17.

24 To Alice Clara Forster

[Cambridge] Sunday [11 June 1899]

Dear Mother,

What shall I tell you first? Yesterday I went to the races with the Fulfords. I had quite a quarrel with Mrs F. because I was going back to supper with Meredith and she had never asked me but expected me to come back with them. She said 'Ah I know what it is: young men have so many invitations, and you do not mind throwing over one to go to another.' Then 'the family' was roused, and I said 'No: I have not thrown over your invitation for you have never invited me: and because you were kind enough to invite me back to supper last year I had no right to conclude that you would do so this.' Flatness ensued but she presently said she must forgive me, and was much pacified by me giving her three tickets for the King's Concert. I am to escort Mrs Woodbury, the Swedish governess and Phyllis. The day was very enjoyable. We were 14 and Mac Munn and I rowed down! Fulford has asked me to go out for the day down the river tomorrow. I ought not to go as there is work and I have also a bad blister on my middle finger, but I think I shall as I have long wanted to and may not have the chance again. The party at Meredith's was chilling. Mrs and Miss Meredith have huge noses and icy manners which reduced Collingham to terrified silence.[1] I think they are really nice, but people have no business to be so alarming. We went to Collingham's room and Miss M. sang. She has a most beautiful voice and would have been a professional if it had been stronger. It is fun making the acquaintance of people's people, but not one looks as respectable as you and very few as amiable! You should see the sights that walk about: the place doesn't look decent. The boat made one bump and was bumped twice: therefore going down one place. In spite of this there was much—I might say excessive merriment—in the evening. They played dance music inside one room, and waltzed most beautifully on the gravel path outside. At a late hour the festivities flowed into Meredith's room and I fled to bed. Today I went to lunch with Miss Darwin and managed to get the two Miss Ommaneys into Chapel when it seemed hopeless, to their great delight. This morning C. Clarke and the friend—whom I couldn't bear—came to breakfast.[2] They departed in the afternoon. Thursday I went to the May Week concert, being given a ticket. We had Verdi's Stabat Mater, Beethoven's Mount of Olives and—what I liked most—Dvorak's American Symphony.[3] All the themes are negro songs, most cleverly worked in. Fulford *is* going to the Clare Ball—you remember the quarrel. I think this is all the news. I hope your gaieties have been as pleasant and as inexpensive as mine. Mr Wedd is distressed that I am not coming on the Long [Vacation]: he says coaching by letter is no good. The place is looking a sight with the preparations for the ball. They are to dance in the hall and have supper in the front court, and the Jumbo house has been fitted up for sitting out.[4] What is the new servant like.

Your loving son.

Oh I nearly forgot: you are indeed a bit of a 'laryer' What a splendid letter you wrote the Provost: exactly what I wanted.[5] All the other mothers have written helplessly to their sons to ask what to answer. Lil knows.

ALS: KCC

[1] Miss Meredith: Hugh's sister Edith. David Horace Collingham (1879–1955) became a physician.

Nathaniel Wedd, EMF's classics supervisor at King's College, Cambridge, who influenced EMF to consider writing as a career. *Below* Hugh Owen Meredith, who helped elect EMF to the Apostles at Cambridge. *Below right* Robert Calverley Trevelyan, EMF's closest literary adviser for a few years from 1902; he accompanied EMF on his first visit to India.

² Perhaps Ruth Darwin: see Letter 15. The Miss Ommaneys: unidentified. Charles Clarke: a family friend.
³ Antonin Dvorak's Symphony No. 9 in E Minor: 'From the New World'.
⁴ Jumbo House: the archway in Gibbs Building at King's, reputed to have once housed an elephant.
⁵ Augustus Austen-Leigh (1840–1905) entered King's in 1859; was Dean, 1871–3; and Provost, from 1889.

25   To Alice Clara Forster

[Salisbury] Sunday [Summer 1899?]

Dear Mother

What rain. I am sorry for you and the Old Boys.[1] I suppose the match could not be played. I have not been able to ride or to see the soldiers: if only the wind drops I might try. I am so glad I didn't bring my bi[cycle]: hiring is so cheap: 6^d an hour 2/– half a day. I went for a nice little walk this afternoon in spite of the rain, and wore my new boots. Maimie seems well and strong, but much pestered by invalids. She wails about M. H. to me and then says 'but she is so unselfish' (which she isn't) 'and it is Mr Coate's fault.' I say 'he is an unscrupulous quack' and she says 'no: he is determined to cure her how ever long it takes.' M. H. is very nice, but Maimie has continually to be sitting with her and when she has headaches—which is often—we cannot play duets. The other invalids are Miss Hislop and Mrs Nihil, but as one is mad and the other decrepit and both bed-ridden, they cannot get to her, and she can see them when she wishes. When you come will you bring Cicero de Officiis—a dark blue book—and Mayor's Ancient Philosophy—dark green—if you can find them.[2] Barnums [circus] comes here next week and Maimie is wild to see it. I wish I were here to take her. She is much amazed at the way the keeper put his head into the lion's mouth without being decapitated. She has however an ingenious theory that his hair is dipped in chloroform, which stupefies the lion! I hear much of Mr Dimbleby, and have tried to read his books.[3] I can't think how Maimie is taken in. Scattered scraps of information such as "in 1903 there will be a second Flood: 'one of the continents' (!) will sink below the sea. In 1910 the world will probably be consumed in the tail of a comet, &^{tc}."

'Dear me' says Maimie, 'to think that we shall be probably alive to see it.'

ALU: KCC

¹ Probably the Old Boys of Tonbridge School.
² Joseph B. Mayor, A Sketch of Ancient Philosophy from Thales to Cicero (1885).
³ Jabez Bunting Dimbleby (1827–19??) wrote millenial books whose titles became progressively longer and more alarming. In 1897 The New Era at Hand, (1898–); or, The Approaching Close of the Great Prophetic Periods, achieved a thirteenth edition.

26   To George Barger[1]

Acton House, Felton R.S.O. [Northumberland][2]
27 July [1899]

Dear Barger,

I will say without preamble that I do absolutely understand and that if I do not treat the subject at very great length it is because you have very much expressed my thoughts on it.

In one way my position is more complicated than yours, for I have much sympathy with the people who do not understand him.[3] If he had not shown some liking for me I should have been as them, and when they accuse him of being conceited—of which I suppose the definition is that he has not any regard for their opinion—I know not what to reply. I did think that I saw what I should call an improvement in him—a tendency to suffer fools more gladly, to not only understand but also to sympathise with the opinions of the 'rest of King's', and Wedd said something to me of the same purport, though in other words, but from your experiences in this Long [Vacation] I fear that at all events the rest of Kings does not see this—beastly profanum vulgus, probably never will.[4] This letter is hopelessly contradictious, coloured too much with the question I am always discussing with myself, as to whether I am conventional or not. The reason that I take so much interest in M's relation to the outer world is that I like him so much that I cannot but wish he was in sympathy with it, & liked by it too. This is coupled with the knowledge that he is immeasurably superior to it, & that this is (in a way) unworthy of his notice. I'm getting in a hopeless boggle. I don't think analysis can be my strong point. If you can't make all this out reserve it till you see me & we can discuss it. I suppose much of the difficulty arises from the fascination you so well, so very well describe, which does not form a good foundation for the discussion of his relations to the rest of people. I said I wd not speak at length but I've been led away. Your letter has just arrived, and when I have finished this I descend to the prosaic but pleasant business of haymaking. My work is not as it should be, but I have done a fair amount lately. I have discovered though the rather pernicious truth that a little exercise is a useless thing and that I only am fit physically when I go out for a long day's expedition and never open a book. If I had discovered this 10 years ago, as most boys do, I should have been— well the subject's too extensive to tackle. I have had a good time in Scotland & here & go home next week. I have just read James' "A portrait of a Lady". It is very wonderful but there's something wrong with him or me: he is not as George Meredith. Now I'm reading the Forest Lovers by Maurice Hewlett, and am a little bored though there is lots of delightful writing.[5] Yesterday I went to Bamborough [sic], saw the castle and the tombs of my ancestors—I've no reason for supposing they are though the name is the same & the *arms* similar, but Bamborough is such a nice cradle for one's race that I shall always call them mine.⁶ Then I paddled on the deserted beach and felt very Calibanish for I had nothing to dry my toes with & the sand stuck them together.⁷ I must stop now. Thank you very much for your letter. I judge better to destroy it, as I am careless in leaving things about. Do as you think best with mine.

Yours very
sincerely
E.M. Forster

ALS: KCC

¹ George Barger (1879–1939), who was half Dutch by parentage, came to know EMF at King's. In 1903 he joined the Wellcome Laboratory as an experimental chemist. He was Professor of Chemistry at the Royal Holloway College, 1913–14; at the University of Edinburgh, 1919–37; and at Glasgow University, 1937–9.

² Home of EMF's huntin' and shootin' uncle, William Howley Forster (1855–1910), younger brother of his father.

³ This discussion about H. O. Meredith seems related to the then current debate among EMF's friends about the contrasting values at King's (humanistic) and Trinity (intellectual). Meredith, in their view, was behaving more like a Trinity man.

⁴ Profanum vulgus: from Horace's *Ode* (Book III, i, 1).

⁵ Hewlett, *The Forest Lovers: A Romance* (1898).

⁶ Bamburgh Castle: Norman castle on the site of the capital of the Saxon kingdom of Bernicia, in Northumberland; bought in 1894 by Lord Armstrong.

⁷ Allusion to Browning's 'Caliban upon Setebos; or, Natural Theology in the Island' (1864): 'Will sprawl, now that the heat of day is best, / . . . And, while he kicks both feet in the cool slush, . . . '

27   To Nathaniel Wedd

West Hackhurst, Abinger Hammer, Dorking
3 September [1899]

Dear Mʳ Wedd,

I have finished all the Latin you suggested—except the last two books of the Nat. Deorum, which I have not been able to get hold of.¹ I am just beginning the Greek, which I hope to get finished by October, as there is not much of it. Ought I to be doing anything about my history yet? I think I am getting to work quicker, which is some comfort. I was away till the beginning of August: three weeks of the time in Northumberland, where I suppose you are now. I liked Acton very much; we spent most of our time netting for salmon—or bull trout: I never could tell the difference—in the Coquet, and got a good many, to the great wrath of the Anglers' Federation, who own the opposite bank and may only use a rod, and have never yet been seen to get a fish. I have not seen anybody from King's except Haward, with whom I spent a morning in London.² Meredith has written once or twice to me: he seems to detest

Malcolm Lyall Darling, a Cambridge friend. He joined the India Civil Service in 1904; he and EMF stayed at Dewas. *Right* Rupert Barkeley Smith, whom EMF met in 1903 and who later joined the India Civil Service. EMF stayed with him in Allahabad. *Below* EMF (seated centre) with Herr Steinweg, Fraulein Backe and Mlle L. Auger de Balben at Nassenheide in 1905, when he tutored the children of the Countess Arnim. The two girls in the background are probably daughters of the house.

Germany very heartily. I am stopping here in Surrey for about a week.

Yours very sincerely
E. M. Forster

ALS: KCC

[1] Cicero, *De natura deorum* ('On the nature of the Gods').
[2] Lawrence Warrington Haward (1878–1957), who entered King's in 1897, was on *The Times'* music staff, 1906–14; then Curator, Manchester Corporation Art Galleries, 1914–45.

28   To Alice Clara Forster

King's College, Cambridge
24 October 1899

Dearest Mother,

You will like to hear an account of the dinner party. I wore all my best things, including those you put ready, and looked very nice indeed—probably I was remarked on though I did not hear it. We were ten in all Mr & Mrs Litchfield, Miss D[arwin], Miss Ommaney, Dr & Mrs Laurence Humphrey, another lady, two more nice dons and myself.[1] I was the only child, so I felt proud. I think I must have been to match Miss Ommaney. We were all very hungry and ate a great deal. I lifted my elbow and did not bite my bread. They talked of the Transvaal war, and were mostly against it; after desert the two dons talked in whispers about a broken 'tibia', which did not sound inviting. Then into the drawing room and more conversation, and one of the dons drove me down to King's. This morning Mr & Mrs Litchfield and Miss Darwin came to see me & my room. They liked it very much. This afternoon I went for a ride with Haward and picked some beautiful autumn leaves. My cold has left me with neuralgia over the left side of my face: it is not really bad but troubles me a good deal in the evening & early night. However there is nothing to be done for it but eat and drink, which I am doing. Hasten up over the coupons: I have [a] most wily plot to make Mrs Fulford buy the other; it is too long to explain, but is in train now, and I hope will succeed.[2] The coupons *must* be sent in within a month or they aren't valid.

To be read aloud: if aunt Eliza & uncle Frank have arrived give them my love and say how sorry I am to miss them, but I do hope they will come and spend a day with me at Cambridge if they can manage it.

--------------------- .. ---------------------

There: am I not an apt pupil of Ma's deceit: but Ma is good as well as deceitful and I am not.

Your loving
Morgan.

ALS: KCC

[1] Location of this party is unknown. Richard Buckley Litchfield (1832–1903) went to Trinity College, Cambridge, and read law but gave his major interest to the Working Men's College in Great Ormond Street, London. In 1871 he married Charles Darwin's daughter Henrietta Emma (1843–1929), the 'Aunt Etty' of Gwen Raverat's *Period Piece: A Cambridge Childhood* (1952). She was a close friend of EMF's Aunt Laura Forster. After Richard Litchfield's death Etty moved to a house called Burrow's Hill in Gomshall, near Abinger. She once told EMF that he would think differently about Egypt and India if he had read the books *she* had read. The Miss Darwin at this party was probably Ruth Darwin. Dr Laurence Humphrey was a Cambridge physician. Miss Ommaney is unidentified.

[2] EMF was meditating vengeance on Mrs Fulford's high-pressure salesmanship at the bazaar; see Letter 18.

29   To Alice Clara Forster

King's College, Cambridge
Sunday [5 November 1899]

Dearest Mother

So they are coming![1] Advice indeed is wanted. Shall I give them a 2/– lunch complete or order things separately, and what? and shall it be hot or cold. Shall they have tea in the Union or in the rooms—and how am I to manage to make friends flit through, and who shall flit. I want a Minstrels gallery like Penshurst.[2] And wouldn't Uncle Frank like whiskey as well. It is the little things that are really important to make them enjoy themselves, and I do want it to be successful. I have heard from Uncle Willie and at the end he says "I hope your mother is better". What does it mean. I do hope you haven't been deceitful and it has got round by Aunt Laura. My suit is quite successful & could be paid for; as for the g^t coat—er—well—I haven't written with one [thing?] & another. Yesterday I went for a walk with Mr Headlam.[3] "Dear, clever people are very strange":— he went straight over ploughed fields with corn just coming up, so that I got muddy to the knees—old-clothes—and trampled on the young crops—but I hope it was too young to be hurt. However I enjoyed it very much & we are to go again. I am going now to play duets which I enjoy. Would you have come here cheap if you had come with the F[ulford]'s? If you go to Putney by any chance couldn't you come for the night?[4] The time seems flying away, and next year if I am here I shall be in lodgings and not worth looking at. I have been reading Bernard Shaw's plays. Wonderfully clever & amusing, but they make me feel bad inside.[5]

Your loving
Morgan

ALS: KCC

[1] Aunt Eliza and Uncle Frank Fowler.
[2] Penshurst Place, in Kent, birthplace of Sir Philip Sidney.
[3] Walter George Headlam (1866–1908), a distinguished classicist and Fellow of King's.
[4] Putney: the home of EMF's grandmother and the Whichelo aunts.
[5] George Bernard Shaw's *Plays: Pleasant and Unpleasant* was published in 1898.

30   To Alice Clara Forster

King's College, Cambridge
10 November [1899]

Dearest Mother,

They are gone—and I really think it has been quite successful. I spent your money without stint. They arrived in shower & we drove to here in a cab, but immediately after it cleared up. On arriving we examined the chapel. Loud were the exclamations of approval. Aunt Eliza repeated "it is so sumptuous, so rich, the glass is so rich—like woven silk, so . ." and she waved her hands. "Fine building, remarkably fine building" kept on remarking Uncle Frank. Then lunch: nice preparation of chicken & pineapple & cream. Whiskey, then white port. After that, coffee. Collingham & Mollison appeared. Aunt Eliza talked volubly, but was not elegant, and amusing; though she chanted about 100 times "I know you will all be sorry to leave this place, that you will." Mollison rose to the situation and explained in simple language the difference of being out & in college. Collingham mumbled to Uncle Frank. Waxing excited, Aunt E. offered to send M. & C. each a pot of Devonshire Cream which they accepted with thanks. Then, when they had departed, she felt dull: had she been free & forward, would they think it ill mannered? but perhaps they would make allowance for country people. I said 'Dear me no', but she shrank from sending it direct, so it is to go via me, & the thanks return the same way. Then we went sight seeing—senate house, Caius, Trinity, Johns, the Backs, the Union, Jesus, Trinity again, & then I was bringing them back to the Union for tea, when they turned tiresome. No they did not want it: they would walk in the direction of the station. I managed to delay them a little over the University Church, & then took them to the tram, for which they wouldn't wait: they would walk. No sooner did they walk than they wanted to drive, so I put them into a hansom, there being no 4 wheelers, & swiftly followed on my legs. In spite of all we had nearly ½ hour to wait at the station, they not getting off past 5.0 I pressed them hard to stay, but they couldn't as they were dining with Mrs Kynsey. "I tell you we *pulled* & *pulled*, but they made us promise." Complements [*sic*] flew amain, and they wanted me to fix the date of a visit for next year, and I had a hard time evading. They are certainly much nicer as guests than as hosts and I enjoyed the visit very much. They liked their time at T[unbridge] Wells.

ALU: KCC

31   To Alice Clara Forster

[Cambridge. 3 December 1899]

Sunday

There now! After all I have got an English Essay prize—and got £4 for Latin Verse as well.[1] About the latter I am much delighted. But not so much about the former, as there are rather heartburnings on the subject. There were, you know, three subjects—Montesquieu, The Future of Africa, and the Novelists. The two best essays were on Montesquieu, but they did not like to give all the prize money to one subject, so gave a prize to one on Montesquieu, and recommended the other to an extra prize—which the college is sure to give. That is all right; but when they decided to whom to give the other half of the real prize, they had to choose between me and the Africa man, which of course was difficult. We know it was touch and go, and I think they had better given it to him, for his Essay was twice as long as mine and he had got up his subject—and besides he had never had a prize before. I have not seen him since the award and he is very queer tempered so I fear he may be angry. The Latin Verse is a great surprise and I am very jubilant: I only got £2 last year. I had intended coming home this next Saturday, but Nicholas has just asked me to spend a night at Eltham which I shall like to do, so I shall wait and go to them on Monday and come home Tuesday. I have asked Fulford and he will like to come, but we have not settled the day. I forgot to answer your question about Xmas. It would be very nice indeed to have 'the boys': I have not seen them for so long: perhaps the Courtneys could come later.[2] I am looking forward to the return. I think it

ALU incomplete: KCC

[1] He won a half-share of the College Prize, with an essay on 'The Novelists of the 18th Century and Their Influence on Those of the 19th' (A MS. KCC).
[2] Courtneys: apparently family friends.

32   To Laura Mary Forster

King's College, Cambridge
27 February [1900]

Dear Aunt Laura

I wonder how you are getting on in this depressing weather. We have had floods here, which put off the Lent races, but the floods have gone & the races began to-day. It was too wet to go down, but I hear that each of our boats have made a bump, which was more than we had hoped for. You will, I know, like to hear what I have got with my prize money—Ruskin's Stones of Venice, Shakespere,

Bryce's Holy Roman Empire, Seeley's History of British Policy, A history of King's by the Provost, and five of Meredith's novels.[1] I have still nearly £3 left. Last Thursday I went to Mr Dickinson's to hear Trevelyan of Trinity read a paper on 'The Uses of History', & very good it was. Last night Trevelyan came to my rooms & asked me to breakfast on Friday, which was very kind of him, as there was no reason he should do it. I know you will be glad to hear this, as I remember you saying you wished we could meet. Which of his relations did our family know especially?[2] I am glad to hear of Cronje's surrender; the news came this morning.[3] I have just been at the Union at a stormy discussion whether Olive Schreiner's husband should be allowed to take part in a debate or not. People objected to him because he had come for propagandist purposes, but the motion was carried and he is at present speaking, tho' I haven't got time to hear him.[4]

Nicolas paid me a visit last Sunday week. We enjoyed ourselves very much in spite of slushy weather. Miss Jorgensen came to tea with Boofie & Nora a week or so ago.[5] I don't think I have any other news to tell you, except that I enjoy myself as much as ever, and do not get as much work done as I could wish—which you will be glad to hear. The weather has been so bad that I have hardly been any bicycle rides, but always for walks. I want to go & see Mr Carter as soon as the roads are less muddy. My Mays come next week & my tripos in May—a depressing prospect![6] I am very anxious to hear how your domestic arrangements are going on. Thank you so much for sending the Punches. They are a public blessing to the staircase!

Yours affectly
E. M. Forster

ALS: KCC

[1] James Bryce's 1863 Arnold Prize Essay, *The Holy Roman Empire* (1864); Sir John Robert Seeley, *The Growth of British Policy: An Historical Essay* (1895); Augustus Austen-Leigh, *King's College* (1899), in the Cambridge College Histories series.

[2] George Macaulay Trevelyan (1876–1962) was Regius Professor of Modern History at Cambridge, 1927–40. He was the third son of the politician and diplomat Sir George Otto Trevelyan, 2nd Bt (1838–1928), and Thomas Babington Macaulay was his maternal uncle.

[3] General Piet Arnoldus Cronje (c. 1840–1911) a Transvaal commando leader, surrendered at Paardeberg on 27 February.

[4] Olive Schreiner (1855–1920), South African pro-Boer crusader and novelist, sprang into fame with *The Story of an African Farm: A Novel* (1883). Her husband Samuel Cron Cronwright-Schreiner (1863–1936) left South Africa for England on 8 January, hoping, as a South African of pure English descent, to get a hearing for the Boers' view of the situation. For one of his English speeches, see *The Pro-Boers: The Anatomy of an Antiwar Movement*, ed. Stephen Koss, pp. 121–6.

[5] Boofie: i.e. Ruth Darwin, and her sister Emma Nora (1885–), later Lady Barlow, daughters of Sir Horace Darwin. A family jest dubbed Ruth and her brother Erasmus (1881–1915) 'the Boofies': hence 'Mr and Mrs Boofie' in Letter 34.

[6] Mays: a first-year preliminary examination. Tripos: in Cambridge parlance, the final examination (or examinations) leading to a BA degree, or the course of study leading to this.

33   To Alice Clara Forster

[King's College, Cambridge]
Friday [2 March 1900]

Dearest Mother

I haven't written for a long time. Our great excitement has of course been the relief of Ladysmith. The beaming Mrs Tabor brought me the news & I ran out about 11. in the morning yesterday.[1] The streets were already full of flags, & all the bells were ringing. In the evening there was a bonfire but I was too late to get out of college, so watched it from the lawn on the north side of the chapel, where it looked most beautiful. The Lent races have been this week. I went down twice & ran. The first boat made 2 bumps & the second 3, so we are jubilant. Tonight they are all having a dinner. Last evening, at 7.15, which is just the middle of Hall, someone—or rather ones—cried out for cheers for the Queen, & the whole company rose to their feets [sic] & finally stood on the forms, singing. Such jack's work!—and the poor dons were so terrified—thought it was a mutiny—but at last detected the noise of the National Anthem and stood up & joined, which was very kind of them. O[scar] B[rowning] and Nixon, who are Pro Boer, were however very angry.[2] This morning I went to breakfast with Trevelyan, who is a Fellow of Trinity, and whose paper on 'The Uses of History' I think I told you Mr Dickinson had invited me to hear. He is a descendant of the Trevelyans the Thorntons knew—Macaulay's great nephew I think. Aunt Laura wanted me to know him so she will be pleased.[3] It was very kind of him to ask me, for he had no reason to do so, having only seen me among a lot of others who were listening to his paper. He is very nice, very clever, and mighty clever! He doesn't seem to have heard of the Thorntons, which would distress Aunt L.! Not much else has happened this week. I had a very nice letter from Nicholas. I am writing to the Postons suggesting I should spend Saturday—Monday with them on my way home.[4] The Mays end on a Friday. If I do that I shall be with you on March 19th—I am not quite sure of the date—if not on the 17th. I have not yet consulted Mr Wedd as to working up here, but I don't think I should as the climate is worse than ever (not that I'm ill!) and I believe that Dr James, the tutor, is very chary about giving leave to stay.[5] However I must do as Mr W. thinks best. You, I find, will never answer my enquiries how you are, and never mention your health except 'a racking head' after your struggle with Milly Ievers: which wasn't surprising.[6] I am writing on a table on my knee which accounts a little for my writing. I find I am quicker in reading classics than I used to be, but I don't think I shall be any more effective in exams.

Your loving
Pop Snake.

Joy! Ickle Lill has committed an error in Orthography. She put 'too' for 'to'! Yes, Gran does sound peevish.

ALS: KCC

[1] Ladysmith, in Natal, was besieged by the Boers from 1 November 1899 until relieved by Sir Redvers Buller (1839–1908) on 28 February 1900. Mrs Tabor was EMF's bedmaker. In 1927 EMF, Collingham, Mollison, George Barger, and H. O. Meredith presented her with a retirement gift. EMF wrote (to Collingham, 7 December 1927. Jane Wedmore) that 'she was most moved and moving. You ought to have seen her start, dramatic yet sincere, when the word "rose bowl" struck her astonished ear.'

[2] On Oscar Browning, see Letter 20. John Edwin Nixon (d. 1916) had been a King's Fellow and Tutor since 1862. *The Times* (14 February 1916, p. 11) described him as 'one of the last of the old type of Eton scholar and Fellow of King's under the Founder's Statutes'. His weekly quartet parties were famous; in the 1870s he reorganised music at Cambridge and was 'largely responsible for the founding of the King's College Choir School'.

[3] On G. M. Trevelyan, see Letter 32.

[4] Charles Poston was a stockbroker and company director who lived at 'Highfield' in Stevenage. The Forsters were friendly with the Postons, and EMF's encounter with Mr Poston's second wife, Clementine, helped to suggest the Wilcoxes of *Howards End*. The Postons moved to Rooksnest about 1909, and eventually Clementine and her daughter were enabled to buy it with EMF's help.

[5] Montague Rhodes James (1862–1936), bibliographer, antiquarian, and writer of ghost-stories; Director of the Fitzwilliam Museum, 1894–1908; Provost of King's, 1905–18; and Vice-Chancellor, 1913–15; later Provost of Eton.

[6] Milly Ievers: unidentified.

THE FIRST NOVELS, 1901–12

Marianne Thornton's £8,000, left in trust, enabled him to postpone the choice of a career, and in October 1901 his mother and he, giving up their home and putting their furniture in store, set off for a year's travelling in Italy. The scheme was, in part, that he should study Italian art and architecture, to equip himself as a university-extension lecturer, and partly that he should try his hand at writing. It proved, as he said later, 'a very timid outing' and was spent entirely in hotels and *pensioni* and largely among other English tourists (who provided copy for his two 'Italian' novels). The trip succeeded, none the less, in both its aims. He made himself a very competent lecturer on the Italian Renaissance. Further, he fell gradually but intensely in love with Italy. And at Ravello, in May 1902, he wrote, with sudden inspiration, 'The Story of a Panic'—a joyful and exciting experience that gave him the conviction that he was a writer. Before the end of their stay in Italy he had drafted a good deal of the novel that, after drastic later revisions, became *A Room with a View*.

On his return to England he began to do some lecturing for the Cambridge Local Lectures Board, and he began, also, on a voluntary basis, to teach classes in Latin at the Working Men's College in Camden Town. In October 1903 *The Independent Review*, a new periodical of Liberal tendency, was launched by a group of his Cambridge friends, and this gave him his first serious outlet as a writer. The magazine lasted only four years, but during these he and Hilaire Belloc were the principal 'literary' contributors, and Forster published a number of stories and essays in its pages.

In 1904, his mother bought a house in Weybridge, where they were to live for the next twenty years. His own next six years were very productive. Life with his mother suited him well at this time, and he was not persuaded by friends who told him that he ought to break away from it. His pattern of life was a gentle one, composed of writing, piano-playing, and visits from relations and family friends, interspersed with lecturing assignments up and down the country, classes at the Working Men's College, and a succession of visits to friends and relatives, walking tours and foreign holidays.

In 1905 he went for five months to Nassenheide in Germany as tutor to the daughters of Elizabeth, Countess von Arnim-Schlagenthin, author of *Elizabeth and Her German Garden*. During this time he completed negotiations with Blackwood's for publication of his first novel, *Where Angels Fear to Tread*. The book appeared in October and received some very warm reviews. Several influential literary figures, in particular C. F. G. Masterman and Edward Garnett, recognised him as a writer of outstanding promise, and he himself, despite severe self-criticism, had by now confidence in his talents. His chief literary confidant at this period was R. C. Trevelyan, himself a dedicated though not very successful writer.

A major event in Forster's private life took place in the summer of 1906, when he agreed to give some coaching in Latin to Syed Ross Masood, a young Indian protégé of the Forsters' neighbour Sir Theodore Morison. Masood was the grandson of the famous Muslim reformer Sir Syed Ahmad Khan, the founder of Aligarh College. A close friendship sprang up between Masood and Forster: this was the origin of Forster's interest in India. In due course this interest was strengthened through his friendship with a Cambridge man, Malcolm Darling, who had joined the Indian Civil Service and had become tutor to the young Raja of Dewas Senior. These contacts with Muslim and with Hindu India made it inevitable that he should some day visit the country.

The great success of Forster's fourth novel, *Howards End*, put it beyond dispute that he had 'arrived'. It also brought him considerable royalties, making a visit to India now a possibility. And it launched him, decisively, into literary society; in the months after the novel's appearance he began to move in the 'Bloomsbury' and other literary circles. This auspicious time was also marked by a curious side-effect: the conviction that he had 'dried up' as a novelist and would be able to write no more. The crisis was complicated by his mother's morbid reaction to her mother's death (which caused him also much pain, for he was greatly attached to his grandmother), and (according to him) their life together was never again so happy.

In 1911 Sidgwick and Jackson published a volume of his short stories, *The Celestial Omnibus*, which earned him the friendship of the Ulster novelist Forrest Reid, with whom, over the next thirty years, he had extensive and interesting correspondence. Forster wrote two plays (unpublished and unperformed), and he embarked on a new novel, now known as 'Arctic Summer', but got into difficulties with it. Thus, when at last he set out for India in October 1912, in the company of his friends Goldsworthy Lowes Dickinson and Robert C. Trevelyan, it was partly in the hope that the experience might resolve his 'writer's block'.

34   To Alice Clara Forster

[Cambridge. 2 March 1901]

Dearest Mother

The enclosed (See end of letter) has naturally perturbed & enraged me. Nothing could have been clearer than the agreement I came to with Winnie, that she was to let me know when she came to Wistow, & I was then to invite her.[1] I am despatching letters of mingled firmness & regret to her, & also to the Hughs, coupled in the latter case with an invitation to luncheon. Is it stupidity or malice? Tear this up.

I went last night to the H. Darwins—present M^r & Mrs Boofie, Lady Farrer, Mr Jenkinson the University Librarian & Mr Newall, the sub astronomer, and his wife.[2] The conversation was elevated but depressing, turning chiefly on the new Star (have you see it? In Perseus), microscopes, prismatic refractors, and Bugs—from the naturalist's not the housekeeper's point of view. Lady Farrer was in a bright mood, but was very nice afterwards. I hope she is coming to tea Monday: perhaps Boofie too.

My visit to Miss Stephen's went off very nicely. There was Leslie Stephen, his son, Trevelyan, & a friend, & Barcroft a King's fellow.[3] They booed down the trumpet, but sounded to say such foolish things that when it came to my turn I refused. I had such a nice letter from Miss Stephen afterwards, saying that the evening had cheered up her brother.[4]

My other experience has been tea at Reddaway's to meet Girtonians.[5] Reddaway was clammy with agitation, for the fire went out nearly & the chaperon arrived without the young ladies who couldn't be found. Finally they were found, and we had tea and played 'Ping-Pong'—table Tennis, a most entertaining game, and I played against a maiden who was actually clumsier than myself, and beat her hollow. We his history class [sic], and chatted most agreeably about Triposes & subjects, till they departed, & we fell on the food & devoured it.

Thursday night was the Brahms Requiem in the chapel, which I much liked. Oh the clacking men![6] never at peace, but always wishing to make their voices heard—for you wouldn't believe it, but nearly everyone in the college is angry because they have the Requiem in the chapel. The Low church people are angry because a Requiem is Popish, the High Church because it was on an Ember day, the Fellows because they hadn't got seats for nothing, the aesthetic people because they said the electric light w^d injure the chapel, the patriotic people because it was against the traditions. A letter has actually been sent by some undergraduates to the Visitor, the Bishop of Lincoln, complaining of it! It is to be hoped he is a sensible man and that his reply will not make them feel martyrs.[7]

I am going out to lunch to morrow at the Frank Darwins.

The cards from the Army and Navy [Stores] have come. Thank you.

I expect I shall be back in about a fortnight. I am afraid I shall have to work hard, for I have not nearly concluded my subjects yet, and must leave all next term for revision. I have written to the dentist to tell him to fix one more interview as he wished it. My teeth haven't ached, but I still only dare to eat one side of my mouth. Very much love to Gran. I hope she will be all right soon.

Your loving
Morgan

P. S. I can't find the enclosure which was a card from Aunt Laura, saying that Lucy had been to tea, & was much aggrieved because I had "promised to ask Winnie to come to Cambridge and had not done so."

ALS: KCC

¹ Probably Winifred Forster (1878–1963), later Mrs Byres-Leake, daughter of EMF's uncle, the Rev. Charles T. Forster of Hinxton.

² This party was at Sir Horace Darwin's. Lady Farrer was his mother-in-law, Katherine Euphemia Wedgwood ('Effy'). Francis J. J. Jenkinson (1853–1923) became University Librarian in 1889. Hugh Frank Newell (1857–1944), Fellow of Trinity College, was Assistant to the Cavendish Professor of Physics, 1886–90, and Professor of Astrophysics, 1913–28.

³ Caroline Emilia Stephen (1834–1909), Quaker sister of Leslie Stephen (1832–1904), and aunt of Virginia Stephen (Woolf) (1882–1941) and Thoby Stephen (1880–1906), Leslie's younger son. Miss Stephen wrote books on Quaker history, engaged in philanthropic projects, and settled in Cambridge in 1885. Leslie Stephen was extremely deaf and used an ear-trumpet in an often disconcerting manner. EMF tried to scrutinise him, but Stephen immediately 'whirled' round toward him. Cf. William Rothenstein's description of his own daunting visit to Sir Leslie in the 1890's, in his *MM*, p. 61. Joseph Barcroft (1872–1947) entered King's in 1893, became a Fellow in 1899, and a leading physiologist, knighted in 1935. The Trevelyan present was probably G. M. Trevelyan.

⁴ Miss Stephen's letter does not survive.

⁵ William Fiddian Reddaway (1872–1949), historian, became a Fellow of King's in 1897. On an encounter with one of these girls in Italy in 1901, see *EMF*, I, 87.

⁶ EMF's adaptation of a favourite phrase of his grandmother, Louisa Whichelo: 'Oh the clacking females!'

⁷ Edward King (1829–1910), Bishop of Lincoln since 1886, was an appropriate seat of appeal for the High-Church faction; he figured in the famous 'Lincoln Judgement' of 1890, which settled a long-standing controversy about details of the Anglican communion service. *The Cambridge Review* (7 March 1901, p. 232) took up safe ground: 'It is a happy thought to celebrate the memory of a good and noble lady [Queen Victoria] whom we are still mourning.'

35   To Nathaniel Wedd

10 Earl's Road, Tunbridge Wells
Tuesday [early March 1901]

Dear Wedd

I went to see the O. B., and found him aimiable but not encouraging. My one hope, he seems to think, is to fortify my degree with a certificate from a training college. He suggested my coming to his at Cambridge, but did not seem particularly enthusiastic about me.[1] However I may as well apply for the papers on the subject. Thank you for the trouble you have taken about me.

I saw your lectureship in Monday's paper. I suppose you will lecture in Greek history.[2]

I leave home next Saturday, and start on my round of visits. I shall try to learn some French in the vac: it is probably the most useful thing I can do.

I remain
Y[rs] very sincerely
E. M. Forster

ALS: KCC

[1] Oscar Browning founded the Cambridge University Day Training College and was its Principal, 1891-1909.
[2] Wedd was University Lecturer in Ancient History, 1901-11.

36 To Alice Clara Forster

Holmleigh, Salisbury [Summer 1901]

Dearest Mother

I arrived here safely on Friday night after a rather broiling journey. Maimie had returned from a visit to the Wildes [Wylds?] just before, & seemed well.[1] Not much has happened worthy of writing. We spend most of our time playing duets and learning Italian. I sympathise with you about mournful topics of conversation. M. talks continually about the end of the world, visits from departed spirits, and Mr Dimbleby. I do trust that I shall drag her down to mundane things.

We went a little walk yesterday, & I called on Miles Williams, who is coming to supper one day this week.[2]

We have just had news of Mrs Nihill's death—I think you know who she is. She has been very ill for some time. "Poor thing," said Maimie, "I shall not have to send her any peaches this year: she will have better fruit"—and then she cannot think why I laugh. Harriet, who lived with her, is to come here for a holiday.

I left Aunt Laura nearly well. Poor thing, it is annoying for her; she has never been bad, but just bad enough to prevent her doing anything with me. And she is always ill during the good weather, and then catches another illness in the bad. She is going to write to Ronald Melville about me and the Education Office, or the clerkship in the H. of Commons, or South Kensington [Victoria & Albert Museum].[3] She won't hear a word about the British Museum, because someone says it is badly ventilated,—quite inaccurate I believe; but if one is to get on by favour one must put up with such things. Having taken a new sheet I have nothing to put on it. I go to Cambridge on the 15th—at least I think so. M. H. comes here then, for goodness knows how long. Miss Heaslop keeps on suggesting herself as a paying guest at 30/– a week, but Maimie still resists.

Your loving Morgan

Maimie utters delightful remarks at times, such as "I far prefer an ugly man who is tall to a short man with the face of an Apollo." Love to Miss Powell.[4]

ALS: KCC
[1] A member of this family, May Wyld, figures in EMF's Indian letters: Letter 107.
[2] Miles Williams: unidentified.
[3] Ronald Ruthven Leslie-Melville, 11th Earl of Leven and Melville (1835–1906), nephew of EMF's great-aunt Marianne Thornton, succeeded his half-brother in 1889. He was Representative Peer from Scotland, from 1892, a large landowner and Director of the P&O Steamship Company, and at one time a Director of the Bank of England.
[4] A diary entry (10 January 1899. KCC) suggests that Miss Powell lived near family friends in Richmond.

37   To Edward Joseph Dent[1]

Hotel Europe, Milan
22 October 1901

Dear Dent
    An engine called Anchises drew us here from Como on Saturday last. Since then it has rained without a break. If the ashes are ever quenched it will be now.[2]
    Saturday we slept at the Hotel de France, that had been recommended by friends. But the bed rooms were so grubby and the dining room so airless that my mother said no she couldn't, and the Sabbath morn was spent in changing habitations. This is comfortable and costly. I hate it. The waiters hand the dishes in white cotton gloves and the bread comes in a silver spoon. I yearn for the attractive looking Biscione, which couldn't take us in.
    But it had better rain in Milan than any where, for as a lady sagely remarked "if it wasn't for the things it contains no one would ever pay it a visit"—and it is not too dark to see pictures and at the same time too dark to see that the Cathedral roof is painted. It is therefore nearly all for the best.
    I have been twice to the Brera, thrice to the Cathedral; and also to the Poldi-Pezzoli, Sta Maria and the Leonardo, and St Ambrogio.[3] The last mentioned has given me more pleasure than anything. Today I was rather weary and did not do much. We stop till Monday next, when we go to Florence, possibly staying two nights at Bologna on the way. At Florence we shall go to the hotel you told us of for a night, and then settle on a Pension. November there,

Dec-Feb. at Rome. I hope to see Pisa Lucca and Perugia somehow, but Siena and San Gimignano and Volterra will have to wait till next year.

We left England on the 3rd, having a devilish start—quite Hawardian that—comprising wrong tickets, unexpected arrival in Paris, sick headaches, quarrelling, lost luggage.[4] We only began to recover at Lucerne where we stopped three nights. Then to Como for two nights. Then to Cadenabbia—for one night as we thought, but it turned out to be ten, so charming was the Hotel Belle Ile (do you know it?) and so attractive the vociferous old ladies. I found it dull at first, but soon got used to doing nothing. My mother was very loath to go, for the weather there was beautiful. But save for a purse that was lost and was found and a flea and a centipede that were found the incidents were but few. I knocked a good many days off Purgatory though, by going to the Pilgrimage chapels round about.

As for fleas—they are nothing accounted of, as you warned me. But with ammonia—your advice—they make very little difference to one's pleasure. What I do mind are the electric trams which disturb by night and terrify by day. The Piazza del Duomo is a horrid nightmare to us.

My Italian doesn't come on, and I shall be unable to talk to the people at the Florence hotel. But I mean there to take myself in hand.

I suppose you are now in Cambridge. How I wish—in many ways—that I was too. It's the one place where I seem able to get to know people and get on with them without effort. When does your dissertation go in?[5] And now it is I who crave scraps of Cambridge gossip, though I cannot repay them by Bædekers up to date.

I remain

Yours very sincerely
E. M. Forster

ALS: KCC

[1] Edward Joseph Dent (1876–1957) came from a landed Yorkshire family and went to Eton and King's College, Cambridge, where he was elected Fellow in 1901. His early work on Alessandro Scarlatti did much to revive interest in music of the baroque, and his translations of Mozart's libretti are still in regular use. From 1926 he was Professor of Music in Cambridge, and he was President of the International Society of Contemporary Music from 1922. He was a virulent anti-clerical and misogynist, with a severe manner and a habit of closing his eyes in company. EMF, who was fond of him and drew on him for the hero in Where Angels Fear to Tread, told PNF that Dent took much interest in him when he was growing up but less later—'after the information was imparted'.

[2] 'Ashes'; conceivably a reference to the scene in Virgil's Aeneid (II, 705–59) in which Aeneas fled from burning Troy with his father Anchises on his shoulders.

[3] Palazzo di Brera: the art gallery. Cathedral: the Duomo di Santa Tecla. Museo Poldi-Pezzoli: former private home and art collection bequeathed to the city in 1879. Santa Maria della Grazie: brick and terra-cotta church built 1466–90, with Leonardo da Vinci's The Last Supper (1495–8) in the monastery refectory. Sant' Ambrogio: built on the remains of the Basilica Martyrum erected by St Ambrose in 386.

4 Alludes to L. W. Haward. Cf. Letter 27.
5 Dissertation on Alessandro Scarlatti (1659–1725), Italian composer on whom Dent became the recognised authority.

38   To Edward Joseph Dent

Albergo Bonciani, Florence
30 October [1901]

Dear Dent

Your very welcome letter came this morning. We go tomorrow to the *Pension Simi, 2 Lungarno delle Grazie*.[1]

We have been here three days, and very comfortable, but my mother hankers after an Arno view and a South aspect, so we are not stopping.

The people here beam greatly at the sound of your name, but I regret to say that at the O. B.'s they stare blankly, and my Italian is insufficient to describe his appearance.[2] It is a fat young fair haired man with a very dress shirt that I talk to. We like the food too, though our ignorance of Italian words and ways makes choosing difficult and sometimes unsuccessful

Everything about the Pension Simi seems nice except the lady who keeps it, who scatters her Hs like morsels and calls me 'the young gentleman'. But perhaps this is fastidious. Jennings Riccioli, alas! was full as regards South rooms. M^{de} J.—or R—has asked us in to tea. We went up to the Bellini, but slunk away when we saw it. Pendini looked nice, but we wanted the Arno.

Thank you very much for the letter of Introduction. I am most grateful for it, as I know no one here. I don't know either of the non-contracting parties in the C-C business, so it should be easy to keep away from it. I am sorry that such storms are following the breaking off of the engagement.[3] I was at school for 3 weeks with Hugh Crofton. He was very much bored, but not as much as I was, and I always remember him as one of the few people who were kind there. I haven't seen him since.[4]

I have done little sight seeing as yet, and my mother none, as we are both rather knocked up, why I don't know. This aft.noon I have been to the Uffizi and saw two rooms of Tuscan pictures.

Yesterday I went to St Lorenzo. I had got ready all the appropriate sentiments for the New Sacristy, and they answered very well.[5] More spontaneous perhaps were my feelings at seeing the cloisterful of starved and maimed cats.

Though one of the many cradles of Italian Art is at the door, we have not yet inspected it properly. Besides, it always seems shut.

We went to the Certosa at Milan, for which I have to thank you; also to Monza.[6] I went twice on to the Cathedral roof, the second time on Sunday, which is not so nice, as the people on the spire spit on you as you come up. I was also much struck by there being a forth on the roof; I don't know whether I am more impressed by the number of the forths in Italy or by their fig leaf character.[7] Talking of fig leaves, how flagrantly indecent are the statues in the Uffizi with their little brown paper bathing drawers. I almost feel that the permanent plaster article of the Catholic reaction is preferable. It did know its own mind.

Thank you for Cambridge News. Have you come across a bye-termist called Daniells?[8] He kept opposite me at 12 K[ing's] P[arade], and I think you would find him nice. He is older than most of us, and hated Cambridge very badly, so perhaps he may not be there still.

I wonder if you would be so very kind as to send me a copy of Basileona when it comes out, and let me owe it you for a rather indefinite period?[9] I am glad you didn't wire to me, as after all we didn't go to Bologna. You'll of course let me know if there's any thing of any kind I can do here. I hope you can read this. The Bonciani pen is rather bad. Their piano though is very good.

Y[rs]

E. M. Forster

I am very sorry indeed to hear about M[rs] Allen's death.[10] Tomorrow I was going to write to her about Italian lessons, so your letter came just in time.

ALS: KCC

[1] The Pensione Simi, in *A Room with a View*, seems to have been based on this Florence pension. Hugh Carey, nephew of Dent's friend Clive Carey (1883–1968), told PNF (letter, 27 March 1971) that he had found in his uncle's diary for 1904 'a description of an incident when he [EMF] & Dent (& Percy Lubbock) were on holiday and had to give up their "room with a verandah", which is I suppose a germ of "A Room with a View".' This passage, as printed in Hugh Carey, *Duet for Two Voices*, pp. 19–20, omits the sentence: 'We moved upstairs, where we had a better view, but a smaller balcony.' See also *RV*, p. 221.

[2] I.e. Oscar Browning, who prided himself on his intimacy with Italy.

[3] Probably a reference to David Horace Collingham and Mabyn Dorothy Crace, sister of a fellow-Kingsman, whose father objected to their marrying. They did so, however.

[4] Certainly a slip for Hugh Croft, who was at Tonbridge School, 1891–93. The School has no further record of him.

[5] Begun by Michelangelo in 1520 and usually called the Medici Chapel.

[6] The Certosa of Pavia, Carthusian monastery near Milan. Monza is a village near Milan.

[7] More accurately, fourth: Cambridge slang for lavatory.

[8] Probably Harold Griffith Daniels (1874–1952), 1901 bye-termist (one who began his academic career a term late) who went down without a degree, owing to illness. He became a journalist.

[9] *Basileona* (Nos. 1–8), then called *Basileon* (1900–14); usefully reprinted 1974, with Introduction by Sir Charles Tennyson, as *Basileon: A Magazine of King's College, Cambridge, 1900–14*.

[10] Mrs Allen: perhaps the mother of Hugh Percy Allen (1869–1946), musicologist and friend of Dent, and Director of the Royal College of Music, 1918–37.

HARNHAM.
MONUMENT GREEN.
WEYBRIDGE.

19/10/08

Dear Dent

No, I don't expect that you will do with the book very well; it does, sincerely or insincerely, commend an attitude that you will think insincere. Only I do wonder that you find it difficult to read — pretty straight forward isn't it, such.

I feel myself that it comes off as far as it goes — which is a damned little way — and that its character of Lucy, on which everything depends, is all right; she and Mr Beebe have interested me a good deal. Cecil (described not entirely from Lucy's point of view) is certainly incomplete. But his 3 proposals don't strike me as unnatural. She may only be a peg to hang his artistic sensations on, but she is a peg he can't reach easily, and this at once increases her value. Of course when his amour propre is wounded it is a different thing — off he goes at the end of the book, & he comes a misogynist. But until that happens, I maintain he will be attracted, and think that he is caring more about her than about himself. You say "if he is too young to realise that he can know no one intimately, he does not seem worth bringing in." Why?

Oh Dent, these slips! What is one to do about them. I laboured so with the Italian, but of course have missed all the points you have mentioned, & I dare say many more. Only I will defend Santa Conversazione; — they are saints talking, not family groups: Filippo Lippi, Andrea del Sarto as well as Bellini.

I got home Friday — straight through from Parma. Have had a splendid time, blessing you most days and, as you may imagine, every evening. I was just going to write

to you about the net. Would you resent it, being washed? I have grabbed it a little, and my sponge has pump shifted over it in one place or so, and I would like to return it clean. Expert opinion says that it a good job can be made of it — except that it may shrink a little, and the mesh be rather smaller. Let me know.

Montagnana was glorious — thanks so much; nor do I agree about Monselice. The walk up the hill amidst statues & cypresses was exquisite. Then I went to Ferrara, Ravenna, Rimini, San Marino, Forli, Faenza, & Parma. I cleverly mislaid the list of hotels you copied out of your Baedeker, & suffered occasionally in consequence. I liked the Maccini at Forli — and such a glorious fresco on the dining room ceiling — style of Guido Reni, I think — Aij. Also in an abundance of soft clouds. How horrid the Corona at Faenza is. I hear that the Vittoria is better. At Parma the Ma>land does very well.

I should like to come & stop some time very much; it is very good of you to ask me. So glad to hear that Howard is picking up at last. I have had a letter from him. What news about Frances Darwin! England seems nasty after Italy, though not as nasty as France. We are going away in a few days, & I trust that Weybridge will air itself in our absence — at present it smells. Do you know of the Rev Courtney Gale who comes here to lecture on music for the University Extension? Would he not be an absolute sell? I hear he spent the opening lecture partly in not being there, and partly in reading aloud the

A letter from EMF to Edward
Joseph Dent (see Letter 72 in text).

39 To Goldsworthy Lowes Dickinson

Grand Hôtel Brufani, Perugia
15 December 1901

Dear Dickinson

I don't at all know where you are, but I hope this letter will eventually reach you. We have reached Perugia in our travels, it is hardly a place to visit in December, though a bedroom window that looks out above and over the clouds, is not to be despised. Perugia would be nicer, I think, if Symonds had not written an Essay on it, or, at all events, if Miss Symonds had not trod so amply in her father's steps.[1] The pall of tragedy has been affixed to the unfortunate city, and the elderly ladies of the hotel make midnight excursions in the well lighted streets in search of blood and adventure, and come back breathing desolation & woe. The exalted level is sustained by an old lady who is understood to be waiting for an inspiration to write a book, and by an old lady who had really written one, which was squashed by the landslip at Amalfi. A welcome addition was a commercial traveller, who spent last evening in proving to me how vile and worthless I was, and I was too frightened to contradict him, though I had just finished a very nice little bit of prose on "Italy in the Autumn."[2]

We went last Friday to Assisi, which is most wonderful. I wish we were stopping there instead of here. I realised for the first time what the interior of an Italian church can look like when it is painted all over, and not merely patches of colour. The light was too bad to see the lower church properly, and the Giotto allegories were almost invisible.[3] I am going again, if only the weather will clear up.

We go to Rome on Wednesday. Letters to the Poste Restante there will find me for the next two months. At Easter I hope I am going to Greece with the Gardner party.[4] Is there any hope of you coming too?

I have done no writing—or hardly any—since I have been abroad. I could not do anything that w^d at all do for the Westminster before I left England: but I wrote to Theodore Davies, and asked him if he would hand on anything I might do later on, & he kindly says that he will.[5] I'm very discontented with the novel. I've tried to invent realism, if you see what I mean: instead of copying incidents & characters that I have come across, I have tried to imagine others equally commonplace, being under the impression that this was art, and by mixing two methods have produced nothing. I think I shall have a try at imagination pure & simple: though the result will be as unsuccessful it will perhaps be more profitable. I think I have the photo-graphic gift of which you spoke: but till I'm sure I can do no better, I don't mean to use it unreservedly.[6]

I should so like to hear about your American expedition if you have time to write. Don't you find that in Italy the average American is much nicer than the av[erage?] Englishman?[7]

Yrs affectly

E. M. Forster

ALS: KCC

[1] Margaret Symonds (1869–1925) was the daughter of John Addington Symonds (1840–93), poet and critic. She and Lina Duff Gordon published *The Story of Perugia* (1898). Symonds' essay: 'Perugia,' in his *Sketches in Italy and Greece*, pp. 68–94.
[2] Eight Italian essays—but not 'Italy in the Autumn', which is lost—survive in manuscript (KCC).
[3] Four allegories glorifying St Francis, by Giotto and his followers, in the lower church of the Sacred Convent of St Francis.
[4] He eventually went on a Greek cruise, in 1903, conducted by Ernest Arthur Gardner (1862–1939), Director of the British School of Archaeology, Athens, 1887–95; Professor of Archaeology, University of London, 1896–1929. EMF knew his nephew, Arthur Gardner (1878–1972), who was at King's with EMF, and became a stockbroker.
[5] *The Westminster Gazette* was a high-minded evening paper printed on green stock, a spokesman for Liberal ideas after the 'Liberal landslide' of 1906. EMF apparently hoped to get some work as a reviewer. The connection of Theodore Llewelyn Davies (1871–1905), uncle of J. M. Barrie's famous adopted boys, with the *Gazette* is unclear.
[6] This attempt was the uncompleted novel known as 'Nottingham Lace'; see *ASOF*, ed. Oliver Stallybrass and Elizabeth Heine, pp. 125–30.
[7] Dickinson went to New York in the summer of 1901 to visit his brother, to travel and lecture, and to jolt himself out of what he feared was the Cambridge rut; see *GLD*, pp. 125–30.

40   To Goldsworthy Lowes Dickinson

42 Piazza Poli, Rome
[*c.* February or March 1902]

Dear Dickinson

I managed to break my right arm and I have waited to write to you till it came out of plaster.[1] It has come out, and I am glad to say has healed up well, but unfortunately it is one of the little reasons that have led me to give up Greece. The others are the abridgment of the expedition, the absences of any friends, and the difficulty of leaving my mother, who cannot speak Italian.

I do wish I was going. Still I have Sicily to console myself with. And the last fortnight Italy has been waking up and I have been waking up too—though all the winter I have slept. Italy in the winter is not nice. It is useless to try & cheat the seasons. Winter should be spent in the north, I think. I don't hate the North as you do; and my love of Scotch cold & chilliness have had gradually to thaw off me before I can like the South. I do believe at last I shall like it very much.

I should like to hear you on America when I get back. But here abroad the English seem even more intelligent: and to the intelligent Rome is a terrible snare. I wish I didn't see everything with this horrible foreground of enthusiastic ladies, but it is impossible to get away from it.

I went to Nemi the other day, & got right down to the temple of Diana. The place is covered now with lilac purple & blue violets, pale blue & mauve anemones, cyclamen, and grape hyacinths. It's a glorious place

ALU, incomplete: KCC

[1] He fell on the steps of St Peter's, and he was further depressed by the dull weather. He wrote to Dickinson ([February or March 1902]. KCC): 'I last wrote under weeping sky & perhaps a little disconsolately. But though I do love Italy she has had no such awakening power on me as she has on you. I believe it is the weather. When the sun is in she is uninteresting & even ugly—perhaps all ought to be—and unless the sun is out *continuously* her beauty never developed. The light is stronger now and I feel that the next month may have much in store.'

41   To Edward Joseph Dent

Hôtel Belle Vue, Naples
[Postmark 11 May 1902]

Dear Dent
    Many thanks for your letter. It is most provoking. By the time you are in Italy I shall be in the Tyrol.[1] I think there is nothing I should enjoy more than to have gone about with you in Italy during a portion of your holiday there; if you would let me come. Umbria rather than Venetia, surely; though the latter I have not yet seen! I much want to go to Gubbio, and at one time meditated being there on the 21st of this month for that curious festival—the Ceri is it? but I forget the name. The festival of S Gennaro dwindled, when we got here, to Ascension day. We went, much disappointed: but there was something after all, for in his chapel they were exhibiting the blood which had been liquified on the preceding Sunday, and was still as runny as ever. It is in a glass bottle which is tied inside a glass compass case, which is tied by a chain to a priest, who wobbles it up and down and occasionally holds a candle behind it. According to my mother, it is coloured gelatine, and the candles is to prevent it coalescing again.[2]
    We are in a state of great agitation. The day after our arrival here, when I went up to bed, my Mother met me with an ashy face saying, "Mr Dent advised us not to come here, but we disobeyed him, and we have been terribly punished." There, in the soap bowl was lying dead a 🐞. My childhood has been so pure that it was the first I had ever seen, and as it is I cannot draw it very well. We hope that perhaps we brought it with us from Sicily, but the next night I found another, which I have not mentioned as a second was to mean flight, which would be very inconvenient. Our gratitude and admiration for the extent and accuracy of your knowledge have always been immense, but now they are mingled with awe. We speak of you in

EMF with Syed Ross Masood, whom he tutored
in Latin in 1906. Their friendship caused EMF
to interest himself in all things Indian.

the words of the hymn: "and soon the people all were dead who did not do as he had said."

I quite understand feeling depressed with Cambridge: indeed I fear that when I come up in October I shall understand it even better than you do. In your case I feel I might offer the conventional, but valid consolation that "you will soon feel different." For, when all humorous remarks have been made, it is a very great thing to be a don. I would have given and would give any thing to be one. I can't think of any body who is in a better position for making new friends and keeping old ones. But, as you hint, the relation of the new don to old dons whom he does not know well already must naturally be trying. And it is true that Nixon, who is made to masquerade as the don of the old school, is the only one who has eternal youth.

Would you kindly ask the porters if they know Lubbock's Rome address, & if they do put it and the two extra stamps on to the enclosed. If they don't would you post it as it is. I shall be there two or three days, and should like to catch him.[3] Letters, for the next fortnight, will be forwarded from here.

Y^{rs} ever.   E. M. F.

You do not say whether your solitary tour is combined with your Venice party; but I rather conclude it is.
No; I had never heard about C's father.

ALS: KCC

[1] Dent was in Paris, pursuing studies for his Scarlatti book; see Letter 37.
[2] At Gubbio the procession of the Ceri on 15 May celebrates St Ubaldo (d. 1160), the town's patron saint and bishop who saved it from Barbarossa in 1155. San Gennaro: the Naples Cathedral, which contains the head of St Januarius and two vials of his blood. The 'miracle' of the liquefaction occurs three times annually, and the city's prosperity is thought to depend on the speed of liquefaction.
[3] Percy Lubbock (1879–1965), literary critic, novelist, and biographer, entered King's in 1896, then worked in the Education Office, London, until made Pepys Librarian at Magdalene College, Cambridge, through the efforts of A. C. Benson (see Newsome, On the Edge of Paradise, p. 190). Lubbock is now best known for The Craft of Fiction (1921).

42   To Edward Joseph Dent

Hotel Stella d'Oro, Cortina [d'Ampezzo]
10 August 1902

Dear Dent

Excuse these ends of paper. I am so glad you found the case. It may enshrine your soap till we meet.

It is church time, but I am reposing after the debauches of Coronation night. The last Coronation I spent at San Gimignano, before Ghirlandhaio's frescoes, and this one is not an improvement.[1] The table was decorated and so were we with red white and blue of horrid crudity, and nasty white wine and another course were added to our meal. Then we had toasts—the King the P. of the U.S.A. the Queen the Emp of Austria and the King of Italy, followed by God save the Kwing played as a violin solo, unaccompanied. Then a pinfire of claps. That was not enough, and many of us proceeded to the Faloria hotel where there was a dance and more national anthem. I wonder whether the Coronation came off.

How disgracefully the Victoria behaved. The boot tariff seems inconceivable to me. I can't belief [sic] it is genuine. I will settle when we meet.[2]

I hope that Weston has turned up by now.[3] The Accademia sounds very fair, and I suppose that we are certain to go to Verona if we go to Italy.[4] What we do I don't know, though it depends on me. Any how we don't move from here for some time, as I have started committing noble thoughts to the green paper and find them entertaining. Moreover travelling is to be avoided, to judge by your experiences. I did fight to the table at Franzensfeste and got what looked to be a slab of chocolate, but was biscuit inside![5]

I travelled part of the way with a vast Italian family. The train gave a lurch and an enormous box descended straight on to a signorina's pink hat, whence it rebounded on to the ground. She became a little pink too, but did not cease eating her ham sandwich. In the diligence I made life long friends with a fat German lady—a further proof of the superfluity of conversation as a means of communication. She stuffed me with peppermints, and I arrived reeking.

I have just had a letter from Mollison, containing no news of any importance. Collingham has gone to Cornwall with Crace. Werner and Clapham are climbing in Switzerland.[6] I climbed too the other day, and was received by a hail and thunderstorms. I defied the elements with selections from La Justice.[7] The Pension is convulsed with brawls, my mother persisting that the English have faults, and they nor few nor small, the others asserting (i) that we have none (ii) that we must not mention them abroad in case foreigners find them out. The confusion has become quite serious, but the Perfectionists are leaving this week.

They have returned from church. There was another Nat. anthem, and on Saturday there is to be a concert. How I wish you were here to help.

Y^rs ever
E. M. F.

ALS: KCC
[1] That is, coronation of Edward VII on 9 August, postponed from 26 June to 9 August because of his appendicitis. Ghirlandhaio's frescoes: in the Collegiata—scenes from the life of Santa Fina.
[2] Victoria: presumably a hotel.
[3] George Benson Weston (1879–1959), an American, received a Master's Degree in Romance

Languages from Harvard in 1898 and taught there from 1906 until retirement in 1941 as Professor Emeritus of Romance Languages.
⁴ Accademia: the art gallery in Venice.
⁵ Franzenfeste: German for Fortezza, village in Bolzano.
⁶ John Foster Crace (1878–1960) entered King's in 1867, later became an Assistant Master at Eton; cf. Letter 38. Charles Augustus Werner (1877–1916) entered King's in 1896, also was an Assistant Master at Eton, was killed in action in France in World War I. John Harold Clapham (1873–1946), at King's in 1892, became a well-known economic historian and Professor of Economic History there, 1928–38. He was knighted in 1943.
⁷ La Justice seems to be related to a fragment, 'At Dinner Margaret', in which Ralph, the hero, after demanding 'Justice! Justice!' names the mountain peak that he is climbing 'Justice' (MS. KCC).

43 To Edward Joseph Dent

Hotel Strauss & Bayerischer Hof, Nüremberg [sic]
17 September 1902

Dear Dent

I can't write to you from Munich, only about it—and that with a vile pen. We left yesterday, so I had not time to use your kind letter of introduction, but I hope I shall come again and be able to. I much enjoyed Munich but spent most of my time in its Museums. The New Picture Gallery and the Schade are much better than the Tate—if such infinitesimal praise is worth giving. The only modern I really caught on to is Arnold Böcklin who pleases me immensely. I saw your distressful shepherd; also what Bædeker calls "An ideal landscape in Spring"—and whenever I see its sky I never mean to forget it. As a white-mutton-chop-whiskered Englishman was bawling out, "many of these pictures would make a sensation even in the Academy."¹

In the Old, I looked with all attention at the Rubens, and came away more understanding if not more appreciative. The rape of the daughters of some one by I forget who is a marvellous picture—even I can see that: and I should say that if you undressed fat women they would look just so—pink and white with blue and yellow here and there.² But why I cry out against Rubens is because he painted undressed people instead of naked ones. If their clothes haven't just been torn off them, they are always wondering where they are, or expecting you to wonder. I don't think it's an epigram to say that he's too prudish for me.

Never will I stop in a German Pension again. It was very expensive & besides opposite the Liebig monument with dinner at midday, and I felt I should never wish to eat again.³ After such distension the nice café you told me of was out of the question. But I enjoyed it, for Fraülein Liesecke is a most charming lady and there were some delightful Americans there. Here we tried for the Victoria (which looks just the right sort, if you ever come) but it was full, and we came here. Rooms fairly moderate. "How I do like a good hotel" said my mother as we descended to eat. "You pay very little more in the long run." We entered the Restaurant, and I noticed that all the waiters had gold braid on one shoulder, as if they had been hung up on pegs. I guessed something was coming. It did. Today we eat elsewhere.

In the train we made friends with a very aimiable old German, who got a porter at Nürnberg station to look after our joint baggage, and marched us off through that endless subway. My mother isn't accustomed "to be parted from her things", and the strain of keeping up courteous converse in French and of wondering whether it was a put up job between the a. o. g. and the porter was almost too much for her.

I offended Nature on Monday by going to Starnberger See, and Providence by going to Die Zauberflöte on Sunday, and between the two I have got a colossal cold. I enjoyed the Opera very much, and as I sat right at the side I had a splendid view of the machinery. But I am as yet too inexperienced a goer to listen properly to the music and singing. I will try to analyse the plot and the motives of the characters, for which I ought to be shot. As it was, I understood little except the tragic death of the boa constrictor in the first few bars.

I forgot to tell you that the Provost, Mʳˢ P, Willie and his daughter all appeared at Cortina.⁴ I went to call and bored the P. exceedingly till he caught sight of my nice umbrella, when he exclaimed "that looks as if it's been up a good many mountains! heugh! heugh! heugh!"

We leave here Sat. morning for Heidelburg. I think Poste Restante Cologne would be the best address

Yʳˢ Ever
E. M. F.

ALS: KCC

¹ Arnold Böcklin (1827–1901), Swiss painter who combined Swiss and Mediterranean landscapes with mythological figures. Here, probably his Die Klage des Hirtes (1866) and Ideale Frühlingslandschaft (1870).

² Peter Paul Rubens, Rape of the Daughters of Leucippus by Castor and Pollux (c. 1618).

³ Baron Justus von Liebig (1803–73), German agricultural chemist, was Professor of Chemistry at the University of Munich from 1852 until his death. His monument was in the Maximilianplatz, Munich.

⁴ Augustus Austen-Leigh, King's Provost, with his wife Florence, his brother William, and William's daughter.

44 To Edward Joseph Dent

Hotel Stella d'Oro, Cortina d'Ampezzo
Tirol, Austria
30 July 1903

Dear Dent

The pens are so vile that I am writing in pencil which please excuse.

Yes, I am still here but on the eve of departure. Tomorrow we fly through to England—unless it's cool, when we may throw in a few cathedrals on the way. I was wanting to write to you, when your letter arrived (Poste Restante Vienna I felt would hardly still find you).

We had a splendid but strange journey from Belluno to the Cadore, with some ladies from Dalmatia, a drunken coachman and a young man travelling in spectacles for a Pieve firm, very aimiable, afflicted with the tape worm, and also drunk. He sang long excerpts from Verdi and then remarked 'English poetry, I know it too', proceeding to declaim with the most exquisite taste "I hard a leetle poney its name was Darple Gree".[1] He loved England, on account of its Bath Oliver biscuits. Up the hill into the Cadore the drunken coachman got down and left the horses to themselves, and they began to stroll towards the precipice for the sake of the view. Loud screams from the Dalmatian ladies, who together with my mother bounded out like acrobats on to the road.

Since then I have lived uneventfully though pleasantly. I've just returned from three days over the border. All the province was full of troops, chiefly mountain artillery.

I was going to Munich for the Ring, but it fell through. Then to Paris, but fear of heat stopped that. So after a day or two at the Kingsley I go to Salisbury, thence to an aunt in Surrey, then to hunt for a house.[2]

Yours E. M. F.

ALS: KCC

[1] In *The Oxford Dictionary of Nursery Rhymes* (1951), p. 143: 'I had a little pony, / His name was Dapple Gray; / I lent him to a lady / To ride a mile away.' Etc.

[2] Kingsley Hotel, Bloomsbury. Salisbury: to Maimie Aylward. Surrey: to Laura Forster at West Hackhurst.

45 To Robert Trevelyan[1]

11 Drayton Court, Drayton Gardens [London] S.W.
5 July 1904

Dear Trevelyan

I'm very glad you like the story better than I expected: I think you do.[2] It was extra good of you to read out loud. I quite agree about the end, and shall try to alter it this morning. But I'm not, yet, dissatisfied with the beginning—at least with its intention. I wanted her to treat the incident in a light, half humourous way. It is no more to her, until she is stirred up, and her past actions group themselves. Then, it is to become supreme. But, certainly the opening conversation does suggest a rather unbecoming sauciness, which I shall try to knock out. I wish you had told me where are the facetiae: they are a most certain fault; and my taste doesn't guide me. Someone told me, many years ago, that I was amusing, and I have never quite recovered from the effects. (This is not a modest sentence.) You don't say, either, whether you think Ch. II a hash: doesn't the conversation with Signora Cantù read poorly?[3]

Another house is ripening, and I don't think that I ought to come to Seatolla.[4] Indeed I ought never to have held myself to you as holding out hopes to myself: (observe the result of the W[ing]s of the D[ove]!)[5] My mother sends her remembrances to you and to Mrs Trevelyan: she hopes you will be at home when she comes in August.

My Ravello story is coming out next month.[6] It's shockingly composed, and I don't know ~~think~~ they ought to have taken it. But I like it more than I ought to.

Thank you very much for the letter.

Yours ever
E. M. F.

ALS: TCC

[1] Robert Calverley Trevelyan (1872–1951) was the second son of the historian Sir George Otto Trevelyan, and elder brother of George Macaulay Trevelyan. Robert went to Harrow and to Trinity College, Cambridge, and on leaving the latter insisted (to the disapproval of his public-minded family) on choosing poetry as a career. He was not a very successful poet, although a poem by him was included in the first volume of *Georgian Poetry*. He published most of his numerous volumes at his own expense. He, however, lived the poetic part wholeheartedly, referring everything in life to books and conversing on recondite matters to anyone at hand. In 1900 he married a Dutch lady, Elizabeth des Amorie van der Hoeven, and they had a house, 'The Shiffolds', built for them at Holmbury St Mary. Trevelyan was a passionate pacifist, and during the first World War he served in a Quaker mission in France. EMF, who knew Trevelyan only vaguely at Cambridge, became very friendly with him after his own return from Italy in 1902, and for a few years Trevelyan was his closest literary adviser. Trevelyan, with Goldsworthy Lowes Dickinson, accompanied EMF on his first visit to India. To some extent, EMF modelled 'Summer Street' in *A Room with a View* upon Holmbury St Mary, which lay a few miles from his Aunt Laura's house in Abinger.

[2] 'The Eternal Moment,' first published in *The Independent Review*, 6 (1905); Part 1, 206–25; Part 2, 86–95, 211–23. See Kirkpatrick, pp. 50–1.

[3] Proprietress of the Albergo Biscione, in the story.

[4] I.e. Seatoller, in Borrowdale (Cumbria).

[5] I.e., in the convoluted later manner of Henry James's novel, published in 1902.

[6] 'The Story of a Panic', published first in *The Independent Review*, 3 (1904), 453–72; reprinted in *The Celestial Omnibus* (1911).

46 To Robert Trevelyan

Harnham, Monument Green, Weybridge
14 November 1904

Dear Trevelyan

I am returning Leonardo with many thanks, and have put 'not to forward' on it, lest you be already abroad.[1] Munich has fallen through for the present: perhaps it will come in the new year.

The above is our amended address: Glendore was a bit too much.[2] It's all quite nice here: the best families are to call presently, and I hope to join the new Literary Society, if I am duly invited.[3]

Tomorrow I go to Cambridge, seeing the Knight of the Burning Pestle on the way.[4] Surely it wasn't you who said that thing was poor? I have a kind of idea it was, though.

I wish you would quickly inhabit your new house: I want it for some people of mine.[5] They are living there at present in the greatest discomfort not knowing which way the front door opens or what the view is like, and till I go there to tell them they will never get straight. If you could also provide one of them with something to do and something to die of I should also be grateful. In other ways, they are as well as can be expected.

I saw George the other day—the first time, I think, for two or three years.[6]

Please remember me very kindly to Mrs Trevelyan.[7] I and Meredith went to call on her cousin—I can say but not spell his name—but he was out: not unnaturally, for I then remembered that he doesn't come up till the spring.

I shall be down at West Hackhurst for the New Year, but by that time I fear there is no chance of you.

Yours ever
E M. Forster.

ALS: TCC

[1] Leonardo: perhaps a book or picture, unidentified.

[2] EMF had written to Trevelyan (25 August 1904. TCC): 'The news is we have got a house, too small and with no garden. Its name is *Glendore* and it is at Weybridge, on *The Monument Green*. It's quite pretty in some ways, looking out behind over a wood and a field full of dropsical chickens. The monument I gather was erected to or by Hanoverian royalty and bears an inscription to the effect that it really pays to do good: the last line is "are registered in courts above." The rent is £55: the villa is detached and has a beautiful brass bound door step, which we are taking on from the last tenant. None of our neighbours have one.'

[3] EMF read several papers to this Society, possibly including 'The Poems of Kipling' (MS. KCC).

[4] Comedy (printed 1613) by Beaumont and Fletcher, at the Royalty Theatre, in a series of Old English Plays; it was repeated in December as a 'Christmas novelty'.

[5] 'Some people': i.e. the Honeychurches, in *A Room with a View*. The Trevelyans were about to move to their house, 'The Shiffolds', in Holmbury St Mary.

[6] Perhaps George M. Trevelyan, Robert's brother.

[7] Elizabeth ('Bessie') des Amorie van der Hoeven (1876–1957) had independent means, and literary and musical interests.

47 To Robert Trevelyan

Harnham, Monument Green, Weybridge
1 January 1905

Dear Trevelyan

Yesterday I saw Miss Vaughan Williams and she had just had a letter from M[rs] Trevelyan, and that made me write at once, since I knew your address, and ask for more news.[1] Of course the arrival, the landslip, the old woman, the book box one knows by instinct. It's probable I did the same myself. But the marriage of maiden Palumba, the treachery of the waiter (whose name I forget) and the whole beer garden plot excites me very much: I only heard a scrap from Miss V. W., and when you have leisure want to hear more. I've always been inclined to croak over the future of Ravello, and unless you stop me shall begin with 'what did I say?'.[2]

It is kind to tell you of the fogs, though you have heard of them already, I suppose. Weybridge got into them all right, and I have had a cold, sore throat, and depressed spirits. All are right except the last, and those are on the mend. I am lecturing at Guildford next term, and possibly in Cornwall.

This afternoon I have been to see Sanger, who was very vigorous against the Pragmatists. I thought of Charles VI's Pragmatic Sanction, and supposed they were something like the Jacobites.[3] It turned out that they are much less important, being William James and some Oxford philosophers who approach truth in the spirit of πραγμα, business. Sanger put it very clearly, but that is all you will get out of me. Besides, he says, they are stale news. A thing you cannot possibly have heard of is my unfinished ghost story, which I destine for Temple Bar.[4] An old man—a very nice one too—has committed, from high motives, a crime: you mustn't mind what. Justice, so obviously immanent in our daily life, compels him to reveal it in pieces: I mean that *he* is in pieces: falls into them when he goes to sleep. His head is shot one night by mistake for a wild duck, and when they call him in the morning he is dead, and no traces are ever found of the murderer. It is called The Purple Envelope. But I somehow think I am too refined to write a ghost story.

I have been to the Confederacy twice since you left England, and to The Maid's Tragedy.[5] The latter moved me a good deal, though it was badly done. I haven't read it yet.

My mother sends all New Year's greetings to you and M[rs] Trevelyan, in which I join. I have no one else to greet at Ravello, but if you go to Pesto remember me warmly to the station master, Amilcare Sabbattini, who will show you shiny sheets of 'uomini celebri' on his office walls. They are his gods, I think: he is a libro pensatore, and does there very well.[6] Before I knew him I stole out of his garden one rose, to fool Bædeker.

Yours ever   E. M. Forster

I am glad to say that my largest cousin has married a man with a crest. I send it to you, and though it is trying to come back to me do not let it.

ALS: TCC

[1] Margaret Vaughan Williams (d. 1931), and her brother, the composer and conductor Ralph Vaughan Williams (1872–1958) lived at Leith Hill Place, Surrey, and thus were neighbours of the Farrers.

[2] It would seem as if the Trevelyans were at Ravello and had apparently encountered real-life events that confirmed EMF's fictional evocations in 'The Eternal Moment' and perhaps in 'The Story of a Panic', in *The Independent Review*, 3 (1904), 453–72; and 6 (1905), 206–15.

[3] Charles Percy Sanger (1871–1930), jurist and statistical economist, was an early member of the Bloomsbury Circle. William James's important 1905 lecture, 'The Pragmatic Method,' was published in 1907 as *Pragmatism: A New Name for Some Old Ways of Thinking*. The Pragmatic Sanction of 1713, which was the attempt by Emperor Charles VI of Germany to ensure his choice as successor, led to the War of Austrian Succession, in 1740–8.

[4] 'The Purple Envelope', published posthumously (*LTC*, pp. 36–54).

[5] Sir John Vanbrugh's *The Confederacy* (1705) and Beaumont and Fletcher's *The Maid's Tragedy* (1611), performed by the Mermaid Society at the Royalty Theatre, December 1904.

[6] 'Uomini celebri': famous men. 'Libero pensatore': free-thinker.

48 To Leonard Woolf

Harnham, Monument Green, Weybridge
1 January 1905

Dear Woolf

I was up for a fortnight, and read the Society a paper, which, if I find it, I will send you, as you have never heard me read. No one thought there was much in it (Strachey, Sheppard, Keynes, present).[1] You may throw it away.

George Trevy, as you probably know, has written on 'Religious Conformity' in the Independent. At one moment I very nearly blasted against it with 'Non-religious Conformity'.[2] It would have been an impassioned and humourous article, but the moment passed, and after all his may not do any harm. 'None at all' perhaps you think, but I am so sick when a thing I love is turned into a 'movement'. Of course it's all very practical, and vulgar Christians will see that they can be quite as aggressive & noisy as agnostics, and wring their brothers' & sisters' hands just in the old way. I'd like to hear what you think of the article, whether you like it, or whether—as I expect—you dislike less than half.

Meredith is going to Manchester, as an assistant professor or that kind of thing in the School of Commerce at Victoria University. I believe the post's good. I am trying to get taken on by the

Manchester University Extension: Cambridge isn't much go, though I have work this time. I have finished a short novel, and if ever it is published will send it you.[3] Just now I am writing a ghost story, but can't. It does require a mind of extraordinary frivolity to frighten people, and I'm rather pleased to find that I can't do it. At the critical moment—in this case a finger promenades by itself, tip to root, caterpillar fashion, over the carpet—one is calmly considering the disposition & appearance of the man who lies in bed watching it.

When you write, don't forget the obvious things—the voyage, your work, the scenery & people. Of course you can omit them—but that's different.[4]

Yours ever
E. M. Forster.

ALS: Berg

[1] I.e. a paper (now lost) read to the Apostles. These members were Lytton Strachey (1880–1932); John Tresidder Sheppard (1881–1968), classicist, Vice-Provost of King's College, 1929–33, and Provost, 1933–54; and John Maynard Keynes (1883–1946), economist, created 1st Baron Keynes in 1942, Lecturer in Economics at King's, 1911–37, and its first Bursar, from 1924. His book, *The Economic Consequences of the Peace* (1919) was at the centre of controversy about rebuilding Europe.

[2] G. M. Trevelyan, 'Religious Conformity', *The Independent Review*, 4 (1904–1905), 374–92.

[3] I.e., *Where Angels Fear to Tread*.

[4] Leonard Sidney Woolf (1880–1969) had been accepted by the Ceylon Civil Service and posted to Ceylon, where he remained until 1911, when he resigned, to marry Virginia Stephen and stay in England as journalist and political theorist.

49   To Alice Clara Forster

[Nassenheide. 4 April 1905][1]

Dearest Mother

My arrival here was beyond my wildest dreams, and I will begin by it. It was 10.0. o'clock when the little tram-railway put me out at Nassenheide—pitch dark, no station, no porter, no one of any kind. What would have happened if the guard had not been extremely nice & talked French I can't think. He arrested the traffic, gave me out Pa, and promised to take care of my big box—where I can't think, but I suppose it will turn up in time.[2] Then he explained to a farm man, who was fetching parcels, and I started with him for the schloss. Slosh! we trod in puddles, there was no road, & when we got to the farm there were the most appalling smells of pig & horse & cow, and we waded in manure. Here we parted and he indicated to me a rough carriage drive, which was better, being only very sandy & full of holes. Presently I hit a large building which had a light in the upper window. I found a bell in it & rang. A hound bayed inside. By this time I was weak with laughter. I rang again, and at last a dishevelled boy, with no light, appeared. Yes; it was the schloss.

What did I want? I said I wanted to live here. He replied that he would see, and got a light, revealing a long low white washed barrel vaulted hall, hung with trophies of the chase, & at the end of it an inscription 'Idiota, insulsus, turpis, tristis abesto' or something of that sort.[3] Turpis I certainly was, for my boots oozed manure. He then awoke the German tutor, Herr Schenk, who seems extremely nice, & took me to his room. The Countess was in bed: she had not expected me till today, having muddled me up with the new housemaid!

Gradually the household awoke. A dishevelled housemaid made me up a bed—and meanwhile another youth appeared—an ex-English tutor who is here on a visit & had the room that will be mine. He too was very nice. My room was large & comfortable but rather cold. I shall go into my proper room this morning.

I had breakfast at 7.30! (but am not yet feeling wan) with May, June, & an unnamed baby; April is in Italy with her father.[4] The French governess also breakfasted. She has been three days here & seems gloomy. 'Mangez Mademoiselle, Mangez!'

'On ne peut pas manger encore: l'appétit n'est pas ouvert.'

'Mais si vous mangez, vous ne serez pas si maigre!'

When the children had gone she informed me that it is 'very silent here.' 'Dans la ville il y a des distractions, n'est-ce pas?' I expect the end shortly.

After breakfast I saw my hostess who is pleasant but rather disappointing, having indifferent false teeth & a society drawl. The children seem delightful, but she says I must be strict with them in lessons (11.30–12.30), as they are tiresome.

It's not quite raining, & the view is woods, a farm with two chimneys, and manure.

I continue this letter after my first lesson. The children were quiet and tearful, owing to the departure of the ex-tutor, whom they like.[5] It all seems very pleasant, & the only thing I'm glum about is the German, for which there seem but poor opportunities. I must talk about it to E.; it is the reason why the other tutor (a very charming person. I have been a walk with him) left. If it turns out a failure I shall not overstay my 3 months but perhaps go into some family for July.

My box has come, so has my hat. I have also got my room—or rather rooms—two most pleasant places, with a noble stove in either. The bed & the crikey are in one, the bath & the washstand in the other, so which is the sitting room I don't know. The garden, of course, is exactly like any other garden. But I suppose it's hardly fair to judge yet.

Besides all this my journey seems uneventful. I had a pleasant time in Berlin, in spite of the pictures being moved to another gallery, which wasted half an hour. They were magnificent. At Stettin I had the hottest & greasiest soup ever set before man, followed by slabs of pig, not so bad. For this and for bread, potatoes and beer I paid 1.20.

At Berlin I was able to register my luggage immediately on arriving at the Stettiner Bahnhof, & was thus saved all bother.

Much love to you M^rs M[awe] & El[aine].

Your loving
Morgan

ALS: KCC

[1] Countess Mary Annette Beauchamp ('Elizabeth') (1866–1941) was an Australian and cousin of the writer Katherine Mansfield. In 1890 she married Count Henning August von Arnim-Schlagenthin (1841–1910); and, in 1916, the 2nd Earl Russell (d. 1931). She and her garden became famous through her *Elizabeth and Her German Garden* (1898). As explained there (pp. 184–6), she maintained a continual succession of governesses and tutors, of whom EMF was now to be one, in order to keep her children out of German schools. It came about through EMF's friendship, which began in 1905, with Sydney Philip Waterlow (1878–1944), author and diplomat, and nephew of 'Elizabeth'.
[2] Pa: nickname for one of a set of travelling bags.
[3] 'Begone the fool, the insipid, the foul, the sad.'
[4] 'Elizabeth' nicknamed her children after the months of the year. 'May baby': Liebet (later, 'Leslie de Charms'); 'June baby': Beatrix; 'unnamed baby': either a girl nicknamed Quiqui or the son, Henning Bernt; 'April baby': Evi. Another daughter, Felicitas, called 'Martin', died at the age of seventeen.
[5] The governess's name was Mlle L. Auger de Balben. EMF's predecessor as English tutor was named Roger Gibb. The German tutor was Herr Dekan Johannes Steinweg (1879–1961), a divinity student.

50   To Alice Clara Forster

c/o Count Arnim, Nassenheide,
Pommern, Germany
9 April 1905

Dearest Mummy,

Hope you are all all right. I expected to have heard from you by now. As for me, I am settled down and I think it is going to be very pleasant. The days are all much alike. I am called at 7.0. and my breakfast comes at 7.30., but my movements are veiled from the official world till 11.30, when I give my hour's English. For breakfast, which I generally eat at about 8.0., dressing after, I have bread butter, jam, egg, and coffee: the latter very weak, but I will try & alter it. At 11.0. there appears a glass of hot milk and a tongue sandwich. We all lunch together at 1.15, and disperse afterwards. At 2.45 I and Herr Steinweg (the real name of the German tutor) go a walk. We talk German one day and English the next. He seems extremely nice, which, as I see more of him than anyone, is fortunate. We return at 4.0, and have tea in his room, during which he reads Keats to me or I the Child's first Lesebuch to him, correcting each other. Dinner at 7.30 and at 9.0. we again disperse to our rooms, which I rather hate, for a liquorice coloured stove, however hot, is too silent a companion in the evening. So I go pretty early to bed.

I have written for a good German Grammar to England. Otto is too tiresome.[1] Herr Steinweg is not inclined to give me lessons, as he is working hard, to take orders. But I can count on him to explain my difficulties, and though it is not what I hoped I must make the best of it.

⟨Here your letter arrived.⟩

I don't see much of E., who is engaged on a book, but when I do see her she is most pleasant and amusing; and I think I shall like her very much. She is, as I rather expected, nicer than her books, and I don't feel in awe of her, and chuttle-pie away, so that if she is meditating to turn me into copy, she has every opportunity. The great news—over which she has been very kind & sympathetic—is that Blackwood has written offering to publish my novel. It was for the Magazine that I sent it them, and the terms they offer are not at all good—I have written trying to do better, and meantime am trying to find out whether Blackwoods as *publishers* are a good firm, as though I don't mind much about money it's important to be in the hands of people who will advertise you well. Methuen or Heinemann are the firms I should have naturally tried first. The title has to be changed, which is very sad, but I see their point of view.[2]

It is the May baby who is away, with her father & the German governess. The other two do their lessons well, and hitherto I have kept them in order, and am trying to break June of slinging her ink over the blotting paper—just as I do myself. I rather feared that I bore & chill them, and that they don't take to me, and I haven't found so far opportunities of being with them in play time. This morning however (Sunday) I had a pleasant time with them in the school room, and consented to bite at a piece of what was most obviously soap, but was offered to me as bread. "All your tutors fall in," they cried. And indeed I could see the tooth marks of my predecessors on the margin. Mademoiselle refused. "Moi même, j'ai porté un saucisson de savon à mon neveu. J'ai dit 'Tiens? mangez!' Ah qu'il m'a battu!" She preferred to distract herself upon the zither. The click of E's type writer was heard in the next room, and a message was sent to ask whether she minded the noise. The answer came back 'Non. Cela me soulage.' Presently the pendant on Mlle's bracelet caught in the string of the instrument. There she was fixed, ~~unmoved~~ immovable, and for five minutes neither the April baby nor myself could release her. Meanwhile June had twisted the leg of Quiqui (the fourth baby) into the back of the chair and the kitten, who had recently taken some pink medicine, began to rock to and fro in the most alarming way. But I left them very cheerful, and

Quiqui writing a letter to her doll. 'My dear Comtesse Jane, I am glad to tell you that it is your birthday. I shall see you in time. I hope you will not die between.'

Sorry about Bædeker. Herr Steinweg wanted to do it up, but I thought it'ld do. I conclude postage not enough. B. & Pike's bill came. Blue suit 4.11.6. It has been snowing a lot; but I have gone some walks. The country is marvellously beautiful, & deer go hopping about like rabbits. In the air are cranes, and the storks are expected shortly. Elizabeth has lent me Erewhon which I am enjoying.[3] I have told Williams & Deacon [Bank] to put £30 to your account.

Pommern has 2 m's. And I believe that 'bei Grafen von Arnim' is the German way of address. And you need not put 'Germania' for if you do you had better write it Deutschland. YA! YA!

ALU: KCC

[1] Dr Emil Otto (1813–78), author of numerous grammars and readers for German, French, and English.
[2] I. e., *Where Angels Fear to Tread*. Blackwood thought that 'Monteriano', the original title, would not sell the book. Cf. Letter 60.
[3] Samuel Butler's utopian fantasy, *Erewhon; or, Over the Range* (1872).

51   To Arthur Cole[1]

c/o Count Arnim, Nassenheide, Pommern, Germany
11 April 1905

Dear ~~Fer~~ Cole—(I started writing to myself: I think it is the hot pickled cabbage that I have just eaten, served with sugar).

Your letter found me in Dresden, half way through the Ring of the Nibelung—the better half way, I think, for I doubt whether any thing is as stupendous as the end of Rheingold, or as heroic as the Act I of the Valkürie. I only care about Wotan and Walhalla: Siegmund is an intruder even, though a glorious one, and as for Siegfried—words fail me, even as they failed you with another fair haired Child of Destiny. He ought never to have got his fellowship: his education was ~~devoid~~ one sided, his dissertation inadequate and his subsequent achievements confer little credit upon the institutions from which he draws his salary. To insist on marrying your half-aunt on both sides and then totally to forget her—this, as far as I can make out, is all that Siegfried does after gaining the Ring, the Tarn cap, and the Sword. But—observing that the Ring was very decently done and that I saw it for 18/–, I will now pass on, omitting my paragraph about Dresden and its crocodiles, and Berlin and its dirt & meanness and streets full of unhappy soldiers, and Stettin, where I had the hottest & greasiest soup yet known, while outside a merry go round played Ta-ra-ra-boom-de-ay with incomparable skill. It was now evening, and having gone from Stettin to Stöven and changed it was now night, and where was the Nassenheide train. I ran up and down the rails shouting 'Wo Zug? Wo Gepack?' and presently I ran into the train, which by some strange chance, had a guard who spoke French. This is why it was all a comedy instead of the other thing, for when we got to Nassenheide there was no one there—not a porter nor a light nor even a platform. (I had been muddled up with the housemaid and not expected till the morrow.) The guard got out & found a labourer who was going to the Schloss. Leaving my trunk in the open country, where it was found all right in the morning, and taking my Gladstone, which was full of Virgils, in my hand, I set forth, and immediately stepped into a deep puddle.[2] I laughed heartily, as young Englishmen do, and my other foot went into some manure. I arrived at the Schloss in a thoroughly eighteenth century condition—to find all dark. They had gone to bed. I rang the bell and a hound bayed. I rang again and a dishevelled youth asked me what I wanted. I said I wanted to live here. He replied that he would see. Then the German Tutor was awoke—and from that moment things have been normal.

The country is magnificent, the weather cold—snow storms most days—, the German Garden I cannot find. Here and there is a bed, and I suppose that in the summer they will be filled with flowers, like other beds. My duties are light, my pupils charming. So is my hostess, though I see her but seldom. My chief companion is the German Tutor, Herr Steinweg, whom I shall like very much I think. I have had an offer to publish my novel in the autumn. The terms are shocking bad. However to have an offer at all is encouraging. I am finding your Sidgwick useful.[3] But I shall certainly return it to you. This letter is posted in England, to save 1/½. I haven't read 'Euripide'.[4] Have you read Erewhon? Now I'm at Marius the Epicurean.[5] Write again soon.

> Yours ever
> E. M. Forster

ALS: John Cole

[1] Arthur Frederick Andrew Cole (1883–1968), barrister and bibliophile, was a Kingsman and a close friend of Malcolm Darling. Cole gave King's its Music Library.

[2] EMF was at work on the *Aeneid*, to be published as *The Aeneid of Virgil*, translated by E. Fairfax Taylor, with Introduction pp. vii–xvii and notes by E. M. Forster; in the Temple Classics Series, edited by G. Lowes Dickinson and H. O. Meredith for J. M. Dent (1906).

[3] Perhaps a text by Henry Sidgwick (1838–1900), Cambridge moral philosopher, author of books on European economy.

[4] From EMF's spelling, a French publication.

[5] Walter Pater, *Marius the Epicurean* (1878).

52   To Alice Clara Forster

Nassenheide.   13 April 1905

Dearest Mother

Very glad of your letter. How tiresome about Miss Parmiter: it looks as if she is trying to hole you.[1] Telegrams are cheap, but I suppose it's even too late for that now. You don't say whether you will travel through, and whether you will avoid Cologne. Pity too about the operas—though I don't pity you for seeing Sampson et Delilah, which they say is magnificent.[2] Meissen sounds nice. I suppose it's too cold for Save on Switzerland. The children's names are Evi, Liebeth, and Beatrix: ages 14, 12, & 11 I think. They have just written me the most charming Essays on Mr Fairchild: 'He knew the whole bible by heart, so pious he was.[3] Each time his children were naughty his face glanced with words out of it; and immediately out came a quotation and it flowed like a river....Perhaps he may have been soaked in religion in his child-days, and then very clear it appears to me that when thinking too much of higher powers his mind became a little disordered, and never would get right again. He is a good man, but I would warn him not to think too much, or his end might be rather doubtful.'

Here is a bit of gossip. It is a real quarrel between B. and Mrs Farmer: I thought so at Dresden. Mrs F. & her sister stayed here, once, years ago, and when the 'German garden' came out, the sister thought she was Minora and made London ring with her wails. B. says she would never be so beastly as to put a guest in, and that Minora has no original. Any how there was a row, of which I have of course only heard one side, from which Mrs F., or rather her sister, sounds to have behaved very badly.[4]

My chief jaunt has been coffee last Sunday with the Pastor at Blankensee—whom I do think the original of Pastor Manske in 'The Benefactress.'[5] The awful part of the meal was the end when, after a long coquettish grace, the Pastor rose and kissed his wife tenderly on both cheeks, and then kissed the children on their foreheads. Every one shook hands with me and I thought I had to go, but no, it was rejoicing because we had had another meal. Then we went into the parlour—the walls were crimson and the floor coltsfoot—and there I sat on a straw chair with arms at the end of the table, and the Herr Candidat, or curate, sat on a straw chair without arms at the side.[6] We talked in Latin 'Venistis in curru?' 'Non. Pedibus veni' and so on. Altogether I talked five languages. Presently the Pastor came and sat on the sofa opposite side to the Curate, and asked me what I was going to do in life. I told him and he said it was not enough. I must get a professorship in Latin. I said I did not know Latin very well, and he said that that was what I said: I ought to get a professorship in Latin: I knew quite enough.

Blackwood's terms are really no money at all; in other words nothing on the first 300 copies sold, 10% on the next 1000, 15% up to 2500, and 1/- a copy on all copies after 2500.[7] They haven't yet said, either, what price the book is to be sold at.

Next week come the Easter holidays, and I have ten days rest; I believe we go for picnics and sit in wet woods. The pony cart known as the Tumbril is to be taken for Mademoiselle and myself; and if we get tired we are both to get in it and be photographed. M[lle] is an endless source of joy: always dressed in navy blue with an embroidered apron and a broad leather belt. She is elderly with strange frizzy hair, and also limps, and has read fewer books & acquired less information than I should [have] thought possible. I suppose she chaperones us all, in the absence of the Man of Wrath[8] who is expected to return on his birthday—Good Friday. Fraulein Backe and Liebeth start from Amalfi today, and travel straight through, arriving on Monday next.

I think, like M[r] Hervey, that I am making progress with my German.[9]

Your loving
Morgan

ALS: KCC

[1] Miss Parmiter: unidentified.
[2] *Samson et Dalila* (1877), opera by Charles Camille Saint-Saens.
[3] Mary Martha Sherwood, *The History of the Fairchild Family* (1818), a particularly pious 'improving' Victorian book for children.
[4] Minora: in *Elizabeth and Her German Garden* (pp. 133-218, 223-4), a tiresome and tenacious guest. It seems plain that 'B.' indicates Elizabeth. Mrs Farmer is unidentified.
[5] Elizabeth [Russell], *The Benefactress* (1901). Pastor Manske is a silly, sentimental man.
[6] On the parson and his family, see *Elizabeth and Her German Garden*, pp. 123-7. According to 'Elizabeth', his wife supposedly 'stirs her puddings with one hand and holds a Latin grammar in the other, the grammar, of course, getting the greater share of attention. . . . If I were the husband, those puddings would taste sweetest to me that were served with Latin sauce.'
[7] I.e. terms for *Where Angels Fear to Tread*; see Letter 50.
[8] Elizabeth's nickname for her husband.
[9] On Mr Hervey, EMF's childhood tutor, see Letter 9.

53 To Alice Clara Forster

Nassenheide. Good Friday [21 April 1905]

Dearest Mother

Your card just arrived & very glad I was to get it. I rather think it has been delayed in the house by the boy not understanding Morgan Forster. I was very sorry for your unprosperous letter & things don't seem likely to go better yet awhile. It is so sad, that poverty seems to bring muddle after it. I don't think a richish person w[d] have made such a mess. I do hope that you will stop a bit in Paris till the recollection of the unpleasantness has died away. There's sage advice! And the weather even here is better, so I do hope you will have a pleasant time. When you are up to seeing things, don't forget Puvis de Chavannes' frescoes of Ste Genevieve—not that I know where they are.[1]

It's all very pleasant here. Yesterday I went to Stettin for the day—a picturesque town, though I really went to shop: a black felt hat, drawing pins, notebooks &^ct. Shops seemed very good &—except for the hat—cheap. I also bought eggs ~~with~~ hares ~~in them~~ for the babies, and also an egg for you, to appease them: they were so horrified that I was going to give you ○ and that in all probability I should get ○ from you. If I can find a match box & if it is not too expensive to post, you will perhaps get it: but I don't suppose that a 10 pf. chocolate egg with a marzipane hare peeping out of it is exactly what you feel like at the present moment; you will enjoy it, even if it is a little wilted, just as much when I return. The babies['] eggs are much superior: one of them being not an egg but a green cabbage with the price written in indelible pencil on the stalk. All these things I bought at the beginning of the day, in the fear that my German would be unwieldy & lengthy: so that I was a quaint &—at the end—a fatigued figure as I strolled about.

I was entrapped into church, & have been chilly a little ever since: and Elizabeth, out of pure sprightliness, has dictated that today we fast and have only fish & eggs. They have been a walk: I prancing on E's second best typewriter, which does my Virgil notes splendidly. Fraulein Backer [sic] the German governess, seems nice.[2] I think we're very lucky to be such a harmonious quartette of menials: not that we've tried each other really yet. Really the charm of the place for me is not its vaunted solitude but the quality of pleasant people. I believe the children like me, but am not sure; perhaps they are a little bored by the host of attendants; they seem to be happiest with each other. Liebeth (May) is pretty, as the books record, but rather fat.[3]

Lately we have been dancing a good deal, I skirling about with E. in the Highland fling or leading the Cake Walk, to the intense joy of the company, while Md^lle. whose head turns, turns the hurdy gurdy. Then musical chairs, & then Oranges & Lemons—or to give it its shocking Nassenheide name—'Tummy-aches & Castor Oil'! You have to choose which you will have. I was the only one who chose Tummy-aches, which was Elizabeth, and naturally we could not pull over the others, who were headed by Fraulein Backer, purple with excitement, and clad in white satin from head to foot. My ancles are quite enfeebled.

The Man of Wrath is expected shortly. He is so musical that hardly any of us will be able to play the piano, and he will not play it himself, though he was a pupil of Liszt, & wonderfully good. The sweet storks have come—but I think I told you that before. Bunny balls, & a few king cups are out, but that is all. Nearly every birch tree has a great bunch of mistletoe on it.

Such a bad pen. Love to Mrs Mawe & Elaine. Your loving Morgan.
You did not tell me G[ran]'s address. I had written to her at
Werter Road.[4]

ALS: KCC

[1] Pierre Puvis de Chavannes' two sets of murals (1874–8, 1897–8) in the Panthéon, Paris, on
the life and works of Saint Geneviève.
[2] Fräulein Backe ('Teppi'), Elizabeth's faithful and much put-upon German governess.
[3] As . . . record': in Elizabeth Russell, *The April Baby's Book of Tunes* (1900).
[4] In Putney, home of Louisa Whichelo and some of EMF's aunts.

54   To Alice Clara Forster

Nassenheide   [c. beginning of June 1905]

Dearest Mother

I suppose you are back again, and perhaps Gran and Percy are
with you. Give them my love. I am glad you found Tanty well, and
hope you took her the drive.[1] Is there any need of money for her? I
prefer to do good in secret, or at all events through the medium of
someone who has lost their character.

The great expedition to the hills came off, and we were walking,
with intervals for food, for nearly 12 hours. No one was dead,
though Fräulein Backe is now suffering from 'bubbles' on her feet.
Unfortunately it was misty, but the hills themselves were
beautiful—covered with magnificent trees, & there were real
mountain brooks in them, which is rather surprising, considering
they are only 300 feet high. We had lunch at an inn: I send you a
photograph, which Md^lle took and gave me. On the seats (from left
to right) are April, June, May & Herr Steinweg. Behind, Fräulein
Backe with a head ache. Myself with numerous family to the right.
The babies and Mademoiselle are not free from snobbishness, and
were a little unwilling to be mixed with the lower herd. Then we
played skittles, and then on again through miles of forest.

The heat is appalling. A large meat-safe shutter has been fastened
over my bedroom window. I did not desire it, but must be grateful.
Elizabeth comes back in a day or two. Tomorrow is 'Himmelfahrt'
[Ascension Day], and we have a holiday. Herr S. & myself have got
to 'R' in the library, but there remains a good deal of work. Next
Sunday he preaches again, and I think I know enough German to try
and hear him.

I have had a civil letter from the publisher, Fisher Unwin, saying
how struck he is with my work and begging me to call.[2] I have an idea
that he is a bad egg, but he is also a large one, so I have written back
also civilly, managing to drop that I had already signed an agreement
for my first novel with some one else. If he will publish my short
stories in a book he shall, but I do not think he will see the fun of it:

no one will read a book of short stories. Tiresome Blackwood won't send my proofs: I wanted to get the correcting done here.

Your loving Morgan

ALS: KCC

[1] EMF's cousin Percy Whichelo (1876–1956). 'Tanty': his great-aunt Catherine Graham (b. 1823).
[2] Thomas Fisher Unwin (1848–1935), noted liberal and founder of the publishing house of his name, in 1882. His letter does not survive.

55   To Alice Clara Forster

Nassenheide   [Week of 12–18 June 1905]

Dearest Mummy

I hope you are both all right. I havn't any news—except that the weather is always beautiful, and that I am said to look very well. Oh yes—of course I have news. This week we had the long expected Schiller-Feier at the Parsonage.[1] The babies looked very sweet as fisher boys and shepherds, and the Parson's child, who was Wilhelm Tell, was allowed to have its petticoats shorter than was expected. The audience consisted of we four, Count & Countess, Pastor & Frau Pastor, the Pastor's neice, and the schoolmaster, Herr Braun. After the play we sat down—fifteen of us—to supper, which was deafening, and then we did our shadow-pictures, which would have been better had not Herr Braun, in excess of zeal, emptied a large watering pot on the sheet to make the shadows sharper. The room being very small, both actors and audience were instantly flooded, and maids had to come and mop, and Herr Steinweg said decisively that there had been rain enough, and that we must go without our storm. (One poured water out of the w-pot into a basin, close in front of the lamp, and it would have been beautiful.) Then we played a distressingly vulgar game called "die Königin von Saba", and then came beer and a hymn which we sung planted in a row along the sitting room wall, the Pastor giving it out line by line.[2] It was time to go, and Elizabeth asked me whether I had any money. With great pride I poured out a stream of silver upon the table. "Wretch!" she hissed; and it turned out that she wanted to tip the servants unobtrusively, according to the German custom, and feared she would be seen getting out her own purse. The Pastor's family stared blankly out of the windows during the gross proceedings. It seems one must always tip if one has a meal, and people who are not quite, will, in their efforts not to be it, even tip for an afternoon call.

E. has, in a fit of enthusiasm, asked me to come to the Stettin races, and I, equally unwisely, have accepted. It will mean they can't take a footman, since I shall sit on the box, and she has no ticket for me either. However, I should rather enjoy it, and if I can't get in can come back by train. Yesterday evening—or rather night—we went a wonderful drive in the forest. The evening before was not so nice, for the Man of Wrath got wrathful with the food, and Fraülein Backe, who is housekeeper, cried, and then outside, I pushed the June baby into a tea rose, & broke the rose and dirtied her dress.

Meredith writes that he is asking to come down if he is going to P^t Elizabeth, what about asking him to go to Mr Stewart?[3] It is quite the thing he might do nicely, & it would be nice to know something about the man's looks, & the little boy.

Your loving
Morgan

Would you post enclosed (German) letter.
Much love.

ALS: KCC

[1] Schiller Festival, involving dramatisation of Act I of his last completed drama, *Wilhelm Tell* (1804).
[2] 'The Queen of Sheba'.
[3] H. O. Meredith may have been considering going to Port Elizabeth, in the Cape Colony, South Africa. Mr Stewart is unidentified.

56 To Alice Clara Forster

Nassenheide.   2 July 1905

Dearest Mother

Thank you for letter v. much. So glad G[ran]'s visit was successful; am writing to her. Very sorry about E. Will write to him. It is a misfortune that he has got hold of vegetarianism.

No news except that the heat is very great—greater with you though, I expect. Unless a storm comes on I & Herr S[teinweg] mean to spend the evening at Blankensee, which—except the Grace—is pleasant, and also good for German.[1] For the last four days I have kept Herr S., myself, and two men servants busy over sending off the Virgil to Meredith. You never saw such a to do. Six times did I go to the post, and when it did start something was wrong, and it got stopped at Stettin, and today everything had to begin again. I could not register it—and therefore had to insure for 400 marks: it only came to 2 marks in all and honest 'Government' has refunded the money I spent on the first try.

I enclose my plain self, with a funny parting on the *wrong* side. It is good of Herr S. and of the hats. Md^{lle} took it and gave it me. Also one of the babies. The elderly lady on the box is April: behind her June & May: and Quiqui at the back with Fraülein Backe. We have got a new 'Mamzell' or cook. The Man of Wrath is getting rather tragic over his victuals, which is trying for Fraülein B. Do you remember a very short story called 'The Helping Hand'? I think it is in the upstairs drawers, and should be grateful for it, though it doesn't matter: it's only for E. to read. The Man of Wrath listens to us with an amused smile as long as we talk literature, but when we come to publishers & prices he objects and says 'I never talk of my potatoes, though they are ten times as interesting & valuable.'[3]

We go to Greifswald Tuesday: I expect it to be amusing, and trust I shall not get drunk.[4] I hear they will be so civil & drink to me, and then I must drink back or they will be offended, and what the end will be, and whether it will take me noisy or take me quiet I cannot tell.

I do hope you will get a servant. It is tiresome for you. It would be all right about Ruth's holidays though: I should probably have been back by then in any case (the Bargers do not come to Norway), and if, as the time gets a little nearer, you still have no one, will settle to return then for certain.[5] Unless I do any thing to myself you will think me looking very well. I play tennis with much energy, and work nearly all the time out of doors. In the evening I read Elizabeth 'Emma'. Liebeth has just drawn me doing it on the black board. So good.

Your loving
Morgan

Your letter & book & every thing just arrived. Thank you very much. I am sure the Guildford registry office will be no good, and unless I hear to the contrary (perhaps if I do) I shall be back for Ruth's holidays.[6] Much love to Mrs Mawe.

ALS: KCC

[1] Grace: devotions at the Pastor's house; see Letter 52.
[2] 'The Helping Hand,' posthumously published in *LTC*, pp. 55–64.
[3] Elizabeth's husband was a scientific farmer.
[4] Greifswald: town sixty-five miles northeast of Stettin, near the Baltic coast opposite Rügen. Its university was founded in 1456.
[5] Ruth Goldsmith: the Forsters' cook, from Tunbridge Wells days.
[6] Registry office: Lily was looking for another maid.

57   To Arthur Cole

C/o Count Arnim, Nassenheide, Pommern
7 July 1905

"Life is better than one expected" said one of my new friends: "I never thought to leave Brunswick, yet here is Greifswald!"

"So it is", I did not reply: "nor did I ever think to see it and and [*sic*] its glorious brick churches and its hospitable university and its intersecting woods. In fact, I never heard of Greifswald and I doubt whether my friend Mr Cole puts his finger on it instinctively. I wish you knew Mr Cole; you would have a great deal in common. Bitte! Oh ja! Rügen! Nein, ich bin noch nicht sea-sick. Wie schön! Bitte! Danke—Verzeihung! Bitte Verzeihung Danke schön. The sail has never swept me into the Bodden (map) yet, and I don't see why it should. If it does, sit tight, and remember that a little life has gone a longer way than one expected."

To this he answered "You will certainly not be back in time to change for the lunch of the Theologische Gesellschaft. So Werner will take you down to his room and lend you his frock coat. That, with the straw hat and flannel trousers, which you have now got on, will be the very thing."

"I'd rather like to have shaved."

"Oh Herr Forster, we are not formal. Bitte—darf ich—Danke. Indeed you will think us impolite, and I must explain something. For this evening we Foxes act a little play in which an Englishman is…is…is ridiculed. Had we known you were coming Never would it have happened. But now it is all ready—rehearsed—music—the dresses—I do hope that…"

Here we grasped each other warmly by both hands, while Werner swished the boat back into what you may call the Cam—a placid stream some two miles long which connects Greifswald with the sea. Of course we were late for lunch, which I attended in the combination ~~about~~ above indicated. After lunch I fell asleep over a paper on Evolution and Christianity which, together with a lecture in the morning—on the Apochrypha—was about the only bit of rest I got. In the evening, a Kneipe, where we drank deep to Theology, and also the play. The Englishman had on a white topper with a blue veil, a white coat like an umpire, check bags, & red socks. He sang a slow & mournful song, with 'Aow yes' at the end of each line. Then the others fell on him—I couldn't see why—& beat him, and then they made friends, I couldn't see why either, and the curtain fell. The singing was really admirable with jolly quick 3/4 time when things got exciting, just like an early Verdi. Then the ladies—for the cloven petticoat was present—went, and we had more beer, and though not drunk, I woke next morning, for the first time in my life, with the real dissipated headache. However the head ache had to go, for there was an Exbummel of men of maidens [sic] to Eldena—a great brick ruined abbey on the Bodden. We went two & two—fortunately the maidens did not go round but I had a rather dreadful man who would make me conjugate English auxiliary verbs. But I think this is my sole black spot in Greifswald. The other might have been a Miss Scott, but I was not introduced to her till too late, and she had scarcely said how nice it was for English people to meet abroad before I had to fly to the train. All this, or some of it, was only yesterday, and it is almost impossible I should ever see the place or the people again.

These then are my thoughts—to dignify or degrade them by that name—and in my present full blooded mood I make a long nose right over to Cornwall, and don't care a 20 pfennig damn about my behaviour. My books are equally stimulating: Wilhelm Tell—which is thought mighty fine—and Northanger Abbey, which I read aloud to Elizabeth in the evenings. Also Thais, but that I am only beginning.[1] Virgil is not long finished, and was much more sweat than I expected. Yes: I tell my public to like Bk II best, and not to take Bk IV too seriously. That, together with taps at Homer, Tennyson, Augustus, and ourselves nearly completes the introduction. I look forward a good deal to Juvenal, whom I never read & thought pretty bad. Satirists always tried me, especially when they denounced indecency and lavish housekeeping, and after a non-perusal of Juvenal I got the idea that he tried less than the other satirists to see what good or inevitable things lay at the back of either. Laughing at mankind is rather weary rot, I think. We shall never meet with anyone nicer. Nature, whom I used to be keen on, is too unfair. She evokes plenty of high & exhausting feelings, and offers nothing in return. To quote the Man of Wrath: "You will never be able to talk of Beethoven to a cray-fish. Even if he hears you, you will never know it, for his bones are outside, and this prevents any intelligent facial expression." But the Man of Wrath prefers the cray fish to Beethoven & me. He would rather be with animals & plants, whom he cannot see at all, than with men, whom he sees through. Do you call this very spendid? I honestly despise him for seeing through me: he is impious: he does it with a lens too little. It is impossible for me—and perhaps you—to say: for I have seen so little of the 'wicked' world: but now it seems to me that we are all much more alike than we suppose, and much better. Whereas literature & conversation dwells on the vices & the differences. Let me inform you that I contain a solid lump of good, in spite of all I know of myself, and that I believe you to be as lumpy or even lumpier. Now I will thank you for having read as far as here.

Proofs of 1st 4 chapters of novel just arrived: the book itself comes out in the autumn.[2] Blackwoods publishers and I have settled into contentment, for really it is wonderful luck for an unknown to get a 10 chapter book taken at all.

I come back August or September, and perhaps you will at all events pay week end visits to Weybridge River, pine woods, spare bedroom with 'The Stepping Stones' on the wall, Literary society, Tom cat who sneezes to come in, Ruth (beloved factotum), and I hope a house maid too, for till we get one you can't be asked.[3]

Yours ever

E. M. Forster.

ALS: John Cole

[1] *Thaïs* (1891), by Anatole France. EMF wrote in his diary (16 July 1905. KCC): 'The idea of a historical novel, long in my head, has taken rude shape with reading "Thaïs".'

[2] I.e., of *WAFT*.

[3] *The Stepping Stones*, a Victorian favourite by the Surrey artist Myles Birket Foster (1825–99), was originally a wood engraving (Plate 22) in *Birket Foster's Pictures of English Landscape* (1862). In later years he based many water colours and engravings on those plates and showed a painting, *The Stepping Stones*, at the Royal Society of Painter in Water-Colours in Winter 1880–1.

58 To Alice Clara Forster

Nassenheide.   8 July 1905

Dearest Mother

Thank you for letter and story. I have had another £7.7 for the 'Eternal Moment'. I expect the whole thing will stand me about £20. (I have put £25 to Poppy's mummy's account) I don't know what my movements are exactly. I very much want to go to Rügen, and thought perhaps of going thence to Stralsrund, Rostock, Wismar, Lübeck (and Kiel, only now it's no good) and returning by boat from Hamburg to England. I may tempt Herr S[teinweg] to go to Rügen with me.

Well, now for what I have done—my visit to Greifswald—one of the loveliest experiences I have ever had. May you be able to read it, for I am writing on a bobbly table in the garden.

We arrived at 5.0 P.M. on Tuesday—apparently in a wood, for the town is built round a great bar (or rather dumb bell) of trees, and you pop out of streets into it in the most curious way. Then we sight saw, and at 8.30 festivities began, with a 'Kniepe' or drinking bout. For the first two hours I was rather bored, but got into the spirit of the thing during the last two hours and a half. We sang, there were speeches, and a professor came in and everyone screamed with joy and danced round him. I sat next to him, & on hearing my name he said 'There is an Englishman named Forster, an excellent oriental scholar, who wrote about the Rosetta stone.'!!![1] Imagine the excitement! He regarded me as a repository of knowledge in consequence. I and Herr S. shared a room—as small as my bedroom at home. There was only one bed, which I insisted on him having, because he sleeps so badly. I had a short sofa, with high walls at each end, over which my feet strayed in the night, and I woke to find them in the wardrobe. I slept like a log, but the night was too short, and consequently I fell asleep over a lecture on the Apocalypse which I attended in the morning. That was at 9. At 10 we were all photographed (I must tell you that all this is a festival of Herr S.'s Corporation, which corresponds a little to a college in an English University. Its name was the 'Theologische Gesellschaft'.) At 11. Herr S. had things to do, and I would not have minded some sleep.

But civility forbad I should be left alone. The freshmen in Germany are called 'Foxes' and Herr S. shouted 'Fuchs!' and up came one running and I was handed over to him. With this Fox, (who did not know Herr S.) I had a delightful time. Together with another, we walked down to the sea and went for a sail, and saw Rügen in the distance. The formal lunch of the Gesellschaft was at 1.0., and being no longer a Fox, I knew we should be late. We were, and I had no time to put on my honorable clothes. But he said 'Come to my room and I will lend you my frock coat.' He did, and in that, & a straw hat, a blue shirt, and flannel trousers I entered the assembly—to discover that I looked exactly like every one else. The lunch cost 1.50, and was in consequence very elaborate. It is impossible in Greifswald to spend more than 1 mark. After lunch Herr S. read on Evolution and Christianity, and I got a little sleep. Then with the Fox I went to a wonderful fair. Imagine a merry go round, the horses going up & down as well and on them enormous fat men in a kind of evening dress with a broad red ribbon, and vast elderly ladies on swans and in boats, and a student, with his face & scalp covered with scars urging forward a revolving pig. I was told that this was the smart day: if so, the behaviour other days must have been startling. Then came dinner which we had together and then another Kneipe (from 8.30 to 2) at which ladies were present. A great deal of beer was drunk, but no one was the worse, and I noticed that much of it was non-alcoholic. More songs & speeches, and my lady & me having bored each other rather badly we parted and I sat with various aimiable new friends, & promptly upset a mug of beer over my own trouser. Then OH! A play in which England was insulted. "Had we known you were coming Never Never would this have happened. But the dresses are all bought and all rehearsed, and would you, could you, pardon our incivility." I tried, and at all events did not flounce out of the room, nor am I writing to the Times. But do ask Mrs Mawe to tell Miss Merryweather.[2] The Englishman was dressed in a white pot hat, with a blue veil, a long white coat like an umpire, check trousers, and red socks. In his hand he carried what must have been a Bædeker, and he sang a song with 'Aow Yes' at the end of each line. They fell on him and beat him; I could not make out why; and then they made friends—I could not make out why—and the curtain fell. The singing was really admirable.

Next day there was a walk of men and maidens to Eldena, a ruined abbey by the sea. I had only time to go, and then had to fly back to Greifswald by steamer to catch the train to Stettin. The others were to spend the afternoon and evening there, ending up with a dance in their boots. This is called an Exbummel. The students were shaggier & poorer than the English undergraduates, but violently courteous—my hat was all day by my knees, and I bow right from the waist—and I think they were very nice besides; their kindness & trouble was endless.

My proofs are arriving at last. E. is very funny over it. She read ch. 1–3, and said it was very clever, but most unattractive, and she felt as if she wanted a bath. Then she read ch. 4, and said it was really beautiful, and she wanted to retract. Now she has read ch 6—you wouldn't remember, but it was the one that you rather liked—and has gone back to her original opinion.

You will be angry, but I've mislaid the pens that you sent out. Would you send more?

Much love to Mrs Mawe

Your loving
Morgan

Who is Ethel Escome?[3]
I put in a card of Greifswald.

ALS: KCC

[1] EMF's grandfather, the Rev. Charles Forster of Stisted, wrote *The Monuments of Egypt and Their Vestiges of Patriarchal Traditions*, Part 2 of his three-volume work, *The One Primeval Language* (1851–4).
[2] Miss Merryweather: unidentified.
[3] Perhaps Edith Escombe, author of *Phases of Marriage* (1897).

59 To Alice Clara Forster

Hotel "Goldener Löwe", Stralsund
10 August 1905

Dearest Mother

I think I did not give this as an address, so I can hardly repine at not hearing. I prolonged my tour at Rügen, to the great detriment of my appearance. I wore my shirt inside out, & then took to my pyjamas. It was so lovely that it seemed foolish to be hurried away by dirty clothes. For my body there was always the sea, in which I bathed often—sometimes several times in the day. I sat so long toasting in the sun that the whole of the skin has peeled off my back & shoulders, and as for my face it is scarlet. As you have the Countess' book it may be worth telling the tour.[1] Binz (1 night): Lauterbach (3 nights, including the Jugdschloss, Vilm, & Putbus): Sassnitz, via Bergen, 1 night: thence by Stubbenkammer to Lohme, where I slept again. The next day steamer to Arconia [Arkona], & thence to Wiek, where I stayed two nights. And last night at Hiddensöe [Hidden See].

I left Nassenheide in much glory: I turn out to be most successful as a teacher, & to have kept wonderful order. The children did behave all right, but I didn't realise it was owing to me. Evi & Liebeth both wrote me valedictory poems—Liebeth's quite sweet—: and Beatrix "tried to think of a poem, but it wouldn't come, so here are gooseberries instead." All these gifts, much beflowered & be pinned & beribboned, were handed to me as the train left Nassenheide. I will put in the Countess' nice letter, if it isn't too heavy. I asked Fräulein Backe about tips, and our ideas horrified her. I ended up by giving Arno 10/–, and dividing 11/– among the others. This will scandalise you, but not more than it would her, it being *exactly seven times* the sum suggested as adequate! Truly this land is modest in its ideas. The 'great expense' of Rügen culminated in 2.50, for a bed. Generally I paid 2.00: the last three nights 1.50, This last night, at Hiddensöe, I made sure I was to be murdered. All hotels were full, and I could only get a room in a villa, whereof the landlord looked mad, & the landlady not respectable. I was not admitted into the room till late, and then found that two men had to come and sleep through me. I tied nosebag to my heart. Of course nothing happened, & I think really everyone was quite nice.

I found my bag here, which encourages me to hope I shall find my box at Bremen. I come back thence, if I can, by steamer to London: if not, via the Hook & Harwich. I shall be home on the twenty-something: it would be earlier, but Mʳ Hervey likes me at Kiel on a Sunday—the 20th.[2] Let no one expect any nice presents. There are none to be got. I found several letters here: one from Gran, not written at her best: smacks all round. My clothes have swelled frightfully, & I have to travel with a card board box, like a true German. However large & heavy, it seems to go by post for 0.50. In Rügen, of course, I only had my knapsack. I am too sleepy to write. Tomorrow evening I go to Rostock. Write to me, in a day or two, at Mʳ Hervey's. There have been so many things lately that I forgot to tell you that the Manchester plan has all fallen through, but that instead I lecture at Hunstanton, which is mad enough to pay my expenses from Weybridge every fortnight.[3]

I wished for you again here. It is a wonderful place, full of old red brick houses, which, though not picturesque in outline like the Nuremburg ones, are more marvellous in detail. Three marvellous churches—one of which, together with the Rathaus, is opposite the hotel: you would enjoy it; & the air always so cool. Love to Rosie if she is with you: ⟨and scoldings to her if she isn't⟩

Your loving
Morgan.

ALS: KCC

[1] Elizabeth von Arnim (Russell), *The Adventures of Elizabeth in Rügen* (1904), account of a trip taken despite her husband's disapproval, around Rügen with a coachman and a maid.
[2] Mr Hervey, EMF's old tutor, was then at Kiel.
[3] Part of his University Extension Lectures series on Italian culture.

60 To Robert Trevelyan

Harnham, Monument Green, Weybridge
28 October 1905

Dear Trevelyan

Your letter was rather what I expected, and very much what I feel about my book myself, though on the whole I am less severe, and inclined, I think, to view my work too complacently.[1] The object of the book is the improvement of Philip, and I did really want the improvement to be a surprise. Therefore in chapters 1–2 I never hinted at the possibility, but at the same time did not demonstrate the impossibility, or did not mean to. In ch. 5 he has got into a mess, through trying to live only by a sense of humour and by a sense of the beautiful. The knowledge of the mess embitters him, and this is the improvement's beginning. From that time I exhibit new pieces of him—pieces that he did not know of, or at all events had never used. He grows large enough to appreciate Miss Abbott, and in the final scene he exceeds her.

All this is what I intended.

But I do begin to think (—I will say 'to fear' for it is a pity it should be so—) that this 'surprise' method is artistically ~~impossible~~ wrong, and that from the first one must suggest the possibility, not merely the non-impossibility, of improvement. I disliked and do dislike finger posts, and couldn't bear in the earlier scenes the thought of inserting "Philip has other things in him besides these: watch him.", however well the insertion had been made. And, when I wrote Monteriano I pushed this dislike to an extreme and should have ~~seconded~~ felt the suggestion that a book must have one atmosphere to be pedantic.[2] Life hasn't any, and the hot and cold of its changes are fascinating to me. I determined to imitate in this and let the result be artistic if it liked. Naturally it did not like.

I too would like to have a talk, and can't get what I want to say on paper. You can gather however that I know I am not a real artist, and at the same time am fearfully serious over my work and willing to sweat at atmosphere if it helps me to what I want. What I want, I think, is the sentimental, but the sentimental reached by no easy beaten track—I cannot explain myself properly, for you must remember (I forget it myself) that though 'clever' I have a small and cloudy brain, and cannot clear it by talking or reading philosophy. In fact my equipment is frightfully limited, but so good in parts that I want to do with it what I can.

Miss Abbott comes to grief for archæological reasons. She was originally meant to turn out smaller and different. About the scene between Philip and Gino I don't, however, quite concur.[3] (Less important than the death of the baby, which is the real crisis.) P. is a person who has scarcely ever felt the physical forces that are banging about in the world, and ~~I didn't forget~~ he couldn't get good or understand by spiritual suffering alone. Bodily punishment, however unjust superficially, was necessary too: in fact the scene—to use a heavy word, and one that I have only just thought of—was sacramental. Nor do I lose interest in Gino after it: here the possibility was hinted at during his intercourse with Lilia.

If you are good enough to write again, I wish you'ld tell me on which pages I am unduly facetious. That is an awful evil, and only you have warned me against it. And I wish, if it was only two or three lines, you would say something about my style. It is scarcely fair though, after all your goodness, to bother you again. You're the only person who has troubled to criticise me in any detail.

Yours ever
E. M. Forster.

When do you go abroad? I am not where I appear, but in the North: I return on the 3rd.[4]

ALS: TCC

[1] EMF had apparently written twice to ask Trevelyan's opinion. For part of his reply ([n.d.] KCC) to the second appeal, see *WAFT*, pp. 150–2. No second reply from Trevelyan survives, but he wrote to Leonard Woolf (December 1905. Berg): 'I wonder whether you will have seen E. M. Forster's novel "Where Angels Fear to Tread": it is worth reading, but some people like it a great deal, others, like myself, only rather.'

[2] Monteriano: original title of *WAFT*. EMF remained undecided almost to the eve of publication and had solicited friends' suggestions. He wrote to Dent (21 July 1905. KCC): 'Thanks most awfully for titles: you're simply marvellous, and left me in as bad a hole, for instead of not knowing what I didn't know which. Finally I sent "Where Angels Fear to Tread" and "From a Sense of Duty" to Blackwood, and he will choose between them.' In 1953 he would ask his French translator, Charles Mauron (1899–1966) whether *Monteriano* might be substituted in the French edition: 'My English publishers refused it. They said it would imperil the already slight chances of success. My friend, E. J. Dent the musician, jotted down some alternatives and *Where Angels*——was chosen hap-hazardly and half heartedly' (20 April 1953. Mauron).

[3] Chapter 9, in which Gino tortures Philip.

[4] At his Uncle Willie Forster's home, in Northumberland.

61   To Goldsworthy Lowes Dickinson

Harnham, Monument Green, Weybridge
9 December 1905

Dear Dickinson

I am wanting to express my pleasure but find it very difficult, for I do not know how far you intend your work to be admired & loved from a point of view so narrow as my own.[1] 'Arguments', to me, are only fascinating when they are of the nature of gestures, and illustrate the people who produce them. The arguments of your people, besides doing other things, do this, and hence my admiration and love. I am glad to see that critics think the other things are good as well.

It is so beautiful—the style, the setting, and those characters whom you have intended to be beautiful: above all Mendoza and MacCarthy. Other people will have written this, and not so crudely. But I'm trusting you not to be jarred. The feelings I'm trying to express now have been in me for years.

E. M. F.

MS: KCC

[1] Dickinson, *A Modern Symposium* (1905), in which participants are analogues for well-known late-Victorian figures. Mendoza and MacCarthy are based, respectively, on Disraeli and Henry Sidgwick.

62 To Edward Joseph Dent

Grand Hotel de France, Blois[1]

3 October 1906

Dear Dent

So glad to hear of you: such news as there may be of me you will have heard from the Bargers.

Yes I did like Subiaco, tho' only there for a few hours. Did you dispute with a monk up at S[ta] Scholastica on the subject of the Hanoverian succession?[2] Neither my Italian nor my arguments were enough to defend it. Then I rode to the Casa Baldi, Olevano: wonderful hills, and an inn on a hill among corn fields. I played on the grand piano to the land lady while the canary sang like mad.

I suppose you know this country. You would hardly know me, so violently has Chartres gothicised me. In the presence of Blois or Chambord I say "Tut! tut! Toys of kings and their mistresses! Where is colour, mystery and the promise of eternity? Where the mediaeval survey of man—erroneous if you like, but a survey—?" In or outside Chartres you can find every human passion. Huysman[s], amid much nonsense, does make this point—that the middle ages did not shirk things. That, he suggests, began with the Counter Reformation. His is an interesting book—I forget if you set me on to it: at all events you first told me his name.[3] Well to Chartres I hope to return, after the 8 or 9 castles on our lists are ticked off: we're just off to Tours. Also I will see Le Mans.

France is full of horrible English.

I overeat. I cannot help it: food is a tiresome business. There seems no escape from Table d'hôte. At this minute I have ten courses inside me—not counting the peaches I took away in my pocket. We're really having a very good time as regards sight seeing and weather. We expect to be back in about 10 days or a fortnight. Any letters should be addressed home, but I can well imagine you're rather busy for writing. I was up at Cambridge to lecture on Richardson.[4] Greenwood & Woolley were up and I had a very good time.[5] Since then I've been stopping with George Hodgkin at Sunderland: I'm not sure whether you know him.[6]

Yours ever
E. M. Forster.

ALS: KCC

[1] EMF and Lily were touring the château country.
[2] Subiaco: town twenty-five miles northeast of Rome; EMF had been there in 1902. Sancta Scholastica is a Benedictine monastery, founded 981.
[3] Joris-Karl Huysmans: pen-name of Charles Marie George Huysmans (1848–1907), Franco-Dutch novelist; author of La Cathédrale (1898), whose protagonist's experiences reflect Huysmans' own return to Roman Catholicism.
[4] This lecture on the novelist Samuel Richardson (1689–1761) does not survive.
[5] Leonard Hugh Graham Greenwood (1880–1965), New Zealander who entered King's in 1899; Tutor at Emmanuel College, 1910–26, and University Lecturer in Classics, 1926–45. Victor James Woolley (1879–1960) physiologist and pharmacologist, was a student also of sexology and spiritualism; Fellow of King's, 1903–9. EMF was with him in Venice in 1908.
[6] George Lloyd Hodgkin (1880–1918) was a Quaker friend of Arthur Bevington Gillett (1875–1954), also a Quaker, and a contemporary of EMF at King's; he lived in Banbury and was a Director of Barclay's Bank. Hodgkin went to Sunderland about 1903 to study civil engineering, and he worked briefly in Gillett's bank in Banbury. He died of dysentery in Baghdad, where he was organising relief work.

63 To Alys Russell[1]

Harnham, Monument Green, Weybridge
30 October 1906

Dear Mrs Russell
    My bag and I arrived safely, and before ten minutes were over I told my mother that she had made me miss the train. She replied "What you want is a proper flat nice dress suit case: I have told you to buy one again and again. How can you travel comfortably unless you have comfortable things?" Who won?
    In Oxford I saw the Shelley: the hip is indeed ugly, and the dome tawdry I suppose, but I do still like it, upholstery and all.[2]
    I enjoyed my visit so much: it was very kind of you to ask me. I hope the cat is well: ours would send kind enquiries, but has just been smacked for eating a beetroot.
    Again thanking you for your kindness,

I remain
Yours sincerely
E. M. Forster.

ALS: Fawcett Library

[1] Alys Pearsall Smith Russell (d. 1951), American first wife of Bertrand Russell.
[2] Lady Shelley wanted to substitute the ornate monument (1892) by the English sculptor Edward Onslow Ford (1852–1901), for the simple slab on Shelley's grave in the Protestant Cemetery in Rome. This brought on a controversy over the land-title of the grave, and the monument came to rest at University College, Oxford, in 1893; see Newman Ivey White, Shelley, II, 383–4.

64   To Edward Joseph Dent

Holmleigh, Salisbury   [late April 1907]

Dear Dent

It's long since I heard from you and the fault's mine: thank you for writing like this—I had no idea how the people who count would take the book, nor much idea how I take it myself. For the B[ritish] P[ublic] it is assuredly a Cross, nor did I intend it otherwise. I have only had two reviews yet—bewildered and respectful.[1] But we must not grow superior—! What you kindly call 'inner meaning' is only clumsiness.

M⟨rs⟩ Failing & Ansell seem to me the two good eggs, but I'm glad Stephen impresses you. There was actually a long 'Panic' chapter about him—rather jolly I thought—but I soon cut it out, for it shifted the vision too far round.[2] So, probably only students of the Master's Juvenilia will now twig what he's driving at.

I am very sorry about your troubles with your mother. I hope she didn't mind very much—which reads like a back-hander, but I am always wondering how much old people suffer. However much you minded at the time, it must now be better for you.

We must fix up a meeting before the middle of May. I go home tomorrow to squire a dull damsel and finish off my work, which is interesting but brings neither fame nor wealth. I hate leaving here, for my friend is letting for a year, or more if she can, and for so long I bid good bye to this wonderful country, or at least to this particular view of it.[3]

Nothing much has happend this year. I have just been with the Merediths in Wales—eight of us pigging it. We were all very nice.[4] I have also become friends with a nice (who isn't, except in novels?) Mohammedan—at least he thinks he's a Mohammedan and that I am a Christian.[5] "I must really bike over to the mosque some Friday" or "Excuse me if I tell you, but I am told that even clergymen find the Trinity hard to understand" or "Let me explain my religion. Not to drink wine. Not to eat the pig. There is one God and Mohammed is one of his prophets. To believe in the Last Judgement. Oh yes, and not to eat an animal that has died."

I have vague ideas about your recent doings? What about Mozart?[6] I will write again as soon as I see a chance of being in town.

Yours ever
Sharp wholesome insect[7]
(*vide* Times critique.)

ALU: KCC

[1] Reviews of *The Longest Journey*: probably the one included under 'Fiction', *TLS*, 26 April 1907, p. 134; and in the *Daily Chronicle* ('A Story of Distinction', 23 April 1907, p. 3), whose reviewer complained that 'in his efforts to be startling [he] fails to be altogether intelligible.'

² A chapter (MS. KCC) in which Stephen is knocked on the head by a bottle thrown from a train-window and wanders naked into the woods, like Siegfried or Adam.

³ My friend: Maimie Aylward. 'Dull damsel': unidentified.

⁴ Besides the Merediths and EMF, the Bargers.

⁵ Syed Ross Masood (1889–1937) was born in Aligarh, the son of a distinguished Indian jurist, and grandson of the famous reformer Sir Syed Ahmed Khan (1817–98). Sir Syed, a leading figure in the Muslim revival after the Indian Mutiny of 1857, founded the Muslim Anglo-Oriental College at Aligarh (later Aligarh University) in 1875. After his death Sir Theodore Morison, who was then Principal of the College, adopted the young Masood, whose father had suffered some kind of mental breakdown. Masood came to England in 1906 to complete his education at New College, Oxford, and Sir Theodore, who had retired to Weybridge and was friendly with the Forsters, invited the novelist to coach Masood in Latin. A strong friendship quickly sprang up between the two, causing EMF to interest himself in all things Indian. It was agreed between them that when Masood returned to India (as he did, reluctantly, in 1912) EMF should come out to visit him and the various Indian acquaintances he had met in Masood's company.

Masood worked for a few years in a legal practice in Bankipore, but through the influence of his British friends he abandoned the law for the Educational Service, and in 1918 he became Director of Public Instruction in Hyderabad State, where he was instrumental in the founding of Osmania University. In 1914 he had married and had two sons, Anwar and Akbar, by his first wife. By 1928 he was in difficulties; he had decided to divorce his wife, from whom he had been estranged for some years, and he lost much money in the Stock Exchange crash. He accepted premature retirement from his Hyderabad post. At this point, however, he was offered and accepted the Vice-Chancellorship of Aligarh University. He had some success in rehabilitating this institution, which had been in difficulties, but he had powerful enemies and resigned in dudgeon in 1934 after being outvoted over a staff appointment. During his last two years he served as Minister of Education in Bhopal, but his defeat at Aligarh had more or less wrecked him. He left a daughter Nadira, by a second marriage. He was knighted in 1933.

Masood was a handsome man, very tall and massively built, with a vivid and exuberant character and inclined to surround himself with a little 'court' of friends. EMF was intensely attached to him and evolved many of his ideas about British–Indian relations from this association. He evokes Masood's personality in his essay 'Syed Ross Masood,' a letter to the journal *Urdu*, 17 (1937), 853–60; reprinted in *TCD*, pp. 285–7.

⁶ *The Magic Flute* was by no means staple operatic fare in England when Dent took a keen interest in it and, with Clive Carey, produced the opera at Cambridge on 1 and 2 December 1911. In 1907 Dent was engaged in the research that led to his book, *Mozart's Operas: A Critical Study* (1913).

⁷ The *TLS* reviewer (note 1, above) wrote that 'Mr Forster fastens himself again, like some sharp wholesome insect, upon the life of the suburbs . . .'

65   To Syed Ross Masood

West Hackhurst, Abinger Hammer, Dorking
8 May 1907

Dear Masood

I arrived safely, and my hookah made me a centre of interest to my fellow travellers. Here too it is greatly admired. I am so delighted with it. My aunt was so pleased with your messages, and sends her greetings to you. Thank you also for the card, which you so kindly forwarded. You need not, by the bye, have troubled to put it in an envelope. The same stamp does if it is re-addressed the same day. See how economical and commercial my soul is? Am I worthy to be shod in golden slippers?¹

I'm anxious to hear from you. It is a difficult business, and I

sympathise with you very much. If only H. does not flare up, it will
be all right, for it is easy enough for him to shift his rooms after his
holiday. Whether your suspicions about the matter are right or
wrong, he ought to go. I am certain of that. I hope that you will
always talk over difficulties with me when you feel inclined. I am far
from being the wisest of your English friends, but I am the nearest to
your own age—and at all events such talk would be a great pleasure
to me.

You hate being thanked, so what am I to say? Well Oxford's not
such a bad place, is it, and you aren't such an intolerable person, are
you? Will that do? No it won't. I insist on thanking you for my
delightful visit.[2] I enjoyed it immensely—boat, walks, talks, and all.
Please remember me most kindly to Hassan & Raschid, and thank
the O'Connors for their hospitality—and don't go to the beastly
bazaar.[3]

Yours ever
E. M. Forster.

ALS: KCC

[1] Hookah: presumably a gift from Masood during EMF's Oxford visit. Slippers: also a gift
from Masood.
[2] EMF tried in various ways to circumvent Masood's embargo on thanks, as in the letter
reproduced in *EMF*, I, 145.
[3] Mohammed Abdul Rashid Khan (1886–1943), housemate of Masood at 12 Edith Road,
Chelsea. Rashid's daughter Amtul was to become Masood's second wife. Hassan and the
O'Connors: friends of Masood in Oxford.

66 To Robert Trevelyan

C/o Mrs Read, Grasmere
[July 1907]

Dear Bob

We're not getting on so badly. It rains all night and every day, but
not always all day. 'Excursions' are impossible but one gets good
walks. I like Grasmere. After the Lowwood Hotel Windermere
(12/– a day—but I must admit they do you prettily there as well as
well—no beastliness: I can strongly recommend it though of course
only to fools)—well after it Grasmere seems seclusion. The
associations are just 'right'. The Billy here is in proportion—
whereas the Billy of Normandy and (I fancy) he of Stratford are out
of it. I have seldom enjoyed a Sight more than Dove Cottage—only
spoilt by the beastly Arnolds—Rugby and Mat—with their low
clerical chins by the side of that sweet fish Coleridge's.[1] Between the
rain we row on the Lake[,] pick Welsh Poppies and buy
gingerbread.

We had meant to drive to Keswick—Borrowdale—Buttermere—
Cockermouth—but the weather is so chancy, & the round so

expensive that it is [*sic*] has fallen to 'round Thirlmere for 3/6'—we start in half an hour: and go tomorrow to the Patterdale Hotel Ullswater—though don't write anything entertaining there, as even *that* may fall through. Thence home.

Where is Joanna's Rock²?

Yours ever

E. M. Forster.

ALS: TCC

¹ 'Billy here . . . Billy of Normandy': William Wordsworth as Lake Country poet living at Dove Cottage, Grasmere, and William the Conqueror. Billy of Stratford is, of course, Shakespeare. EMF had always found Matthew Arnold an unsympathetic character, as also his
² Joanna's Rock: Wordsworth, 'To Joanna' (1800).

67 To Edward Garnett

9 Wolseley Place, Withington, Manchester¹
28 October 1907

Dear Garnett

You said I might write to you about *The Breaking Point*.² I think it wonderful, and unlike anything I have read before. One receives images from some books, and yours suggested a vase in the hands of a clumsy person which will be dropped sooner or later, but when, one cannot tell. I had this image even before I came to the broken glass in the first act.—Of course, this is only a roundabout way of saying that it is tragedy.

I hardly know whether you have gained or lost by not having it acted. Most decidedly it is an acting play and all your points— particularly such points as Sherrington's first serious remark, and Agatha's uncanny muddle about the carriage lamps—should come out tremendously on the stage. But, in the present state of acting, I feel it might have got terribly spoilt—Grace Elwood especially. She is so unlike other stage characters that I feel—perhaps fancifully— that you want for her someone unlike other actresses—someone inexperienced & sincere.

Those who are reading the play here share my admiration. The only criticisms that seem to stand are, (i) we wish the play was longer wh. is only another way of saying that it is an acting play, and (ii) whether Mʳˢ Sherrington need have appeared. Might she not have merely written to S., and the (slight) gossip about Grace be heard in the village by Aunt Dorothy?—But this is criticism of a narrow type, for Mʳˢ Sherrington, as a character, is splendid. You have shown in her that the unimaginative willingly joins hands with the religious.

All this is very scrappy, but I have taken advantage of your invitation. I wouldn't have let loose on you otherwise.

Yours sincerely
E. M. Forster.

ALS: HRC

[1] H. O. Meredith's address.

[2] Drama written in 1906 by Edward Garnett (1868–1937), publisher's reader and critic. After the Lord Chamberlain denied it a licence, it was published as *A Censored Play: The Breaking Point* (1907). Samuel Hynes, in *The Edwardian Turn of Mind*, discusses the episode as a paradigm for authors' troubles with censorship (pp. 216–22).

68 To Robert Trevelyan

[N. p. 20 January 1908?]
Per Mr Forster, who will come on Sunday.

Sir

I hesitate to address you but you have again confused me with my young cousin Miss Honeychurch ('Lucy'). I am of no consequence, I do not matter, living in a very quiet way as I do at Tunbridge Wells, and I really write to you on my cousin's account. It is not fair on her. She is most sensitive and accomplished, and alas! I rub her up the wrong way only too often. Our tour to Italy was not the success I hoped, for I do not understand the modern girl, and I have Lucy's own word for it that I bored her, that day of the dreadful expedition to the tomb of Cecilia Matilda. Now our ways have parted and it would gall her beyond measure to be confused with her unattractive old cousin. I beg you therefore for her sake to remember that I am

CHARLOTTE Bartlett.[1]

APCU: TCC

[1] Character and events from *A Room with a View*.

69 To Edward Joseph Dent

Harnham, Monument Green, Weybridge
10 February 1908

Dear Dent

Is the Owlet sustentation fund still going? If so, please accept the enclosed trifle for it. The fruit I had consecrated to Melpomene (pretty) has just arrived: I wish it was a bigger bunch.[1]

I have long been intending to write to you and among other things—to thank for a p[ost] c[ard] you sent me long ago with a parallel to 'The Longest Journey' on it.[2] Now that I do write, I feel stupid and tired: I am very busy in a scrappy way with a new course of lectures and with teaching Latin at the W[orking] M[en's] C[ollege].³ I suppose that you're very busy too with the house which I know only as the page of an exercise book; and I hope that the furniture won't swell when it arrives and refuse to fit into the appointed squares.⁴

I have not seen many people lately—Laurence [Haward] at Götterdämmerung on Saturday, and last month I went to stop with the Waterlows at Rye. There I had a very good time the 'feature' being tea with Henry James. I was preceded by a little story that I had written, and so was particularly nervous in case I didn't come up to sample.⁵ H. J. received me with much civility and warmth, laying his hand on my shoulder. I thought 'Hooray—he likes it—I really *am* great' when he said 'Your name's Moore' which was a pity. Then he said 'Where do you live?' My tongue clove to the roof of my mouth, and he thought I answered Wakefield. 'How do you like Rye?' was the next question and I think I replied 'Very happily'. It is a funny sensation, going to see a really first class person. I felt all that the ordinary healthy man feels in the presence of a Lord. And H. J. had the royal power of convincing one that one's idiocies didn't matter. I did enjoy the visit very much [word inked out and illegible] indeed.

Do you know of a Miss Marie Motta, who is bringing a string quartet down here next month? I heard her last year and thought her good.⁶

Yours ever

E. M. Forster.

If you are telling Carey the names of his well wishers, of course tell mine: one anonymous person is rather a frost. But if there have already been anonymous donors, I should prefer to be classed among them.

I don't really mind: I am trying to think which would be the least nuisance for him.

ALS: KCC

¹ Dent organised a subscription for Clive Carey (1883–1968), who was trained at the King's College Choir School and entered Clare College in 1901. They collaborated on various musical enterprises, and Carey became known as a collector and performer of English folk songs. He later taught singing in Australia and in London. 'Owlet': from Carey's role in Aristophanes' *The Birds*, set to music by Sir Hubert Parry (1848–1918), Professor of Music at the Royal College of Music, and performed in Cambridge in 1903; see Hugh Carey, *Duet for Two Voices*, pp. 10–13. 'The fruit . . . Melpomene': perhaps money due to Forster that he intended to put aside for Carey.
² Only one postcard to EMF is extant, 3 August 1907 (KCC): not the one referred to here.
³ The 'new course' was probably for the Cambridge Local Lectures Board.
⁴ In 1907 Dent returned from the Continent to King's but decided to move to a house in Cambridge, at 4 Belvedere Terrace, Panton Street.
⁵ Wagner's *Ring* was being performed at Covent Garden. Sydney Waterlow had married Alice Isabella Pollock, daughter of the famous jurist Sir Frederick Pollock (1845–1937). The

Waterlows settled in Rye, where Sydney was acting as a kind of Boswell to Henry James. For a description of EMF's visit to him, see also *EMF*, I, 163–5. The 'little story' was 'The Celestial Omnibus', in the *Albany Review*, 2 (1908), 459–75.

[6] Miss Marie Motto's Quartet had given a concert series at Queen's Gate Hall, in South Kensington. The only notable member of the group was its violist, the composer Frank Bridge (1879–1941), then only five years out of the Royal College of Music.

70 To Edward Garnett

Harnham, Monument Green, Weybridge
6 June 1908

Dear Garnett

I am in London next Wednesday and should much like to call at one; I may be a minute or so late.

Granting that your play[1] was bad—I need hardly say I don't grant it—; some criticisms that I read still remain inexcusable. Full bloodedness and vitality are all very well, and perhaps I admire them more than you do and more than one ought. But to demand their insertion in such a scheme as yours—! Words fail me. I did not see the performance, but it seems to me impossible that the first scene should fail to move. I can only conclude that critics found the movement shocking. People hate to be reminded that many actions and speeches are directly physiological. They like to think that life comes straight from heaven.

Yours sincerely
E. M. Forster.

ALS: HRC
[1] See Garnett, *The Feud: A Play in Three Acts* (1909).

71 To Hugh Walpole

Harnham, Monument Green, Weybridge
19 July 1908

Dear Walpole,

I can say without preamble that it's good—the theme is ample and fills the book properly, the development holds one, and though the future is always hidden, when it arrives it always seems inevitable and natural.[1] The interest does persist to the very end. I did put the book down, because I went to bed, but I finished it first thing in the morning. You ought to get it taken all right—though of course one can't ever speak for certain about that. To call it "promising" sounds impertinent, but I mean that the most ambitious scenes in it are the best—e.g. *all* the scenes in which Dahlia appears, and the row between Harry & the family.

As for the defects, I fancy you've tipped them for yourself. Your method, while avoiding all obscurity and affectation, is at times in danger of missing mystery also. In spite of your obvious delight in beauty and antiquity, one sometimes felt their presentation was not quite successful. This is intangible criticism, and on the other hand to say that "certain clauses were redundant" is almost too tangible! But I remember ⟨e.g.⟩ a comparison of a deserted mine to a temple which would have charmed me more if the end of the sentence had been topped off: I refer to it not out of captiousness, but to show the sort of feeling that's in my mind.[2]

The ages of the characters are certainly not always convincing. Mary is old, Harry is young, and his development is just what one might expect in the 20's,—not in the 40's? My own notion of them is that though men may keep buoyancy, freshness & charm, they *must* lose adaptability, and Harry is so adaptable—as if he were Robin's brother. But your notion may be right.

One general criticism. Haven't you tried to treat as related, two problems that are really distinct? Isn't "Harry v. the family" one case, and "The Cove v. Pendragon" another? It's impertinent of me to speak about Cornwall, when I've only been there once, but to me Harry doesn't = it: he's Anglo-Saxon, and likelier to sail on the boats of Lowestoft than of Newlyn. Still less do the Trojans = progress and electric trams, and I felt it unreal when Clara defended them, however languidly, and when Garrett grew keen on sanitation—though perhaps it was pure self advertisement in his case. I mean by all this that there's a discrepancy between your actors and their backgrounds, and, if I'm right, one or the other must suffer. It seems to me that the backgrounds suffer, and that the atmosphere of your story is not as successful as its action. Personal scenes—getting back letters etc.—are admirable; but when the characters try to express the vast forces that move behind them—forces that move behind us all and the expression of which is one of the highest aims of literature—I've got this sentence tied up, but it amounts to this: you haven't succeeded in doing a very very difficult thing!

You must take the above as the result of one reading at full speed. I shall read in the book again before I return it, and may regret my criticisms. But I wanted to write straight off about it—it interested me so. Yes, the title is all right.

I should like to hear what the other two men say.

Yours ever
E. M. Forster.

ALS: HRC

[1] Hugh Walpole (1884–1941), New Zealand-born novelist, was educated at Emmanuel College, Cambridge. He tried teaching school but turned to writing as a career. EMF writes here about Walpole's first published novel, *The Wooden Horse* (1909), about a Cornish family, and first called 'The House of the Trojans'.
[2] In *ibid.*, pp. 192–3.

72 To Edward Joseph Dent

Harnham, Monument Green, Weybridge
19 October 1908

Dear Dent

No, I don't expect that you will do with the book very well: it does, sincerely or insincerely, commend an attitude that you will think insincere. Only I do wonder that you find it difficult to read—pretty straight forward isn't it, surely.[1]

I feel myself that it comes off as far as it goes—which is a damned little way—and that the character of Lucy, on which everything depends, is all right: she and Mr Beebe have interested me a good deal. Cecil ⟨described not entirely from Lucy's point of view⟩ is certainly incomplete. But his 3 proposals don't strike me as unnatural. She may only be a peg to hang his artistic sensations on, but she is a peg he can't reach easily, and this at once increases her value. Of course when his amour propre is wounded it is a different thing—off he goes at the end of the book, & becomes a mysogynist. But until that happens, I maintain he will be attracted, and think that he is caring more about her than about himself. You say "if he is too young to realize that he can know no one intimately, he does not seem worth bringing in." Why?

Oh Dent, these slips! What is one to do about them. I laboured so with the Italian, but of course have missed all the points you have mentioned, and I dare say many more. Only I will defend Santa Conversazione's—they are saints talking, not family groups: Filippo Lippi, Andrea del Sarto &^{ct} do them as well as Bellini.[2]

I got home Friday—straight through from Parma. Have had a splendid time, blessing you most days and, as you may imagine, every evening. I was just going to write to you about the net. Would you resent it's being washed? I have grubbed it a little, and my sponge has pump shitted over it in one place or so, and I would like to return it clean.[3] Expert opinion says that a good job can be made of it—except that it may shrink a little, and the mesh be rather smaller. Let me know.

Montagnana was glorious—thanks so much; nor do I agree about Monselice—the walk up the hill amidst statues & cypresses was exquisite. Then I went to Ferrara, Ravenna, Rimini, San Marino, Forlì Faenza, & Parma. I cleverly mislaid the list of hotels I copied out of your Bædecker, & suffered occasionally in consequence. I liked the Masini at Forlì—and such a glorious fresco on the dining room ceiling—style of Guido Reni, I think—Apollo in an abundance of soft clouds. How horrid the Corona at Faenza is. I hear that the Vittoria is better. At Parma the Marchese does very well.[4]

I should like to come & stop some time very much: it's very good

of you to ask me. So glad to hear that Haward is picking up at last. I
have had a letter from him.[5] What news about Frances Darwin?[6]

England seems nasty after Italy, though not as nasty as France.
We are going away in a few days, & I trust that Weybridge will air
itself in our absence—at present it smells. Do you know of the Rev.
Courtney Gale who comes here to lecture on music for the
University Extension? Would he not be an absolute rotter? I hear he
spent the opening lecture partly in not being there, and partly in
reading aloud the whole Abt Vogler.[7]

Yours ever
E. M. Forster.

ALS: KCC

[1] *A Room with a View*, published 14 October 1908.
[2] See *RV*, p. 235 note.
[3] 'Pump shitted': EMF's misspelling of 'pumpshipped'.
[4] Masini, Corona, Marchesa: hotels.
[5] Haward's letter does not survive.
[6] Frances Darwin (1886–1960), poet; daughter of Sir Francis Darwin and granddaughter of
Charles Darwin. In 1909 she married Francis Cornford (1874–1943), classicist and Fellow of
Trinity College, Cambridge.
[7] The Rev. Courtenay Gale (1857–1937) was Vicar of Christ Church, Sutton, Surrey, for
fifty years. He was something of a local legend, and a successor, the Rev. Frank S. Lewis,
recalls stories about him as a 'very colourful personality' who 'claimed to be a Platonist and
was very musical and something of a mechanic. He used to go out to mend the very fine organ
during the service and emerge into the pulpit with very black hands which he used with
considerable effect in his sermons, ... ' (F. S. Lewis to ML, 29 August 1982). Hence, a
certain logic in his devotion to the organist of Browning's poem 'Abt Vogler' (1864).

73   Syed Ross Masood

Harnham, Monument Green, Weybridge
2 July 1909

Masood!

Where's my cap! What a fellow it is. Don't send it now, for I'm
getting a new one, which I will wear cursing you. Wear mine—and
try to be methodical—like me—!

I enjoyed the play awfully, and dinner perhaps even more. It was
decent getting you to talk with again; Weybridge has been a
different place since you ceased to inhabit it: there's no one I care for
living here now. I have been gardening and making up lists of
magic-lantern slides all to day—neither very exciting occupations.[1]
But something exciting is coming on—did I tell you? The Minister
for Foreign Affairs has read the works of your humble servant, has
approved of them, & has asked me to dinner in consequence. Did
you ever! I am looking forward to it, and am not in a funk, for Grey
is not only charming, but simple, I hear: I do know his brother &
sister a little. It comes off on the 12th.[2]

I was interested in your music-hall experiences, but that side of
life seems more interesting than it really is. If you want to feel sad,

think about poverty: that is interesting almost to madness if it grips you once. As for those women, isn't it rather rough luck on them to study them? It is as if one went into a shop, took up people's time, and came out without buying anything. There's also the chance of getting into a mess. With which priggish reflection I will conclude. But the subject *is* an interesting one, though I've just said it isn't. Wish we could have another talk. Why don't you get bored with Ghent & come to London for a bit? I would if I were you.[3]

E.M.F.

ALS: KCC

[1] Slides: for his extension lectures.
[2] Sir Edward Grey, later Earl Grey of Fallodon (1862–1933), Secretary of State for Foreign Affairs, 1905–16. Which brother and sister EMF knew is unclear.
[3] Masood wrote (6 July. KCC) that he *was* bored with Ghent, where he was supposed to be learning French.

74   To Malcolm Darling[1]

Harnham, Monument Green, Weybridge
14 October 1909

Dear Malcolm

You'll be glad to hear that Hilton Young & I arrived alive.[2] He was wonderful. After a few miles we took to the grass and with compass & bicycle lamp he steered us through a black night and torrential rains, and was only half a mile out at dawn. We broke into Stone Henge at midnight, and ate on the altar stone, which may have been sacrilege but was more probably the other thing. Poor Stone Henge has been ruined these 5 years, but it got its own back that time. I don't ever want to see it again. The other wonder was the glare of Salisbury, which could be seen for nearly fifteen miles upon the southern sky. I suppose that rum expeditions like these are part of your daily work, and you may smile slightly at the idea of anyone getting wet through for pleasure. Certainly I don't think that any one except Englishmen (and possibly Germans) would take them. It was about 30 miles; at 9.0. we reached the so called cottage—thatched it is true, but replete with hot baths and the novels of Arnold Bennett.

Since then King Lear has been my chief excitement; the scenery Druidic and the weather in appearance even worse than ~~life~~ Salisbury Plain.[3] But it makes a difference whether the rain falls down your neck, or only on to tea trays in the wings. The performance was very fine. I have never seen Shakespeare performed Elizabethanly, but my present wish is for the scenery to be very good *but* simple, and this is what one gets at the Haymarket now. I was in London for three days, stopping with Thompson. He had been to stay with Jermyn Moorsom in someone's cottage in Hertfordshire.[4] They all sound well.

I am muddling away with lectures &[ct]. Do let me hear soon. I am very anxious for a long letter. I saw Dickinson last week. He has tried to like America but cannot—still feels sadly that he ought to like it.

My brain is in a pap, and unless I stop I shall go on to tell you about the Mouse, which has eluded five people, two mouse traps, and a cat for the last six weeks, and was caught yesterday, amidst universal joy.

Yours ever

E. M. Forster.

ALS: HRC

[1] Malcolm Lyall Darling (1880–1969), the son of a clergyman, was related to the famous Indian expert Sir Alfred Lyall, after whom he was named. Malcolm went to Eton and to King's College, Cambridge, and joined the Indian Civil Service in 1904, at which time he began to correspond with EMF. At the end of 1906 Darling was appointed tutor to the young Raja of Dewas Senior; between these two a close friendship sprang up. In letters to EMF he described this tiny state and its curious and Gilbertian constitutional relationship with the neighbouring state of Dewas Junior. In 1909 Darling was made an Assistant Commissioner and assigned to Simla, and, in February 1911, to Lahore. From 1916 onwards his principal duties and interest lay in the Indian cooperative movement, and he became Registrar to the Co-operative Societies of the Punjab. He was Vice-Chancellor of Punjab University in 1931 and in 1937–8, and in 1940 he retired. He was nominated by the Government of India, however, to be head of the BBC Hindustani Service, from which he retired in 1943. He was knighted in 1939.

In 1909 he married Jessica, daughter of Lord Low (a Scottish Law Lord); they had two sons, John Jermyn and Colin, and a daughter, April. Jessica died in 1932.

The scandals and disasters that overtook the Maharaja of Dewas, and led to his death in exile in 1937, disturbed Darling deeply. He made heroic but unavailing efforts to intercede on his behalf with the British authorities.

As a young man Darling was somewhat stiff and conventional in outlook, but in later years (partly perhaps owing to his friendship with EMF, to whom he was devoted) he broadened greatly. His long letter to EMF about the Amritsar Massacre (1 July 1919, CSAS), and also some details of his personal troubles at the time of the Massacre, seem to have had important influence on *A Passage to India*. Darling wrote a memoir of his early career in India, *Apprentice to Power* (1969), and a number of works on agricultural cooperatives.

[2] Edward Hilton Young, in 1935 created 1st Baron Kennet of the Dene (1879–1960), attended Eton and Trinity College, Cambridge, where he was elected President of the Union. He became a barrister and financial journalist, with varied business interests. He had a distinguished war record with the Naval Mission to Serbia and at Zeebrugge, where he lost his left arm. In 1915 he began a parliamentary career, first as Liberal, then as Conservative, that culminated in the post of Minister of Health, from 1931–5. Young was on the fringes of 'Bloomsbury' and for a period let his cottage, The Lacket, in Wiltshire, to Lytton Strachey. In 1922 Young married Kathleen, née Bruce (1878–1947), widow of the Polar explorer Captain Robert Falcon Scott. EMF, who liked and respected Young, noted in his diary (20 August 1910): 'I do not know why he likes me; has even suggested I should share their house in town. He reminds me, in appearance and mind of R. B. S[mith].' On Smith, see Letter 116.

[3] The production was notable, not only because it was the managerial début of Herbert Trench (1865–1923) at the Haymarket Theatre, London, but for the eloquent simplicity of the acting and of the sets by Charles Ricketts (1866–1931), painter and stage designer.

[4] Edward Vincent Thompson (1880–1976), a nephew of the ceramicist and novelist William De Morgan, was a friend of EMF from Cambridge days, and a Civil Servant in the Treasury Solicitor's Department. Jermyn Moorsom (d. 1951) studied medieval and modern languages at King's, then became a solicitor, but he disliked the law and became a sheep farmer in Scotland. The enterprise failed in the 1920s, and after World War II he moved to Ireland, where he died. He was a close friend of the Darlings, who named their first son for him.

75 To Malcolm Darling

Harnham, Monument Green, Weybridge
10 December 1909

Dear Malcolm

I owe you not only long letters, but delightful ones, and don't feel able to repay either debt. I have looked you out on the map, and found your border-state and the great Mountain, and the gorge of the Sutlej. What incredible places, and what luck you both have had. I like that little stream in which you bathed too—and now you will be elephanting for Xmas at Dewas—to which my nearest parallel will be riding on the top of an omnibus in Paris with Masood! It is just possible that I may join him for a few days; I have never been there yet.

So you see how little I have to talk about.—I have sent you a story about Machinery though, in which I talk only too much.[1] The description of the Himalayas will open your eyes, I assure you. I was at Cambridge about 10 days ago. 'Conversation' doesn't exist out of it, I am sure; certainly not in London. Dickinson was there, vainly trying not to dislike America; also Nixon, Reddaway, and many other old friends, all going strong. The latest now is that undergraduates have been 'stag' hunting—i.e. prodding and torturing a tame deer, to make it run; and when a by stander protested, he was answered with cries of 'Yah, socialist!' The sport has been stopped now, thank heaven. One says 'Yah socialist' to everything in these days: if you think the omnibus fare is 1^d and it turns out to be 2^d, you say 'Yah socialist' to the conductor! You, being really a socialist, yah, would have a hot time: all respectable people sympathise with the Lords in their attempt to overturn the poor and the constitution!—You will see that I am a keen if inexpert politician: the issue does seem clearly marked, for once in a way.[2]

Your mother most kindly asked me to supper last Sunday. I could not go, but look forward to calling, and sending you news of how they all seem.

As to books—'my days are spent among the dead'—I have been reading Frank Harris' 'Shakespeare'. It is amusing, stimulating, and contains some truth, though far from true as a whole.[3] His theory is that S's life can clearly be traced in the plays. Of course this involves a second theory—what S's life was—but Harris has a fertile, if not a delicate, imagination, and has plenty to say on both points.

14 December

Still this letter isn't posted. I finish it with the thrilling news that I *am* going to Paris,—or rather 'Parry', for I have never been there before. I start tomorrow morning, and hope to be there a week. If I see any very beautiful picture postcard, I will send it you for a new year's card!

Every good wish to you both.

Yours affectionately   E. M. Forster.

Yes isn't Rolland's Michel Ange good: so glad you like it.[4] He has the true attitude towards genius—as rare as genius itself.

ALS: HRC

[1] 'The Machine Stops', *The Oxford and Cambridge Review*, No. 8 (1909), 83–122.
[2] Lords: controversy over Lloyd George's famous Budget, passed by the Commons on 4 November 1909 but rejected by the Lords on 30 November. This precipitated a General Election, which the Liberals won. In April 1910 they passed a Bill limiting the Lords' power of veto.
[3] Frank Harris, *The Man Shakespeare and His Tragic Life Story* (1909). Harris (1856–1931), if a notorious womaniser and prevaricator, was seldom dull, and his editorship of *The Fortnightly Review*, 1887–94, and of *The Saturday Review*, 1895–8, launched or consolidated many important literary careers, G. B. Shaw's among them.
[4] Romain Rolland, *Vie de Michel-Ange* (1906).

76 To Syed Ross Masood

Harnham, Monument Green, Weybridge
30 December 1909

Dear Masood

I enclose money order for the 10/ + 5.00 fr. that I owe you. Take it to the central post office (I don't know the address of any other), and present it, with your visiting card—that's the way I do it at least. Also give my name if asked.

Let me know if you're running short of money. I know that you have been sending some to a friend. I can easily let you have some, and indeed debated whether I should make this money order out for a larger sum, but it's a bore to be lent money before you've said you want it, so I didn't

Many thanks for the Xmas cards. We all three thought them so pretty. It's awfully good of you to think of giving me a birthday present. I am looking forward to it. Even more important is it that you let me know what day you return to England. We mustn't quarrel about sentiment![1] We agree that it is the greatest thing in the world, and only differ as to how it's to be made the most of, and while I was reading your letter I didn't even differ. Who wrote 'Each time that thou goest out of my sight—'? It is very beautiful.[2]

We had a quiet but orthodox Xmas. Did you buy a plum pudding? I am also anxious to know the result of your battle with *Madame*. If you *havn't* fought, my advice is *don't*, for the sum is small, she seems very kind, and furthermore you didn't recapitulate the terms, or make her repeat them after you, before you took possession of the rooms, and so the thing was not fixed up very tightly. I was a little nervous when I found you hadn't, and if it's only 3.50. more per week than you expected, I think you've come off pretty well.

Don't forget the big *Rubens*, & take your history book with you when you look at them. As for Versailles, go in the middle of the day and have—or take—lunch there, so that you may get a good light: it's not much good making expeditions in the afternoon, this time of year. S⁺ Cloud might also be useful to you.

Do you know how to scan French poetry? There's a rule I'd meant to tell you of: Final e-mute counts as a syllable, though it mustn't be pronounced.

Les sanglots longs...   = 4 syllables
Bless*ent* mon coeur   = „   „
D'u*ne* langueur [. . .].³ = „   „

All these lines are (metrically) of the same length.

But when the e mute comes before another word beginning with a vowel, or comes at the end of a line, it doesn't count.

À la très bell⟨e⟩, à la très cher⟨e⟩.⁴ = only 8 syllables.

Your friend E.M.F.

ALS: KCC

¹ They *had* quarrelled about sentiment; see *EMF*, I, 145–6.
² On New Year's Eve, EMF wrote in his diary: ' "Oh love, every time thou goest out of my sight, I die a new death." How can I keep quiet when I read such things? My brain watches me, but it's literary. Let me keep clear from criticism and scheming. Let me think of you and not write. I love you, Syed Masood; love.'
³ Paul Verlaine, 'Chanson d'Automne' (1866).
⁴ Charles Baudelaire, 'Hymne,' in *Les fleurs du mal* (1857). The first line, however, is 'A la très-chère, à la très-belle.'

77 To Syed Ross Masood

Weybridge.   14 January 1910

Dearest boy

I am just back from a harassing day; on my arrival this morning we had lunch and all three went off to Putney in a beastly motor that bumped and stank and gave us head-aches. However, it was a great thing for my grandmother, and we left her well and safe at her house. Then we went on to a long tea party at my aunt's near, and then up to Waterloo again, and then down to Weybridge with more people; and now would to God I was just arriving at 82, and beginning to talk to you.¹ This letter is to do instead—not that it will. Well, you know that I was happy with you, and I've no need to say it, and that I think Ste Genevieve most beautiful and most beautifully framed as does my mother. But you ought not to have spent such a pot of money over me.—I know this will make you cross, but you oughtn't. It's far too good for me. I write looking at it.

It's a pity the glamour went off Paris. But nothing influences one so much as fright, and with your experience, I should have felt the same. Perhaps you aren't fair to the French. They have an interest in human capabilities and in ideas that may be often applied wrongly but is in itself essentially good, and civilised. When M. Constantine said that his countrywomen had beautiful legs he was better than the English, who pretend that women have no legs at all! Though best of all are those who take legs for granted.[2]

I meant to have asked more about the man in whose face you threw the change. It was a risky thing to do. Did you actually hit him with it?

Good night. I am sorry that I fidgeted about the train, but it would have been grave to miss it, as it would have upset my mother and grandmother, and thrown out their plans. Give my best remembrances to your two companions. I was so glad to see them both again. I did enjoy stopping with you immensely. Good night again.

> from Forster, member of the Ruling Race
> to Masood, a nigger.

And let the latter buck up and write. And let him have a good time at Oxford. And let him and all his be happy. Otherwise:

Forster will never travel in the same railway carriage with him again.[3]

TTr supplied by J. A. Kidwai

[1] EMF's Aunt Rosalie (Alford) had moved to Richmond.
[2] M. Constantine: apparently a Parisian acquaintance of Masood.
[3] For one of Masood's railway-carriage incidents, see *EMF*, I, 144.

78   To Malcolm Darling

Oxford and Cambridge Musical Club,
Reynolds House, 47 Leicester Square [London]
20 January 1910

Dear Malcolm

I began a line to night, in spite of incessant chatter close to my ear on the subject of art and that. You praise me for my generosity in writing, but how far you have left me behind—two long & delightful letters, and three articles are all on my mind. So female suffrage leads to polyandry—! I did so enjoy both—and enjoy and approve of the first. (This is not to imply that I disapprove of the second). The fair at Rampur also charms me.[1] Thank you so very much for it, and for sending the other two. The idea of the hill country that you convey to me is grandeur with peace. Is that right? Since reading your letters & the articles I have supposed myself to feel at home there. The Alps and other mountains that I know feel like boundaries—barriers between two countries rather than worlds by themselves—but the Himalayas, partly from their size, partly from their construction—can hardly give the sense of anything behind, across, them—they must feel like the 'sea that ends not till the world's end'. May I see them before I die—the gorge of the Sutlej in particular. You have given me tremendous pleasure.

I can only write for a little, having as usual put things off till next day. I had the luck to find your mother and sister in the other day—they both seemed well. So am I. And happy if it were not for politics. The German scare and snobbery seem doing their worst, and the appeals this election are made to lower instincts, than heretofore.[2] Dishonest, illiberal, the spirit of the petty tradesman, who doesn't mind if he's found out to morrow, so long as he cheats you today—that's the spirit of both sides as it appears to us: and I have continually to remind myself that there must be honest effort & conviction somewhere, hidden behind the froth of either party.

What a rotten letter! But I want to greet you in the spirit, and accept that though the words are worthless. I will write again—by next mail—and tell you all about Paris, where I have been with Masood.[3] Also about India. I am reading two books on it at once, and expect to be most helpful to you. Meanwhile tell me a little more about it yourself.

Your affectionate friend
E. M. Forster.

ALS: HRC

[1] India has at least three Rampurs; this is plainly the one in the part of the United Provinces, now named Himachal Pradesh, at the foot of the Himalayas. It was also relatively near the Darlings at Lahore, where Malcolm was Under-Secretary to the Government of the Punjab, 1911–13.
[2] Probably an allusion to a current controversy about building dreadnoughts, to compete with Germany. This was the General Election precipitated by the Budget Crisis of 1909.
[3] EMF and Masood went to Paris on 15 December and stayed there for about a week. On 15 December EMF recalled (diary, KCC) that they had talked of 'the day when I shall go to India'.

79   To Malcolm Darling

Holmleigh, Salisbury.   10 February 1910

Dear Malcolm

I owe you a letter oh this long while. I left off the last saying that I was going to tell you something special in the next, and now for the life of me I can't remember what it is. It's a comment on our civilisation. This reminds me: of my story being read to the Rajah.

Well I never! I don't know why it should make me smile, but it does. That he, sitting in the heart of poetry, should tolerate it seems odd.[1] Perhaps he would think it odd to read a book about Indian Art, as I have been doing—by Havell.[2] A little petulant in tone, but fascinating. Have you ever been to Sanchi?[3] It doesn't look far from Dewas on the map.

This letter is already getting scrappy, as is the way with mine. Yours really do tell something, and the description of Dewas and of the way thither is so clear that I could get there with my eyes shut. The yogi must have been wonderful. I expect that to you two such an attitude seems steadily beautiful. Or do you have your moments of repulsion and think 'What shall it profit a man to gain his own soul, if he lose the whole world?' It is curious how one's little feelings are connected with the immense past, for I am sure that the repulsion of which I speak is our heritage from Graeco-Roman civilisation. Logically, the yogi must be right. Wealth, success, friendship, love, are all one illusion, and reality, (whatever it may be) is obscured by them. But in practise one shrinks from this conclusion. The Western world, and in particular the Latin races, have too vivid a sense of surface-values. How wonderful—and how comforting—that the yogi should be illogical at the last moment too!

I thought of you yesterday, for between the hours of 6.50, and 8.19. I made great friends with the man who was sitting opposite me in the railway carriage; and I think you can do that. We actually exchanged cards, and think what a wrench that is for English people—not but what he was Irish which accounts for the whole affair. If I say that our literary, political, and social judgments concurred, you will think we were a pair of prigs, but really honestly we weren't he was as different to me as possible, so at the most there was only one. I do not *think* he will pick my pocket or murder me—in the British mind there always lurks this fear—and this morning I have written to him suggesting a meeting in London. If it ever comes off, I will tell you about it. He was a very charming fellow on the surface, and there's no reason he shouldn't be further down.

Now I am in the train again returning to London. No prospect of life long friendship here. My companions are two soldiers, who will not talk to each other so it is not likely that they will talk to me, and a young lady with the wings of many blue birds in her hat. The train is just going over Wiltshire Gap at a frightful lick. and I am writing very well considering. The sky is grey, the earth brown. The only approach to colour is in the valleys, whose green is ruled with the silver lines of the irrigation: and in the cuttings, where the chalk is eternally white. Here is Andover. The nicer of the two soldiers has got out, and it has begun to rain.

I dined with Thompson lately.[4] He tells me that J. Moorsom is well. Have you heard from him? Cole I met for a second not long ago. He has been a recluse since his marriage. Speaking generally, our mutual friends seem all right. Dickinson asked me to go to Italy with him this Easter, but I couldn't. He has been electioneering, and I ought to have done the same, but do dread it, and am so ignorant and incompetent. Hilton Young stood against Austen Chamberlain. He was defeated heavily, but I don't know what he expected. It may have been satisfactory to him. I am just going to tea with another vanquished Paladin in the shape of Sir Frederick Pollock—or rather with his wife & daughter & Sydney Waterlow, for I do not expect the warrior himself will be there, and when he is he always frightens me.[5]

Oh I almost forgot. I have *not* sent Lady Low a card about the O & C. review.[6] I really cannot. I only inflicted the story on you because we had talked about the Mechanical together. There is no reason that a perfectly innocent person should suffer. I will do anything else for you.

Yours affectionately
E. M. Forster.

ALS: HRC

[1] Perhaps 'The Machine Stops': note 6 below.
[2] Probably *Indian Sculpture and Painting . . . with an Explanation of Their Motives and Ideals*, by Ernest B. Havell (1861–1934), Superintendent of the Madras School of Art, 1884–92; then Principal of the Calcutta School of Art, 1896–1906. His protest against the utilitarian bias of art education in Government schools in India was the impetus for William Rothenstein to organise the India Society in London in 1910; see *IE*, pp. 2–8.
[3] Sanchi is a Buddhist archaeological site in Madhya Pradesh, dating from the second and first centuries BC, with remains of one of India's largest stupās, or funeral mounds commemorating the Buddha's death. A. L. Basham (*The Wonder That Was India*. p. 368) calls Sanchi 'the crowning achievement of early North Indian sculpture'.
[4] Presumably E. V. Thompson.
[5] Rt Hon. Sir Joseph Austen Chamberlain (1863–1937), at various time Chancellor of the Exchequer and holder of other key positions, was firmly settled in as MP for East Worcestershire, 1892–1914. In 1910 Sir Frederick Pollock was Chairman of the Royal Commission on Public Records, and, in 1911, was made a Privy Councillor. In 1902 his daughter Alice Isabella had married Sidney Waterlow.
[6] I.e. 'The Machine Stops', in *The Oxford and Cambridge Review*; see Letter 75.

80 To Ottoline Morrell[1]

Tyn-y-Gamdda, Llanfair, Harlech, Wales[2]
2 April 1910

Dear Lady Ottoline
I am here, and on Friday go to Italy for a month. I would like very much to come & see you when I return, and wish that it could be earlier. It is most kind of you to ask me: I will write & suggest myself.

I am reading Les Frères Karamazov, but am so far a little

disappointed.³ It seems sketchy, though I have no notion what I mean by that useful word; not 'insincere' by any means.—But criticism, or rather critics, are such nonsense: their nerves are upset by half a sentence, and they haven't the peculiar will power to put them right. Hasn't the reception of 'Chantecler' been humiliating—all the literary people had wrought themselves into such a state that disappointment was certain.—And so myself after reading Crime and Punishment.⁴

But Dostoieffskie always makes one feel 'comfortable'—again difficult to define. Tolstoi doesn't. Henry James does. George Meredith doesn't. Swinburne does. Browning doesn't. There certainly are 'dears' in literature, and a man may [be] a dear in any line, and it has nothing to do with niceness or the drawing room table. But whether it has anything to do with literature—. I have been muddling round this point for some time now, but can't get it clearer.

Again thanking you, and with many regrets:

Yours very sincerely
E. M. Forster

Hugh Meredith, with whom I am staying, & who is also a friend of Dickinson's, would very much like to see you. Might I bring him some day—?

ALS: HRC

¹ Lady Ottoline Morrell (1873–1938) was the half-sister of the 6th Duke of Portland. She was a patron of artists and writers, and a founder of the Contemporary Art Society. Flamboyant in appearance, she was both generous and vulnerable in personality. Her husband, Philip Morrell (1870–1943), was an MP from 1906–18, and he put pacifist principles ahead of career.
² EMF had just handed a rough draft of thirty chapters of Howards End to Edward Arnold, his publisher. He relaxed with a walking tour in Wales before going on with the novel.
³ Dostoievsky's classic novel was then available only in the French translation. The first English translation, by Edward Garnett's wife Constance (1861–1946), was not available until 1912.
⁴ Chantecler, Edmund Rostand's last complete play—an allegorical verse comedy in which the characters are barnyard fowls, with the cast literally in full feather—opened at the Porte Saint Martin Theatre, Paris, on 7 February 1910. The misgivings of The Times' dramatic critic, that the play could not measure up to advance publicity, were more than fulfilled. The 'greatest "first night" of modern times' was marked by diminishing applause, 'a sense of disappointment', and cries of 'Author' that were 'few and obviously half-hearted'; see ' "Chantecler",' The Times, 8 February 1910, p. 11; 'M. Rostand's "Chantecler",' 9 February, p. 5.

81   To Malcolm Darling

In a hotel   Baveno, Lake Maggiore¹
[15 April 1910]

Dear Malcolm

I received your letter with even greater pleasure than usual, as the news Hasluck told me made me uneasy.[2] Being first in Wales, and then here, I had not the opportunity of calling at Green Street, & though Hasluck's second letter was so far reassuring that the subject was not mentioned, I am more glad than I can say to be reassured properly.[3] I hope I shall soon hear again: what a wretched time you must both have had: my love to you both.

We have been here a week, and if a note of petulance creeps into my remarks, put it down to the rain, which has continued without a break for 60 hours. 'Non semper imbres—', & it promises to clear now.[4] The place is glorious, though the beauties are a trifle well ordered, or seen from a somewhat well ordered foreground perhaps, as we are entirely surrounded by English people mostly of middle age. A curate, who is almost too stupid to be alive, is close to me, & pointing out waterfalls to him is his wife, who is haughty & cautious, & not sure whether my mother & myself will do. In the hall other guests are making bead necklaces or playing poker-patience, or deploring the vulgarity of Lloyd George, and the rest are sleeping.

Has it ever occurred to you that the south coasts of Europe & of Asia are analogous—three peninsulas, with the chief mountain chain knotted up at the head of the middle one? I am accordingly now in the Himalayas, while Dickinson is in Ceylon![5] I should like to have been with him, but my mother was persuaded to come abroad, & I am with her—she is enjoying it, in spite of a bad attack of lumbago.—I was amused & delighted with your description of your state. Really you do have—luck I was going to say, but it is scarcely the word I mean. I hope that you keep a diary—except that your letters will make up that deficiency. You must have seen more than any one of our time at King's. I like 'do Taubacca' as a measure for distance, & the people who have never heard of the Great White Queen.[6]

We go on—if mother is well enough—to Parma, Pisa, Siena, Florence, and get back the end of May. I am anxious to see Hasluck. He seems to have had a topping time.

Did I tell you I stopped with Dickinson at Cambridge? He was in very good form, and *cannot* swallow America, try though he does.

Your political reading chides me. I ought to, but continually postpone. Just now I am enthralled by Gibbon's Autobiography. There are passages in it that are more than 'correct', and on the border line of beauty. What a giant he is—greatest historian & greatest ~~figure~~ name of the 18th century *I* say; whether it is his greatness or his remoteness that makes his goings on with religion so queer I do not know. That such a nature should be pre-occupied at all with it personally puzzles me. It is a sort of jig saw puzzle that he plays with a little when not occupied with more important things, but he genuinely regrets that the pieces will not fit.[7]

Write again soon.

Yours affectionately
E. M. Forster

ALS: HRC

[1] EMF went to Italy with his mother hoping to finish *HE*.
[2] Frederick William Hasluck (1878–1920), archaeologist, expert on Italian influence in the Levant; entered King's in 1897 and joined the British School at Athens in 1901.
[3] Green Street: London address of Darling's mother.
[4] Horace, *Odes*, Book II, No. 9, ll. 1–2: 'Non semper imbres nubibus hispidos / manant in agros.' (Not for ever do the showers fall on the sodden fields.)
[5] That is, Dickinson was in Sicily.
[6] 'do Taubacca'; Hindi or a dialect thereof: literally, 'two Tobaccos', presumably the distance measured by two pipes or cigarettes.
[7] Darling replied (3 May 1910. CSAS): 'Of course directly I read what you said about Gibbon I wanted to fall upon the Decline & Fall with the autobiography you speak of as a succulent entrée. But I am summoned by books still unread.' *War and Peace*, he wrote, was 'still the biggest thing I have ever read'.

82   To Malcolm Darling

West Hackhurst, Abinger Hammer, Dorking
29 June 1910

Dear Malcolm

A letter, not to say two, should indeed be on its way from me to you, but I seem to have done so little lately, and one that I have begun is left unfinished at home. This will be an anxious month for you, and I need not say that my thought & sympathy have been & will be with you both. It is terrible to hear of so much discomfort and suffering, though I can imagine with what courage it has been born[e]. You say that neither of you have been anxious for a child: when it comes surely you will feel differently, and realise it is the greatest of blessings. Children are so delightful—and something more besides.[1]

I called at Green Street not long ago, in the hopes of gleaning some news about you both, but didn't:—the less as Mrs Darling was then away at Ober Ammergau. I was delighted to speak directly to your sister on the subject that I knew was occupying her mind as well as mine, but feared that she might think me intrusive, and perhaps resent it in other ways. When I am in London again—the end of July—I shall call again.

I am just going to Harrogate for a fortnight—a horrible & expensive experience, but my mother has been ordered there for gout, and if I do not lead her to the waters, will not drink them. I shall have my work, and they say the scenery is fine and the invalids genteel, but I would give up all and the 80 mineral springs thrown in, for one hour's ride with you in your hills. Don't I recollect

Bashar—(though I spell its name from memory)—?[2] You leave off at an exciting moment. Were you backed up at Simla or did (forget his name) manage to get round people there? To be continued in our next, I hope.

Let me tell you a little about India. I am reading Manucci's 'Storia do Mogor'—a most entertaining book if it comes your way.[3] He goes via Persia and arrives in time at the court of Shah Jahan, afterwards fighting against Aurangzebe whom he loathes. He is so amusing & vivid about the Indian character that I can't believe it's all lies, though it is said to be partly. Now I will tell you about China & Japan. I have been to Shepherd's Bush, but was disappointed—the painting huddled away among the commercial work, & not catalogued.[4] Then to the B[ritish] M[useum], which, with coy dignity, has brought out *its* Chino-Japanese pictures, and simply knocked Shepherd's Bush into a cocked hat. I never imagined such beauty poetry & humour—at least I knew from specialists they were there, but never imagined I should see them. The Chinese things in particular are as easy to love as Fra Angelicos, or Botticellis—a 'fairy walking on the waves'—; the 'Paradise of the West'—gods & goddesses in a bowery garden, even too happy to drink their cups of tea. The 'garden of the 100 children' who are playing endless games without a single grown up. How unlike the "Organised Play" which it was my fate to witness at a Whitechapel Board School!

I saw Masood yesterday—much flustered about the advancing Missionary methods; but he generally is flustered over something. He complains does not mind the old type, who slammed the heathen on the head with a bible, but resents the sympathetic person who dons native dress and says Siva is another and but an imperfect name for Christ. I don't know. What do you think of missions? I should be grievously sorry if the whole world became Christians, but within certain limits missions have their value. E.g. in Northern Nigeria the missionaries would do something to raise the population, while the government (if I may judge from a friend of mine) resents all attempts to make the native think or feel, because it may increase the difficulties of administration.

It is stormy and cold, but beautiful: dog roses, foxgloves, and blue ancusas in the garden; also strawberries. I must stop now, & do some work.

With all messages & wishes:

Yours affectionately
E. M. Forster.

ALS: HRC

[1] Darling confessed that at first he had 'no spark of paternal feeling at all. India is hard enough on married couples, but it is downright cruel to the children. This is in fact no country for them. And we were much too content together to wish for a third, at least for some time, till we had grown even more into each other. . . . it is almost a patriotic duty for people with our advantages to have children' (M. Darling to his mother, 15 February [1910]. CSAS).

² Bashahr was a hill station in the lower Himalayas, 'quite different from anything I have experienced in India,' Darling wrote to his mother on 3 October 1909 (CSAS), and reminiscent of Switzerland.
³ Niccolo Manucci, Storia do Mogor; or Mogul India, 1653–1708, trans. William Irvine (1906–8).
⁴ This was the art section of the Japan–British Exhibition. One critic called the Japanese section short of 'the expectations—perhaps too roseate—provoked by Japan's position as the one country in which, in modern times, art has been in some sort indigenous'. As for the British section, it was a 'slightly purged Royal Academy exhibition . . . ' (C. K., The Athenaeum, 28 May 1910, pp. 647–8).

83   To Malcolm Darling

Harnham, Monument Green, Weybridge
12 August 1910

Dear Malcolm,
    This is all splendid. I was very anxious to hear, and partly knew all you were both going through. I am pleased about the baby, of course, and more pleased than I can say that his coming has made other things better. He is the future, & our love for him is still hidden in it: I never can look beyond the present, and the present is you two. I am distressed about your deafness, & wish you would tell me more about it. Is there discomfort too? And how is your general health? I will not let anything go further if you do not wish.
    As to being godfather, I have thought it over during the week, & have decided to say no. I have only once said yes, and that was to parents whose atheism was even more pronounced than my own. I do thank you both from the bottom of my heart for trusting & honouring me, but in spite of possibly seeming ungracious, I cannot feel that I had better accept. I hope & think that you will understand. If I am lucky, when he grows up he will like me and I may be of use to him, but I must leave it there. (And, outside my family, no grown up person was ever of any use to me—what one really wants is a god-brother, not a godfather).¹
    I stopped a night with Hasluck last week, and saw picture p.c.s. of India that made my mouth water. My goodness what a place! But those Dravidian temples are nightmares. "Obviously devil worship" says H. and they look it, tho' I can't believe they really are.² It is so difficult to imagine any one glorifying what he knew to be Evil, and if Satanism was studied carefully (I leave the field open!) it would surely prove to be a revolt—however misguided—against the conventional ideas of good. Blake and Carducci are clearly this.³ One glance at the fields or the sky ought to prove the non-existence of spiritual evil. There is disease or decay, but they are incidental, and the spiritual power behind them is either Nothing or Good.—This is a long cry from Hasluck, and atheists were ever adiabolists, so I'll go no further.

Next Sat. I go for the week end to Hilton Young's cottage, and if the weather holds shall walk away from it on the Monday for 2 or 3 days, or longer if people will give me food and shelter, but there is something very awful in my appearance when I walk alone, and very often they won't. Ten days later, if weather still holds and various other things go right, I may walk again under the aegis of E. V. Thompson. Every one will take me in then.

Do you get any time for reading? I am taking huge chunks of Mat Arnold. He's not as good as he thinks, but better than I thought. His central fault is prudishness—I don't use the word in its narrow sense, but as implying a general dislike to all warmth. He thinks warmth either vulgar or hysterical.

Well good night & good bye. I do hope you understand about the godfatherhood. To be asked did give me great pleasure.

Yours affectionately
E. M. Forster.

ALS: HRC

[1] The baby was John Jermyn Darling. The Darlings had asked EMF, in addition to being godfather, to write a dialogue or 'godfather catechism' for which they suggested the idea. He wrote to Malcolm (22 September 1910) that he was glad Darling did not think him 'a pedantic ass. I have been worrying myself stupidly about it. I wish you would take the job out of Plato's hands, and write the dialogue yourselves. It is most beautiful; willingly do I subscribe to it. It is the only reasonable justification of the office—so obvious as soon as it is stated, . . . And a child ought to realise that he is a "pignus", though he cannot realise in how many senses until he is older.' On 19 November EMF wrote to Josie Darling, who was in Scotland with her parents, that he had just composed a catechism based on 'a beautiful idea about parents & godparents that you & Malcolm sent me— . . . I did it quite quickly this evening—as if the suggestion was at last inspiring me.' On 21 November he wrote that he would 'like to be J.J.'s x-father after all; adding that 'I was not the least ashamed of my conduct in refusing & prevaricating at first, but felt that I had done quite the proper thing throughout; I hope you will think so too. For it is difficult to accept such a post quickly when one is definitely not a Christian.' They must bear in mind, he wrote, that they were ' "calling in" one who does not accept the Christian metaphysics, & only part of the Christian ethics.' The dialogue, between the Mother and the Son/Boy, is about living and growing. A manuscript, in EMF's hand, bears the caption: 'Liking Being Alive. A Catechism, by M. L. and J. Darling. Written out by E. M. Forster, 20/11/10' (MS, and these letters: HRC). A sample of the style: 'The Mother: Tell me first: what is a father? / . . . The Son: Why a father's Father. That's easy enough. Father is a father. . . . / The Mother: Wait a minute. Have you ever thought how you came to be alive? . . . listen. Your father also liked being alive. When he was your age he too, thought that there was nothing so wonderful as riding on a horse. He liked to camp out. As he grew older, he began to care for other things. He read books, and because he read them properly he liked being alive more and more. . . . / Godfathers and godmothers are to tell you about the things that they have liked in life. Being alive is so great, that no one person can understand it all.' In the end, EMF declined to be godfather.
[2] Hasluck, the trained archaeologist, falls into the European habit of drawing parallels between Indian representations of gods and Christian notions of satanic creatures. For an extended discussion of this subject, see Partha Mitter, *Much Maligned Monsters* (1977).
[3] Giosuè Carducci (1835–1907), Italian poet of pagan tendency, won the Nobel Prize for Literature in 1906.

84   To Robert Trevelyan

Harnham, Monument Green, Weybridge
18 August 1910

Dear Bob

My aunt has not been well enough to have us, and all our plans have gone to pieces. I may be walking for a week this month, but if I don't (& perhaps if I do) should like to come to see you. I will write again shortly. I am so glad you are all well. I have just been to stop with E. H. Young near Marlborough, and thence walked to the White Horse, Wantage, & Goring, along the Icknield Way, in furious guise along the Icknield Way.¹ It is glorious country. I got home last night.

Private

Sidgwick and Jackson are nibbling, though feebly, at my short stories. They suggest illustrations. That I won't have but have no objection to 'End Papers.' To come to the point: would it vex Fry if they asked him to design one?² Does he feel for the stories anything the least approaching enthusiasm? I know that he wants money, but would rather he went without it than that I procured it him by means of uncongenial ~~and~~ or "contemptuous" work. I think the stories good myself, so do not mind learning the opinions of others. If Fry has had one, and you know it, I should be very grateful.—This idea has only just occurred to me: I have mentioned 'End Papers' to S. and J. in the vague, but breathed no further word, & please don't you.—Also would they object to Fry's charges?— That's all. I expect nothing will come of it. I enclose S's letters, which please return or burn.

Hellfellows is an awful work of Housman's which they would have liked me to look like—'minor redemptions'—you never tasted such bilge.³

Marguerite was well rid of Mat.⁴ It is certainly interesting.

Yours affectionately
E. M. Forster

That poor poet Stokoe seems in a muddle—he proposes to take a B. A. degree & take to pedagogy; at 28 that isn't a good plan, I should say.⁵

ALS: TCC

¹ Edward Thomas, who walked it before writing *The Icknield Way* (1913), describes it as 'the chief surviving road connecting East Anglia and the whole eastern half of the regions north of the Thames, with the west and the western half of the south of England' (p. 84). It runs east from the Norfolk ports and into Wiltshire.

² *The Celestial Omnibus and Other Stories* (1911) has end-papers by Roger Fry (1866–1934), painter and advocate of Post-Impressionism.
³ Laurence Housman, *All-fellows: Seven Legends of Lower Redemption with Insets in Verse* (1896): parables, pseudo-Biblical and pseudo-mythological.
⁴ He was writing on Matthew Arnold, for the Weybridge Literary Society. Cf. Letter 66.
⁵ Frank Woodyer Stokoe (1882–1956?), author of poems, fairy stories, and a study of German influence on English romanticism. He became a lecturer in French at Cambridge and had been one of the succession of tutors at Nassenheide.

85   To Syed Ross Masood

Harnham, Monument Green, Weybridge
18 August 1910

Dearest Boy

Are you angry with me for what I couldn't help, or are you up to your old pranks? In either case you're an ass, and I shan't write again until you write to me.

I am just back from a wild walking tour in Wilts and Berks.¹ I was three days alone, and in country so deserted that all day I never passed through a village. It isn't bad being alone in the country—the nearest approach we Anglo Saxons can make to your saints. There's such a thing as *healthy* mysticism, and our race is capable of developing it, I think. But perhaps you don't understand, and if you did, it isn't likely you'd agree.

I have been writing letters all day, for correspondence—mostly tiresome—has piled up in my absence. Now I have proofs to correct, and with luck I shall finish them next week, and perhaps go walking again, with Thompson (no, you don't know him).

Poor Brussels! But if there had to be a misfortune I would rather it happened to that pretentious bastard tippling discourteous nation than to any other.²

I am interested about these letters from English sympathisers, (alleged to be) discovered when Mitter was arrested, for I know one of them—Philip Morrel[l]—a little, and his wife pretty well. I don't believe it. Is it likely that the police would at once communicate such a piece of news to the press? It is more likely a piece of blackguardism, engineered by the anti-liberal party. Morrel[l] lost his seat in the last election, and they hope to lessen his chance of regaining it in the next.³

Venus is radiant, but sends you no message until you send one to her. We talk over you a good deal—!⁴

Yours with love,
E. M. F.

TTr supplied by Akbar Masood
¹ This was the three-day walk from Hilton Young's Wiltshire cottage; see Letter 74.

[2] On 14 August, a great fire at the Brussels Exhibition destroyed much valuable property, including the entire British Section.

[3] Philip Morrell was adopted in April 1910 as Liberal candidate for Burnley. In August letters from him to an Indian nationalist, Krishna Mitter, were seized during house searches in Calcutta. Morrell had written that he hoped 'the authorities would release those unjustly detained and would hesitate before again resorting to these oppressive and unjust measures'. See 'The Seizure of Letters in Calcutta', *The Times*, 24 August 1910, p. 3.

[4] Venus: a statue, apparently a gift from Masood.

86   To Malcolm Darling

Harnham, Monument Green, Weybridge
22 August 1910

Dear Malcolm

I am so pleased to get your second letter, but its reference to the godfathership makes me write again. I do trust and think that you will both have understood why I have refused—how deeply I was moved at your asking, how carefully I thought it over, how thoroughly I agree with you that it is a grave matter. I know that I may have put you to incidental inconveniences too, but that is little in comparison with my fear that you will have thought me indifferent. If all goes well, he will like me and I may be of use to him. I couldn't be of less use to him than my own official godparents have been to me, and perhaps it's the emptiness of my own experience in ~~my own~~ this direction that makes me behave like such a prig now.[1] Promises are too tragic, considering what life is. Just give him my hope and my love.

No, mugs wouldn't have entered my head, I am ashamed to say! The only present I ever feel inclined to give babies is to take away some of their toys. I do wish I could see him—even in this demned damp moist unpleasant stage which even *he* cannot be avoiding.[2] I am very fond of babies. Though I can't help laughing at them—they will more than pay me out for that in the future—!

Thank you for asking about my mother. Harrogate hasn't made her worse perhaps, but not the very least better.

I have been for a week end to Hilton Young, & thence walked in hilarity and solitude from Marlborough to Goring—three days, and on the chalk downs all the time. It was fine.

I am bringing out a stodgy novel this autumn, but I think I told you this. It's called Howards End, and dealeth dully with many interesting matters. I am correcting proofs now.

What *is* a cream pudding! ⚱ or 🥣 or 🏺 or 🍮 ? Or is it more like a boiled cream tart? And what is that like? Any how I am glad you enjoyed it. I must get to work now, & as it is have missed out two important matters—Bashahr, and your own health.[3] Do keep me posted as to both. It is a relief to know that you are a bit better.

Yours affectionately
E. M. Forster.

ALS: HRC

[1] One of EMF's godparents was Henrietta Synnot, sister of Maimie Aylward's first husband. As her influence was usually overpowering and sometimes ominous, the precedent for godparenting was not an auspicious one; see *EMF*, I, 10.
[2] 'Demned . . . stage': EMF echoes Mr Mantalini, in Dickens' *Nicholas Nickleby*, Chapter 34.
[3] Bashahr: see Letter 82.

87 To Edward Marsh[1]

Harnham, Monument Green, Weybridge
22 August 1910

Dear Eddie

I meant to write before, though what's the good of meaning.[2] I liked Pompey, though not as much as Nan.[3] Masefield has chosen such an impossible hero. Pompey *was* a muddler, and the play is consequently a muddle. As for Maradick, he contains nothing that I value—they can't even get married but the clergyman's fireplace has tiles of the 'right blue'—but all the same, it is full of merits and easy to praise.[4] I am afraid he does not know how bad it is essentially, and until he does, will scarcely do better. It is a great pity, for he is both copious and constructive in his methods.

I know some of the places you're going to—at Rimini the best hotel is the best. You will also be comfortable at San Marino. Beyond that things looked grim and Baedeker began talking of 'quarters at Letitia someone's'[.] Gubbio disappointed me—a city built ill, though the hill behind was pleasant and the picture by Nelli charming.[5] Borgo San Sepolcro and C[itta] di Castello were both pleasanter. Heaven help your poor feet.

I have just been 4 days walking in Wilts and Berks, mostly alone. One never gets that awful toe-tiredness in England, and the scenery was something special all along. Thank you very much for offering to put me up again: I should like to come sometime very much.

I wish you would walk outside Sidgwick & Jackson's offices shouting nonchalantly "short stories are what *we* want".[6] They are considering mine, and even nibbling, but oh so feebly, and I am afraid that only those to which we refer as 'of a mythological nature' will be published, if published they are. They talked of illustrating them, but I do not want that.

Now I must try and write a paper for the local literary society on Mat Arnold.

Yours ever
E. M. Forster

[Pencilled note in another hand added:] Maradick at 5.0 will appear in Oct.

ALS: Berg

1 Sir Edward Howard Marsh (1872–1953), Private Secretary to Churchill, 1905–8 and 1917–22, and to Asquith, 1915–16; editor of the influential anthologies, *Georgian Poetry* (5 vols., 1912–33); patron of artists and writers. EMF had known him since 1909.

2 Phrase picked up by EMF from his grandmother.

3 Plays by John Masefield: *The Tragedy of Pompey the Great* (1910) and *The Tragedy of Nan* (1909).

4 Hugh Walpole, *Maradick at Forty: A Transition* (1910).

5 Probably *Madonna and Child with Angels, Saints and Worshippers* (1403), by Octaviano Nelli (d. 1444), in the Church of Santa Maria Nuova at Gubbio, which in the fourteenth and fifteenth centuries was the centre of a branch of the Umbrian school of painters.

6 Sidgwick and Jackson were slowly considering publication of *The Celestial Omnibus and Other Stories*. On 28 June they asked to see the stories, despite the disabilities suffered by short fiction in the view of the general public. On 1 July the story 'Mr. Andrews' was pronounced 'most amusing—and instructive' but in danger of being thought blasphemous. The firm's reader was to be consulted. On 9 August EMF was informed that 'you can understand I hate giving a definite refusal to publish a book I wd. willingly buy and enjoy to read—if only somebody else wd publish it, ... ' (Bodleian Library. Sidgwick and Jackson Papers.)

88   To Teodor de Wyzewa[1]

King's College, Cambridge
3 November 1910

Dear Sir

Some time ago I heard a rumour that my novel *The Longest Journey* had been mentioned in the *Revue des Deux Mondes*.[2] Naturally I was much pleased, and tried to find out in which number the criticism had appeared, but without success. You can judge therefore what pleasure your letter has given me. I like the book myself—in the peculiar way in which one does like one's own work—having feared that it was provincial rather than intimate, and would only interest the limited circle of my friends. Leaving aside the high authority of the *Revue des Deux Mondes*, it does touch me very much that a reader, not an Englishman, should care for my book more at a second reading than at a first, and should detect in it a few of the qualities that I prize myself in the books of others. I would like to thank you for your letter, and to add that I have never received a letter that has encouraged me more.

You are also kind enough to ask about my other books. About two years ago I published *A Room With a View* (Arnold: 91

Maddox Street, Bond Street)—a slight sketch of bourgeois life in an Italian Pension and at home in Surrey: I do not think that it would interest you. And last month I published a more ambitious work called *Howards End*. Of this I am venturing to send you a copy—not to secure a mention in the *Revue des Deux Mondes*, because it is only too probable that you will not think it worthy of this, but in order that I may make some slight acknowledgement of the pleasure that your letter has given me.

Believe me

Yours truly
E. M. Forster.

TTr: KCC

[1] de Wyzewa (1862–1917) was a Polish-born critic who settled in France in 1882. He entered Mallarmé's circle and, in 1885, was a founder of *Revue Wagnérienne*, later the *Revue indépendante*.

[2] de Wyzewa, 'Le Roman Anglais en 1907: Les Nouveaux Venus', *Revue des Deux Mondes*, 42 (1907), 896–920; on *Le plus long Voyage*, pp. 916–17.

89 To Edward Garnett

Harnham, Monument Green, Weybridge
12 November 1910

Dear Garnett

With the possible exception of the Times, which avowedly omitted bad points, your criticism is the only one that strikes me as just.[1] I only hope I may profit by it in the future, and a writer can't say more. Though whether I can profit is another matter. It is devilish difficult to criticise society & also create human beings. Unless one has a big mind, one aim or the other fails before the book is finished. I must pray for a big mind, but it is uphill work—!

Yours very sincerely
E. M. Forster.

Do you remember some short stories of mine? I have at last entrapped a publisher into taking them. I am very glad, for I think them better than my long books—the only point of criticism on which I have ever disagreed with you![2]

ALS: HRC

[1] For this review of *Howards End*, see 'Fiction', *TLS*, 21 October 1910, p. 412. Garnett's review: 'Villadom', *The Nation*, 8 (1910), 282, 284.

[2] This was *The Celestial Omnibus and Other Stories*; the publisher, Sidwick and Jackson. See Letter 87.

90   To Syed Ross Masood

[N. p.]   21 November 1910

Dearest Boy,

I was so glad to hear that you were not vexed with me. It is such a difficult subject and we shall not make anything of it until we talk together even more freely than we have before. There are two sides to it—firstly, it is an experience for you; secondly, you may do good to her. Now, in this latter side I don't think there is any point at all. You will not do any good to her. I am absolutely certain of it. It is not your fault, or hers; but because you are the age you are, you will always be arousing hopes of another kind in her. This is natural. The only good you can do is indirectly—through men. Vice can only be suppressed through men. Tell every one you know that it is a horrible disgusting notion that love can be bought for money. The more men believe this, the fewer poor women will be forced into a life of debauchery and disease.

There is still the other side of the thing, but enough. I was very thankful to get your letter. It is making me very happy.

Now, we must meet next Wednesday. I am engaged all day, but will you meet me at 10.30 P.M. sharp—if anything a little before—underneath the clock inside Charing Cross Station; it isn't a very big clock, but it is easy to see—right in the middle of the inside of the facade. Because I feel like you, I am sick of the old conventional surroundings, and another sight of 47 Leicester Square is more than I can at present stand.¹ So meet me where I say, and if it is fine we will walk, and if it is cold we will go and have sandwiches somewhere, and in either case we will pretend it is Constantinople.

I must tell you one more thing. My book is selling so well that I shall probably make enough money by it to come to India. There will not only be an American edition, but a Canadian, and perhaps a translation into French.² I do not tell most people this because they would think I was bragging, but I know that you will understand, and feel what I feel.

Let me hear at once about Wednesday.

Your affectionate E.M.F.

TTr supplied by Akbar Masood

¹ I.e. Oxford and Cambridge Musical Club, where they used to meet.
² *Howards End*, first American edition by G. P. Putnam (1910, i.e. 1911). There was no separate Canadian edition. The French translation as *Le Legs de Mrs Wilcox*, by Charles Mauron, appeared in 1950.

91 To Arthur Christopher Benson[1]

West Hackhurst, Abinger Hammer, Dorking
13 December 1910

Dear Mr Benson

Thank you for your letter, and for the extract from Mrs Benson's letter; I need not say how flattered I felt by them and how much they interested me.[2] Their tone, though, was much too *respectful*; while reading them, I felt as if I had made some serious contribution to thought or literature, but I know that I have not. Thus, I agreed with you that the book is poetical rather than philosophical. This sounds arrogant, but one's confused little mind is visited by impulses of beauty, whereas systematic thought can only come to the mind that is both strong and orderly. However, it is great fun writing, and I am sure I do not want to run myself down! The house certainly would not appeal so strongly to the idealists; I had not thought of that. Indeed, though the supernatural element in the book is not supposed to be 'compulsory', I'm afraid that only those readers who 'take' it, will get through with any ease.

Again thanking you for your encouragement, and for all the trouble you have taken in writing to me.

I remain
Yours sincerely
E. M. Forster.

It would be a great pleasure to come & see you when I am in Cambridge next.

ALS: Cambridge University Library

[1] A. C. Benson (1862–1925) was the eldest son of Edward White Benson (1829–96), who became Archbishop of Canterbury in 1882. Arthur was a master at Eton, 1885–1903, and became Master of Magdalene College, Cambridge, in 1914. He wrote biographies, poems, and belle-lettrist essays, but his most substantial contribution is his journals, in 108 volumes, edited by David Newsome as *On the Edge of Paradise* (1950).

[2] Benson wrote to EMF (9 December 1910. KCC) about *Howards End* and quoted a long extract from a letter from his mother, Mary Sidgwick Benson (1840–1918). She defined EMF's moral theories as Pragmatism, as if 'situations make their own ethics; . . . It certainly hits the want of elasticity in some codes, . . . but it also has tremendous dangers?"' Benson himself stated that the book stirred him but that 'the appeal of the *house* was a little strained—I should rather have expected the *conventionalists* to have felt that than the *idealists*. . . . the book interested me very greatly, & gave me the beautiful sensation of a sudden *uplifting* of thought every now and then, like a mountain breaking out of a cloud.'

92   To Syed Ross Masood

[N. p.   Mid-January 1911]

Dearest Boy

You asked me to see the Morisons and to write soon. So, in both I obey. I have just had a very pleasant visit to her—learning among other things, that she liked Mirza very much.[1]

I write with a clinical thermometer in my mouth, for I am not clear of Latham yet. I have to take my temperature for a week, & then see him again. Drops of my blood have gone (at a guinea a piece) to the laboratory, and though no traces of tubercle have been found in them, what is termed 'the resistant power' is rather low, and L. wants to send me for a short period to a Sanitorium. I think it is all rot, & shall persuade him against it if I can. It will be expensive & depressing, and a real worry to my mother, who will regard it much too seriously. You won't do that, but still you won't want to think of me sitting in a draughty verandah with a purple nose and an overfilled stomach and an empty brain, and people who are really ill sitting round me. So I shall get off if possible.[2]

How can Cambridge remind you of Heaven, and yet of Oxford too?—! (Who's got a nasty one this time?) I am glad that you have seen a real University at last.—As for LL. D. [G.L.D.?] I have sent him a line, asking him to write to you if he has leisure to see people. Sometimes he hasn't, being a busy man, so you must not think it indifference should you not hear from him. I know he wants to see you if he can.

My mother returns tomorrow. I don't think we can imagine at all how unhappy she feels. We have never yet lost anyone out of the first rank of those whom we love. I will give her your message.

I am reading Lyall's hand book about the English in India—the sort of thing I required.[3] Also have failed to read another of Alice Parin's novels called *Idolatry*.[4] The other I tried was good, but this is about missionaries & wicked Hindus and most tiresome.

When will you be back from Cambridge? I think it's a very good idea to be there but mind you work. Do you not address your letter from the hospitable mansion of Beg?[5] Is this wise—?

Yours affectionately & forever
M.

TTr supplied by Akbar Masood

[1] The Mirza brothers, Ahmed (untraced), Sajjad (1898–1974), and Abu Saeed (1891–19??), were among EMF's closest Indian friends. Ahmed and Abu Saeed were in England at the same time as Masood, Ahmed studying engineering at King's College, London, and Abu Saeed studying law at Lincoln's Inn. In 1909 their father, Moulvi Mohammed Aziz Mirza, who was Home Secretary to the Nizam of Hyderabad, lost that post as a result of intrigue and had to leave the State. They returned to Hyderabad in January 1921 and were close to Masood, who by then was Director of the Educational Service.

² Despite EMF's disclaimer, the ailment was probably psychosomatic, the result of a run of griefs and worries: his mother's misgivings about *Howards End*, the death of his grandmother Louisa, his fear of drying up as a writer, and uncertainty about the friendship with Masood. Latham was a specialist whom EMF had consulted.
³ Sir Alfred C. Lyall, *British Dominion in India* (1893). EMF was reading, as well, Lyall's *Asiatic Studies: Religious and Social* (1882) and G. F. I. Graham, *The Life and Works of Syed Ahmed Khan* (1909). He wrote to Masood (4 February 1911. TTr supplied by Akbar Masood): 'India, you see, is already occupying me.'
⁴ Mrs Alice Perrin, *Idolatry* (1909).
⁵ Beg: possibly an *Arabian Nights* nickname. 'Beg' was the title of the lieutenant of a province under the Grand Signior.

93 To Syed Ross Masood

Walker's Temperance Commercial Hotel
2, High Street, Devizes
24 March 1911

Dearest Boy,
    This is wretched news. Don't worry, for God's sake, and if you find yourself thinking about books at night, think of people instead; it's a good cure, and sends one to sleep. You know how sorry I am about your crocking up, so I won't go on: indeed by this time you are probably set up again by the sea air. If I can, I shall look in at No 12 on next Wednesday, but I cannot be sure when I get to town.¹
    We (Greenwood & I) started walking yesterday in a thick mist from Swindon to the cottage of a friend of mine near Marlborough.² It was rather beastly, for we got right up in a cloud, and should have lost our way but for having a compass. We did about 14 miles, arriving for tea. There were two or three others stopping there, and one of them, Davies, reminded me that you had introduced him and me at *Le Bourgeois gentilhomme*. Do you remember? His face came back to me when he told me. I liked him extremely.³ How much more grown up Oxford men are than Cambridge! It is a thing I sometimes don't like in them, but I liked it in Davies. He is a clever chap, is he not?
    Today G. & I have reached the above pleasing address; but do not write to it, for we leave tomorrow; Westbury, Wincanton, & Sherbourne is probably our route, should your enfeebled frame be able to open an atlas, and your brain be strong enough to look at it! I wish I could go walking with you, but fear you would not care for it—you athletic brutes are so slack when it comes to the point: it is fragile creatures like myself who take their 15 miles a day for a week and thrive on it. This reminds me—I meant to have said it before—my aunt wants us to fix some day for your visit to her when you can. She has no engagements, so any time will do; her kind remembrances to you, & she much wants to see you again.⁴ She was well, though in bed most of the time: it is more comfortable for her

till the weather is settled. My mother's lumbago is also better; she is now at Salisbury with Mrs Aylward. This makes me easy, and able to enjoy my walk, as I know she is with some one whom she likes. If I knew you were all right, I should feel A. 1.

This letter, stupid as it is, is intended to cheer you. I am pleasantly tired, and G. is strumming little tunes on the piano. By the way I have been playing THE WALZE the strange harmonies of which occasionally are beyond me. Still, it isn't likely one would take in the great oriento-occidental music of the future at once. Besides I am forgetting that damned middle part of the tune again.[5]

I suppose you aren't down at Ramsgate alone—at least I hope not. Well, goodbye. With all that I always feel whenever I write to you; + wishes for recovery & good luck in your exams.

Morgan

ALS: KCC

[1] Masood's London address: 12 Edith Road, Chelsea. He was studying for law examinations.
[2] EMF's friend: Hilton Young; his cottage: The Lacket.
[3] Davies: apparently an unidentified Oxford friend.
[4] Probably EMF's aunt Laura Forster.
[5] Howard Ferguson suggests that this may have been a composition using Indian and Western motifs, sent to Masood by an Indian friend.

94   To Malcolm Darling

Harnham, Monument Green, Weybridge
29 July 1911

Dear Malcolm

You have been a slack correspondent lately with reason; I without. There is no reason that I should not have written you a long letter every week, full of wit and body. I have been thinking of you all, but that is no excuse, for it is easy, indeed inevitable, to think of those one loves. I wish you did not feel parted from your hills; but it's a feeling that we must all go through. It is tempting to proceed "But they will come back to us more glorious for the separation", yet I won't, for hills, whether of earth or of the imagination, are too big to play cup-and-ball with in this comfortable way.

I write to you for ¼ hour; then I go down to the river, to row my mother & a friend about. My mother is about the same, thank you very much. I can't persuade her to take a change. I am going to Italy myself on Monday—she will have visitors here.[1]

It's so hot that the pen (now that I have taken it up) clings to my recreant fingers. We went to town yesterday to see the Russian Ballet, after which a thunderstorm broke, flooded the streets and the tubes, sopped me through, and caused Hasluck, who met us at tea, to take a taxi, unheard of portent. It looks about to do likewise now, yet I suppose our heat is nothing like yours.

I will now tell you all about Bashahr. It is a very remarkable place, and extraordinary figures may be witnessed at the Rampur fair. The religion of the country is not Buddhism as Mr Emerson (an honest but superficial observer) supposes, but Di-theism; there being two supreme gods, the Sutlej and the Kailas, the one proceeding out of the other. (Do not confuse Di theism with Dualism, as was recently done by the Bishop of Lahore). The Sutlej consents to an occasional garland of wire rope: the Kailas are worshipped without ritual.[2] There are places in Bashahr that might have dropped out of Switzerland, and other places that actually have dropped out of the moon—desert after desert of mountain ranges heaving. Politics are complicated: I will deal with them next time. Oh and as for some photographs I have received I glanced at them ~~with condescension,~~ but they are very far from giving the spirit of the country, let me tell you once and for all!

How much more of this are you going to stand? See the results on the human brain, when it is not set to work at files occasionally; and further more when there is going to be a thunderstorm. How undignified! How unworthy of our Island Race! Let me hasten to reintroduce those photographs properly. Thank you for them very much. They gave me a very good idea of Bashahr, and I am sending them for safe keeping to your mother; she also has very kindly lent me some.

By now—or during now, if there is such a phrase—I have taken my ladies on the river, and the storm, whose effects you have already felt, is bursting, or rather popping, with a maximum of bluster and a minimum of rain. I have been reading Kipling's child's history of England with mingled joy and disgust.[3] It's a fine conception, but oh is it necessary to build character on a psychological untruth? In other words to teach the young citizen that he is absolutely ~~like the~~ unlike the young German or the young Bashahri—that foreigners are envious and treacherous, Englishmen, through some freak of God, never—? Kipling and all that school know it's an untruth at the bottom of their hearts—as untrue as it is unloveable. But, for the sake of patriotism, they lie. It is despairing. How slowly righteousness works up against the tide.

I couldn't on the other hand read the New Machiavelli, finding it too fretful and bumptious, and very inartistic, but must try again—the more so as Wells, in an article in Le Temps has mentioned me among the authors qui méritent être mieux connus en France; on which the New Age remarks "to recommend Forster ~~or Galsworthy~~ to the French Nation is to insult its intelligence; ~~they~~ he simply does not count."[4] The best novels I have come across in the past year are Rosalind Murray's The Leading Note (Josie might like it); and

Wedgwood's *Shadow of a Titan*—unfortunately written in an affected and unreadable style.[5]

So glad JJ. is well & happy. What are his movements? Can you have him with you all the year, or does the climate make it impossible? Wish you well through the Durbar. Poor George & Mary will be ~~more~~ almost dead before they reach you. They looked at their last gasp when I saw them at the Coronation Procession— his face bright red, hers white, and both without the slightest expression.

When you have a spare day—only then—do send me some Indian Papers—the Pioneer, and if possible something Nationalist & semi-seditious. I have read Chirol's book, and am anxious to taste the Journalism direct—just specimen copies.[6] I can't get hold of anything over here.

Yours affectionately
E. M. Forster.

ALS: HRC

[1] On 31 July EMF and Masood left for Tesserete, in the Italian Lakes. He was in somewhat low spirits on the eve of departure and remarked in his diary (30 July. KCC): 'Glad on the whole I am going. Shall hope to think over my messy life. Its apparent success is over. Is it to be a real as well as an apparent failure in the future.' In retrospect, however, it stayed in his memory as one of the high points of his friendship with Masood.

[2] On Bashahr, see Letter 82. Mr Emerson: character in *RV*. The Rt Rev. George Alfred Lefroy (1854–1919) was Bishop of Lahore, 1899–1912. The Sutlej, Indus, and Brahmaputra Rivers spring from the Kailas Range of southwest Tibet.

[3] Kipling, *Puck of Pook's Hill* (1906).

[4] H. G. Wells, whose *The New Machiavelli* was published in 1911, lectured to The Times Book Club on 18 May 1911, on 'The Scope of the Novel', which he revised as 'The Contemporary Novel', in *The Fortnightly Review*, 96 (1911), 860–73, and published in *An Englishman Looks at His World*, pp. 248–69. Alfred Richard Orage (1873–1934), who edited *The New Age* from 1907–22, intensely disliked Wells's ideas about the novel as a medium of propaganda. Orage's staff writer, John McFarland Kennedy (untraced), in 'The Last Straw' (9 [1911], 232–4), commented similarly on Wells, quoted *Le Temps'* introductory remarks to its translation (18 and 21 June) of the Book Club lecture, retranslated large parts of it, and closed with the comment: 'As for Messrs Galsworthy and Forster, it is an insult to Modern French literature to say that there [*sic*] names mériteraient d'être mieux connus en France".' The writers named by *Le Temps* were Arnold Bennett, Joseph Conrad, John Galsworthy, EMF, and, of course Wells. *Cf.* 'L'Objet et le Development du Roman contemporain en Angleterre,' *Le Temps*, 18 June 1911, p. 2; 21 June, p. 3.

[5] Rosalind Murray, *The Leading Note* (1910). A. Felix Wedgwood, *The Shadow of a Titan* (1910).

[6] Valentine Chirol's *Indian Unrest* (1910) was a considerable contribution, in Indian opinion, toward increasing that condition.

95   To Jessica Darling

[N. p.]   24 September 1911

Dear Josie,

Your letter arrived today, and in a flood of gratitude I take up my pen. Now why don't you write oftener? I extend to you the courteous invitation. Simla sounds trying. No, I shall *not* take over the house keeping when I come to stop with you, good as I am at that sort of thing. I came home last week to find the housemaid in hospital, and we are running this house on a cook, which, small as this house is, means 'planning' and all that is sobering and unpleasant. So I shall *not* help you. I had much rather overlook your mistakes with a courteous smile.

It's something to be near fine country. Beastly children! Why didn't you turn them into the rain! Whether it is something to have the novels of Hardy with you, I doubt. He is a poet, and the few novels of his I've read were unsatisfying. However serious the edifice, the ground plan of it is farce. He's a poet (I repeat; having got my previous sentence rather cock eye)—and only comes to full splendour in his poems. In them his narrow view of human, and especially female, character doesn't matter, and Wessex and Destiny at last stand clear out of the mist.—This sounds arrogant, but it is much quicker to be arrogant; and even where I don't read Hardy, I have idolatrous reverence for him. He is one of the few writers one trusts. What he said to a friend of mine is very illuminating: "I am a very stupid man." He lacks the all-round intelligence that one expects as a matter of course in this cultivated age—a lack that is often a sign of creative power. Michelangelo lacked, so did William S.; Goethe is the only genius who was not stupid. Malcolm was very entertaining and just about T. H. and Destiny's clothes in his last letter—received a week ago. I am writing to him soon. Meanwhile will you thank him for it and for the Indian Punch.[1]

I had a glorious time in Italy—such weather water and woods. I was in the Lakes all the time, except for excursions to Milan and Bergamo, and managed to keep clear of 'resorts'. When you and Malcolm take your Italian villa, I know which Lake it ought to be on, but shall not commit its sacred name to paper.[2] Much did I bathe, much eat, and lived in a dream till I fell suddenly into England on Basle station—hundreds of tourists struggling for half that number of seats on the midnight train, and shouting that all would be well if the others would behave like Gentlemen. The sacred word re echoed loudly. Eight in the carriage, still chanting it, we started, our legs intertwined like spillikins, so that if one ~~person~~ gentleman moved in the night, all the other seven woke up. The train was two hours late, the boat later.[3] I returned a little discontented to Albion, and still long for the beautiful forms of the Italian hills.[4]

Thank you for what you say about my short stories.[5] I would rather people praised them than anything else I wrote. But I *have* a tall hat (only used for funerals however), which shows that one can get the best of ~~we~~ both worlds.

If any thing in this letter is unintelligible, remember that it refers to something in your letter to me, which you have forgotten. In common fairness, foreign letters ought to [be] returned to their writers to elucidate one's reply. This however I do not intend to do.

I expect to be at home for some time now, varied by lecturing at Harrow &ct. The weather is very cold.

With many thanks

Yours ever
E. M. Forster.

ALS: HRC

1 *The Indian Punch* (1859–61, and n. s. 1862–3), published in Meerut [Delhi], superseding *The Delhi Sketch Book*.
2 This was Lake Orta. EMF stayed on after Masood left.
3 He used this episode at the opening of 'Arctic Summer', p. 120.
4 He returned a good deal discontented and in four days succumbed to gloom: 'Till today, should have written cheerfully of home also for the first time this year, but have returned after two days at Aunt L[aura's] to the familiar morbidity' (diary, 27 September 1911. KCC).
5 Jessica Darling's letters to EMF do not survive.

96   To Rupert Brooke[1]

Harnham, Monument Green, Weybridge
24 November 1911

Dear Brooke

I have this moment decided to put all I can remember of your paper on art into a novel—and as I remember it.[2] You have not to mind. "It will never get written unless."

Yours
E. M. Forster.

ALS: KCC

1 Rupert Chawner Brooke (1887–1915) entered King's in 1909. He is now best known for his war poems.
2 This was 'Democracy and the Arts', delivered to the Cambridge Fabians on 10 December 1910, about six weeks after EMF had stayed with him in Cambridge; see Elizabeth Heine, Introduction to *ASOF*, p. xviii. The novel was EMF's uncompleted 'Arctic Summer', in which, under Brooke's influence, the central socialist concern of the hero becomes 'State Subsidy for Literature'.

97   To Forrest Reid[1]

Harnham, Monument Green, Weybridge
31 January 1912

Dear Sir,

I have read The Bracknels, and wish to thank you for it. Most books give us less than can be got from people, but yours gives more, for it has a quality that can only be described as 'helpful'. I do not use the word in the vulgar sense. Denis is no more likely to be prosperous after death than before it; but it does help one to distinguish between the superficial and the real, and to some minds there is something exhilarating in this. You show so very clearly that intelligence and even sympathy are superficial—good enough things in their way—they do what they can and would gladly do more; but the real thing is 'being there'; and the worst of it is that no two human beings can be in the same place. The book has moved me a good deal; it is what a friend ought to be but isn't; I suppose I am saying in a very roundabout and clumsy way that it is art.

The only point where I do not follow you spiritually, is in your introduction of visions of evil, but perhaps I am trying to define too much; at all events Denis escapes into a confusion that is not of this world.[2]

The other qualities of your work—realism, character drawing, construction &[ct]— seem to me admirable, but I have dwelt upon the one that interested me most. I hope that you will excuse me for having written to you.

Believe me
Yours truly
E. M. Forster

ALS: Stephen Gilbert

[1] Forrest Reid (1875–1947), novelist, was born in Belfast of an impoverished professional family and was apprenticed to the tea trade. In his twenties, on the strength of a legacy, he went to Cambridge University. He had published his first novel, *The Kingdom of Twilight*, in 1904, and after graduating from Cambridge he returned to Ulster and devoted himself to writing, his novels being centred mainly upon boyhood psychology. For some years he shared a house with the three Rutherford brothers, James, William, and Andrew, but after the death of Willie Rutherford in 1918 and James's marriage he lived alone in Belfast, paying occasional visits to friends in England, notably to Walter de la Mare, and competing in croquet tournaments. He was a book-collector and published a study, *Illustrators of the Sixties*, in 1928. In later years he rewrote his novels *The Bracknels* (1911) and *Following Darkness* (1921) as *Denis Bracknel* (1947) and *Peter Waring* (1937).
[2] Denis Bracknel is a boy with a strange inner life, whom a young tutor tries, but fails, to rescue from his uncomprehending family.

98   To Jessica Darling

36 Botanic Avenue, Belfast[1]
6 February 1912

Dear Josie
    Are you an Honourable? I hope so, and in any case shall continue to put it on the envelope, for you are my only chance.[2] And is JJ an Honourablino?—But enough. I am really writing to thank you for a long letter which gave me great pleasure and which I should have answered before. I remember two things in it distinctly, though I have it not with me here—your just remarks about hanging pictures, and your rather unjust remarks about The Shadow of a Titan, which is bad in the ways you say—indeed I never to the end found out whether it was about two young ladies or one—but so very good in

the imaginative treatment of landscape: the paragraph about the Andes is unequalled in modern literature, don't you think.[3]

Before I get off books, I will put down the names of one or two that I have enjoyed lately. George Moore, *Ave*, William James, *Memories & Studies*, G. L. Strachey, *Landmarks in French Literature* (price 1/–, and oh so good), J. T. Sheppard, *Greek Tragedy* (also 1/–; Malcolm knows him), Foemina, *L'Ame des Anglais*, André Chevrillon, *Dans L'Inde*, Forrest Reid, *The Bracknels*, Lascelles Abercrombie, *Emblems of Love*, Edith Wharton, *Ethan Frome*, Max Beerbohm, *Zuleika Dobson*.

Now for myself. I am in Belfast, and all inadequate to the historic occasion. What does interest me is to see the effect of politics in the home. We went to tea on Sunday to a pillar of the Ulster Reform Club. "Belfast," he told me "will listen to anyone except a Judas; or a turncoat" (I glanced nervously at my own, which has been turned so often that I forget which side was which originally). Then "We are not acting in accordance with any principle, and we do not pretend that we are;" this very majestically. "It just shows the uselessness of principles," cried the exultant little wife, and passed on the glad news to her baby. There are all sorts of rumours about the Churchill meeting. According to some, the employers have served out clubs and revolvers to their men and the tent will be set on fire in the best Durbar style. Fear not for me: I have promised my mother that I will not go! Whether at the last moment I may not yield to curiosity is possible, but I think it may take the form of going to the Protest meeting in the town.[4]

I heard Christabel Pankhurst the other day. She was very able, very clever, and very unpleasant; she talked a certain amount of rot about Indian Women & her idea of progress is that females should meet together in vast masses and orate. But I agreed with most of her remarks, and her tone did not unconvert me.[5]

I stop here for a fortnight, and then expect to be at home for some time. I am hoping to persuade my mother to come abroad—perhaps to Spain. There have been no great excitements lately—except the performances of The Miracle and Oedipus, and of these you have probably heard from others.[6] Christmas we spent very pleasantly at a London hotel.

I hope that you and Malcolm will be writing again, now that the Durbar is past.[7] You must have been pretty well done up, both of you. I wish you would spare me a photograph of JJ—preferably in some manly occupation: also that you would sketch—as far as you can—your movements for this year & next. I expect it would be better to make up my mind to come to India this autumn, as I have always hoped to do: it will be as difficult to leave my mother next year as this. All the same, I want to know all that I can before deciding.

Roger Fry, the semi-post-impressionist, has painted my picture. I like it, but it finds little favour with the relatives. He put it in an exhibition together with many beautiful landscapes.[8]

Now I must stop. After a high tea my friend (H. O. Meredith, who is Professor of Economics at the University here) reads a paper on the Economic Aspects of Class Distinctions. It should be interesting.

Yours affectionately
E. M. Forster.

ALS: KCC

[1] Hugh Meredith's address. During this visit EMF met Forrest Reid. He wrote to his mother ([Feb. 1912]. KCC): 'The other excitement—there have been so many—is the discovery that Mr Forrest Reid, who wrote The Bracknels, lives at Belfast. I went to lunch with him on Tuesday: he lives with a curate [i.e. James Rutherford], & a great many books, a great and dogs and cats; a nice and very ugly man. He and the curate came to tea here yesterday; Meredith liked them both and pronounced it "one of Morgie's finds": the University always declares that there are no literary people in Belfast, & I have routed them out. If it does not rain I am going to Newcastle, Co. Down, tomorrow with Mr Reid; it is said to be beautiful.' The curate was James Rutherford (1878–1942), then Assistant Presbyterian Minister at Newtownbreda Parish Church. He and Reid had shared a house since 1908, an arrangement continued from about 1912 until James married. On Reid and the Rutherford brothers, see Brian Taylor, The Green Avenue: The Life and Writings of Forrest Reid (1980).
[2] Jessica Darling's father, Lord Low, was a Law Lord: a life peerage accompanying services as a Senior Judge.
[3] A. F. Wedgwood's The Shadow of a Titan (see Letter 94) is a novel with setting divided between an Edwardian country-house and a South American revolution. The paragraph on the Andes, p. 265.
[4] Churchill had just finished terms as Secretary of State for the Colonies, 1906–8; as President of the Board of Trade, 1908–10; as Home Secretary, 1910–11. In none of these had he pleased the Ulster Irish. He fared little better as First Lord of the Admiralty, 1911–15. On EMF's obedience to his mother, see Letter 99. 'Durbar style': during the Delhi Durbar in December 1911 fireworks exploded prematurely, a half-hour before fire broke out in the Fort, and the quarters of Lord Crewe's private secretary burned during investiture of the Queen as Knight General Commander of the Order of the Star of India.
[5] Christabel Pankhurst (1880–1958) was a daughter of Mrs Emmeline Pankhurst (1858–1928), and both were intrepid crusaders for votes for women.
[6] The Miracle, a Gothic miracle-play by Viennese producer Max Reinhardt (né Goldmann) (1873–1943), was a production tour-de-force involving 2,000 players, an orchestra of 200, an invisible choir of 500, and some £40,000 for an eight-week run at London's Olympia from December 1911. His Oedipus Rex, another extravagant spectacle, opened in January 1912 at Covent Garden, although Reinhardt would have preferred the Albert Hall. His most distinguished enterprise, however, was production of Richard Strauss' Der Rosenkavalier (1911).
[7] The Coronation Durbar of King George V and Queen Mary took place in Delhi on 12 December 1911. On its manifold political and social ramifications, see Robert Grant Irving, Indian Summer: Lutyens, Baker, and the Building of New Delhi (1981). On 4 February Darling wrote to EMF (CSAS): 'At the time I had an uneasy feeling that the realities that lie behind politics are pretty thin, & looking back that must, I think, explain why as a whole the recollection of it gives me no proper frisson, except one thing, & that was when the people, the real India, surged past the old Fort walls upon which the King & Queen sat alone panoplied in all the cumbrous additaments of their calling. I could not see them, but I did see perhaps 100,000 people washing up to the walls in great waves of many-coloured humanity and emotion breaking from them like foam in the music of uplifted hands and voices. That was a superb & most moving spectacle.

'The Durbar itself also was a fine spectacle, but a spectacle & nothing more; in fact Drury Lane at its best; no Drury Lane cld. never be as good [though] it would like to be. The one thing lacking was fine music. There were bands enough—'1500 performers' so the newspapers said—& they performed very well, but they forgot to bring music with them. Political shows to have any meaning want the adjuncts of religion.'

8 For this oil portrait (1911–12), reproduced in colour, see the jacket of *EMF* (English edition). After it was exhibited at the Alpine Club Gallery, EMF bought it for £17.10.0; now in a private collection. Frances Spalding (*Roger Fry*, pp. 150–2) states that Fry was exercising his 'new severe style', and doing so with 'energy and conviction'.

99   To Alice Clara Forster

36 Botanic Avenue, Belfast
9 February 1912

Dearest Mother,

Thank you for your card. I am glad you got to Miss G's lecture, though I fear you would have found it more interesting if you had known the subject before hand. We had an interesting day yesterday.[1] I went down to the [Grand Central] Hotel, which was full of people & got further as the morning wore on. I didn't get at Marsh till the end owing partly to the crowd, & partly to the stupidity of the hall porter: then I had a little talk with him. There were two doors to the Hotel, & everyone said Churchill would slink out by the back. However he came forth between us in grand style, looking very pale—sea kail colour. An enormous crowd outside began to boo, and then the hotel vomited its contents behind him, all booing as well. He brushed against me as he went out: I lifted my hat with great intrepidity. Meanwhile Marsh was manoeuvring on the pavement with police & motors. Mrs Churchill was already in, and off they went, very slowly because of the crowd. People said he would never get to the Football Field, but as usual people were wrong. It appeared to be a very cheap sort of motor, which poured out smelly blue smoke behind, & kept the crowd away a little[.] As soon as he had gone, the Unionist leaders—Carson Londonderry &^{ct}—appeared in the windows of a club, and there was great cheering and singing of Rule Britannia. I went for lunch to a restaurant close by, & saw the whole scene from the first floor window: the Police had a great bother in carving a way through the people for the trams. The meeting, according to Meredith, was a great success: no interruptions except from suffragettes, & I have not heard of any rioting in the evening. For that we have to thank the troops. What I said is quite true—the Unionist leaders refused to issue any peaceful announcement until they heard the troops were coming.

We are going to Dublin this evening & return Monday.[2] If only the weather improves, it will be very jolly. It does look a little

ALU, incomplete: KCC

[1] Churchill came to Belfast to speak on 8 February, for the Home Rule Bill. Four thousand

troops were on duty and the atmosphere was tense after thousands of Unionists signed the Ulster Covenant, a pledge to oppose the measure. The speech, planned for the Ulster Hall, in Unionist territory, was moved to the Celtic Road Football Ground, in a Catholic workingmen's neighbourhood, where cheers replaced threats. Edward Henry Carson (1854–1935) became head of the Ulster Unionist Council in 1912. Charles Stewart Henry Vane-Tempest-Stewart, 7th Marquess of Londonderry (1878–1949), who later held a variety of important Government posts, led the Unionists. Londonderry and Churchill had had a tense correspondence about this speech, with Churchill defending the rights of Belfast citizens to assemble for public meetings and discussion (see Randolph Churchill, *Winston Churchill*, II, 445–50). Events soon confirmed EMF's first impressions of Belfast, recorded in his diary kept during this trip (KCC): 'A pious and self conscious city—more apathetic than I had expected, but less apathetic than she seems—at least so an inhabitant tells me. Except for a few "No Popery" inscriptions at street corners, and for a banner of Latimer & Ridley burning in their night shirts, there is little trace of enthusiasm out of doors. / But indoors—!' At a luncheon he was advised to listen to the orators on the Custom House steps. 'This I did. . . . The first orator was inaudible; the second was a clergyman with a bullying roar of a voice who was showing off three converts, and causing them to recount their salvation. The crowd threw pennies. It was an ugly sight: the converts performing like whipped curs. The third was a Socialist, the fourth another preacher supported by a lady on a chair, the fifth a seller of patent medicines. The sixth, who drew an immense crowd, was politico-religious, such as I had gone out to hear. His argument was "You have won the first victory, & driven Churchill from the Ulster hall: leave the rest to the Almighty who will send a snow storm from heaven when he tries to speak in the Football Field." ' The Lord obliged with a downpour, but 5,000 turned out to hear Churchill speak.

[2] The reason for the Dublin trip is unexplained.

100   To Syed Ross Masood

Hotel Russell, St Stephen's Green, Dublin
11 February 1912

Dearest boy

Thanks for your Paris letter.[1] You can never miss me more than I do you. I mind it the more because you're absolutely useless at a distance—so damned slack that I may not know whether you're alive or dead for months. I mean to write every week, in my cold regular Western way, and please, SRM, do write pretty often back, for life will be pretty blank without you, and London never the same again. I'm thankful to have come straight to Ireland—it gives me other things to think about, and as we were on the edge of civil war at Belfast it was exciting enough.

All is over now, and Churchill safe back in England, but I really think it is a pity things didn't come to a head—there is sure to be trouble in the future. I have heard a lot of talk, both from Unionists at Belfast and from Nationalists here, and had no idea how high feeling ran.

I go back in another week. My mother is at Salisbury with Mrs. Aylward. I have been corresponding with Lady M. about a German governess for Dorothy.[2] I have heard from Pino, damning you for not telling him about your exam.[3] I replied that you served every one alike! That is about all the news, except about Irish politics & Ireland, which will not interest you. The Irish view of the English character resembles the Indian: they say we are such hypocrites, and that we should be better, if we did not pretend to be so good. For my own part, I think that we should be worse; hypocrisy is a sort of cement that holds one's wretched little character together. I met H. W. Nevinson last night; he says that now it is too late, Grey is trying to do something in Persia.[4] Foreign affairs get filthier every day; our English bishops, &[ct] have been overeating themselves in Russia, and pretending to represent Parliament. The King is back, and has dismissed the Lord Chamberlain—at least so people here say.[5]

Let me know whenever you want any commissions done in England, of course. I have forgotten when you reach Aligarh; do fulfil your promise of writing your first impressions to my mother; it will give her so much pleasure. I think of you every day. I think of your mother too. Do not forget to give her a message of respect from me. Good night, dearest boy. I can never say what it has been to me knowing you. Good bye, and my love.

Yours forever
Morgan

Address all letters
Weybridge of course.

TTr supplied by Akbar Masood

[1] Masood had just returned to India.
[2] Lady Margaret Morison was the wife of Sir Theodore (1863–1936), who was so important in the lives of Masood and his family; tutor to the Maharajas of Chhatarpur and Charkari, 1885; teacher at the Mohammedan Anglo-Oriental College, Aligarh, 1889, and its Principal, 1899–1905; Member, Council of India, 1906–16. Their daughter, Dorothea Cotter Morison (d. 1928), married Richard Bevan Braithwaite (1900–), University Lecturer in Moral Science, Cambridge, 1928–34; Knightsbridge Professor of Moral Philosophy, from 1953.
[3] Pino: Signor Ithen, their host at Tesserete.
[4] Henry Woodd Nevinson (1856–1941), foreign correspondent and staunch civil-libertarian; on the staff of The Nation, 1907–23. In July 1911 the ex-Shah had tried to invade Persia but gave it up, under British and Russian pressure, in July 1912. A 'Parliamentary visit' by the Speaker, financiers, and clergy including some Anglican Bishops, went (despite Liberal protests) to try to improve British relations with Russia; but the real purpose seems to have been to attract British capitalists to Russian market possibilities.
[5] The King and Queen had by now returned from their Coronation visit to India. Lord Spencer, Lord Chamberlain since 1905, was replaced, 'due solely to considerations of health' (The Times, 10 February 1912, p. 8), by Lord Sandhurst.

101   To S. R. Masood

[N. p.]   8 March 1912

Dearest Boy,

Have just dined with the Morisons—a very interesting evening, and I had a long talk alone with Miss Wright about her writings.[1] We got on very well; at least I felt we did. She showed me that dream poem that we had at Tesserete. It is altered—the Lover cut out—and I think very good indeed. She has also done a little story about two people who shoot themselves sooner than grow old. Not bad, but she has chosen to write it in a very difficult way, so that one doesn't know whether they shoot themselves, or one another, or neither, or whether one shoots the other but isn't shot, etc., etc. She was amused at our mistakes and is trying to get it clearer.

I am writing a three act play.[2] The first two acts (The Reign of Love and The Reign of Force) are in the remote past; the third act (The Reign of Reason) is in the remote future! It amuses me very much and I don't think it's bad, but doubt whether it will ever grace the stage. I am just doing a procession of Kings in the third act, all renouncing their crowns at the feet of the Spirit of Man, and at the same time making little speeches, in which they say what they have done for the enrichment of that Spirit; and you will be delighted to hear that when the King of Albion spoke, I could not think of anything for him to say! This brings me to your voyage out. I am so sorry to hear from Lady M. that you had a rotten time, and disliked your fellow passengers—Anglo Indians presumably.

Luncheon bell. Must stop. Love, as always,

Morgan.

TTr supplied by Akbar Masood

[1] Miss Wright: unidentified.
[2] Unpublished 'prophetic morality-play', depicting the rise and decline of civilisation (MS. KCC).

102   To Malcolm Darling

Salisbury.   12 March 1912

Dear Malcolm

I have now had four letters in succession from you, but they are not with me here, and I may forget all the points. But the better news about Josie—I am so thankful and bless the egg that produced that tempting guinea fowl. Your sister has kindly said she will write again, so I am safe for news if you do not have time to write to me direct. It is a very great relief. What did JJ think when his black nursey disappeared? But there, who cares about JJ.

In my hurried note, I think I never alluded to your disappointment about the other child. I was so grieved.[1]

Then there was a message in the first of your letters about something that I could do for you: you would explain what next week. This you never did. Do you remember what it was, and can it still be done?

Goodall's engagement. I had heard the bare fact, but was much interested in the details, and that Miss Walker was a cousin and friend of Josie's.[2] Josie must be most cock-a-hoop at her insight. Perhaps when I come out she will find a wife for me. Not Miss Christabel Pankhurst, please, I am definitely off with her, not so much for her window breaking as for the moral windows that she broke in me at Belfast when she suggested we should all be beastly together.[3] I suppose I've got elderly and law abiding, but I weary of this lack of the elements of patriotism, which seems growing daily. Every one says 'wait till I've got what I want: *then* I'll be patriotic.' But that moment never comes—it is for all human beings at the bottom of the rain bow.—Of course I'm not referring only or mainly to the Suffragists (to whose principles I stick as formerly); but to Orangemen, Syndicalists, emissaries of the National Service League, mistresses who can't stick on Insurance Stamps, &c[t]. &c[t].

As for myself—not that I have in any way shunned that subject in the previous pages. But about India. Your definite statement that you come home in April brings matters to a point, and I hope to write in a week or two. My mother is not well—nothing definite, but loss of spirits since her mother's death a year ago, and I doubt whether she will ever recover them entirely.—⟨This need not go farther than yourself and J.⟩ —You see how difficult it all becomes. I know that she will mind me going even if she urges it, and that she will be lonely without me; and yet the problem will be no easier another year, and no one can help me with it. I must muddle it out myself. I long to see India steadily. It's out of the question that she should come with me.

I seem to have read several good books—William James's *Memories and Studies*, Walter de la Mare's *The Return*—supernatural, profound and fine—: *The Reward of Virtue* by Amber Reeves—refreshingly free from Heart or Podge or whatever it is the young are free from. Foemina is interesting on *L'Ame des Anglais*, though she theorises too much.[4]

Did I say Roger Fry has painted me? I couldn't have said I have acquired the same, having only just done so. Advanced people love it but relatives wail. It represents a brilliant and somewhat pleasing youth with a green face and pink eyes. One cheek is shaded yellow, the other purple; only the left hand has been stricken with diabetes, and the general effect is nonchalant and gay. If it photographs well, I will send you one.[5]

Ever yours affectionately
Morgan

How very kind of Lady Low to say that I may come to see her. Please remember me to her if she is with you still.

ALS: HRC
[1] Jessica had apparently suffered a miscarriage.

[2] Charles Henry Goodall (1882–1968) had been Darling's fellow-student at King's, after which he joined the Bombay and Burma Trading Company. The Maharaja of Dewas Senior, who came to know him through Darling, honoured his marriage to Mary Walker, Jessica's cousin, with a splendid banquet on 29 December 1912; see *HD*, pp. 25–6.

[3] On Christabel Pankhurst in Belfast, see Letter 98.

[4] Recommendations for current reading are a feature of the correspondence with Darling. William James's *Memories and Studies* comprises essays on peace, personalities, and education. *The Return* (1910) is a novel by Walter de la Mare. *The Reward of Virtue* (1911) by Amber Reeves, has a wry title in view of the fact that she had given birth to H. G. Wells's child in December 1909. Foemina: pseudonym of Mme Augustine Bulteau; her *L'Ame des anglais* (1910) appeared under another pseudonym, Jacque Vontade, and with the title, *The English Soul* (1914). She *does* theorise at length, on love, beauty, friendship, and duty.

[5] On this portrait, see Letter 98.

103   To Leonard Woolf

(On journey).   [Before 24 May 1912]

Dear Woolf

It's a good story. Try the English Review—I know of no other magazine that will pay for erections and excrement. Suggestions. New title. Shorten the Introduction and simplify its style, e.g. 'content not to know (thought he didn't)' sets a wrong atmosphere. What about missing out the first 'I' altogether? What does the reader see through his eyes that he could not see without them?[1]

I enjoyed the story more the second reading, but still feel the touch of 'scold' about it, that often goads me in Kipling. Indignation pierces through writing so easily and inevitably that the ~~words~~ writer need never trouble to cut a special channel for it, and your man who has done & felt things is a little too anxious to give those who haven't a bad time. Those who haven't (in his sense) include me, so I don't offer this as an aesthetic conclusion. Only just possibly it may be one. Contrast the last section of Karain.[2]

I hope you'll show me anything else you feel inclined. You seem a very good writer! tippy at describing the scenes I most want to see— e.g. the two deaths at the end.

I'm in a state of peevishness for which you are partly responsible. Conrad induces the same. Why ever do you want to stop in England? I'm on my way to Oxford to stop with a friend whose wife has never sat in darkness, and feel ill prepared to stand her.[3]

I wish now that you had come to my lecture at Morley as it was rather good and no one there, as term had scarcely started.

Please let me know your movements—whether & when you go back to Ceylon. I'd like to see you again soon.

Yours,

E. M. Forster.

ALS: Berg

[1] This may be a reference to a draft of Woolf's novel, *The Village in the Jungle* (1913). He had left Ceylon in May 1911 on leave from the Civil Service and began writing it while awaiting

Virginia Stephen's decision to marry him. That novel had no other title, and nothing appeared in *The English Review*. The manuscript (264 pp.) was given in 1974 to the University of Peradeniya, Sri Lanka.

2 Joseph Conrad, 'Karain: a Memory', in his *Tales of Unrest*, pp. 1–79.

3 These Oxford friends are unidentified. 'Sat in darkness': see Psalm 107, verse 10.

104   To Forrest Reid

Harnham, Monument Green, Weybridge
19 June 1912

Dear Reid

I am anxious to hear how your new book will fare. I can't imagine it won't get published, considering how good your 'press' was for the last; but if such a fate should await it, I claim the right to read it in M.S.¹ I don't expect to like it as much as The Bracknels, not from any thing that you have told me about it, but because of human nature's inability to admit this. We should hear less of writers 'falling off' in their work if they would.—As for 'story' I never yet did enjoy a novel or play in which someone didn't tell me afterward that there was something wrong with the story, so that's going to be no drawback as far as I'm concerned. "Good Lord, why am I so bored?"—"I know; it must be the plot developing harmoniously." So I often reply to myself, and there rises before me my special nightmare—that of the writer as craftsman, natty and deft.—But I know it isn't a nightmare that many share with me, and will check myself.

The day before yesterday I read The Ghost Ship by R. Middleton.² I expect you have done the same. I thought it very good, and it added to the other qualities I want in a supernatural story, the quality of good temper. The others in the same book did not look as interesting.

I saw the Abbey players last week, and liked better the secondary company that I saw in Dublin. They did Kathleen ni H. and The Playboy. Tomorrow I'm going to the Russian Ballet—lucky to get a seat.³

Yours ever
E. M. Forster.

ALS: Stephen Gilbert

1 The new book was *Following Darkness*. 'I claim the right': it was to be dedicated to him.

2 Richard Barham Middleton (1882–1911), *The Ghost Ship and Other Stories*, published posthumously (1912).

3 W. B. Yeats's *Cathleen ni Houlihan: A Play in One Act and in Prose* (1902), in which the mysterious stranger, the Poor Old Woman, represents Ireland. It opened on 3 June with John Millington Synge's controversial *The Playboy of the Western World* (1907), at the Court Theatre, London. The Russian Ballet, starring Karsavina and Nijinsky, which opened at Covent Garden on 13 June, shared the bill with Wolf-Ferrari's *Il Segreto di Susanna*. EMF wrote in his diary (20 June. KCC) that at the Ballet '[Lytton] Strachey, looking like Jesus Christ, attracted much attention between the acts. I met him with [Henry] Lamb the painter bounding like kittens in the corridor.'

INDIA, 1912–13

Forster set out on his long-prepared-for visit to India in October 1912, accompanied by Dickinson and R. C. Trevelyan and (for the sea-journey only) another Cambridge friend, Gordon Hannington Luce, who was to take up a post in Burma. The friends joined the ship in relays: Trevelyan and Luce in England, Dickinson in Cairo, and Forster himself, on 7 October, in Naples, after bringing his mother and her friend Mrs Mawe to Italy with him for a holiday. On arrival in Bombay Dickinson and Trevelyan set off for the famous cave-temples of Ajanta and Ellora while Forster went to stay with Masood in Aligarh. His first weeks in India were thus spent in Muslim India, and moreover in a circle of active Muslim nationalists, for Aligarh University was to a considerable extent the home of the future Muslim separatist movement. When, in late October, Masood took him to Old Delhi, they stayed at the house of Dr M. A. Ansari, one of the moderate leaders of this movement.

From Delhi Forster went to Lahore, to stay with Malcolm Darling, who was Assistant Commissioner there, and to rejoin Dickinson and Trevelyan. While in Lahore, the three friends went to Peshawar to visit their shipboard acquaintance, Kenneth Searight, and with him they went to see the Khyber Pass. Forster then set out alone to Simla in mid-November, taking up a casual invitation from the novelist 'Sara Jeannette Duncan'. From there he made a brief sight-seeing safari towards the Himalayas.

The three travellers assembled once more in Agra, and on 27 November they arrived in the remote princely state of Chhatarpur as guests of its eccentric Maharaja, an old friend and former pupil of Sir Theodore Morison.

After Chhatarpur the three friends split up finally, Dickinson and Trevelyan setting forth to South India and eventually to China. Forster, who was to spend Christmas with Malcolm Darling at Dewas, employed the intervening days in a circuitous journey through Rajputana.

His very happy stay at Dewas, which is celebrated in *The Hill of Devi*, was his real initiation into Hindu India. It was also the beginning of his important friendship with the Maharaja of Dewas. His route from Dewas took him through Allahabad and Benares to

Bankipore, where Masood conducted his legal practice. Forster drew heavily on this ugly town for the fictitious 'Chandrapore' in *A Passage to India*, and upon the Barabar Hills, which he visited on his return from Bankipore to Allahabad, for suggestions of the 'Marabar Caves'. His stay in Allahabad with his friend R. B. Smith, who was Assistant Magistrate there, gave him some not-very-favourable impressions of British officialdom, again reflected in *A Passage to India*

There followed a visit to Patiala, for a stay with the teacher and author Edmund Candler, a brief reunion with the Maharaja of Dewas in Delhi, and a tour through Jaipur and Jodhpur, and on to Bombay State to see the Jain temples at Mount Abu. On 20 March he set off for the last lap in his travels, a visit to Hyderabad, the Nizam's Dominions, where an English friend, May Wyld, was Principal of a girls' school. He saw also an Indian friend, Abu Saeed Mirza, one of a family of brothers with whom Masood was intimate and whom Forster had known slightly in England. Abu Saeed was a junior magistrate in Aurangabad and invited Forster to his home, as a jumping-off place for the cave-temples of Ellora. Fragments of his conversations with Abu Saeed, and of the latter's outbursts against British rule, are recalled in the final chapter of *Passage*.

105 To Robert Trevelyan

Harnham, Monument Green, Weybridge
26 August 1912

Dear Bob
  I'll begin a letter while I remember what I want to say.[1]
  (1) Will you kindly take my pith helmet on board with you—it's quite light and will be in a cardboard box. If you'll tell me where to send it to meet you, I'll do so. Where will you start from in London? N[ational] L[iberal] Club?—*You'll* do better to buy helmet at Port Said. But I have one.
  (2) What about deck chairs? If you like, I'll buy you one when I get mine, and have them packed together and delivered (to you) on board.[1] This should be cheaper than buying separately. At the A[rmy] and N[avy Stores], the simplest kind cost 4/– about; those in which you can lie down 11/–.
  (3) As soon as you get on board, you must see the head steward, and arrange that ultimately we are all put together for meals. I don't expect that this will mean you'll have to sit alone till we join you, as there'll be plenty of room to go where you like up to Naples; but I understand that one has to come to some understanding with the steward before the first meal comes off.
  (4) If you want to be inoculated go to S[t] Mary's Hospital Praed

Street, where a very charming Captain Hayden will say to you 'Shall
I do you in the belly?' Reply 'No: in the arm place please.' Then go
at once to bed. I was sore & inflamed for 36 hours: some for 48 hours
or longer. In about 8 days you go to him again. Being done in the
belly makes one unable to move.—I wish I hadn't let him: it
wouldn't have been anything otherwise.—There are no tropical
specialists in London now, though Charles will be back at the end of
the month.[2] Sir Arthur Bramfoot saw me at the India Office as a
friend's friend, but he is not practising.[3]

(5) See A[rmy] and N[avy] list for Tea Baskets, &[ct].
  Cummerbund—Sir A. says important for night in train.
  Keatings.
  Chlorodyne
  Quinine
  Your favourite Pill.
  Avoid celluloid *under*clothing
  Plenty of visiting cards.

Yours affectionately
E. M. Forster.

ALS: TCC

[1] Trevelyan and Gordon Hannington Luce (1889–1979), poet and orientalist, were to board
the *City of Birmingham* in England, EMF at Naples, and Lowes Dickinson at Port Said.
Luce was en route to Rangoon, where he married a Burmese lady and became a noted
authority on Burmese history. See *Essays Offered to G. H. Luce in Honour of His
Seventy-Fifth Birthday* (1966).
[2] Charles: unidentified.
[3] Sir Arthur H. Branfoot (1848–1914), Surgeon-General and President in 1911 of the
Medical Board, India Office.

106 To Florence Barger[1]

S. S. City of Birmingham off Perim[2]
[c. 17] October 1912

Dear Florence

I send a line—a little confused, for I sit, alone in morning dress, in
the midst of bridge-players. We began all by not dressing, but the
others have gone over to Society. I find that I really don't mind the
singularity, and since I can't find my evening tie, let Fate take its
course.

Well, I am very well, and usually happy. Drawbacks—military
element predominating, poor food, cabins small & full. Advantages—presence of Dickinson, Luce, & Trevelyan, beautiful seas
full of flying fish, fine weather, steady boat. The voyage has been
wonderful—especially the coaling at Port Said. (This is not a joke:
barges of coal with Arabs lying on it were tugged up and woke into
life; endless procession of men—& women—carrying coal in
baskets over planks to the light of antique lamps, held out by other

men; all chattering & shouting, & at times stopping their work to clap hands in unison. It is said to be the best coaling system in the world: it's certainly the merriest!) The canal after Port Said was in a way disappointing, for the East has been so painted that nothing was new. It was like sailing through the Royal Academy—a man standing by a sitting camel, followed by a picture of a camel standing by a seated man: picturesque Arabs in encampment, ditto in a felucca. Scene of Pharoah's mishap. Mount Sinai & god on the top in a cloud.—But to be serious: it is a wonderful canal, much longer than I realised & full of variety. Now we are leaving the Red Sea. The heat has always been bearable, and today, with a brisk wind & breaking seas, it has been delightful, and I have pranced about most of the time in much physical fitness.

They think us very queer on board, but are not uncivil & term us 'the professors'. The women are pretty rotten, & vile on the native question: their husbands better. The only person I am intimate with on board is a young officer. Sounds queer, doesn't it, but not as queer as he must sound to the army, for he reads, writes rather decadent stories, knows Pushtu, Urdu, Russian, Arabic, Italian &^{ct}, and hates society, God, & authority. He suits me very well. I've only known him a very short time of course, but shall try to go to see him in Peshawar, where he is quartered. He is very intimate with natives, & might show me a lot.[3] Truly there are more fish in the sea than were ever dreamed in our philosophy.—But George will wince—. Or is Hamlet not a classic, and so open to parody?

This is a a foolish & hastily written letter, but you will like to know that I am well and to receive my love

AND MY LOVE FOR HAROLD and for Evert since he cannot read XXXXXXX

They are all looking over me and interfering in the children's messages. I shall stop. ~~There is wild talk of sending~~ or

All too silly. I write no more.

Morgan.

ALS: KCC

[1] Florence Emily Barger, née Thomas (1879–1960) was of Welsh origin. She attended Liverpool University, where she studied the theory of education, and for many years she did part-time work as a school inspector. In 1904 she married her cousin, George Barger, EMF's undergraduate friend at King's; thus Florence came to know EMF. The Bargers had two sons, Evert and Harold, and a daughter Margaret. They were very friendly with the family of H. O. Meredith, whose wife Christabel was a fellow-educationalist. However, the two families indulged in a good deal of mutual criticism of their respective ways of bringing up children. Florence was a high-minded and sometimes censorious crusader for causes such as the Labour Party and feminism. EMF described her political activity as 'rushing about to interview people, denouncing others, and losing papers' (to William Plomer, 7 December 1960. Durham University). He and Florence developed a very close friendship; on the eve of this first visit to India, and for many years she was his closest woman friend and his principal *confidante* about his affair in Egypt with Mohammed el Adl. After George's death in 1939, Florence came to live in Hampstead. He told Plomer: 'She was my confidante, and as sometimes happens to

people when they are confided in, she became very broad-minded; less so in later years; but a
heroine and a darling always.'
² Perim: small island off the coast of Arabia.
³ This was Arthur Kenneth Searight (1883–1957), who joined the West Kent Regiment in
1904. He settled in Rome in 1926. He was good-looking in a Byronic way, and, as soon came
out in conversation, was a dedicated homosexual and kept a voluminous confessional diary.
He was stationed at Peshawar in 1912.

107   To Mary Aylward

In Doctor Ansari's House¹
Close to the Mori Gate   DELHI
30 October 1912

Dearest Maimie
   Thank you for your sweet letter—it nearly made me cry it was so
sweet. I wonder if you remember what you wrote though!
   Well what shall I write to you? My time since I landed a week ago
has been so marvellous that it will read like a dream. It has been one
ceaseless excitement and surprise, and I have fallen straight into
Indian (i.e. Native) life, which is a piece of luck that comes to very
few Englishmen.
   I'll begin with a bald catalogue of my doings
   Oct 22–23ʳᵈ at Bombay.
   23ʳᵈ & 24ᵗʰ in the train—the most comfortable I have ever travelled
in. I went straight to Agra, changed there, saw the Fort by
moonlight (but not the Taj), and reached Aligarh at 2.30 in the
morning of the 25ᵗʰ: there Masood met me and I have been staying
with him till this morning, when we both came to this friend of his at
Delhi—a most charming Doctor, and as hospitable as he's
charming. In three days I leave for Lahore.
   That's the outline of my doings; I have just written a long letter to
mother, and I think I'll describe to you what I *didn't* describe to
her—then you can exchange letters. I'll tell you about the shooting
expedition—you need not be disgusted; scarcely anything was shot,
and of course I didn't even try.
   We left Aligarh at 4.30. in the morning in a sort of starved
omnibus—I can't describe it better—very narrow & hard & angular.
Four of us were squashed inside, and the moonlight cast on the road
the shadows of many more who were squatting on the top among
the food. Dawn came—the great mosque of Aligarh looked
magnificent against the glow—and then we were in a country that
was flatter than anything you can imagine. It is as if you took a steam
roller over Salisbury Plain. After two hours the road ended in a huge
mud village, where we were welcomed by the local dignitary, a fat &
very kind Hindoo, who provided us with Bullock Carts and again
we went forward through clumps of pampas twelve feet high and

fields of cotton and castor oil plants, and ponds full of delicious 'water nuts'—the fruit of a reed, which the servants gathered for us and peeled. Presently we came to a village of converted Moham-medans where it had been arranged that we should eat the English food that we had brought with us, but they were so delighted to see Masood & my other companions that they insisted we should eat *their* food at *their* expense, and prepared a sort of municipal banquet in the square. The Head man's house had a broad arcade in front of it, in which they had ranged a row of beds for us to sleep on after lunch, and what I took to be a large bed to hold 10 little nigger boys all in a row, but this last was really the dinner table. The others squatted on it: I, being a heretic, could not squat, but perched on the edge, and in the middle was an extraordinary medley of food; you seemed to eat anything with everything or all at once. Cakes of maize and chili served with white curd sauce—these were so hot that my eyes poured water; but most of the food was very good, and we had three or four kinds of chupatties in which we wrapped the meat before swallowing it. After lunch we fell asleep on the beds, with the whole village looking on, and discussing us, but quietly, so as not to disturb us. They had—the old men especially—such beautiful manners, and thin fragile faces that seemed full of intelligence; though I suppose they are just the equivalent of a yokel on Salisbury Plain. Shaking hands was curious—they put both of theirs in yours, but without the slightest pressure; it was like saying how dye' do to a Greek statue. Hookahs were passed round, but not to me, because not being a Mohommedan, I should have defiled it and the village would have had to throw it away.

On we went again—still the enormous plain with birds in every direction: two cranes with their darling baby stalking between them, green parrots, mynas, countless doves, jays, water wag tails—all of them worthless from the sporting point of view, and an extra joy to me. Camels strolled about in a dégagé way, people with beautiful brown skins were working in the fields, and a cool refreshing breeze never stopped blowing, though the sky was cloudless. I am told the weather just now is perfect: it certainly seems so. As the sun set the moon rose, and wisps of blue mist came out of the pools—I did not fear them, having stuffed myself for this expedition with quinine: indeed I was particularly fit after it.—The moon was quite unlike your English article, which, as you know, I have always been so rude to. It coloured all the sky near it a wonderful pearly yellow and the sky beyond it was pale purple. I will never speak against the Indian moon. Now we returned—first to our lunch village and then to the village I first mentioned where the Hindu, dressed in a night shirt, sat under a straw canopy in a court yard, surrounded by screaming geese, and did the honours of another meal, while our belongings were shifted out of the Bullock

Carts into the omnibus. What a long confused sentence, but it was also a long & confused affair, for the Hindu, though forbidden to approach our table by his religion, yet did so out of politeness, darting forward to give us now some betel nut (which I liked) now some musk pills of his own making, which were not bad either, now some scent,—I enclose two examples of the scent. He talked English quite well, and I told him that, after I had enjoyed his present, I should send it to friends who would value it at home. It comes just as he gave it to me. No doubt the straws will smash in the post and the scent evaporate, but I know you would like something really Indian, given to me under that glorious moonlight. The rest of our expedition was less pleasant. We drove back in the omnibus to Aligarh too much scrunched up to fall asleep. We had been driving &ct exactly 22 hours![2]

I must end now—abruptly but with much love. I have written to May.[3]

Your loving & very happy
Morgan.

ALS: KCC

[1] Dr Muhktar Ahmed Ansari (1880–1936) was trained at Edinburgh University and settled in Delhi in 1910. He led the Red Crescent medical mission to the Balkans wars in 1912. He was a moderate in the Pan-Islamic movement and in 1918 helped to organise within the Khilafat movement constructive ways of bringing Hindus and nationalist Muslims together politically. He served as President of the Muslim League in 1918 and was President of the Indian National Congress in 1927.

[2] Nural Hassan Khan, a Deputy Collector of Aligarh, took EMF on this expedition to Khair (the first village visited) and to Jamon (perhaps the second village described here), south of Khair.

[3] May Wyld (d. 1970s), when both she and EMF were about twelve years old, came to know him and Lily through Maimie Aylward. She wrote (to PNF, 2 July 1971) that she remembered how Lily treated Morgan 'as if he were a piece of Dresden china. . . . I was already helping to look after five young brothers. Naturally I had no use for what seemed to me to be a lot of fuss about one boy who should be able to look after himself and I wondered why he did not rebel, throw away the shawls and mufflers and come out in the garden to play with me. Of course it was not really his fault. He had been cossetted all his life and knew no better. He did not even know what he was missing.' Miss Wyld lost touch with the Forsters for many years, and at the age of twenty-eight she went to India to be Principal of a girls' high school in Hyderabad, which, it turned out, did not exist. She therefore set out to create the institution that became the Mahoobia School for Girls. As the girls she attracted were from the 'better' families, they were strictly subject to Purdah, and May, who was plainly a fighter, resolved to try to accelerate history: 'I must support Purdah strictly so as to win confidence, I would somehow get the school going in spite of the prejudice of centuries, and I would start to make them want to break through to freedom themselves. I thought it would take some 150 years. Largely owing to two world wars it took about 40. . . . I would not allow myself to consider that I was attempting the impossible.' After ten years, chronic malaria forced her back to England. 'I fought through every kind of intrigue, secret and open, bias and prejudice, but by the time I came home I had a recognised school of over 100. We were still Purdah but they could no longer shut us down.' EMF's letter suggesting that he visit her presented problems, since she had no room in her bungalow, there was no hotel, and few English residents lived nearby. In her view: 'An Indian household was quite out of the question.' She could not have known then how easily he took to Indian ways. Cf. Letter 126.

108   To Laura Mary Forster

C/o Doctor Ansari (a friend of Masood's)
Close to the Mori Gate   Delhi.
31 October 1912

Dear Aunt Laura,

I forgot and began to write the way you dislike—hence the odd position of the address. We arrived here yesterday after a delightful week at Aligarh, and on arrival went to the Kutb Minar in a motor car.[1] This is sacrilege, but Masood has so little time, and it was a treat to make the expedition with him, he was moved so deeply by all the relics of vanished Mohammedan greatness with which the road is strewn. It seems foolish to describe to you what you can read in any book, but the drive is so fresh in my memory that I cannot think of anything else, and I don't think even the Taj will be more amazing. If one compares the country around Delhi to the Campagna (though as a matter of fact there is a touch of soft English blue in the distances)—then our 11 miles drive will stand for the Appian Way, but an Appian Way of incredible splendour, bordered with tombs of red sandstone and marble. From the greatest of these—the Emperor Humayun's—there is a view over the plain, covered with domes and ruined forts and mosques as far as the eye reaches, and in the distance modern Delhi, topped by the enormous Marconi apparatus that was used for signalling at the Durbar.[2] I am thankful to have seen the country before the new capital is built, for though it is supposed not to interfere with the Antiquities, there are terrible rumours of tidyings up and conversions, and of a Mint that is to be built in old Delhi, now a ~~ruined~~ deserted fortress with a glorious mosque. The Editor of the 'Comrade', Mohammed Ali, in other ways a most ~~offensive~~ untaking man, was talking about it to me last night; no doubt the Society for the Pres[ervation] of Old Buildings has its eye on the danger, and will do more good than the protests of M.A.'s ~~somewhat~~ petulant though clever paper.[3]

I sit—having after all never got you to the Kutb Minar but Sir F. Treves will do that much better—:[4] I sit in the verandah of the house of Masood's friend, with now a chicken running past and now a squirrel, and listen to the doves and green parrots making conversation in the garden. Twenty yards off is the city wall above which nothing is to be seen but blue sky and kites manoeuvring. Both garden and house are small, and it is a great kindness on Dr. Ansari's part to have put me up. Though a young man, he has already a large practice, and is at present out at a case. He seems as competent as he is charming, and I think I would as soon rely on him as on certain paler skins at home, whom I might mention by name but will not! After three days of his hospitality I go to the Darlings at Lahore, and Masood goes to Bankipore to his work.

Altogether I am charmed with India, and have had the rare privelege [sic] of dropping straight into native life. At Aligarh I was a guest at a village feast far out in the country. We banqueted in the public view on dishes of strange food, and slept afterwards, equally publicly, on beds that were drawn up in a row on the loggia. The manners of our hosts were perfect—courteous & grave—and one thought with shame of their social equivalents in modern England.—I also saw a good deal of the Aligarh College Professors, English & Indian. Masood's mother I did not see, but she sent me messages, and also a message for you, much wishing that your health could allow you to take so long a journey, as it would give her so much pleasure to welcome you in her house.

I must stop now, as breakfast—that is to say lunch—is at hand. It is a curious life, reminding one in some ways of the 18ᵗʰ century: for instance there are two 'poor dependents' in this house, distant cousins of Ansari's, who, though in no sense servants, will run messages, pick up fallen books, &ᶜᵗ, and who feed apart from us and sit on the more distant and uncomfortable of the chairs.

It sounds conceited, but I should be so glad to see my own letters again when I come back! my diary gets behind, and what I write to you and mother will be the freshest chronicle of my doings. I wonder what your weather is—here we have uninterrupted sun. I think I did acknowledge the long letter from you that I had at Bombay. I was so glad of it, and I wish that you were with me in my happiness.

Yours ever affectionately
E. M. Forster.

There are warm messages of greeting from Masood.

ALS: KCC

[1] Qutb Minar: tower of victory 238 feet high, with five storeys, associated with the Quwwat ul Islam Mosque, begun by Qutb-ud-din Ghori after the capture of Delhi in 1193.

[2] Humayun (1508–56), father of Akbar, was the second Mogul ruler. He was born in Kabul and ruled from 1530 until his death.

[3] The Comrade was a militant Muslim newspaper published at Aligarh, 1912–14. The editors were Mohammed Ali (1878–1931) and his brother Shaukat Ali, militant Muslim nationalists. 'Society . . . Buildings': apparently a reference to the Society for the Protection of Ancient Buildings, which is still active, with headquarters in London.

[4] Sir Frederick Treves, 1st Baronet (1853–1923), Royal physician of 'Elephant Man' fame, was also a world traveller; see his The Other Side of the Lantern (1905).

109 To Florence Barger

Doctor Ansari's House, Mori Gate, Delhi
2 November 1912

Dear Florence,

I have had enjoyed & mislaid your letter. I left Bombay before that mail arrived, but it greeted me soon after. I do hope that your cold gave way—it was evidently very bad when you wrote. As for Christabel, I wonder whether she may not soften to the situation when it approaches:—you or I should, but perhaps we are incapable of tragedy. It is awful should she continue to think that her life is ended. I am glad to hear the good account of Ralph & moderately good account of Sidney.[1]

As for myself—I am in the middle of a very queer life, whether typically Oriental I have no means of knowing, but it isn't English. I went straight from Bombay to Masood, first at Aligarh, his home, with its interesting of [sic] public-school-y college for Mahommedans; and then we came on to stop here with a friend of his. The house is small, and full of people who come in without being announced and sit over the room, or even on one's bed: I had three there last night, visiting Masood who lies sick of the plague-innoculation in the bed adjoining. They were nice chaps & talked English, and we had quite a merry time. Presently food was brought—this I am told is unusual—and they ate that on the bed too, sitting cross legged and shoeless. Then the dog came in, and then some one brought a cockatoo, and then—O Mercy!—I saw & slew a bug on my pillow. All the time I was half undressed, and the curtain being drawn—exposed to the view of other guests or patients or poor relations who were grouped on the sitting room sofa. Everyone was there but our host who was rambling over Delhi in a fly on his rounds, while little black boys here called wildly for him down the telephone. The climax came when—Oh mercy again!—the Cockatoo— —only on the mosquito curtain though.

Yesterday was altogether curious. Nothing happened, yet I enjoyed it greatly. We went to our host's rooms for M[asood] to be inoculated, and we waited—I do not exaggerate—three hours. The rooms are in the Bazaar, at the top of the Chandi Chauk [sic] which was the Piccadilly of the place in the days of the Emperors, and for most of the three hours I sat in a balcony watching the East pass.—[2]All this has been described, & I won't renew the attempt—merely selecting an old man, nearly naked, who held his grand son by one hand and an enormous sugar cane in the other, which he used as a walking stick. Behind us was the doctor's court yard with invalids sprawling over the floor awaiting their turn; and he seeing patients in semi publicity behind a straw curtain.—He is a good doctor from the European point of view, I believe, and certainly a nice chap.—At last I grew weary, & went to the Mosque. They said I should never find my way there, but by getting into a queer carriage & uttering its name, I arrived in ten minutes. A most glorious building—the courtyard raised on huge basement, colonnaded with sandstone galleries, and paved with marble. A tank in the middle, gateways on three of the sides, and the mosque proper filling up the fourth. You will have seen pictures of it, but they miss the colouring and accentuate its chief defect—the square screen that cuts the line of the central dome. (—But M.'dans here say it isn't a defect but a beauty. Their view of art is the patriotic, however, as are all their views. They are wild over the Balkan war, and with Grey for having hastened to acknowledge Italy in Tripoli.)[3]—I then saw the Friday prayers—impressive yet ridiculous to see hundreds of people squatting at once, with their faces on the ground. Some of the 'effects' were most dramatic. In the midst of the exercises a late comer would burst in through one of the doorways and fly like a maniac over the pavement, his bare feet slapping the marble. Or some little Harolds & Everts, instead of forming up in line like their elders, would do their prayers at an immense distance, out in the sun.[4] Sensible people kept in the cool, and the shadow of the minaret was full of them up to the tip.

I go to Lahore and Anglo-India tonight, but before I start my friends are having a nautch, mainly in my honour.[5] I wish they would not, partly because it will cost them so much, partly because I do not know the exact degree of festivity it connotes. It will be interesting though to experience really good Indian dancing & singing—one of each is to come—and I can be sure that it is the genuine article not one made for tourist consumption. It is to be in a house near. Our host's wife—whose aimiable presence manifests itself through gifts of cigarettes, betel nuts, and scent, but not through the flesh—says that she would not mind it here, but there is an English lady next door who might overhear, and spoil the doctor's practice by gossiping!

No, I didn't get an opportunity of talking to my mother about Weybridge. Perhaps I ought to have made one, but it was such a relief in Italy to see her dropping all domestic cares that I didn't like to.—Perhaps it *wouldn't* do to mention it to her under these circumstances, unless the conversation so turned that you could refer to it on your own account, without mentioning your talk with me.—I have asked her to let you see some of my letters some time—here & there they may interest you, but I'm bad at writing for more than one person at a time.

I'll end by remarking that I have enjoyed myself in India ever since I landed. It is quite different from anything anyone says, but of course I have had great luck. When I happened to say on the boat that I was going to stop with a native, my table-neighbour was so horrified that after one gasp she changed the conversation. One was also told that Indian food is impossible—quite untrue; now and then a dish is too rich or too hot, but one can always pick good things out of the fare, and the puddings are always delicious.

To end, with love to all.
Morgan.

ALS: KCC

[1] There was a prolonged debate in the Meredith family as to whether Christabel should continue her professional career as an educationalist. Christabel, who was born in 1876 and died in 1945, went to Newnham College, Cambridge, in 1898 and was Lecturer in Education at Liverpool University, 1905–6; Mistress of Method at Homerton College, Cambridge, 1909–12; and Lecturer in Educational Psychology at the Roehampton Froebel Institute, 1928–38. She married H. O. Meredith in 1906, and there were problems about her combining a family with a career. Meredith tended to take her side. She was politically left-wing and became even more so after a visit to Russia in the 1930s. Ralph and Sidney were twins born in 1908.
[2] Chandni Chowk: main business street of Old Delhi.
[3] By the Peace of Ouchy, 15 October 1912, Turkey relinquished Tripoli and recognised Italian control there. England had followed suit.
[4] The Bargers' sons: Harold (1907–) and Evert (1910–75).
[5] Lahore: EMF is off to stay with the Malcolm Darlings. Darling was then Assistant Commissioner at Lahore and an Under-Secretary to the Government of the Punjab.

110   To Alice Clara Forster

Nabla House, Lahore.   6 November 1912

Private Sheet.

Dearest dearest

Had your letter of Oct. the 17th yesterday. I wish I had warned you more about the delay there would be in hearing from me. I really became quite anxious about my own safety when I read of your anxiety. Poor dear! I posted at Port Said on the 11th, but my letter evidently had to wait for a mail boat—they don't run daily.

Am delighted to hear of your successful stay in Rome, & feel so proud of my part in getting there—the other part is Mrs Mawe's: she always thought it would be nice to go. Thank her too for her letter. I wonder what you will do with your little gifts.

As for W[illiams] & D[eacon's Bank] I am telling them to put £25 more to your account. How glad I am that I remembered to send the other £25. I am *almost* sure that I have paid the Sept. payment before leaving England. That would have been £35. You can find out quickest by asking them. I also enclose a note to them which you can send if you want a larger sum—it is so wretched to be tight, and you might have something you wanted to do at Xmas. It had better be sold after Jan 1st though—the interest would then not be lost.

I wish that you would go to Maimie's for Xmas. Surely Aunt Eliza would understand that you would prefer not to be at Plymouth *then*. Could you not put it openly? When I left we left England, you had already thought it possible that you would go to Maimie's. Do tell Aunt E. that you think you will. You see, if you are at Weybridge, you will either have someone to stay, which I don't think you would care for, or if you do not, you will be pestered by Rosie, Werter Road, &ct, to go over to them. I am sure that Maimie's is much the best plan. I do hope that you will do this. There! I grow quite like a female, underlining my words in my attempt to persuade sweet Mummy.[1]

The shortest way to the Sistine Chapel! Well I never! To think it still goes on. I am sorry you sparred over the guide book, but it is a common battle ground. In her letter to me she says you are splendid at knowing Rome—an amende honorable, I think. Now for a more public sheet of paper.

I think I last wrote from Delhi, but soon after my arrival. I had a very happy four days there in rather a poky little house belonging to Masood's friend. He is a doctor, and I imagine very good, and quite charming. The life is impossible to describe—every one here says that I must have been treated with real intimacy; it certainly felt intimate. You had food when you liked, and very much where. Whenever I came in, tea & poached eggs came on a tray or else I found luke-warm pilau and chapatties in the dining room. These appeared to be the chief form of nourishment. There were three dogs, a cat, & a cockatoo, all loose over the room, to say nothing of unbidden guests, like lizards; the garden was full of queer carriages & the sitting room full of queerer people who came in unannounced and sat about on sofas and chairs—not invalids, I think, for Doctor Ansari's rooms were in the Bazaar, but the friends of invalids. Meanwhile Masood lay sick—not very sick—of the plague-inoculation, and all his friends came to see him, and sat on his bed and on my bed—we shared a room—and on the luggage, and on one another's laps, and more food came in and the cockatoo screamed for grapes.

Of course I did some sight-seeing, and saw the stone elephants and the place on the wall where the King & Queen showed themselves at the Durbar, but the Fort at Delhi was rather a disappointment to me. The buildings, though beautiful, are small & scattered, and overshadowed by ugly barracks. I preferred the Great Mosque and—best of all—the country outside the city, which is like a glorified Appian Way. My best time was at the end, when Ansari, who had not been able to see much of me, insisted on treating me to a Nautch.[2] I did not want him to, partly because of the expense, partly because I was a little nervous at the exact degree of festivity I was in for! However all was perfectly comme il faut; a modern ballroom is shocking in comparison. It took place in the middle of the Old City, a most romantic place,—on the roof of a house belonging to one of his friends. The ladies—two—salaamed us on arrival—one with a queer but charming face and delightful manners; the other less charming, in white knickerbockers, and enclined to en bon point; she wore a nose ring. There were five musicians and several attendants who robed the dancers. We sat cross legged or as cross as we could on the floor, and as I knew every one there—about 9 or 10, all Indians—it was really a very homely and pleasant evening. "Was it beautiful?"—Well the noise was often excruciating—the musicians seemed out [of] tune and playing in different keys, I could never seldom follow the rhythm, and the ladies' voices went into my ears like battering rams; but the dresses & gestures were so lovely, and the singing was clearly so emotional that I did get a great deal of pleasure from it. For instance, the charming one did a peacock dance; very slow, scarcely moving the feet, but gradually a shawl of scarlet and gold over her head. This was the peacock's tail, and at the climax of the dance she let a wonderful gold border appear at the edge of the shawl, and made it quiver between her outstretched hands as though it was alive. Then she did a dance in which she flew imaginary kites—first letting them out & then pulling them in; most delightful. Her songs began—as is usual—with exercises to show the flexibility of the voice; then came a mystic address to God in the classical style and then human love songs, which were easier to follow, and which she gave sitting in our midst with her lovely robes spread around her. The second singer—who had covered the knickerbockers with a blue dress—was not as good. The entertainment lasted 3 hours—that is to say as long as I stopped; I was the chief guest. I complimented the chief lady as well as I could through an interpreter, upon which she shook hands. I think they had told her it was an English custom. It was now midnight. I drove on to the station with Masood & Ansari, and there sat Baldeo with all the luggage, and I got straight into the Lahore train, undressed, and had a very good night. Is it not a queer life!

Malcolm met me at the station, since when I have had one round of dinner parties, visits to educational institutions, &ᶜᵗ. I'm all in a whirl. The house is charming, but Lahore is a beastly place—I wish for selfish reasons that they were not here. Dickinson says it is like an American town endless broad dusty roads with half finished buildings in desolate gardens. None of the cabmen know where anything is, and much time is spent jiggling about in search of colleges &ᶜᵗ. We are late for everything, but I gather everyone is in India when they aren't too early.

I have broken off to illustrate my own words. We were due to dine with Mʳ Turner, a missionary, head of the Y.M.C.A. here; Dickinson & Mʳˢ D[arling] drove off in the carriage, while we went for the equivalent of a cab.³ Nothing came. We sent out one servant after another (1) the groom (2) the messenger (3) Malcolm's private servant (4) the 'thief catcher', who is himself a thief and is paid to guard the house from his friends—and heard them all screaming in the darkness. At last a carriage came—but it belonged to our host who had sent it for us. We arrived a mere 40 minutes late for dinner.

The missionary was so nice: quite the most charming man I have met there. He knows Indian life much better than the civilians, and was most sympathetic, and full of fun. Though a missionary he is also rich, having married an American heiress: I think he too was American. He will take us through the native city at night after we return from Peshawar. We have already driven through by day. It is far queerer than Delhi—indeed it is said to be the most interesting in India after Peshawar & Hyderabad—but it is some way from these desolate streets of the English quarter.

My plans have altered. After Peshawar I go with D[ickinson] & T[revelyan] into Rajpootana, and end up at Dewas, returning after Xmas to Lahore for my main visit. I enjoy stopping here. Mrs Darling or 'Josie' as I entitle her is so very nice—I like her more & more. Malcolm isn't very well—just recovering from fever & overwork. The little boy too is very backward and peaked; poor baby, he had enteric of all things when they were in Simla this summer. He is two and only says the word of words as yet—I mean of course 'puff puff'. But he is robust on his legs and takes long strolls with us.

Baldeo continues satisfactory. The Darlings approve of him, but not of Dickinson's & Bob's servant, who cheats them more than one ought to be cheated, and last night was either drunk or else very queer; the other servants, who hate him, say the former. B's cheating is most moderate; "he keeps to the *custom*" is the phrase the D's apply to him; this is the equivalent of having a good servant. It is also the custom for the employer spasmodically to protest, and yesterday I selected 3 dusters for the battlefield which ought to be 2^d each and had been charged 3^d in the bill. A rending scene—he produced the dusters, which certainly were good ones. However I wasn't there to be reasonable, and as I knew that the other charges were also a little higher than they should be, I kept to my point. He is said not to mind at all, and doesn't seem to. I like him much better than any other servant I have seen, and when you come in tired and want to be treated as a baby, it is very nice to have someone who will do it, even if he's paid to.

7 November 1912

Thursday morning—7.30.
I am in bed. B. has brought me tea and I have explained successfully that he is to stop here while I go to Peshawar: there seemed no need to take him. We go at 12.0. and arrive towards midnight. Friday we go up the Khyber Pass with Searight. It will be most thrilling.

Bob is not here but with friends of his own a couple of miles off. We arrange joint expeditions. The country round is as flat as Aligarh, but more beautiful for there are fine trees. On the whole I am disappointed with the vegetation—It looks like England until you look into it; very seldom a palm or even a cactus. I believe the south will be different.

Dickinson is in good form. He was funny the other day about the 'cool note' that Swinburne wrote to Emerson. "I was annoyed with Emerson so I wrote him a cool note....I reminded him that he was an old and now toothless ape who had hoisted himself on the shoulders of Carlyle to a platform of his own finding and fouling!"[4]—Talking about Apes, the other morning a beautiful man in a purple turban appeared outside my window with two and a goat, squatted down and began to play on a drum that was shaped like a dice box, and to sing in sweet tones a mixture of English & Urdu about Mon kee. I thought this was a usual event. Not at all. Monkey man never been there before. Great excitement. M[rs] Darling ran for her child, all the servants came—and then alas! we of the quality had to go to breakfast, for there were visitors, and all through the cultured conversation we could hear the monkey man's drum in the distance. We were told that the monkeys did wonderful things. At the end they were married and sat together on the back of the goat, and finally all three salaamed. I can't think why one entertainment is so delightful and another a bore. We all agreed we could [have] listened to that particular man for a long time.

I must stop now. I am only taking a little luggage to Peshawar, & must pick it out myself. B. packs very nicely. Have had a card from Ruth. Much love again to you both.

Loving Morgan.

ALS: KCC

[1] It was a relief to EMF that Lily had distractions from his absence and from the recent deterioration in their relations.

[2] Another guest was the Muslim nationalist, Mohammed Ali, who was next door contemplating suicide after hearing of the Bulgarian army's approach to Constantinople. He was saved 'by the unexpected appearance of a Muslim friend [Masood] who had graduated from Oxford not long before and was on this occasion accompanied by an English fellow-graduate of that University who was his guest [i.e. EMF] and had expressed a desire to see an Indian *Nautch*. Arrangements had been made *sub rosa* [because *nautch* dancers were not acceptable guests in a respectable home] and the place selected was the house of a barrister who was my next door neighbour.... my friend would not take any denial and almost bodily ... carried me by main force to the private *Nautch* party next door' (Ali, *My Life: A Fragment*, p. 36).

[3] Colonel George Douglas Turner (1880–1945?) was a lay missionary. His wife Mary Borden Turner (1886–1968) wrote under the pen name Bridget McLagan.

[4] Dickinson takes his cue from Edmund Gosse, *The Life of Algernon Charles Swinburne*, Bonchurch Edition, XIX, 193: 'It was a courteous and reasonable letter [that Swinburne wrote to Emerson]' after an anonymous author wrote that Emerson had 'condemned Swinburne severely as a perfect leper and a mere sodomite, ... ' (This was 'Emerson: A Literary Interview', in *Frank Leslie's Illustrated Newspaper* [3 January 1874], p. 275.) Actually, Swinburne wrote no such letter.

111   To Alice Clara Forster

                                          Lahore. 12 November 1912

Dearest Mother

Your Perugia letter has come. What a dreadful nuisance about the luggage at Rome. I think that if once they had given the 'scontrino' they had no right to reject it, but of course it is no moment for rights. I'm so sorry the weather was bad. Sneak never mentioned that she had had indigestion, but kind Mrs Mawe, she told me!!¹ I often wonder about your rheumatism, but feel sure you will never let me know if it is bad, in case of worrying me!

Well, instead of badinage, I must begin, for there is so much to tell and so little time. Plans again altered as a most kind invitation has come from Mrs Cotes ('Sarah Jeannette Duncan') to stop with them at Simla; I am going up by the night train while D. & T. go to Delhi, and I rejoin them at Agra.²

The chief excitement since I last wrote is of course Peshawar. I longed for you to be there. We drove into the borderland between India and Afghanistan, which belongs to neither and is guarded by the 'Khyber Rifles' twice a week so that the caravans may pass. It is the most thrilling thing I have ever seen. We lunched on a patch of grass at the bottom of a ravine, and watched all the peoples and animals of Central Asia pass closely by us. Camels of two kinds—the ordinary and the splendid Bactrian—donkeys with hens and puppies and children all tied together on their backs, horses, goats, sheep, buffaloes. The people, especially the men, were most beautiful and walked like kings. They dressed in every kind of garment or its absence, and always successfully. The children were also charming, and as fair as English people. The ladies, poor dears, were the least attractive—of course they had the most to do, so it was not surprising. The procession went on for an hour and a half, and in both directions. Many of the mountaineers were coming in to spend the winter in Peshawar, so it was a particularly fine caravan, and as Searight could talk their language—Pushtu—we learnt something about them. Each caravan was closed by an escort of Khyber rifles, and at 2.30. the Pass was cleared, and left to barbarism until the next caravan day. We drove back to the frontier—Jamrud—where all new arrivals were disarmed—and in spite of jibbing horses and breaking traces were back in Peshawar for tea. I ought just to describe the scenery. Peshawar lies in a pocket among the mountains. The plain is a flat desert, and the high lands begin suddenly, like scenery on the stage, and the Khyber Pass goes straight into them, as a road goes into a gate way and does not begin to rise until a mile or two further on. It is not fine scenery, but very impressive.

EMF wearing a Mahratta turban, perhaps in Dewas. *Below* The palace of Chhatarpur, where he stayed with Trevelyan and Lowes Dickinson in 1912.

I am describing every thing backwards. Dickinson and I went alone to Peshawar, leaving Bob behind, as he was said to be suffering from German Measles. He was stopping with a friend of his here, isolated in a tent in the garden from which he was always bursting to talk to people, and we left him very peevish saying 'Well if the whole regiment *did* get it, what would it matter? I feel all right, & why shouldn't I come?' I said to Dickinson 'I'm sure Bob means mischief', and sure enough when Searight met us at Peshawar station he had a wire saying 'No measles, am coming to morrow morning.' It turned out that the nursemaid of Bob's friend's children had told him that she was quite sure he had not the measles, ~~armed~~ comforted by which he sent for the doctor again, and made him agree with her, and was just in time to catch the night mail. I never thought myself he had them—it was so very slight—and I admire his perseverance in trampling difficulties.

He had to go to the Hotel, but D. & I put up in the Regimental spare room, behind the Mess. I feel compelled to alter my opinion of soldiers, these were so charming, and without the least side, and their hospitality passes anything I could have imagined. Not only did they want to drive one everywhere & pay for everything, but one of them after half a day's acquaintance begged me to stop with his brother in Bombay when I went there again, and Dickinson, after not half a day but half an hour, is in the possession of an introduction to the brother of another in Hong Kong. The first night was a guest night; the band played during dinner, and afterwards they danced pas seuls up and down the verandah to its music. Dickinson and the one elderly officer sat indoors like two pa's, but the rest grew friskier and friskier: they were very young for the most part. Searight would make me dance with him, and also rode on Bob's back. Every one got covered with white wash stuff and the clothes of some were torn by the spurs of the cavalry. We then played an absurd card game, but not for long, and ended with supper, where a charming & reckless boy would prepare me a 'Prairie Oyster'—quite the most horrible & senseless thing I have ever swallowed—a raw egg rolling in vinegar, red pepper & sherry. In spite of their folly, many of them were sensible talkers and had even read a good deal. Searight's Bungalow was close to the Mess Room, and we spent any spare time there was in his charming sitting room. It was very good of him to have us, for we were queer fish to be in such a place, to say nothing of the expense. Dickinson was called 'The Don', and I overheard one saying to the other about me "Oh I say—! Will he put me into a book?" S. did us proud to the last, driving us over the native city and seeing us off by the midnight train. D. and I took his servant with us, and left Baldeo behind here; I was glad to be back to him, for D.'s gives me the shudders and is—according to ideas out here—im-

pertinent: he comes into the room with his shoes on unless re-
buked!³

We had a pleasant night in the train, and were met at Lahore
station by Turner, the charming missionary I have already
mentioned to you, who arranged to take us over the native city here
the same evening. We had tea with him, drove to one of the gates,
and plunged into it on foot. We went into Hindu Temples & saw the
priest, naked to the waist, singing hymns to Krishna. We went into
the Arya Somaj building—the reformed Hinduism, which is to the
old thing what Protestantism is to R[oman] C[atholic]'s.⁴ Then to an
opium den—nothing much, and Turner was very sensible about the
opium. He says that the Indian, unlike the Chinaman, understands
it use and does himself no harm, and that the Government, by
discouraging it, are driving the natives to alcohol, which they do *not*
understand. He is the only Englishman I have met who seems to care
for the people. The officials &ᶜᵗ may understand them, but it is
always against the grain in their case. Turner lived in the city three
years before marrying his heiress. He showed us his old house, and
his neighbours seemed delighted to see him again. He told us how he
used to hear them discussing him. One said 'He is a government
spy'. The other said 'No—he has committed some grave sin, and is
living among us as a punishment'! Then we met a young barrister
friend of his & went into *his* house. The entrance was dark and
narrow, and on either side of the passage ran an open drain. Upstairs
we sat on chairs round a low table on which a lamp sputtered sadly,
listening to our host's description of his day. He had defended a
client who had bought a wife for 50 rupees from another man. "Ah
Krishna, Krishna!" said Turner, the missionary suddenly popping
out. "Did I not tell you that you would rue the day that ever you
entered this damnable profession." Mʳ Krishna smiled gently, and
feeling that he ought to be confused, covered his face with his hands.
Then he took us on to his balcony, which, like all the wood work in
the city, is beautifully carved, and we looked up and down the
marvellous street and heard the conches and drums sounding from
the temples and the chatter of the people. It was now quite dark, and
we went by back alleys to our carriage, buying some pictures of gods
on the way. My feeling about India is that if one *hadn't* introductions one would miss all the best things; it is impossible that
the ordinary tourist should do all that I have done, and I do feel
lucky and grateful.—

From the Native city we went on to a dinner party, and here
'the force of Nature could no further go' I nearly fell off my chair
with fatigue during dessert. Fortunately it was not formal.

Yesterday was fairly light. Someone to lunch, out to the Club for
tea and a dinner party given to us at a Hotel by Mohammedans in the
evening. Today is lighter still. ———

Off to Simla. Great haste. Servants in rows wanting Tips.

Love,
Poppy

ALS: KCC

[1] Scontrino: ticket or receipt. Sneak: Lily, scolded for her slyness.
[2] Everard Cotes (1862–1944) was Managing Director, Eastern News Agency, 1910–19; and on the London staff of *The Christian Science Monitor*, 1927–39. Sara Jeanette (Duncan) Cotes (1862?–1922), Canadian-born novelist and journalist.
[3] For Dickinson's description of this visit, see his *Autobiography*, p. 178.
[4] Arya Samaj: Hindu reform movement founded in 1875 in Bombay, by Dayananda Saraswati (1824–83), based on the undiluted authority of the four Vedas.

112   To Alice Clara Forster

Agra.   21 November 1912

Dearest Mother

Your sweet and long letter awaited me here. I have only read it once yet. Yes, I do well remember Nov 1st at Florence, but fancy it being 11 years ago. I was so interested in all you told me, and especially that you had found new things to see. I wonder whether you will have given up Venice. I hope so, though you will hate Montreux. I had a letter from Aunt Laura too, the rest of my mail was poor, dear Ruth having sent notices from W[orking] M[ens'] C[ollege], Buenos Ayres Railway, Society for [the Protection of] Ancient Buildings, Charles that he had new patterns, &ct.

I wonder whether you will go to Maimie for Xmas. I do hope so. I am sure *she* wants it.

I am very sorry that you are both San Bernardino's.[1] Don't overdo it—though when you read the rest of my letter you may say 'Who am I to talk!'

This being a private page, I will tell you about the Indian tuffet. It is quite nice—a little 'carry away' in a wooden box, and as every house has a man whose sole duty is to wait on its pleasure, it does get carried away. It lives in the Bath room that is attached to every bedroom, and, holding its hand, is the bath—a large tin tub standing in an enclosure, with a stone ridge like a fender fencing it off from the room, and with a hole in the wall behind, through which the water runs, when Heaven knows what becomes of it. Hot water is brought on the tuffet man's back in a large tin, embossed, I know not why, with the figure of an elephant. Cold water lives in an earthenware urn by the side of the bath. 'Drinking' water in the familiar bottle.

I am very well always, and I think enjoying India much more than the others: very much indeed, in fact, and I wish my letters might help Mummy to share my pleasure.

Well, contrary to all my theories, I have been wanting you to be

EMF, wearing R.B. Smith's jodhpurs, in Allahabad. *Below* Vishwanath Singh Bahadur, Maharaja of Chhatarpur.

here all the week, and especially at Simla! Imagine my lovely bed
room—a blazing fire one end, and French Windows opening on to a
terrace of roses the other, beyond which I saw 70 miles of hills to the
main chain of the Himalayas. Always bright sun, and though it was
freezing in the shade, there was no wind, so one did not feel the cold.
I was never in such a delicious climate. One had all the joys of
summer and winter at once. Simla was deserted, though the
Government was still there in theory, and there were none of the
smart people whom I feared to meet. But I will go back to Lahore.

We all left it by the night train—Dickinson & Trevelyan in the
Delhi carriage and I in the Simla. I slept nicely, and got out at the
junction for Simla early in the morning. There I got into the
mountain railway, which takes 7 hours more—too long to admire
scenery however splendid—and I fell asleep again till we stopped at
a station for breakfast. Such a twisty woggly journey; some people
get ill with it. The engine turns round and looks into the carriage in
the most alarming way.

Simla is on a very thin ridge, so that you get views both sides. No
one is allowed a carriage except the Viceroy, the Governor of the
Punjab and the Mail; and every one else goes about in rickshaws,
drawn by four men. The Cotes sent theirs for me, and an
assistant-journalist, Digby by name, also met me.[2] I did not like him
at first, but he turned out nice, with a voice & jokes like Arthur
Gillett's. M[r] Cotes himself was charming—the vigourous athletic
type, but not the least alarming. He took me a delightful ride. M[rs]
Cotes was clever & odd—at times very nice to talk to alone, but at
times the Social Manner descended like a pall. Her niece completed
the household; they were busy packing up for Delhi, and in great
excitement over the change of capital, as are all. Their Simla house is
quite English, with a hall, staircase of dark wood, &[ct]: indeed all the
time I was in Simla, I forgot I was in India; there is nothing there but
government & scenery.—Oh I forgot though: I did go to an
'advanced' Mohammedan wedding. Very queer it was. In a garden,
with crowds of guests, some of whom, we heard afterwards, were
hostile. The bride wore no veil and sat with the bridegroom on a
hideous sofa in the garden, while the moulvi (=priest) sat on an
armchair opposite, very ill at ease, because it is the first wedding
without Purdah that has ever taken place in the district, and he
feared a row. The stage directions were given by the bridegroom's
brother in English, which every one understood: every sort of
religion was present, as they had scattered invitations all over Simla.
We had verses from the Koran, a poem on 'Conscience'—for which
there is (significantly) no Urdu word: the poet had to use the
English one. His poem was translated line by line by a friend. Then
the Moulvi married them and then he delivered an address to the
audience, justifying himself for having done so. But there is a fearful

row about it, I hear, and some of the Moslem congregation are trying to excommunicate him. At the time they seemed ~~peaceable~~ quiet enough, and partook of luke warm tea, as we did. Proceedings ended with a gramophone. Next day the bridegroom's brother came to thank us for countenancing it. It was very interesting, and he was a worthy man, but a more higgledy piggledy undignified performance I have never seen. As Mrs Cotes said, it was like George Trevelyan's marriage, with a service tinkered up for the occasion by Mrs Humphry Ward.³—Another day at Simla I went up the hill behind the town that is full of monkeys. A holy man is on the top, and if you pay him he feeds the monkeys and calls them with his little drum. They even come into the town, and I was woken up every night with one dancing on the corrugated tin roof of the house. They are most naughty.—But my best time was at the end. Malcolm Darling had told me what to do, and the Cotes were very kind in helping me. I hired two coolies at ten pence each, put my bed clothes and Baldeo's on their heads, and walked for four hours into the mountains, up the Hindustani–Thibet road. Then I did long for dear mummy again: the road was smooth and not steep, and she would have come in a rickshaw. The last four miles were the most impressive I've ever walked—the whole range of the Himalayas along the horizon and between them and me the queer crinkled outlines of the lower hills, coloured purple and dark brown. The Himalayas too were odd shapes—one like a Landseer Lion, another a house with a gable, a third like a volcano—and all were covered with snow which turned pale rose at sunset. They were—see earlier parts of letter—nearly 70 miles away, but as clear as the houses over Monument Green. At sunset I reached the Dak Bungalow or Rest House—to which I had previously telephoned. Baldeo and the coolies had arrived, a fire of deodar logs was burning, tea on the table, dinner cooking, every thing most comfortable. There was a broad verandah, where I sat till it grew too cold, watching the mountains in the moonlight. Dinner—very good—then bed, and all my clothes + an eider down of Mrs Cotes' kept me warm. In the morning, after tea in bed, I walked to the edge of the ridge down which the Hindustani road falls before it makes its next rise into Thibet. I passed a thorn bush, covered with scarlet & white rags. This meant it was sacred. At the root were one or two stones, painted red. A little boy sat guarding the shrine, and salaamed me very politely. I also met a three legged dog who came with me wherever I went.—However, all this only took ½ an hour. I went back to real breakfast at the Bungalow, and there Mr Digby joined me, having risen at 6.30. and ridden out from Simla on a horse. We walked back, disputing most of the way on the nature of the Universe—he is a scientist, or, rather, has the scientific mind.—and reached Simla in time for lunch. I left it by the evening train, changed into the Agra train down in the Plains at 1.0. in the morning, reached Agra in another ten hours, and, though I slept as usual, must acknowledge that I am a wee bit tired, especially in the muscles of my feet and knees. The mountain air is so good that one notices nothing at the time, and the great height—nearly 10,000 feet or over twice as high as Cortina—did not trouble me as it does some people.[4] In fact I'm in love with the Himalayas and think I should have gone further towards Thibet if I hadn't promised to join D[ickinson] and T[revelyan] there.

Now you will want to hear about Agra & the Taj. Well, I don't intend to be original. It is certainly one of the finest buildings in the world. Of course you know it to weariness in photographs, but they never convey its size. Each side of the tomb itself is as big as the façade of a great Cathedral, and the tomb rises on a platform of marble which platform is as big as a Piazza, and at each corner of it is a minaret. All this is white marble. Then the platform itself is raised high above the ground on marble walls through which staircases are cut, and the ground itself is a garden full of fountains and cypresses and sweet smelling trees, with raised tanks and terraces—again of marble—so arranged that one may get beautiful views of the tomb. This sounds all, but it is not. Round the garden is a boundary wall of red sand stone, broken here and there by the most magnificent gate-ways which would be a show by themselves in any other place, only here we all hurry through them to reach the tomb. I forgot to say that the further side of the tomb is washed—or to be accurate—sanded—by the River Jumna, and being placed at a bend is seen for a long way up and down stream.

There! yet another description of the Taj has been written. After that, I won't go on to describe the Fort, which we visited this morning and which I liked more than the Fort at Delhi, though they say I am perverse. Anyhow it is very fine: I will send you a p. c. that brings in both it and the Taj. Agra is the only place that provides good post cards. There are several tourists here—the first I have struck. This afternoon we drove out to another tomb, of which much might again be said, but I won't. Considering I only arrived at midday yesterday, I have not done badly. We are in a Hotel—the first I have had to go to since Bombay. It is very comfortable.

Plans are all in the melting pot again—it scarcely seems worth while mentioning. Bob is in one of his fidgety moods and feels he shall never get in China if they don't hurry up, so he is rather hustling poor Dickinson. Rajputana is off for them—not for me, as I shall see it after Xmas—and we now go to Gwalior and to Chattarpore. What a name, and what a place! It is the abode of Morison's Raja ('My dear King') and I have just written him the most amazing letter, pronounced by the others to be thoroughly oriental and very good.[5] "I should further be grateful if Your

Highness would tell me the name of the railway station nearest to Your capital" is a good specimen sentence. Going there and seeing the Khuharajo [*sic*] temples will take at least a week, and then I expect to part with T. & D. as they are going too far East. I shall go I don't [know] where—perhaps to Bhopal—and must rather beat time till the 20th of December, when I go to Dewas. Or if the Rajah of Chhatarpore is nice and asks me to, I might linger there. I gather from Morison though that he is more likely to ask me to than to be nice, as he *will* talk Herbert Spencer and Marie Corelli till one nearly screams.

I meant to chatter further to my dearest, but sleep overcomes me and I must finish a letter to Aunt Laura too. I do hope that you will hear from me as usual next week, but the postal arrangements at Chhatarpur may be queer, so don't be anxious. Three of my letters (all to people in India) have miscarried, so I feel sceptical. Perhaps they are in Baldeo's pocket, though he says not. He continues a great comfort to me. My love to Mrs Mawe.

Yes we *must* go to Assisi &ct together. How sweet of you to suggest it, *and* how rash, because I shall keep you up to it. I was much amused at your account of the Simi. How little it changes. Yes, is not Mrs Tribe repellant. Much love again.

Poppy.

ALS: KCC

1 The travellers had apparently encountered some exorbitant charges in Italy. Saint Bernardino (1439?–95) was a crusading reformer and preacher against usurers.
2 This may have been Everard Digby (1882–19??), who was Assistant Manager of the Associated Press in India.
3 In 1904 G. M. Trevelyan married Janet Ward, daughter of the novelist Mrs Humphry Ward (1851–1920), who wrote an idiosyncratic marriage service and had it performed by her favourite Unitarian clergyman, Dr Estlin Carpenter of Manchester College, Oxford.
4 Cortina d'Ampezzo, in the Austrian Tyrol, where the Forsters stayed for some time in 1902; see Letter 42.
5 This was Vishwanath Singh Bahadur, Maharaja of Chhatarpur (1866–1932), Sir Theodore Morison's former pupil. The Raja was a fantastic and somewhat muddled personality who turns up in various memoirs of Indian travels. See, for example, William Rothenstein on his visit there in 1910 (*IE*, pp. 28–31). The Raja is the original of the 'Maharaja of Chokkrapur' in J. R. Ackerley's *Hindoo Holiday: An Indian Journal* (1932).

113   To Alice Clara Forster

Guest House, Chhatarpur, Bundelkhand,
Central India.   1 December 1912

Dearest Mother
    Letters reach this paradise slowly, and I may have to post this before I receive your (third) letter from Florence. I seem to keep on saying 'this *is* the best of all', but really Chhatarpur <u>is</u>. The scenery, of which I have often complained, is here most lovely. The Guest

House stands on a ridge, and from its broad Verandah we look down on the temples of the city, rising out of trees, and over a green plain out of which rise other ridges, and hills like the Dartmoor Tors. The whole country is Jungle. Tigers—(but far too well mannered to eat men)—reside quite near, and monkeys of the sweetest sort come & sit in the trees half a dozen yards away. The ladies sit with their babies clinging to them; the gentlemen swing about in search of tropical fruit. Half a mile off is the Palace, where we go daily, and between us and it is a tank in which the population bathes. The nearest Englishman is 15 miles off, and the nearest Ry Station 35. So we have gone & done it.

We arrived at the station 4 days ago, in the evening, and the Maharaja's motor met us—the servants came on with the luggage afterwards. It was a wonderful moonlight drive. Bob's hat flew off. At the Guest House we were welcomed by many officials but no supper. It came at last, but oh so slowly, and we got to bed very late. The bedrooms are large & airy, and we also have three sitting rooms. The food is not up to sample, and whether owing to it or to something at Gwalior, Dickinson has had a bad digestive upset. The Doctor (Indian of course) is an able man, and I think he has had every comfort, but it is very unlucky for him and even unluckier for the Maharaja who is thirsting for philosophic talk with him: they have only met once. I think he is better tonight, but remains in bed. Bob and I are very well. Finding the place so pleasant and the Maharaja so hospitable and charming, I had at once determined to stop on when D. and T. left, as it will fill up my gap between this and Xmas; and now they too are stopping on owing to D's illness, and will also stop after his recovery to see the Khujraho temples. Bob has quite changed—no hurry—plenty of time. So the atmosphere is restful.

Well, I will describe a typical day, for we are already settling into a routine. Baldeo brings tea at 7.0—I often have it on the verandah and see the sunrise: a new experience for me. Breakfast about 9.0, and then the Doctor and Private Secretary drive up—the first a Hindu, very fat, but charming and kind, the second a Hindu-ised Mahommedan who was educated at Aligarh. He is an able and entertaining man, and, being Chief Magistrate as well, is very important in the state. We drive away with him after a time, and come back to lunch. Then the Maharaja's carriage comes for us—perhaps at 2.0. perhaps at 4.—so crowded with menials to do us honour that the horses can scarcely draw it—coachman, coachman's companion, footman, messenger, most of them in rags, and the carriage itself—(a landau going to seed)—smells of grease most terrible. As we go through the town, every one bows. The Palace is white washed; a very beautiful entrance hall in native architecture. We are set down here while the messenger goes to the Maharaja and returns with the message 'He sends his salaams.' We go down the hall into a courtyard, where the ugliest little man you can imagine greets us under an enormous umbrella. It is more like a tent without sides than an umbrella, and when the conversation is above my head, as often, I raise my eyes to it—most gorgeous: tigers elephants deer &ct interlaced by foliage: it must be a priceless piece of work. We sit on chairs: His Highness squats on a cane lounge-chair: the Private Secretary sits like Buddha on a rug at his feet. The interview is very queer and sometimes lasts three hours. The chief subjects are philosophy and religious speculation, in which I do not shine; in fact I haven't made as good an impression as the other two. I gathered from the Morisons that the Maharaja is absurd, but this is quite wrong. He has certainly read bad books as well as good and—(like many would-be[']s nearer home)—can't distinguish between them; but he is so sensible and shrewd, and so full of fun, that listening & talking to him are both delightful. He would be a remarkable man in any country, and out here is very strange indeed. He hates ruling, and I think rules badly, and here he is in a wild jungle with no one to talk to on subjects he cares about. He is pleased with us, for he has let us see his Mystery Players—scarcely any Englishmen have done this, the Private Secretary tells me. His dress is a frock coat of dark buff, buttoned to the throat, knickers of thin white stuff embroidered, and socks. He wears little earrings, and at the base of his snub nose yellow paint is smeared, in honour of Krishna. He cannot eat with us, receive us inside the palace, or offer us his own cigarettes; but he can discuss why he does not do these things, and his mind is more fresh and tolerant than the average European's. His kindness is tremendous—but this, I believe, is usual in India. We are driven everywhere and offered everything, and he is now wanting to wire for an English Doctor, but this won't be necessary, for I'm glad to say that (since I began this letter) D. is much better. To conclude our day. When he has had enough he dismisses us with 'But I will not tire you longer' or something of the sort, and we drive up to the Guest House again. If the sun hasn't set, we then go a little walk; the colours are wonderful.

The Khajraho expedition is waiting for D's recovery. Tents are already there, officials too, and we have given everyone, the Private Secretary in particular, much trouble: I am glad that I had a separate introduction to him through his brother at Aligarh. Khajraho (8th cent. Temples) is 20 miles off—a motor road—and we were to spend the night there. I do hope we shall bring it off soon. I am so afraid of making the State Bankrupt for it is very poor and would show a deficit if it hadn't dug up an enormous treasure of gold coins in a deserted building two or three years ago. It exports betel nut and bones, but gets nothing for the bones for no Hindu will touch them, and outcasts from other states come & pick them off the fields &ct

for nothing.—On the other hand it is a very healthy place—plague & cholera are almost unknown among the people, however poor, and even malaria is uncommon. There is no religious bitterness, such as I found at Lahore, and (as far as I can see) no irritation against the English. The climate is charming—sun and a gentle breeze.

The Mystery Play was at night on a terrace at the top of the Palace.[1] Poor D. couldn't go, and Bob and I saw it alone with the Private Secretary. It was very impressive. The musicians salaamed when we entered, but the actors sat on their thrones—Krishna, Rad[h]a his wife, and four attendant women. As soon as we arrived they began by dances, at the same time singing—not words, but sounds. The musicians also sang, and the performance worked up to a real crisis, like the Russian Ballet, after which they returned to their thrones. After two such displays, the play came—a Nativity Story, reminding one of the Magi. A blue shawl edged with gold was held up by the attendants at the other end of the stage. This symbolised the wall of a house, behind which was Krishna as a baby in the arms of his mother. We could see their heads, but they were not supposed to be seen by the other actor—an old Hermit who comes to see the child: in his hand is a cobra (papier maché of course). The mother calls from the house 'No, you cannot see him—you are a demon with snakes about you & will harm him.' He explains that he has only disguised himself for the journey, but she still refuses. Then he cries 'I want to see him, for he is my god.' ⟨K. is one of the incarnations of Vishnu.⟩ 'Your child is a god and you do not know it, but I do.' She answers 'Hush—go away—you will frighten the baby—he is too young.' He answers 'He is not too young, for he is divine.' Then they drive him away, and he goes saying 'He is my god and will come after me', and as soon as he is out of sight the baby begins to cry! They can't stop him and have to call the hermit back, and the blue shawl is dropped to the ground. The mother carries Krishna out and the Hermit adores him. She then begs him to stop there for ever. He answers 'I cannot do that, but I will come whenever the Baby cries.'!—It was more of an opera than a drama: there was a running accompaniment on the orchestra, and the Hermit all through danced,—not in the Western fashion, but he moved with elaborate and dignified little steps. It was a beautiful little play, and the music was seldom uncouth—it is 'male music'—the actors being boys and different to the 'female' nautch music, which is all that I have heard in India so far. Much of this was in our own major & minor keys, whereas Heaven only knows what the 'female' was in.—I have written rather a long account because I seem to have seen something very uncommon and I wished to write it down. Missionaries often censure Krishna, but his conduct was impeccable on this occasion. When the Maharaja is there, he takes the performance very seriously, sitting on the floor out of respect to the actors and garlanding with marygolds at the end. I think that is why he would not witness the performance with us. We asked the Private Secretary to compliment the Actors for us, but he addressed not them but their teacher, who sat among the musicians. They remained expressionless on their thrones.——Then we went down winding stairs through the Library where Herbert Spencer & Huxley mixed with Indian Bedclothes, lay in piles on the floor. The only conclusion I come to is that His Highness has really first class taste. The whole performance was very good, and whatever ornaments &^{ct} I have caught sight of in the palace are beautiful. The next day he showed us some pictures of Krishna. These too were good. It is a relief after the hideous big palace at Gwalior.

Yesterday morning we went on an Elephant into the Jungle, the Private Secretary with us. Elephant was a dear, and walked quicker & more easily than the lady of Gwalior. When he came to rocks, he hated it, and felt everything with his trunk. He also made a queer vibrating noise—rather like the rumbling at the beginning of Reinhardt's Oedipus—which I thought might be a distant tiger and the P. S. did too for he asked the Mahout, who replied No, it came from Elephant's own inside, and he made it when he hoped he was getting to the end of his journey.[2] We stopped at the bottom of the shrine to the Goddess of Rain, which stands on a crag in the wildest part of the jungle, and climbed up to it. There was a splendid view. Bob wanted to bring out his poetry there. The Brahman who should have been in attendance was away gathering wild fruits, so we had a good view of the Goddess—an elementary person, painted vermilion. The shrine was between enormous boulders, over which were twisted the roots of a tree. Returning, we found Elephant up to his knees in a marsh, lunching off reeds and very happy. More splendid trees by its edge and many water birds; there was even a tank in which Bob was allowed to bathe.—This is the place where an annual fair is held during the Rains. The people all make merry with rain falling gently on them, which they like, the Raja comes out of Chhatarpur to look at them, and the Brahman gets rich with tips.

I must stop, though there is heaps to tell: e.g. I have inspected the Hospital & the Jail—the latter a most cheerful place: the people in India live so simply and eat so little that it is impossible to punish them. They sat about in the sun, talking as much as they liked, and working gently at carpets. I bought a 'durry' or light rug—it is quite cheap and washes: not a bad design, though too mattress-like in parts. Measure, about 7 feet by 4. I don't know what will be its fate, but it will have pleasant memories.

Oh I forgot! At Simla I met William Archer—he who censured Howards End—and he turned up again at Agra, where we saw a good deal of him.[3] I liked him very much. I don't know whether he remembered he had written about me. We shared carriages with him several times, and on leaving he gave me some introductions for Hardwar that will be very useful to me—to the Arya Somaj College, but it's too late to explain what that is.

Well—since beginning this letter, I have had yours, to my great delight—the one in which you say that you have just heard from me. How long it all takes! A pertikly interesting & amusing letter. We were thrilled by your romantic adventure near the Carmine and wonder whose the house was. Miss Breton sounds trying.[4] You must be a mistress of languages now—Italian as well as French. I think I could have got on with Urdu if I had had a decent grammar, but there seems none. I have to learn by asking people the words. I'm anxious for your next letter, as it may tell me whether you will risk Venice. I hope not, as you know. It too may reach me here, as I have only Bhopal and Indore to 'put in' before Xmas, and my other luggage has been sent for from the station.

Good night, dearest mummy, from your loving Poppy.

ALS: KCC

[1] They were seeing an enactment of the central metaphor of the Vaishnava cult, an important medieval *bhakti* (devotional) movement still very much alive, being most influential in northeast India. Its followers worship Vishnu, the Preserver in the Hindu Trinity, and they welcome all comers, without regard to origins or sex. They describe the relation between God and the soul through the episodes in the love story of Krishna, seventh avatar of Vishnu, and his milkmaid lover Radha. Uncounted thousands of splendid lyrics on this theme explicate Vaishnava philosophy and comprise songs of worship. See Edward C. Dimock's Introduction (pp. vii–xx) to *In Praise of Krishna: Songs from the Bengali*, trans. Dimock and Denise Levertov (1967).

[2] On Reinhardt's *Oedipus Rex*, see Letter 98.

[3] William Archer (1856–1924), influential dramatic critic of the *World*, 1884–1905, and translator of Ibsen's *Collected Works* (11 vols. 1906–8). He wrote *India and the Future* (1917), which many British critics found tactless and blustery. Neither the editors nor Frederick McDowell, the Forster bibliographer, have been able to trace this criticism.

[4] Miss Breton is unidentified: perhaps another tourist encountered during Lily's travels.

114   To Alice Clara Forster

Guest House, Chhatarpur, Bundelkhand,
C[entral]   I[ndia]
9 December 1912

Dearest Mother

This will reach you about my birthday. How strange that seems! I wonder where and with whom it will find you. Give them my New Year's love, and take much of the same from your dearest. My character is quite deteriorating!! Whenever I see anything nice I always think "How I wish Mummy was here to enjoy it too." There is so much that you would like. You must think of me as spending my birthday at Dewas, and by then I hope that I shall know where to think of you. I may ask you to pay Meredith £35 for the child at the end of January,—I do not know yet—and if I do this you will certainly have to sell out the Rio Janeiro Bonds for which I sent you an order in a previous letter, even if you have not done so already.[1] I am giving no Xmas presents, but hope to write letters to those people sometime. I had a lot of nice picture post cards, but they are in my luggage at Harpalpur. And though I sent for my luggage, did they send it? No. They mixed it up with the others though I had taken great care to book it separately, and Dickinson's book box and the bag of his servant were sent out instead. Such is India—the word that always rises to one's lips is 'fecklessness.' But I will go on on another page. There are private kisses and love to Mummy on this one. Dear Ruth has been sending such silly things lately, even to duplicate halfpenny circulars.

Chhatarpur [16 December 1912]

We are still here—no difficulty in stopping but much in getting away. Dickinson's poor inside is as well as it can ever expect to be so far East, and we should have left today—Monday. "No, no, I cannot have it, I will not speak of it. Journeys begun on Monday always end disastrously." Then Bob flew into a passion—fortunately when we left the Maharaja's presence. "I simply *will* go on Monday. I don't care what he says—we've given in too much already and he thinks he can behave as he likes. You & Dickinson can stop, but I shall just go on alone." So it was agreed to stand firm, and then when we went to the Mystery Play again last night, the Private Secretary stopped me at the Palace Door with "Oh Mʳ Forster, His Highness is so unhappy, and though I have warned him not to persist, he will. Do, do, intercede with your friends to grant him this little favour." I said "I'm afraid they must go." However they haven't. They gave in, and Bob is now quite happy again. Well, well. I am very glad to stop on myself, being very fond indeed of the Maharaja, and the two chief officials of the State—the Private Secretary and the Prime Minister—are also ~~very~~ nice, though fortunately more practical than His Highness, who is the Prince of Muddlers, even of Indian muddlers. Nothing ever happens here either when or as it is planned. Khujraho has at last been accomplished, but with endless bungling, Bob and I going to sleep there in tents one day, and D[ickinson] being sent alone in a motor the other. The temples are very wonderful but nightmares—all exactly alike and covered with sculptures from top to toe. There are about 30 in all, mostly deserted.[2] The tents were ~~quite~~ comfortable, though Bob had rats and birds and a dripping lamp in his, and slept badly. I did very well.

We see the Maharaja every day, and he usually takes us a motor drive. A 'poor cousin' comes too, and carries his opera glasses, cigarettes, betel nut, umbrella, stick, and State sword, together with a bundle which I suppose contains food, but he always eats in solitude. Poor cousin sits in front with the chauffeur: we and the Maharaja are squeezed behind. Here and there about the roads we come on State carriages, who would pick us up if the car broke—very necessary, for there are no garages. The roads are very good and the country in parts superb. Bears, tigers, leopards, are said to 'rebound', but it is difficult to believe, and as they never attack man, one is perfectly safe. The only surprises are the monkeys, who go about in flocks. There are two kinds—the grey apes with black faces are dears, but they are not as sacred as the others, because they ran away from a battle in which they had promised to help Rama, and their faces turned black as a punishment. The brave monkeys, who did not run away, have red faces, and are horrible. There are also the most wonderful birds. When we were sitting on the roof of a deserted palace upon the side of a hill, one perched on a tree close against us. It was like a swallow in shape, but twice as large, and crimson. The Maharaja exclaimed 'It flashes like a jewel—it must be a Robin Redbreast.' He loves scenery and architecture and all that is beautiful in a way that is very rare for an Indian.

I go on after an explosion of wrath with the Munshi (head servant at the Guest House), who has, for the second night running, left some of the lamps without wicks and the rest without oil. Smell and darkness all over the house. They have not treated us well here, and, being guests of State, one naturally did not complain; but we have been urged to do so not only by other passing guests but by the Private Secretary himself, who says that the State will be charged for all sorts of things that we have not had ('This is inevitable') and that we are to insist on everything being right. So my few words of Urdu are useful, and I wish they were more. The Munshi is a venerable and very tiresome old man. When I complained of the lamps yesterday he said the Prime Minister would not let him have any oil!

Another disappointment is that my mail has not reached me here, so that I write without receiving your 4th letter from Florence; it will wander after me to Bhopal. I do hope it won't go astray. I am so anxious to hear whether you kept to your plan of Venice. The journey to Bhopal will be horrid. I have to sleep in the waiting room at Jhansi, and then either travel in a '3rd Class only' at 5.0. next morning, or else hang about Jhansi station till 4.0. in the afternoon. Sad dilemma. Howsomenever. One can't get off the beaten track without these difficulties, and I have had a lovely time here.

Sanchi, near Bhopal
The journey was not better than it sounds. I caught a train at 3.0 in

the night from Jhansi, as, though very slow, it had 2nd Class carriages in it, so that I could lie down and sleep again: the first instalment of the night my bed was made in the waiting room. Now I am waiting between trains to see the famous Sanchi Tope.[3] It is on a hill close to the station, with charming views from it, but is even queerer than the Khujraho Temples—a mound of earth like a gasometer stands in the centre, which once held Buddhist relics, and circling this, with a passage between, is a rail of great stones, a little like Stonehenge. This rail has four gateways, one at each point of the compass. They are carved with huge elephants and birds and stories of Buddha and are much higher than the rail. Those as likes can see models of them in the India Museum at South Kensington. I go to Bhopal at 8.0. The jaunt has been tragic for Baldeo, who can get no Hindu food at Sanchi, and has had little to eat all day. He sits on the luggage at the station, holy and cross. The one man who could have sold him uncontaminated food here has unfortunately gone for a drive. They certainly act up to their religion, though it is hard to make head or tail of it. The Maharaja will probably never come to England, though he longs to, because of the ritual difficulties. Even the Private Secretary, a man of the world and a Mohammedan, thought that 60 or 70 servants was the least H. H. could travel with. Imagine the scene when he arrived in London or called on us at Weybridge which he wishes to do. Special food & water would have to be brought from India, and all the time the M. doesn't think these observances are any ~~real~~ good, but he has become used to them and hates to stop. Talk of a grove! It is a forest.

Our parting was very sweet. He gave us each a photograph of himself, expensive & hideous—I want to throw it away—: a little Japanese box, and some Jeypore paintings—probably valuable 18th century things. Bob admired them and he said 'they are yours.' I don't know whether they really were. These things are very difficult. The Secretary afterwards said that they were. Anyhow we have each two—I like those of the others better than my own unfortunately. They are small, on tattered pieces of paper.— Chhatarpur has indeed been a find, and I am proud to think that it was I who insisted on going there. Did I tell you in my last letter about the serpent in the paradise—the 'P. A.' (Political Agent who is appointed by the British Gov^t to look after the native princelings?)[4] There is naturally always friction, and we have only heard the princeling's version, but the man must be a trial, for he is really dotty on the subject of theosophy, and perhaps elsewhere. Whatever one says he retorts 'Ah—that is because you have not eliminated the Self'—or 'But can't you see? Everything is all one,' and he confided to me that the sun's rays shone only where there was some solid planet for them to shine upon, since they were ~~really~~ probably composed of Spirits, who would be disinclined to expend their radiance vainly. Did you ever hear such talk? And it comes from a retired colonel of sporting instincts—that is so odd. In our last conversation he proved to me that conscription was necessary because it imitated the example of ~~the denial~~ self-denial that is set to us by the Infinite. I had expected to find queer Englishmen in power, but this man is a stumper.—Then there is the Army Chaplain from Nowgong, a bounder with no manners and no inside, who bullies the Maharaja and his ministers in their own palace.[5] No wonder the M. cries pathetically 'Ah M[r] Dickinson, if only you were in power what a different world it would be.'

We have been many times to the Dances and Plays—5 in all—and in each have found new beauties. The last was a 'swing dance'. But they have no feeling against repetition and seldom any dramatic feeling. With the exception of the dance I described last time, they never come to a crisis, and are as unlike Western things as one can imagine. This type of performance is called 'Lila'.[6] As I said, it is sacred, and very few have seen it who are not Hindus. Krishna and Rad[h]a always appear, though the connection with them is often nominal, and the performers are always men or boys. There are also Nautch girls in the Palace, but we did not know about them until it was too late to ask to see them.

I think I shall finish now as I am in a fright about missing the mail. It is a different day in ~~eae~~ every town. I am sitting in the office of the polite [sic] station, while he sends telegrams close to me, and this will be posted in Bhopal. I feel it has been rather a sight see-ish letter with little 'food for thought' in it; and I do wish my mail had caught me at Chhatarpur. It will take so long for the letters to hark back to Bhopal that I may receive two mails together.

The Express—now due in half an hour—has been stopped for me. I found in the Time Tables that it could be done, in spite of 'doubtings.' But we shall see if it does stop. If it flies past, there is a good Guest House near the Tope. I always go 2nd now, and take the whole of my luggage in the carriage. No one objects and it saves much money. There is always ample room, for Indian Railways are everything Italian aren't. How I long to hear how your tour ended, though it is not ended at the moment I am writing. I expect and hope.

Your loving Poppy

ALS: KCC

[1] EMF was helping to finance Meredith, whose wife Christabel had had twins in 1908, another child, Adam, in 1913, and twins again in 1916.

[2] Khajuraho is a village in Chhatarpur District which had eighty-five temples, of which twenty survive. They are famous for great intricacy and richness of sculptured ornament, including a variety of erotic sculptures.

[3] This is the Great Stupa (or Tope) at Sanchi, built between 185 BC and 320 AD. Cf. Letter 79.

⁴ Lt Col. Charles Hamerton Pritchard (1863–1916) was Political Agent for Bundelkhand in 1899 and again in 1912–14.
⁵ This was Walrond Lugard Clarke (died 1954?), Chaplain at Neemuch in 1912–13.
⁶ 'Lila' is not the type of performance, but the state of joyous empathy with the divine engendered by enactment of the Radha-Krishna stories.

115   To Forrest Reid

Guest House, Bhopal
13 December 1912

Dear Reid

I have read *Following Darkness* again, and am happier than I can tell you to be connected with it. Initials are of no importance—it is the knowledge that I have helped in it.[1] Besides, your books have a knack of opening in my hands when daily life has gone wrong: *The Bracknels* came when I was particularly wretched, and this too comforts, though not in any vulgar sense.

I now understand it better than I did, and, though still requiring extra pages at the end, have a clearer idea of your scheme. Now I will tell you what your scheme is! The book is a discussion. You are talking—very quietly and beautifully, but talking—about the chasms that surround us. You are describing spiritual scenery, and though you are too skilled a novelist to paint the figures in that landscape as generalities, they are most significant when they remind us that we walk in it too. Peter doesn't matter as much as Denis—he ~~is less of a hum~~ has less actuality.[2] On the other hand, what may happen to him matters more. Well what do you think? It seems to me that, without any fuss, you are doing work that is not only good but new.

Now, if you go on this way, you'll find 'passing life' more & more intractable. That is your difficulty, as it has been mine. Your knowledge of social distinctions and age-distinctions will always be getting in your way. And, dramatically, one could criticise this book more severely than *The Bracknels*. The characters are often too intelligent for their position and their years, and speak with too much polish & experience at one moment; while the next they are doing sums on a slate or are puzzled by R.S.V.P. I don't criticise it from this point of view, because you are not concerned with passing life but with the scenery over which it passes. Yet it does interest me to see whether you'll handle the difficulty in the future with more or with less skill.

I don't want it, nor would you give it, as a compliment, but if you wish to dedicate the sequel to me also, you may know how I should accept it. I am writing very openly here, because if you don't dedicate it, I feel sure you'll know that I shan't feel I've been snubbed. God! To be frank one must be very lengthy, but such is the nature of things.

The grotesque condition of my front page is due to *Tanglefoot*, a sticky substance which the Begum of Bhopal spreads about her Guest House to catch flies. No doubt Miss Izzy stocks it.[3] I've pasted tissue paper over to give you the chance of unfolding my letter.

My home address always finds me.

Yours ever

E. M. Forster.

ALS: Stephen Gilbert

[1] Initials: EMF's, in the dedication of the novel.
[2] Peter Waring: central character in *Following Darkness*. Denis Bracknel, central character of *The Bracknels*, is a boy growing up motherless, bookish, and moody.
[3] Miss Izzy: lady shop-manager in *Following Darkness*, prim, bossy, and pseudo-genteel.

116   To Alice Clara Forster

Laurie's Great Northern Hotel, Allahabad
5 January 1913

Dearest Mother

So much happens that I must send you an Allahabad letter as well as a Benares one this week, though as it is written in bed you will scarcely thank me for it.

We left Dewas the evening of the 2nd, dreadfully sorry to go; I never thought to feel a wrench when parting from a court, but when they thronged round our motor in the porch of the New Palace, garlanding and betel nutting and attar-of-rosing us, it felt like parting from old friends.[1] Johnny—the Darling baby—woke up in his mother's arms and created a great sensation by salaaming with both hands. We got off—late of course—and heartrending misfortunes ensued. The motor was lent by the neighbouring and more powerful state of Indore, but the tongas that took our luggage were—alas!—native to Dewas, and when we reached the Ry station, 30 miles distant, one of them had strayed from the way so that 1/3 of the luggage missed the train. All mine caught it, but Malcolm's clothes and bedding are heaven knows where. The train waited 40 minutes for us because we were white while the motor scoured the darkness tooting for the tonga, but in vain. We ended in a row with the station people about Malcolm's tickets—incredibly stupid!—and then the Ayah was cold and incompetent because she had never wrapped up in the motor though begged to do so, and when I tried to make Johnny's bed she had wrapped dozens of mechanical toys up in the blankets and they poured on to the floor. He at once desired to play with them and the hour was late.

Bed at last; changed at Bhopal next morning and travelled with the Darlings till 3.0. in the afternoon. Then I changed into the Cawnpore train, arrived there, and as soon as my bed was made up in the waiting room found that I should have to rise at 6.0. next morning and drive to the other station. This too I did but passed two fragmentary nights.

Allahabad though has been delightful. I had wired to Ahmed Mirza, one of Masood's friends whom I knew slightly in England, and he not only met me, but insisted against all my protestations that I should be his guest at the hotel. I think he likes having me though and I certainly like going about with him; and the hotel bill won't come to much and ought to come to less for it's a bad place. Allahabad is the capital of the United Provinces, and Ahmed Mirza is in the Public Works Dept here. I hired a bicycle and he took me round the principal buildings all of which were new and one of which—very beautiful—he was superintending. He's the first Mohammedan I have met with any feeling for Art. We spent an afternoon interesting enough to keep me from falling asleep.

I returned home expecting a restful & solitary evening. It was not to be. Baldeo met me much excited. 'Ismit Sahib' (Smith) was in the town—he had heard so from another servant. I cried 'summon a carriage' and off we rolled—miles & miles into the dark and drew up opposite a large house and in a bedroom, Smith did sit. He had just arrived and was stopping with the Collector (an official superior) till he could find a house for himself.[2] Much rejoicing. He looks but I fear doesn't feel quite well. I wanted to take him back to the Hotel but the Collector & his wife—neither nice—asked me to dinner instead and I had to stop and hear them despise natives.

Then I did sleep! And this morning the gallivanting began again. Smith came to breakfast with me, and then Ahmed Mirza turned up—he lives in wretched lodgings somewhere—and I spent the rest of the day with him. He had got me an order for the Fort and we went there before lunch—little to see, but it stands finely, where the Ganges and Jumna meet. It was my first sight of the Ganges, but I could not be impressed for it was not there at all: a mile broad of sand and fields and at the further side a crack of trickling water. The Jumna was clear green and very fine. After lunch we took a boat on it. This was delightful. I brought out tea apparatus which boiled beautifully and biscuits and we feasted under the sunset sky. A man and a boy rowed us to the place where the two rivers meet and where a third—sacred and invisible except to the eye of faith—is said to rise from the middle of the earth to meet them. But be all this as it may, we never saw anything meet anything for the man and boy grew tired and said now that it was a long way to the Ganges and now that we were in it all the time and now that if we were in it it would sweep us away, and in any case that it was late. So we went back to our bicycles. Riding to the hotel, we came on a wild procession; a huge acetyline lamp, very bright, was carried in the midst of dancing howling men while a band thundered. "Religious of course." Oh no. It was a wrestler who had just won in a contest, Mirza replied, and his school fellows were taking him home!

7 January 1913

I am at Benares now but will finish off Allahabad. The evening of the 5th I dined with a friend of the Morisons, Burn by name, a high official but very unofficial and nice.³ Next morning Mirza came very early with a gift of guavas wrapped in a towel. Allahabad is famous for guavas and these were certainly less nasty than any I have tasted before, but it puzzles me how they ever turn into anything as nice as guava jelly. We rode out on our bicycles to see a garden & some tombs and then he took me to his lodgings—two bare rooms five miles from his work. There are none to be had in Allahabad except with Hindus and they would not let him eat meat if he came, so he is in great difficulty and has tried to live with Eurasians but he despises them & they him so that didn't do either. People in Allahabad spend most of their time despising. Mirza who has spent his life first in Hyderabad where his father was Minister and then in England is miserable there, and hasn't a single friend of his own age. We went on to breakfast with a middle aged Indian—M. thought the hour was 9.0., I 9.30., but it turned out to be 10.0. Other Indians were there—all eminent I believe, but most of them could not talk English. They were full of the new Councils—the Reform scheme of Lord Morley's—which are about to meet.⁴ After buying a hat—a round cloth thing such as they wear out here: my straw is no more as someone trod upon it—he saw me off by the train, leaving me with strong impressions of his kindness.

P.S. Will you send a 'Sirram' 4/- tea apparatus to him from the A[rmy] & N[avy Stores]. It ought to be packed carefully and postage may be a good deal, but it doesn't matter.

Address

Ahmed Mirza, Esq.
  High Court Works
    Allahabad.
      India. U[nited] P[rovinces].

Private   [9 January 1913]

I will write properly about Benares later, when I see more of it. I went to the Hotel, and a few hours afterwards a man to whom

Dickinson had given me an Introduction came round and with extraordinary kindness insisted I should come and stop in his house.[5] In many ways this is delightful for he is nearer the sights than the hotel—distant 3 miles—and he is a real good sort with a heart of gold. But alas 'I do not like you Doctor Fell', the reason being that he is a schoolmaster who chirrups and contradicts and lays down the law. Anyone more unsuitable to see Benares with (and through) couldn't be imagined, but here I am and he stifles me with kindness. I went to bed last night quite shivering with temper.

Have just had your letter saying you are home. I am so glad Percy met you, and since you *would* go back I am piously pleased that you are back safely! This will arrive late for your birthday, but it contains my love 'and a squeeze and a kiss *and* a hug' as Harold would say. Thank you for getting me presents for the maids. As for Aunt G's piano, I wish it could be arranged that I paid for the tuning always.[6] Is this possible? I'm afraid the piano isn't quite a success—the treble needs some hard playing to tame it in. One other thing—when you have time, do go to David Thompson & have that tooth screwed in again. It isn't only that it's a convenience to have it, but I am so afraid that stuff will get into the root & decay it unless it is cleaned out and filled up.

Have heard from Maimie that she fears May & I shan't meet—Hyderabad so far for me &[ct].—But I have been trying to get answers from May for the last two months, and if only I can hear from her mean to go to Hyderabad before I sail. It isn't her fault really, for her first letter was lost. I have also been trying to meet her at Benares—she was passing this way on a holiday tour.[7] I meant to tell you & Maimie all this later when my sailing is fixed up. I expect to leave Bombay either on the 1st of April or the 15th, getting to England about 3 weeks later. Goodall is fixing it up for me, but I want to hear first from May. The plan is to get down from Lahore to Bombay about 10 days before boat sails and then run to Hyderabad & back. It means a good deal of time & expense (see map), and I don't contemplate it unless I am sure of finding May when I arrive. I am doing it on Maimie's account and of course want to do it, and when I write to her shant let her see that there have been any difficulties.

What else? Oh yes, I will send Meredith the cheque for £35. Goodall is financing me—i.e. he will always cash cheques through the post at full exchange value. This is a great convenience as I now need not order out money from England through Cooks. I owe you £10 still—I'm 'afraid' not more. Mind you sell out the Rio Trams if you want to.

How nice that your tour ended well. No doubt M[rs] M[awe] likes bossing it and that, with the rest, has raised her spirits. You did sound to do a great deal.

Am hoping I shall get through my visit without a coolness with my host. He is touchy as well as dictatorial, so life is difficult. Will you thank Percy for Kolynos, just safely received. Other sheets *not* private.

Benares.   9 January 1913.

Let me add a line about this queer city. I have now been three times to the river side, which is the most interesting part of it, and am losing my first feeling of disappointment. According to Hindu religion, it is a merit to build but none to repair, and the whole river front is either in ruins or else under the hands of contractors. The mess is unbelievable—temples tumbling, stair cases leading no-where, stacks of wood for funeral pyres, sacred wells, trees, shrines; and scrambling up and down the chaos, or perched on stone platforms in the midst of it are the holy men and other worshippers, while the river itself swarms with bathers, muddled up with landing stages and boats. Most visitors see all this from midstream, but it is only when you go among it that it can be understood in the least, and consequently I have enjoyed this morning's visit more than the others. I managed to find the Fakir to whom Rothenstein gave me an introduction.[8] Yesterday I tried in vain, and only was shown a bed of spikes on which they assured me he usually sat, but he was out for a walk just now. Having gathered that he was not the sort who sits on spikes, I felt doubtful, but they were confident, and pointed out his house close by. The door was locked but of course it had a hole in it through which I put my card, giving my address and saying I should call again. But this morning, when I did call again, all the inhabitants of the neighbourhood met me with the news that the spike-sitter was not my fakir at all, and led me to ~~quite~~ another part of the Ghat. There, half way up a huge flight of steps you spring to the right on to a narrow ledge that leads round a temple on the further side of which is quite a nice residence with tomatoes drying on its roof. Out of this the fakir came, with ~~very~~ few clothes on but in other respects not unlike Tom Walker.[9] I only stopped a minute, as he had friends, but he seemed a very nice sort of gentleman. Dickinson & Bob, he said, had sat with him a long time and I am to do the same tomorrow. He had received a letter I wrote to him from Allahabad, and was about to call at the hotel on me!—Later on we passed the house into which I had poked my visiting card. The door opened and the *wrong* fakir came out—a terrible creature whose face was smeared with ashes and red paint. I fled, like Hansel and Gretel from the witch. No doubt he is a nice gentleman too, but I hope *he* won't call at the hotel.

By this time I had quite a train of boys—polite and harmless little creatures—and we all went up the minaret of the mosque. When we came down they asked for bakshish, severely reprimanding each other for their bad breeding as they did so. I pointed out that the baby, who was stark naked and had never come up at all, really could have no claim. This was thought just. To the boy who had helped me not to bump my head I gave one anna. He said it was little, I said it was enough, and he agreed. The other boy had carried Murray so I gave him two, but he too said it was little, on the ground that he had also accompanied me on the expedition to the Fakir. On this I asked his name. He answered 'Baldeo'. I told him that was my servant's name too, and he was so struck that he forgot about the money and engaged in social talk. At the end he said 'Presence, two annas are not much. Can I have four?' 'O Baldeo, two are plenty.'—'Plenty, did you say? Oh, very well,' and he went like a dear. How much better this is than combining extortion with self righteousness!

Tomorrow I go to Bankipore, then to Gya and (just possibly) to Calcutta. Feb 1st I am due back at Allahabad to stop with Smith: a most delightful piece of luck. He is looking after the great pilgrimage camp at the junction of the Ganges & Jumna and has managed to get me a tent there as well. I have just heard from him—he was trying to arrange it but was not sure.

Now I must stop. Love, Morgan.

ALS: KCC

1 The state of Dewas Senior is so fully described in EMF's *The Hill of Devi* (1953) that letters included there are not, in general, repeated here. However, its Raja became so important in EMF's life that some portrait of that fascinating figure must be presented. Tukoji Rao (Puar) III (1887–1937), commonly referred to by EMF as 'H.H.' or 'Bapu Sahib', was head of that small Mahratta state in Central India. Malcolm Darling became his tutor in 1907; they developed a lifelong friendship, and it was Darling who introduced the Raja and EMF in 1912. Tukoji married, in 1908, a princess from the powerful state of Kolhapur, and their son Vikramsinha later became Maharaja of Kolhapur. Within a few years, however, the marriage broke down, and the Maharani returned to Kolhapur, which thereupon became intensely hostile to Dewas, and Tukoji replaced her by a morganatic wife—thus creating dynastic problems. His main interest in life became, increasingly, the state's religious ceremonies, which grew more elaborate year by year. These, the building of a new Palace, and the maintenance of an extensive spy system directed against Kolhapur, were helping to ruin the state, and the British authorities began to intervene. Then in 1928 a disastrous scandal occurred when Vikramsinha, now married, fled the state, taking sanctuary with the British and accusing his father of trying to seduce his wife and to poison him. From this point onward Tukoji's position grew desperate, and in 1933—his state bankrupt and his reputation in ruins—he absconded to Pondicherry in French India, bearing with him the state's few remaining treasures. His last years were spent in unavailing pleas and protests to the Government of India and in penitential fasting. EMF, who related his story in *The Hill of Devi*, blamed the British handling of him as 'impeccably right and absolutely wrong'.

2 Rupert Barkeley Smith (1883–1970), born in Quebec, entered the ICS in 1897 and in 1908 was posted to Meerut. After war years in England and in the army, he returned to India in 1919 as Additional Sessions Judge at Aligarh, then as District Magistrate at Agra in 1922. He then left the Service and set up as a businessman. He and EMF met during the Greek cruise of 1903 (see Letter 39), and again in India, in both 1912–13 and 1921. Smith's rudeness to Indians in 1912–13 was evidently a source for *Passage*, although he had mellowed by 1921. PNF notes that EMF once said to Smith: 'Why are you so much less than you might have been?' Smith took offence at *Passage*, which he thought a slur on the ICS and on himself, since the Turtons' house in the novel (Chapter 3) is a close likeness of his Agra house. However, he and EMF were reconciled in the 1940s.

[3] Sir Richard Burn (1871–1947) entered the ICS in 1891, became Under-Secretary to the United Provinces Government, 1897; superintended the *Census*, later the *Imperial Gazeteer*, 1900–5; and filled other responsible posts until retirement in 1927.

[4] The 'Morley-Minto Reforms' of 1909, proposed by Lord John Morley (1838–1923), Secretary of State for India, 1905–10, and by the 4th Earl of Minto (1847–1914), Viceroy of India, 1905–10, enlarged the legislative councils and allowed them to vote on administrative matters. They added an Indian member to provincial executive councils and to the Central Government. Their good effects were soon vitiated, for, from 1907, the British accepted the two-nation theory of separate Hindu and Muslim electorates, with Muslim communal awards on the basis of 'political importance'.

[5] Dickinson's friend was William Stavely Armour (1883–1933), Principal of Queen's College Collegiate School, Benares, 1910–21. An unkind remark attributed to him by PNF (*EMF*, I, 245) was actually by Barré Cassels Forbes (1879–1946), EMF's host at Lucknow.

[6] Percy: his cousin, Percy Whichelo. Harold: probably Harold Barger, Florence's son. Aunt G: Lily's sister, Georgiana.

[7] On May Wyld, see Letter 107.

[8] William Rothenstein (1872–1945), the English painter and lithographer, and Principal of the Royal College of Art, 1920–35, was one of EMF's forerunners in India. In indignation at the reception of Ernest Havell's ideas about art education in India, and after initiating the India Society in London (see Letter 79), Rothenstein himself went to India in the winter of 1910–11, to paint and to meet Indian artists. Sir Theodore Morison was the link between Rothenstein and Chattarpur, and Rothenstein became the link between the Bengali poet, Rabindranath Tagore (1860–1941) and literary circles in the West, with a campaign of introductions and contacts that culminated in Tagore's winning the Nobel Prize for Literature in 1913, the first such award to an Asian. The 'fakir' was Nrusinh Sharma, on whom Rothenstein had called in 1910; see his *Men and Memories*, II, 243, 244, 249. The visits of Dickinson, Trevelyan, and EMF threw Sharma into a state of high enthusiasm; afterward, he wrote to Rothenstein: 'So far as my humble abilities go I can rightly assert that not only is India benefited by the Benign British Rule but I personally have been greatly benefited as by the Special favour of the Almighty I came into contact with men like you through whose influence also with other noble types of humanity whose hearts as it were melting with love and fellow-feeling and whom I would never forget because of the indescribable pleasure I received from their lucid conversation while sitting in my humble cottage' (3 February 1913). Houghton Library, Harvard.

[9] Possibly the Rev. Thomas Walker (d. 1918), a Master at Tonbridge School, 1884–1901; Sub-Warden, St Augustine's College, Canterbury, and Vicar at Hougham-by-Dover, 1903–18.

117   To Alice Clara Forster

Bankipore.   15 January 1913

Dearest Mother

Somewhere or other is another letter that I've begun to you. I hope to find it and put it in. Now for my news.

From Benares, where every prospect pleased me and only man did rile, I have come to its opposite. This place is horrible beyond words but I am having a pleasant time here. It consists of a street 14 miles long edged with hovels, from which it is impossible to escape, because the Ganges stops you on one side and rice fields on the other. I couldn't believe it until I took a bicycle ride and tried. The house is attractive in its bare way, and looks into one of the two open spaces of Bankipore, so that I leave it reluctantly, and generally to roll through the slums in a carriage to the other open space, where we walk round and round in the evening. Between the two are the Library, with fine Oriental M.S. in it, and the Law Courts—these latter hovels also but more scattered; and on the dusty ground between them squat the litigants waiting for barristers, while the barristers, waiting for litigants, sit inside. The Ganges is close by but you can't see it—you never can see it except in the rainy season when it overflows its banks and turns the dust to mud. There are also fine palm trees, but behind walls so high that you only see the tips of them nodding. Oh yes, and there is a building that has an echo, but you can't hear it because the key of the door is lost.

Masood flourishes in the midst of this desolation amazingly. He has made a good start with his work and is gay and well. How long he will keep well without exercise I don't know. There appear to be no means for an Indian to get a game of tennis, but I expect something will turn up. None—no barristers at all events—are admitted into the English club where such things go on and though Indians form clubs of their own and stump up subscriptions willingly, they somehow fail to turn up and take advantage of them.

Interruption.

Enter three youths to call on Masood who is out. I call for chairs to be brought them. They are much impressed and ask me my 'honourable name', and then various questions about Cambridge life and the foreign policy of Sir E. Grey. They were very intelligent and somehow or other I rose to the occasion and achieved a long address on our Foreign Policy and its difficulties which they assured me had indeed been a pleasure to listen to—interests of British Empire so complex, policy based not on hatred of Islam but on fear of Germany and all the rest of it. It is very easy to talk politics when you meet some one who knows less than you do, but this has never happened to me before. The eldest youth, on leaving, delivered *his* speech—so eloquent that I could scarcely believe he had not expected to find me here. He dwelt on their great good luck in meeting me, on my literary eminence (having taken my own word for that), but above all on my affability. The British Empire might last for ever as long as it produced gentlemen like me. Then they chattered away off down the drive.

Like you, I have less to write about now, as there has been less sight seeing since my last letter.[1] I found the Fakir at Benares on my last morning. He did *not* sit on spikes and was very charming. We had a long talk chiefly about 'inspiration'—i.e. the mental process through which one goes during the act of writing. I have written some account of it to Aunt Laura. I was interested to find that it was the same in his case as in mine, though I produce novels and he Sanscrit Poems.

Yesterday we went to lunch with Hubback, a man I knew at King's, who has been transferred here from Gya recently, and lives in luxurious tents until he can find a house.[2] The others I have seen are all Indian. We often go to tea with a man who has a strange if admirable idea of that meal: it begins with a plate of green peas cooked deliciously in butter and then we eat guavas sliced and peppered and tangerines. The tea comes last, like a liqueur. Here too the cooking is Indian, and as Masood curbs the cook over sugar and chillies, it is very nice and I relish my victuals more than when they were done in the Anglo-Indian style.

The wind has begun, meaning a change in the weather, so the ceaseless sunshine of the past three months will break. I have never undone my umbrella since leaving Italy.

This is a large house, even according to Indian notions, and might be made nice, but as the Gov^t. will probably acquire the site, no one is inclined to put money into it. Down the middle run two big broad halls with an archway between them: to the right of them the rooms in which we live—M's office, which is often pleasantly full of clients—then a long dressing room, then our two bedrooms. To the left of the central halls are the clerk's room the dining room and two other bedrooms. All the back part of the house will be occupied by his mother when she comes, and furniture has to come too. Two verandah and a roof—discovered by me—which is very fresh & nice in the morning: sometimes we have tea &^{ct} up there.

The other night a marriage procession passed—not large but the effect was fine. They know how to use lights so splendidly out here; a few torches in front and then two huge pyramids of candles in shades, they looked like burning trees and owing to their size and the darkness of the road the wedding guests looked unnaturally tiny and gnome like; the sort of effect that Gordon Craig tries for in his scenery.[3] Queer music, seeming never to get further than the note below the keynote, went on all the time. It is just the beginning of the Indian wedding season, so I hope to see many more.

Bob writes that there is nothing to see in Calcutta except people and the tapirs in the Zoo. He gives me introductions to the former, but it is 12 hours journey and 14^s/– a day at the cheapest hotel, so I'm probably not going. The Goodalls, who would have put me up, are themselves homeless. Bob and Dickinson have got to Madras, where they were caught up into the highest Anglo Indian circles, and are probably nearing Columbo by this time.[4] They are having a good time, though D's health is often not very good.

Have just been out on bicycle and knocked down my first Indian. I only wonder it hasn't happened before. They take no notice of the bell until you are passing them when they rush quickly into you and hit you on the ancle. This one—a boy—came to no harm, as I always go very slowly. They do say that you ought to call out "Out of the way brother" or "Mother, do not take up all the road" and things like that, but I can't remember the words.

Your loving
Morgan

ALS: KCC
1 This letter failed to arrive. On the fakir, Nrusinh Sharma, see Letter 116.
2 Sir John Austen Hubback (1878–1968) entered King's in 1897 and the ICS in 1901. He served in Bengal, Bihar, and Orissa, 1902–36; was Governor of Orissa, 1936–41; and adviser to the Secretary of State for India, 1942–7.
3 Edward Gordon Craig (1872–1966), son of actress Ellen Terry and the architect Edward Godwin, made innovations in impressionist stage and scenery designs and in lighting.
4 From Madras Trevelyan wrote to his mother (14 January 1913. TCC) that from 10 to 16 January they had been with ICS officials, including the Governor of Madras. 'I wish,' he wrote, 'we did not have to see so much of second-rate Anglo-Indian society here. That is the worst of staying with Anglo-Indians.'

118   To Robert Trevelyan

P. O. Mordapore, Bankipore[1]
21 January 1913

Dear Bob

Thanks for your letter and the introductions, which, having troubled you, I am not going to use. Both tapirs and Tagores tempt terribly, but samples of either can be met in England, and as I shall be moving about a great deal during the last six weeks of my time and spending much money, I shall remain here till I go to the bathing festival at Allahabad.[2] I am having the usual bother over my passage and may have to sail from Karachi. Goodall is fixing it up. He didn't call on you at Calcutta because he wasn't there.

I wonder how you like Southern India. I must make the roofs of Bankipore do instead. There are so many Toddy Palms and malaria-melon trees that the views from them are quite tropical. (In case you puzzle over malaria-melon, it is a tree with fruit as big as melons which are good for malaria.) Foul as the place is, there is enough going on to amuse one, and I have met several people, not all very nice. Nice are *Russell*, a professor at Patna College, archaeologist and political economist, who has lent me Hsien Tsang; Johnstone—you dined with him; and the *Raja of Canika*, a young Orissan magnate who is here for the opening of the council.[3] Even as I write the council is opening—in the College, as there is no other room. Some times I bicycle, some times by the tide of Ganges do complain.[4] I see steam boats on it, but it is difficult to find when and hence they go and whither.

Masood thanks you and D[ickinson] for your messages. "When they went away I missed them most intensely" he has just dictated. He has a reasonable amount of work and is gay.

I do hope the Karamazov family have arrived. I sent them registered to Madras the same time I sent D. a letter. I am sending a line to Trichinopoly too, as he directed.

Yours
E.M.F.

ALS: KCC

[1] Masood's address.
[2] Tagore's progressive school was at Santiniketan, near Calcutta, and Trevelyan, who had met him, sent this introduction. 'Samples': i.e. tapirs in the London Zoo, and Tagore's poems, *Gitanjali*, published in England in 1912.
[3] Hsuan-Tsang (*c.* 596–664), Chinese traveller in India and Central Asia, studied Buddhist philosophy, translated some of the Buddhist sacred writings, and described his travels in *Si-yu-ki. Buddhist Records of the Western World*, trans. Samuel Beal (1884). Charles Russell (d. 1917) joined the Educational Service in 1889 and in 1909 was assigned to Patna College, Bankipore. At the time of his death in action in the World War, he had become Principal of the College. There was no one named Johnstone on its staff in 1912–13, but this may have been James William Douglas Johnstone (untraced), who had retired in 1910 after serving as Inspector-General of Education in Gwalior State since 1894. The Raja of Canika would have been attending one of the new legislative councils set up under the Morley-Minto Reforms.
[4] See Psalm 137, verse 1; 'By the rivers of Babylon, . . .'

119   To Alice Clara Forster

                                        Gya, Behar.   29 January 1913

Enclosed is a leave from the sacred Pipul Tree at Boddh Gaya. I have two & send you the best one—![1]

Dearest Mother

Another "effelant" day yesterday, and if I had had more to eat between 6.0. in the morning and 2.0. in the afternoon than a dab of omelette, I should have called it a perfect day. As it was, I enjoyed it. Leaving Bankipore at an unearthly hour I was met at a little station called Bela by a friend of Masood's whose name is Nawab Syed Imdad Imam Saleh; I took it all down as I want to write to him. He was an active young man of seventy—rich, aimiable, well read in English Poetry, and great on sport. He brought two nephews with him, who were not so nice and, it then being 10.0 o.clock, we mounted the elephant. It kneels down. You tread on its poor hind heel—that is the first step. For the next you tread in its tail which a servant holds looped in a festoon. The third step is more like a scramble. Ropes hang down from the Howdah over its person, and you haul yourself up by these. Then the final heave, and we had a fine view of the plain and the Barabar Hills where we were going. One of them called The Crow's Swing is this shape ⤳. Well I've exaggerated, but it is as steep as the Matterhorn though not so high, and as it comes straight out of the flat, looks amazing. It ends in a huge thumb shaped stone on the top of which stood a little one balanced so well that a crow could swing on it. Too heavy a bird must have tried for it has fallen. On one side the rock comes down smooth and rounded like an inverted saucer and plunges into the earth of the plain. Beyond this—alas some way—were the other hills—and at their feet in a grove of palms, the tents were pitched. But breakfast—mockery of a name!—was not ready, and it was suggested we should visit the Buddhist caves while it was cooking. Here again were rocks, steps had been cut up them and in much heat and internal emptiness I climbed. The caves are cut out of the solid granite: a small square doorway and an oval hall inside. This sounds dull, but the granite has been so splendidly polished that they rank very high among caves for cheerfulness. Date—250 B. C.; as early as anything in India. One often has a frieze of elephants over the door, but in the rest the only decoration is the fine Pali inscriptions on the sides of the entrance tunnel. Standing inside one sees these in the strong sunlight, and beyond them the view. We lit candles which showed the grain of the granite and its reds and greys. The nephews also tried to wake the echoes, but whatever was said and in whatever voice the cave only returned a dignified roar. We saw seven of them, but no, breakfast was *not* ready when we returned. I ate a Brazil Nut. 'A nut and a slice of bread keep me going the whole day,' said the Nawab gaily.

Having fed, we went to another cave, and then there was a talk of panthers. Plenty about, it seemed. Maimie will be shocked to hear that I was all for going after them. But they don't appear till 5.0. P. M., and as we were not sleeping out we had to leave the hills by that hour or fail to reach Bela owing to darkness. One lives a third of the way up the Crow's Swing, but the villagers whom we asked in passing said they never knew nothing about it.—They always make this reply about a panther, fearing it will overhear them and take their cattle as a punishment. Arrived at the Bungalow of one of the nephews, we had another long wait for food, and I caught a train that brought me to Gya at midnight:—Baldeo went there straight by the morning train: and when I found the Rest House which wasn't easy, as there were two, I went to bed. I write in the resthouse now—it is a wretched little place as the good one is full but I leave early tomorrow.

Well, as to today. Masood has again arranged for me and I am now sponging on Nawab Syed Zafar Nawab Saleh, in whose carriage I went to Boddh Gya. Boddh Gya—not to be confused with the Vishnu temple at Gya about which I wrote to Ruth & Agnes—is the place where Sakya muni (as he was then called) obtained enlightenment—i.e. became Buddha; and it is the most sacred place in the Buddhist religion. Buddhism, though it started in India, has now died out from it, and so the pilgrims to the Boddh Gya temple are all from distant countries e.g. Burma and Tibet. Tibetans were there this afternoon, squat people with rough hair, filling the ante chamber of the temple and crouching between the barbaric pillars. Beyond them the shrine was a pool of fire. They had lighted hundreds and hundreds of tallow lamps, and above the radiance sat the giant statue of Buddha, pointing to the earth to bear him witness that he had gained enlightenment, and covered, like the pillars, with gold leaf. Over his head, dimly visible, swung canopies and streamers, waving in the hot air that rose from the floor— Meanwhile the Tibetans chanted or turned their prayer wheels or clashed cymbals, blew on horns of shell and beat gongs; or there were strange rituals—e.g. each looked into a bowl of water intently and at a signal drank a little.—I fancy the water reflects the universe and that by drinking it they draw up knowledge but I must find out. At the back of the shrine outside the temple, grows the sacred tree under which, or rather under the ancestor of which, Buddha sat. Squares of gold leaf have been stuck on to the trunk and boughs. The temple, together with several acres of garden full of trees and flowers and votive stones, chapels, bells, and statues, lies in a deep courtyard below the level of the surrounding country. The view when one drives up and sees everything suddenly from the edge of the embankment, is, as books say, 'not easily forgotten.' There can't be anything like it in the world.

On my return to Gya I paid a call on Nawab *no* II. He knew no English so most of our conversation was through an interpreter. He was very pleasant and gave me a cup and saucer of polished black stone, such as is made in the town. The handle is already off the cup so I am hopeful no more would happen. Then I went back to the Rest House wrote a little (I am writing *this* on the following day now) and went to dinner with the Chief Engineer of the East Indian Railway, a friend of Hubback's and a very fine chap. I knew his brother at King's too—Hindley the name is: I might possibly have mentioned him.[2] Dickinson & Trevy had stopped with him and he would have asked me but didn't know until too late. He was very funny about Bob—wondered how he *could* be so full of information when he did all the talking.

Then—oh horrible start!—this morning I rose at 5.0. A.M. dressed by a smoking lamp and caught the Bombay Mail to a place called Sassaram. You will scarcely want more sight seeing nor will you be intimate with Sher Shah, whose tomb is the sight. He was one of the Emperors. The tomb—a huge dome with cupolas and pavilions grouped round it—stands on an island in a tank. A causeway leads out to it. There are many palms, both fan- and date-, and many water birds swimming about, and charming hills with other tombs and small temples in the distance. I was there an hour between trains, and now I have brought myself up to the present moment. I sit in Moghul Serai Junction waiting room, until the train for Allahabad arrives. I will finish this at Allahabad. I am going to call on some friends of Hindley's who live close to the station, & must go.

Allahabad.   31 January 1913

Here I am and not only did Hindley's friends give me tea but they introduced me to a high official on the East India Railway, who raised me out of my grubby 2nd Class carriage to travel with him in his private car. It was at the end of the train with windows at the back and armchairs facing them: what luxury! No wind and a view of everything. He was a nice old fashioned sort of old gentleman—gold rimmed spectacles, fob, &ct—and very amusing about the high personages whom he has escorted. 'All the Viceroys are alike—all affable; Curzon, Hardinge, Minto—if I shut my eyes I shouldn't know which I was listening to. And all the Vicereines are charming.' He told the Hardinges that the transfer of the Capital would make no difference to the Calcutta retail trade as the Govt people spent very little time there as it was. Lady H. exclaimed 'Quite true, quite true. I get all my hats in England through my sister and she has my measurements too.'—He and I talked about the bomb outrage. I believe in the theory advanced by Malcolm who visited the scene afterwards—that the bomb came not from the Bank but from the trees on the other side.—But hardly anyone considers this.[3]

My kind host gave me dinner before we got to Allahabad: I was glad of it as Smith is in tents a long way from the station. I'm afraid he is overworked & not very well. He is already down at the Fair. I stopped in bed after my strenuous yesterday.

The chief excitement of my last days at Bankipore were the adventures of silly little Mahmoud.[4] An old man of ruffianly appearance turned up to beg for subscriptions—bearing a (forged) list. Mahmoud gave something on which he said 'You are a barrister, sir; you need a clerk. I will be your clerk.' He continued to sit, presently remarking 'And when will dinner be ready?' Dinner was announced and he went in. 'I could not be inhospitable' said Mahmoud, 'and I felt sure he would go after it.' As indeed he did, but at midnight a cab rolled up out of which he got with all his luggage, saying 'and where is my bed?' He was given a bed. He kept the servants up half the night cleaning his hookah and complained of them in the morning. Mahmoud ran wailing about Bankipore. On the evening of the second day when we called he was still there. Mahmoud, his brother, Agarwalla, Masood myself and he all sat round a small table—the oddest & most uncomfortable party you can imagine. Next morning he called on Masood who had enquired meanwhile into his career and made short work of him, and in the afternoon he ended his career as far as Mahmoud was concerned by entering one of the servants' room and stealing two rupees four annas from his coat pocket. Mahmoud, polite to the last, said to him during the row, 'there seems to be some misunderstanding—I think you had better not stop.' 'Yes,' replied the villain. 'I cannot bear to stop where there has been a misunderstanding.'—This little incident

is typically oriental. It couldn't have happened in the west—though
let Maimie take warning![5]

~~Oh dear oh dear have just heard this will miss the mail I mean~~

(Loving Morgan.)

ALS: KCC

[1] The tree under which the Buddha is supposed to have sat when he received enlightenment.
[2] Sir Clement D. M. Hindley (1874–1944) was an official of the East Indian Railway,
1897–1928, being, in the last six years of his career, Chief Commissioner of Railways for
India. His brother, Oliver Walter Hindley (1877–1944), had entered King's in 1898, and the
ICS in 1902. In 1923 he became Superintending Engineer for the Punjab Irrigation.
[3] On 23 December 1912 a bomb was thrown at the howdah of the elephant on which Lord
and Lady Hardinge rode into Delhi to observe officially the transfer of the capital from
Calcutta. The Viceroy was injured; an attendant was killed.
[4] On Mahmoud, see EMF's 'The Suppliant', in 'Adrift in India', *AH*, pp. 315–18.
[5] An allusion to Maimie's strong tendency to adopt waifs and strays.

120   To Forrest Reid

Sohbatia Bagh, Allahabad
2 February 1913

Dear Reid
     Your letters have a knack of coming when I'm depressed, and
India is too exciting not to bring reactions.[1] I can't answer this last
properly as *F. D.* is away on tour over the peninsula. The critics
though—come come! They did you both well and promptly in the
Times. I wonder if it was into the hands of the obscene A. M. that the
C. O. fell; the review was coy and favourable and very hard to
bear. I sent *F. D.* to a woman of another kind and have just heard
'I am still haunted by it—it interested me very much—it is
extraordinarily intimate and has a certain distinction & beauty that
attract me ⟨*inspite* of—(crossed out)⟩ together with a certain brutal
reality. My impressions are complex and I don't express them well. I
do think it quite extraordinarily good.'—Lowes Dickinson liked it
too.[2]
     How cordially I agree that stories should not click and Freya of
the Seven Isles is fashioned of base metal besides.[3] Your autumnal
tale is the sequel of this, I assume; go on with it and with the spring.[4]
You ask about my work. I feel you too sympathetic to keep silent. I
am dried up. Not in my emotions, but in their expression. I cannot
write at all. You say I helped you once—have a shot at helping me
for I need it. Please do not mention this, as few people know. It often
makes me very unhappy. I see beauty going by and have nothing to
catch it in. The only book I have in my head is too like Howards End
to interest me; a contrast again; between battle and work; the chief
figure a Knight errant born too late in time who finds no clear issue
to which to devote himself; our age demands patient good tempered
labour, not chivalry.—But this isn't good enough.[5] I want

something beyond the field of action and behaviour; the waters of the river that rises from the middle of the earth to join the Ganges and the Jumna where they join. India is full of such wonders, but she can't give them to me.—To have done good work is something and I don't the least doubt that I have done some.

I hope you will be in town when I'm there, but don't stop too long in it. All the boats are full, but I may get back in May. Do write again.

Yours ever
E.M.F.

Have you read *Where Angels fear to tread* yet? If not I will give it to you.

ALS: Stephen Gilbert

¹ Not merely excitement caused a reaction. He was staying with R. B. Smith (see Letter 116) and that day wrote in his diary (KCC): 'R.B.S. typical civilian. Protects ryots [small farmers] but hates any class that can criticise him. Invited Ahmed Mirza to lunch but would not talk to him. Declared that Germany could make a fortune out of India by torturing natives till they gave up their hoards. Is curt & insolent to the pleaders in his court. Very bad—worse than I had feared. Grew too depressed to sit with them in the evening, and tried to get through to Mango Trees & stars. Letter from Reid helped me.'

² F. D.: Reid's *Following Darkness*. The *TLS* reviewer ('Fiction', 17 October 1912, pp. 443–4) welcomed it because of 'its obviously fine intention'—of which it fell short. 'Nevertheless, once read, "Following Darkness" is not a book that will be easily forgotten, and that is becoming rather a rare tribute for a novel.' A speculation about EMF's speculation might be that Alice Meynell wrote the *TLS* review ('Fiction', 22 June 1911, p. 238) of *The Celestial Omnibus and Other Stories*. It refers to EMF's 'elfish sharpness' and complains that criticising the stories is difficult because they are 'all so lightly fitted together and airily thrown off' so that it seemed 'brutal to hold them down and examine them'—in which case one would find that 'some of them are very loosely written.' The 'woman of another kind' is unidentified but may have been Florence Barger.

³ Joseph Conrad, 'Freya of the Seven Isles: A Story of Shallow Waters', in *'Twixt Land & Sea Tales* (1913).

⁴ Reid's 'autumnal tale': *The Gentle Lover: A Comedy of Middle Age* (1912), about a solitary middle-aged man attracted by a young girl. Spring: Reid's *Pirates of the Spring* (1916).

⁵ 'Only book': 'Arctic Summer'.

121   To Alice Clara Forster

c/o Smith, Sohbatia Bagh, Allahabad
5 February 1913

Dearest Mother

I have one interesting thing to tell about this week—the bathing Fair—but nothing else of note, so this will be a short letter. I am so vexed that mine of last week missed the mail: hopeful Indians misled me.

I think I told you that the Fair is on the holiest spot in India—where the Ganges & Jumna meet.—Unfortunately for all concerned the spot is always changing. The Jumna keeps fairly steady but the bed of the Ganges is between 2 & 3 miles broad and it wanders over it. One year it joined the Jumna on this side—close under the Fort: this year it is far over the sand, on which, and not on the solid embankment, the Fair must be held. Imagine the difficulties with which Smith and the other officials have to contend. Roads have to be made, shops let, bathing boards & boats arranged and licensed—and then without any visible cause the Ganges changes its course, washing away the Fair in one place and leaving it high & dry in another. At present the Sangam (holy place of junction) is over a great backwater through which the pilgrims wade—shallow for the most part, but containing one or two nasty holes and watercourses which have to be fenced & policed. The Sangam is only 1 foot deep, but it shelves suddenly to 10, and alters its position about 20 yards every day. Drop upon this scene about one million men and women, most of whom do not mind whether they get drowned or not! Up to now no one has succeeded.—A most remarkable feat! remarkable!

I ride to this Fair & back every morning on the kindest horse. No contretemps, and Smith's Jodhpurs fit me exactly. The first 'bit o' fun' one meets is a Fakir, swinging head downwards over a fire. Another Fakir pushes him. As his head is in a bag the smoke does not bother him, but I marvel how he keeps it up. Further down, another Fakir, doing the same, another banging broomsticks at idols, others squatting in groups their faces covered with clay. On great years, the Fakirs go in procession, and fight with one another & the police, but this is a small year. Farther down the central road are the shops—the chief sweet shop is willing to pay Gov a rent of £160 for the 8 days of the fair, so you may imagine the trade—and beyond them the flags of the priests and the enclosures where the pilgrims have their hair cut. An Indian's chief attraction is his thick black mop, and when it is shaved close except for one long strand in the crown by which he is pulled to Heaven, he looks plain indeed. The state of the hair-enclosure is repellant [sic]—piles of dirty locks, barbers quarrelling over customers, customers arguing over fees; I saw a poor baby squealing while its mother was pulled right & left between rival firms. Then they go to the rivers and bathe—the hair goes separately, in large bundles,—and after bathing they eat and all look so happy. This morning—which was the greatest, but tomorrow will be greater still—we sat on an observation platform at the edge of the backwater, in the midst of a square mile of bald and almost naked people. We saw whole villages enter the water at once in long chains, like the Tonbridge ladies at the Diamond Jubilee. The rich go in boats (as we shall go tomorrow) and the very rich go in boats with removable bottoms so that they can bathe unseen. Some give the rivers marygolds; others set rafts afloat on them for luck; others sit in them holding the tail of a calf which has been brought down by others again who hire it out for that purpose. By the evening, dust and smoke cloud the whole plain. I have just been looking down into it from the embankment, and it was like a pale blue sea with people crawling as shrimps on the bottom. They camp on it and all over the country: a grove near ours is full of watch fires. I am lucky to have hit one of these great Fairs; there can't be anything like it elsewhere.

Naturally Smith is very busy, and as Ahmed Mirza is busy too, I am rather at a loose end for the rest of the day. Our mango grove is not very nice as they are building near, and though we have 29 tents in it, all are hot and small. Three other people also connected with the Fair are stopping in it—all nice, and one of them has a charming & amusing wife, but I don't see much of them. Tomorrow is a public holiday so Mirza will be free and we are to do something together.

I enclose a couple of letters that may amuse you. I have at last fixed my passage on the *City of Marseilles*—arriving Marseilles on April 21st—but may yet come by the later boat (*City of Lahore*) arriving May 1st, as the *City of Marseilles* sails not from Bombay but Karachi which is inconvenient as I shall have to trans-ship there. According to present plan I go to Hyderabad for a couple of days on March 20th, and then to stop with Mirza's younger brother, whom I also know, and visit the Ellora caves.[1]

I do hope that Masood's present may yet reach. He declares he packed it properly.

Loving Morgan

ALS: KCC

[1] Abu Saeed Mirza, Ahmed Mirza's younger brother, went to London at the age of eighteen, was called to the bar at the age of twenty-one, and in 1913 was a *munsif*, or district judicial officer, in Aurangabad. Eventually he became Chief Justice Saeed Jung.

122   To Laura Mary Forster

Lahore.   19 February 1913

Dear Aunt Laura,

Thank you for your letter. I was entertained by your account of the Edser household. Though not in love with Addie myself, I am sure that they have been slandered.—Yes, is it not irritating when outsiders suddenly try to play the good fairy.[1]

The above is a little incoherent, but the Darling baby, house bound by rain, is sporting round me, and shouting at the top of his voice to the servant who shouts back in Hindustani. It is delightful to hear such gaiety, for the poor little dear had enteric last summer, and was peevish & weak when I arrived. Now he has completely recovered into a noisy & affectionate little boy.

For the last six weeks I have been in British India, hearing more politics and business talk than I am capable of understanding, and passing to and fro between the Indian camp and the Anglo Indian. There is much bitterness in either, which has been increased by the Commission; each party has been invited to hold forth on the faults of the other. Indians complain that the only result enquiry will only result in an increase of pay for the officials, Anglo Indians that it means further jobs for Indians, whatever the evidence offered; but I suppose the result really depends on what government is in power when the report is submitted.[2]

The atmosphere in this house is delightful. I enjoyed it on my first visit, but did not realise how unusual it was in British India. Darling and his wife are the only officials I have met who care to see anything of the educated Indian socially; others see him, but at formal garden parties and banquets. Here there are little lunch parties once or twice a week, and as they are not conducted in the 'missionary' spirit, but from sincere desire for a better acquaintance, they pass off cheerfully and well. It is true that Darling is well happily placed; his post of Under Secretary makes Indians anxious to know him, yet does not give them any opening to ask him political favours. But I attribute his success chiefly to his wife, who is unlike any other Anglo-Indiana I have met, and partly to his happy experiences at Dewas. Granting that Native States are worse governed and hot-beds of petty intrigue, they are yet more comfortable socially. The Englishman gets on better with the Indian there, and the Mahommedan with the Hindu, and even the poor people show a cheerfulness and self r air of self respect that one seldom notices in British India. I am glad to think that I shall be back among the native states again before I leave. Next week I have an invitation to Pattiala (Sikh) and go on to Jeypoor where I have an introduction to the Prime Minister, and to Jodhpur, which promises to be as interesting as anything from the social point of view; English men and women and Indians share one club in perfect harmony. I end at Hyderabad, Deccan (Mahommedan).

I have lost my white writing paper, and must use your hated grey. I am so glad that my letters have given you pleasure. It is indeed a pleasure to write them, and I am proud that you should have had passages typed.

Do you know Sleeman's *Rambles & Recollections of an Indian Official*? It is a charming book to read in, but the best chapter, about a Suttee on the Nerbudda, you would perhaps be inclined to skip. I have also been reading *The Private Life of an Eastern King* by E. W. Knighton who was librarian to one of the Kings of Oudh, a very entertaining and interesting little book, and it rings true.[3] It is certainly out of print, but may be in the L[ondon] L[ibrary].

Lahore, though wet and cold, is full of flowering trees, pear trees and Bougonvillea [*sic*]. The tennis tournament is at hand, and while the Darlings practice I walk in the public gardens that surround the courts and listen to the students crooning over their lesson books among the flowers.

Yours ever affectionately
E. M. Forster.

ALS: KCC

[1] Edsers, Addie: unidentified.
[2] A Royal Commission on Indian Public Services, headed by John Poynder Dickson-Poynder, 1st Baron Islington (1866–1936), was appointed on 5 September 1912 to consider advisability of allowing Indians into high echelons of the ICS. Exclusion had long been a sore point with educated Indians, as was inclusion among most Anglo-Indians. The Commission stayed in India for two years, and its report was published in 1917, by which time the European war and rising tides of Indian nationalism had made it largely obsolete.
[3] Sir William Sleeman, *Rambles and Recollections of an Indian Official* (1844): on suttee, Chapter 4. E. William Knighton, *The Private Life of an Eastern King* (1855). Oudh: i.e. Bengal.

123   To Alice Clara Forster

Lahore.   26 February 1913

Dearest Mother
    After all I have plenty of news for my letter. To begin backwards, we went to a romantic dinner party by star light yesterday. It was in the Shalimar Gardens, 5 miles away, and we drove through seas of mud, for the rain had been heavy. The Gardens were built by the Emperor Shah Jahan for the lady who was afterwards buried in the Taj. From the entrance we walked beside a ribbon of water between high trees and this led to a pavilion and vanished beneath it. In the pavilion we found our hosts, Colonel and Mrs Sitwell, but never a light and no food.[1] They led us groping to the further side, and we found ourselves high over a sheet of water which a causeway crossed and round which other buildings glimmered, and in one [of] these, like a meal for fairies, our dinner was laid, the lamp on the dinner table shining through the arches and illuminating the water & the trees. The moon, who was supposed to rise, forgot, but I always bear her absence gladly, and the stars, very large & numerous, contented everyone. What luxury! To sit in an exquisite pavilion with the plashing of fountains and the calling of wild animals coming out of the darkness, and to drink really hot soup and eat really hot food. Indian servants are wonderful. Mrs Sitwell had only to say 'dinner for six at 8.30. in Shalimar Gardens,' and all was done. They think English people mad and this is an advantage, for no one thing we do seems odder than another. In these surroundings I ate my first mango.
    As they said of my short stories 'it didn't compel' but had a subtle and delicate flavour which pleased me.
    In the afternoon I was taken by Mir (whom I knew in England) to

have tea with an old Mohammedan gentleman who had asked to see me.[2] Both tea and old gentleman were ~~ver~~ nice, but almost too much of the latter who prattled without a break for an hour and a half. "Oh I am so happy, so very happy—the Government has been so particularly good to me. It has provided for all my four daughters so that they are not on my mind, and appointed me A.D.C, to many celebrated men. When I travel about the world, as I can do for Government has provided for my daughters, I call upon these celebrated men—it is my duty—and they give me interviews sometimes of one hour, sometimes of two sometimes of three. I intend to write a book about these interviews. Oh what a very happy life." At last I rose—there was no other way—and he exclaimed "I have tired you. I have talked too much. Alas, I always do, and now you are going. It has been a great pleasure to receive you in my house, but I wish you were more fat. You are not as fat as you should be, I am sure." Escorting us down the garden he remarked "And here I listen in the evening to my nightingales. All men are not good but all birds are good. There are no wicked nightingales, not one." Rather a dear, but we came away with reeling heads.

I have also dined with Mir at his house—all ~~rather~~ very Anglicised, though we ended with some Indian dishes. The company were feeblish folk except for one remarkable young man; I don't know whether he was an angel or the other thing, but feel sure he was one or the other. Generally one has to handle Indians carefully in conversation but he was as tough as nails and full of fun and wit. I haven't met any one like him, and his education has been purely Indian which made his assurance & vigour the more interesting.

Then I have been to the two enclosed entertainments which tell their own tale on the back, and we had Indian dinner & lunch parties here; even a lady has come.[3] She is very clever and suspected of sedition. Josie [Darling] says she only needs a little attention & hospitality to make her loyal, which is quite possible. The other guests were the lady's husband and a gentleman who is a Hindu by profession & a Buddhist by faith. I asked him why the Tibetans at Boddh Gya looked into water bowls, and he says it was to see whether their souls were pure.

Furthermore I have been to see an artistic 'Chelsea' sort of couple [several words inked out and illegible] to whom I will give the feigned name of Stephens who have been blackballed by the English Club here because his hair was too long and her evening clothes lost in the Railway Strike. I liked them—her especially, and am going to supper tomorrow with a walk in the city first. The Darlings are ideal hosts and friends. Not many Anglo Indians would encourage a guest to do queer unusual things, still less join in such themselves. Everyone is in such a terror of being out of the ordinary. Classical music, literature, intellectual tastes generally—as a rule all is dropped in a couple of years, and husbands and wives, when their day's work is done, meet other husbands and wives in a dense mass at the Club. One is told that all this has to be, and of course the outsider can't know, but it is refreshing to find people who stand up against it.[4]

At 9.0. A.M. Monday I read a paper to students of the Gov[t] College on 'How to enjoy English Literature', and catch a train to Amritsar at 10.30.[5] Having seen the Golden Temple, I go on in the evening to Patiala, & stop two nights with the principal of the College there, a writer named Candler—good I believe, though I don't know his books, and certainly kind.[6] I hope to have a day in Delhi and see Rashid who has written a nice letter to me. Then wildly through Rajputana. Must stop to see tennis played.

Much love
Morgan

ALS: KCC

[1] Constance Talbot Sitwell, née Chetwynd (1887–1974) was a cousin of Edith Sitwell, and the second wife of Brigadier-General William Henry Sitwell (1860–1932), most of whose military career was spent in Africa and the Middle East. He was on the General Staff, 1909–13. EMF wrote a Foreword (pp. 7–11) to Mrs Sitwell's *Flowers and Elephants* (1927), which annoyed Edith and Osbert Sitwell.

[2] Mir: unidentified.

[3] At one of these entertainments, an old gentleman named Godbole sang *ragas*. This was at a reception given by the Brahmo Samaj, another Hindu reform movement, founded in Calcutta in 1828 and closely associated with the Tagore family. It rejects the authority of the Vedas, and in its worship and theology is somewhat similar to Unitariansim.

[4] Unfortunately, they are unidentified.

[5] This was 'The Enjoyment of English Literature', read to the BA and MA classes at the College (A MS, dated by EMF, 3 March 1913. KCC). His listeners were most of them unsophisticated country boys. The invitation came from Gerald Anstruther Wathen (1878–1958), a friend of Darling who later was Headmaster of the Khalsa College in Amritsar; he had so much influence on the boys that at the time of the Massacre in 1919 there was no disturbance in the College. Wathen is thought by some to have been the original of Fielding in *Passage*. He returned to England in 1927 and taught in a school in Hampstead, London.

[6] His host was Edmund Candler (1874–1926), author and traveller, foreign and war correspondent. He was Principal of the Government College at Patiala, 1906–14. He had come to India in 1896 in candid pursuit of the romance of the East; however, his novels on Indian subjects are far more realistic than romantic. On this independent and interesting personality, see Benita Parry, *Delusions and Discoveries: Studies on India in the British Imagination, 1880–1930*, pp. 131–63.

124   To Alice Clara Forster

Jaipur.   10 March 1913

Dearest Mother

I leave this fraudulent place this afternoon. In the first flush of arrival I sent my clothes to the wash, and couldn't get away till they returned. It's a tourist centre and sports three large hotels and there is—I grant!—one nice expedition to Amber, which I took yesterday, and a fine modern museum. But it puzzles me why tourists come here & miss out Muttra or Sanchi or Gwalior or Gya. There's nothing but a laid-out town, painted blotting paper pink, traversed by streets as wide as White Hall [sic] and intolerable with dust and sun. Even from this the hotels are distant three miles, and carriages at one Rupee per hour are the only means of reaching it; I am in one of the Hotels, but my chief solace is a beautiful garden close by, belonging to a Captain Hartley, a friend of Darling's.¹ I have been to dinner here twice, and am writing in it now.

                                        Jodhpur.   11 March 1913
    This will be a scrappy letter, scarcely worth circulating, for I must jump on to say into what a glorious place I have fallen. Hasluck told me of it first, and I also knew it as the home of breeches, but, though not difficult to reach, it is off the main route and few visitors come. I arrived at 6.30. this morning, and we were waking up the inhabitants of the Dak Bungalow in the twilight to let me in, when up dashed another friend of Malcolm's in a motor and took me off to his house. It's now nine, so I haven't any experience to go on, except a view over a plain, out of which in every direction, square-topped hills rise. On the nearest hill—much the highest—is the enormous fort, covering miles of ground, and cut off, when I saw it first, from the lower earth by the smoke and mist of morning. The white town lies at the foot, and camels stroll about in the foreground, while the whole plain is cooing with doves. My host, Goyder, is Financial Adviser to the Jodhpur State: I have only seen him a few minutes but liked him.² I hope that he will take me to the Club, for English & Indians mix there, I am told, in great comfort. The regent, Sir Pratap Singh, encourages this. It is a Rajpoot State—home of good manners, high birth, and loyalty, but not particularly of brains, and the Raja, who is a Mahratta, was poking fun at it at Delhi.³ "A fine straightforward chap. Oh yes—that is what the Government wants a chief to be. A fine chap like a Rajpoot who notices nothing—Well, I must try." The chief Rajpoot states are Udaipur, Jodhpur, Jaipur, and Bikaner: Chhatarpur and the neighbouring states are also Rajpoot, but of less antiquity & fame. The Mahratta states rose in the 18th century on the ruining Moghal Empire: Gwalior, Indore, & Baroda are the chief; Dewas and Kohlapur of the best lineage. We really conquered India from the Mahrattas, and they don't forget it. The Rajpoots have never done anything but sit tight in Rajpootana. Both sets of states are Hindu. Dear me! How instructive I grow.
    Yet again I go on after a few hours, which have produced a piano, horses without limit, and a very kind invitation to stop several days, which, if I can find out that it would not really bore them, I shall accept and miss out Ahmedabad. Goyder shares the house with another man—I have forgotten his name, but he is building a new

railway into the desert and has offered to take me there on a trolley, and on camels too.[4] He plays the piano quite well. I have just been to call on two other people to whom I have had introductions in the place, but do not like them as much as my hosts. The social atmosphere is unusually pleasant: the English form one happy family, and even when they don't care for Indians can keep off nagging about them. It is so rare in India to find anyone, black or white, who isn't grumbling; a sign of the general 'unrest' I suppose.

I must go back to Delhi. On the second day the Raja paid some official calls, and I drove round with him but did not go in, remaining in the carriage with 'Lady' the elderly pug, who goes every where, I can't make out why. We ended up at the Cotes', whose acquaintance, as friends of Malcolm's, he wished to make, and then, like a boy loose from school, he grew mad with joy that his duties were over, and bounced up and down among the cushions. We drove into the City, and came across his brother and various members of the court who had been shopping. Much excitement, and we drove on, but no sooner had we gone twenty yards than he thought it would be fun to have them all with us. But they had got into the electric-tram to have the experience, which was new to them, and we followed madly in their wake, blocked by buffaloes and camels and goats and cows and sweetmeat sellers and pariah dogs. The tram was disappearing but the coachman, at the Raja's orders, leapt from the box and pursued it on foot, shouting. After five minutes he came back leading the whole procession who got in, together with their purchases of briar pipes, tobacco, mechanical monkeys for the children, writing paper, ink, paper parcels of every size & shape. In all we were ten—the horses were strong and went slowly—and if you had seen us it would have looked like a car in a carnaval. I sat between the Raja in a huge pale yellow turban and his brother whose turban was purple and who was trying to smoke his English pipe. Opposite were doctor in a red Mahratta head dress, a secretary who wore a shallow cup and saucer, and the court buffoon, on whose knees Lady lay, indifferent to everything. Coachman, another attendant, and footman made three on the box, while the groom hung on behind. We attracted, as far as I could make out, no attention at all, though they all talked louder & louder as Indians do when they are happy. We got back at about 7.0. when a scene of great confusion followed. I wanted to make my own arrangements for getting to the station, which thanks to Baldeo always work without the slightest hitch—I've only to name the train, and when I arrive five minutes before it goes there he is with all the baggage in the carriage & the bed made if it is a night journey. But no—I was the Raja's guest and he would arrange—two tongas for the luggage, and he and I alone in a phaeton, while the court, who were going to bathe in the Ganges at Hardwar, should follow behind—the Hardwar train left 2 hours after mine. But the court had got under way and out of hand, and no sooner did a carriage drive [up] than they and their dogs and their parrots and their men servants and their maid servants leapt into it and were off before Baldeo could get the luggage down. Nor could he find any one to carry it. Nor did the Raja lose the extra opportunity for confusion which was presented by two entrances to the garden, sending Baldeo to one while a carriage waited at another. At last all grew deathly quiet—every one had gone but ourselves and the Rani who was dressing, helped by a hand maiden. Taking B. aside I said "Let us not trouble His Highness any more: make any arrangement that you can." The story should end with him doing this, but just then a decrepid band-ghari (= 4 wheeler) came up into which I and the luggage got: not the Raja who had to stop behind to start the Rani, there being no one left to do this. It's so typical of the Oriental who makes a howling mess over one thing and does another with perfect ~~grace~~ success & grace, that when I reached Delhi station an official met me with railway tickets for myself & Baldeo to Jaipur: the Raja had ordered them. It is a usual if overwhelming courtesy in the East to do this, and a deadly insult to ~~protest~~ refuse; and indeed I was pleased to be given tickets by ~~some~~ any one whom I like as much and who is as rich as this man; but I have found it trying when an obscure Indian whom I didn't care for once bought my ticket for me—fortunately only to the tune of ninepence. The tickets—mine first class as against my usual 2ⁿᵈ—did not bring their full joys, for as it was late the train had filled up and I could only get an upper berth, and Baldeo no seat at all. The court, entangled with other courts who were also leaving after the chiefs' conference, ran up and down the platform looking for trains. Rashid came too very kindly to see me off, and on top of him the Raja having landed the Rani safely. Off my train went before I was on it—handshakings, messages to you, cries. I caught it up, and proposed to take Baldeo, whom the guard could get in nowhere, into the carriage, but my ass of a fellow traveller protested, and proposed that Baldeo & his own servant— we were in the same plight—should travel on the foot board at the end of the carriage—they were Continental shape—facing full all night to the wind. He said "it would not do—they would not understand"—that argument so dear to fools. Technically he was right, so I could only point out how inconvenient he would find it if his servant fell on the rails in the night or got ill. At the next station—15 minutes on—I prepared to hunt for the guard again, but by now he had come to his senses, and remarked that it did seem rather cold, and that if I was willing to abandon the conventions, he also. So the servants slept on the carriage floor, and whether or not they understood, arrived at Jaipur without pneumonia. The man, I discovered, was an American. Cheers for Democracy! He seemed absolutely English—upper class. Oxford manner—and had evidently moved in high circles at Delhi, dining with the Viceroy and the chiefs according to his own account. I must try to track him down.

So much to say that I must miss out Amber—I think Treves describes it—and the crocodiles at Jaipur.[5] My paper to the students at Lahore pleased me and I think them, and Wathen told me I had hit the right nails on the head which was gratifying. I will send it you, but it is minus quotations, which lengthened it by ¼ hour.

Now I must stop. View more splendid than ever. Tea.

Loving Morgan

ALS: KCC

[1] This was Alan Fleming Hartley (1882–1954), who was with the Rajputana Cavalry and Transport in 1913 and in 1942 was His Excellency General Sir A. F. Hartley, Commander in Chief in India.

[2] George Barrett Goyder (1872–1952) joined the ICS in 1895 as a member of the Indian Financial Department. He was posted to Jodhpur in August 1911 and became Chief Auditor in 1921. He retired in 1923.

[3] Sir Pratap Singh (d. 1922), great-uncle of the Rajah Sir Umaid Singh, was President of the Council of Regency until that ruler succeeded to the Jodhpur throne in 1918.

[4] This was M. Spartali (untraced), at this time Resident Engineer of the Jodhpur-Bikaner Railway.

[5] I.e. Sir Frederick Treves, *The Other Side of the Lantern*; see Letter 108.

125   To Laura Mary Forster

Jodhpur, Rajputana.   12 March 1913

Dear Aunt Laura

I'm so sorry the ~~letter~~ fakir is lost, for though I say it as shouldn't the letter was interesting and I can say so without contradiction as it is all too unlikely that it will turn up now.[1] I find I had made a few notes on him in my diary, but nothing about his picture of the Tree of the Universe which he explained to me, and the details of which now grow rather dim. Our best talk was about literature; the state of ~~mind~~ a man's mind at the time that he is actually writing. We discovered that though we described our experiences in different words, they were the same, though I wrote modern novels & he Sanskrit poems! He was very friendly and approachable.

I will bring the coins—Rs. 1/–/–, and 8, 4, and 2, annas in silver, and ¼ anna in copper are those in ordinary use. I will also bring a Rupee of Victoria as Queen—i.e. an East India Company issue—but not complete sets of Victorias, Edwards, Georges; a mixed set made up of them all will be equally instructive & less ruinous! Over Rs 1/–/– the issue is in paper notes.

Jodhpur is—after Agra—the finest place I have been to yet. Please tell this only to the very nice or the very feeble, for it is undiscovered so far by the tourist, and all the inhabitants, English & Indian, tremble in fear of his irruption. I wish I could draw what I see now from my host's verandah—parallel strips of green plain, white town, and grey rocky ridge; and rising out of the ridge above the town, the enormous fort, itself grey, and looking less like masonry than an upper stratum of the hill. It's difficult to describe because letters can't convey how large things are. This fort is very *very* large, and I must leave the rest to you. The big palace only fills a corner of it, and the batteries of mediæval guns another corner.

We went there yesterday—it is about three miles off in a straight line. My companion was a garden-architect who comes out every year from Kew; a pleasant little man.[2] He is planning a public garden for Sir Pratap Singh, the Regent, who sent us up in a motor. The Fort has several children at its feet, perched on little hills, and one even broader than the hill it perches on; and all the surrounding ridges are crested with walls for miles. It is entered by I forget how many gates, but after several the motor stopped, and there were palanquins, had we cared to take them, but we walked up by the ancient paved approach, winding steeply between cliffs of masonry and under cavernous arches. As I say, it suggests not a building but a mountain; even when the work becomes delicate, as it does at the palace where the plain surfaces break into filagree, it is still immensely old, untouched, and grey. The jewelry and armoury were open for us, but these are delights over which I don't willingly linger, though it was amusing to see the little mallet, studded with rubies and worth Rs. 5000, which had been made as a toy for the present Maharaja, and which he had broken at the age of three by whacking too hard at the ruby studded ball! He is now a boy at Wellington! I wish you would say a few words to him in season. His palace is at present almost entirely unspoilt, but I fear it is unspoilt by ignorance rather than design. The interior decoration is very gorgeous and purely Indian; round the reception room are pilasters of red and gold, supporting a heavy cornice of red gold & blue, and the cieling [*sic*] has arabesques on white, encircling medaillions [*sic*] of the gods, with a central span of gold filagree through which a looking glass glimmers. It is really splendid in its contrast to the grey of the outside—colour running riot suddenly. But such a room ought to have one good carpet in it and no chairs, and even Lord Roberts, seated on his favourite charger, could be dispensed with. I'm afraid Wellington will not tell the young Maharaja to take him down, nor warn him generally against the Tottenham Court Road.[3] As you say, it is our fault: Indians tell me that they give up their turbans for solar-topees (in which they look particularly plain) because, when Europeanised, they are treated by the police &[ct] with more respect.

My hosts, to whom I had an introduction from Darling, are named Goyder and Sparlati. It sounds like a Bond street firm, but the first is adviser to Jodhpur State, and the second an engineer making a new railway. Both are particularly nice; fond of music, and happy in their surroundings,—state of mind too rare in India. Sparlati [sic] takes me in a trolley today along his new line into the desert, so I shall see untouched country. Trolleys and horses are the main means of locomotion: last night I actually rose to dinner in evening dress

S. calls me. I end in haste & with love.

Yours affectionately ever
E. M. Forster

ALS: KCC

1 I.e. Nrusinh Sharma, at Benares: see Letter 116.
2 The garden-architect is unidentified.
3 In London, traditionally the location of the retail furniture trade.

126   To Forrest Reid

H. H. The Nizam's Mint, Hyderabad, Deccan[1]
23 March 1913

Dear Reid

I shan't let you read my fragments. It was called *Arctic Summer*—the long cold day in which there is time to do things—and its hero one who did not want to do things but to fight. From boy hood he asked for straight issues—to lay down his life for God or King or Woman—and has to learn that in this latter day straight issues are not provided.

Your advice is good and goes as far as advice can. As for school stories, I might write them if I could write freely, but this is impossible in the Public's present state, and it bores me to write insincerely. It's all right touching off girls and boys in a short story, with fantasy instead of psychology to float them.

I must keep myself from trying to look round civilisation. I haven't the experience or the power, & the influence of Galsworthy Wells &ᶜᵗ is certainly bad for me. *Arctic Summer* would have involved the look round. Well good bye and thanks awfully. Such a letter does help.

Yours ever
E.M.F.

ALS: Stephen Gilbert

1 May Wyld had solved the problem of accommodations, and EMF was the guest of Robert Lorraine Gamlen (1874–1937), Head of the Hyderabad Mint, for the State had its own coinage, and some 500 men were employed there. May wrote to PNF (2 July 1971) that she had heard comments about EMF's visit from persons who 'had wondered what the English visitor wanted to know. They did not find him as easy to talk to as the Englishmen who lived in India. This would be natural. The Englishman whose home was in India would talk to the Nawab or the Maharajah as he would talk to another Englishman.' She regretted *A Passage to India*, which in her opinion gave a mistaken impression of relations between English and Indians.

127   To Syed Ross Masood

S. S. *City of Marseilles*, at Red Sea
11 April 1913

Dearest SRM,

I'm having a pleasant voyage, you'll be glad to hear and find 2nd class pleasanter than 1st as the people are more friendly. I am hoping to see Cairo and the Pyramids as we stop for cargo at Port Said.

I forget whether I wrote to you from Bombay—an awful scramble to catch boat, so perhaps I didn't. I was very sad to leave Saeed: his kindness was great and he was much more of a man than I remember him in London. Do speak to him about his extravagance. He tells me he is in debt, and yet he takes no trouble. I was very much worried because he would let me pay for nothing, and the tongas for Ellora alone must have come to 30 rupees or more.¹ You know how I feel about these things, and I think you agree. However, it is better to ruin your host than to offend him, so poor Saeed is ruined by me.—Of course, I haven't nearly as much in common with him as with Ahmed Mirza. All the same, I like him very much, and hope his wife and friends will steady him down a bit.

I've heard from Agarwala and must answer him: more news in his letter than I shall ever get through your's.² So your house is plag[u]e stricken and deserted and still contains a single rear, if that.³ How I wish your mother and yourself would settle up your affairs and join. It's an awful pity when people who love each other and might live together don't. I'm coming to live with you in our old age, but till then you must make some other arrangement.

Yours for ever,
Morgan

TTr supplied by Akbar Masood

¹ Tonga: light two-wheeled carriage. Ellora: site of Hindu cave-temples, nineteen miles from Aurangabad.
² Agarwal[l]a: see Letter 119.
³ Rear: slang for lavatory.

128   To Alice Clara Forster

S. S. City of Marseilles
at Red Sea.—so cool!
13 April 1913

Dearest Mother

After all I write you another letter. It is said, if posted at Port Said, to arrive in England before I do, so I will try. The boat is behind time and will scarcely reach Marseilles before the 22nd, nor I London before the 23rd or 24th, but I will wire day & hour from Marseilles.

There are no time tables on board, and every one, including the captain, is uncertain: he won't even say there will be time to visit Cairo, though I'm sure there ought to be, as we stop to unlade cargo both at Suez & Port Said. So we shall none of us go, and all the plans of seeing Pyramids & Sphinx by moonlight have collapsed.

I am enjoying the voyage more than I expected, though it is 2nd instead of 1st. Both the people, the food, and the cabins are better than on the voyage out. The disadvantage is the deck which is small & swarms with children: the noise is ceaseless & awful, and as nearly everyone is a mother no one tries to stop it. Those of us who are not mothers are fairly good tempered young men who fix up swings &ct, and join in the games. We sleep on deck and the various children sit on our beds and talk to us in the morning: my favourite is a double jointed little boy named Henry—the only intellect of the party. We were watching the bath-water pouring out of the escape-pipe yesterday back into the sea, and he remarked 'Water is the home of water' which I thought good. Nor does he believe that the ship is tied to India by a long rope, and that when she is making 12 knots an hour it means that the rope has been knotted 12 times; a report had been spread among the weaker intellects that this was so.

I can't remember when I wrote last; I expect from Bombay or from the Karachi boat; nor what I said, but I had your letter at Cook's, and have left orders for any others to be forwarded home. Bombay was a horrid scramble—the boat left *12 hours earlier* than they had told me, and I caught it only by rushing myself and Baldeo dead. No time to buy photographs or eat mangoes or repack comfortably or go to the Elephanta caves, nor even to buy cakes for kind Saeed and his friends at the smart confectioners, which I particularly wanted to do; they have been so good to me and love little cakes[.] I stopped with him (at Aurangabad) over a week, and was embraced in the Indian fashion at the Railway station and hung with three garlands of jasmine and marigolds ending in tassels of pink roses. The station master delayed the train ten minutes that all might be accomplished properly. I also had three huge 'papais' (like melons, only they grow on trees), which Baldeo put among books and boots—not the best neighbours. However the biggest survived, and I ate it on the Karachi boat—it was quite a companion. Baldeo saw me on board—our parting was very pleasant. I paid him to the end of the month & gave him 5 rupees extra. He was much pleased and putting his hands together as in prayer made a short speech about my goodness. He was extremely useful during the scuffle for the boat. The hotel too behaved well, letting me off half my 'pension', though I had engaged the room till the following day. I only ~~knew~~ guessed the boat was going because I happened to see someone else's luggage for it being put on to a cab. The agents had written to me but I never got their letter.

I will leave this open & add to it—I don't think I said anything about the Ellora caves to which we went for three days from Aurangabad—Saeed, Mohammed Ishaq, and myself.[1] I wished you were there very much—they *are* caves!

at Suez Canal   15 April 1913

Yes, this will be posted at Port Said. I wish I had asked you to write there as letters would have been brought on board. My trunk and bedding & deck chair, by the way, will go round by sea to Liverpool. This will be cheaper & less troublesome than taking them across France, though I shall have to send my key to Cook's or some agent in Liverpool when I return to clear it through the Customs. Deck chair comfortable but rickety. We must tinker it up if ever it reaches us alive. The children have weakened its constitution; children very noisy today; revulsion of feeling on part of grown ups. I have played chess most of the day with a nice Lancashire man—very amusing & good humoured. I see most of him and of the other rough diamond—a retired sailor, now in some engineering post at Karachi. But everyone is pleasant, and not even the military men stand off; it is good for their manners to go second class. No Indians, which makes for social comfort, and not many diatribes against them from Anglo-Indian ladies.

I had some more riding at Aurangabad, including a tumble. The horse, supposed an angel, bucked me off in the middle of the bazaar. I fell in a sitting posture, not ungracefully, and when he tried again, managed to lash him and stick on, after which all went well. Saeed remarked 'I am thankful to God that it was no worse.' To Ellora we drove—a tremendous expedition all very Indian & amusing. We stopped at Daulatabad to see the Fort which is on a mountain so precipitous that it can only be reached by a spiral tunnel through the rock. The exit of the tunnel was covered by a grating on which a fire was lighted if the enemy had effected an entrance. 'Hot pies on Morgan's head': it fell on to them through the bars. Mohammed Ishaq, my joint host, knew the custodian of the Fort, and much time was wasted in civility and in waiting for breakfast, which we had brought with us, very nice, but which the custodian would provide, very nasty, from his house. As he only spoke Urdu I could not figure, but sent a message that I wished I could. He replied that such exquisite manners and such modesty were sure signs of noble birth. Coming back from Ellora, two days later, I was alone, and to my horror had to call upon this gentleman—he would have taken it unkindly if I had not. It was a funny conversation. He made long speeches in flowery Urdu, and I never understood a word; it turned out he was asking me to stop the night with him; ~~an onlooker~~ a stranger in the room interpreted!

After all I have never described Ellora. The caves are cut in a semicircle of hills, overlooking the Deccan plain, so that the place is beautiful to begin with: there are thirty or forty of them, as large as parish churches, and carved with pillars & cornices and giant statues of the gods. The most amazing, the Kailas, is a temple made of the rock; I mean a pit was excavated in the mountain and cut away so as to leave a huge rock standing, which was then carved into this monstrous masterpiece, hollowed out into rooms, decorated with enormous elephants and dragons and tigers, while rocks on either side of it have been shaped into obelisks and pedestals on which stand even more enormous elephants, trumpeting. Oh yes, and the walls of the pit itself have been scooped into cells, out of which horrible gods look down.—I saw it first from above, at sunset, quite unexpectedly, and surprised them by crying 'this must be the Kailas'; they thought me very well informed. The stone is black, tinged by the light here and there with crimson; it is the most wonderful thing I have seen in India, but too diabolic to be beautiful. I went in after twilight, not being afeard of such things, but Saeed soon rushed after me, lest a leopard might be lurking in one of the cells; they do sometimes. I have never been able to imagine these great wild beasts in India, though I have often been among their haunts. Saeed took the greatest care of me, and after the Kailas was very unwilling to let me stay behind at Ellora an extra day; being a Mohammedan he had no great use for the caves, which are Buddhist & Hindu, and he had to get back to his work. Next morning we all went down again with guides, and they were charming with him, and made him sing Hindi songs which he did quite well, pouring out one after another in the cool recess we had found to rest in. We were out four or five hours, but the caves were so numerous & so weird that I was determined to see them again; according to original plan I was to have spent several days alone at Ellora and gone direct to Bombay, but Aurangabad was pleasant and they seemed to like having me, so I settled to go back there until I had to leave. So I did stop at Ellora the extra day: they left me with both their servants, one tonga, and their blessing, and I saw all the caves again.

It's funny to write this long letter when we meet so soon, but I know we shan't talk coherently when we do meet, so I put it all down; my last three weeks in India have been as delightful as any, and the Deccan is so dry that I did not mind the sun which brought the thermometre up to 100 in the shade.

ALU: KCC

[1] Mohammed Ishaq: unidentified.

THE FIRST WAR, 1913–20

His return from India marked the start of a period dominated by war and its effects. Forster went with his mother to Harrogate; while she took a cure, he fulfilled a long-standing intention to visit Edward Carpenter, who lived on a small farm at Millthorpe in Derbyshire. The encounter with Carpenter, poet, polemicist, the prophet of 'The Simple Life' and 'homogenic love', and with Carpenter's working-class lover George Merrill, had a powerful impact on Forster and gave him the idea for a novel on a homosexual theme. This was *Maurice*. He set about writing it at once and, contrary to his usual practice, completed it within a few months and more or less in a single burst of energy and enthusiasm. He had no thought of publication and indeed was not sure he would show it to anybody; soon, however, he began to lend it to certain close friends.

War came in August 1914, and with it for Forster the realisation that to have written an unpublishable novel had not, as he had hoped, helped him toward writing a publishable one. He was thus plunged into gloom, for both public and private reasons, and decided that for the moment creation was impossible.

As a gesture toward war-work, he took a part-time job as cataloguer at the National Gallery, and when G. M. Trevelyan invited him to join an Ambulance Unit in Italy, he was tempted to accept. Eventually, he refused, out of concern for his mother. Then, in the autumn of 1915, came the idea of going to Alexandria as a hospital-searcher, in the newly-formed Wounded and Missing Bureau of the Red Cross. ('Searching' meant interrogating wounded soldiers and sailors for details of missing comrades.) He accepted, expecting to be gone for three months but in fact remained in Egypt for the rest of the war.

The Red Cross work suited Forster, as did the relaxed atmosphere of Alexandria, and he formed an agreeable cosmopolitan circle of friends. It included Robin Furness, who ran the Government censorship department; a Greek business man and aesthete, Pericles Anastassiades; a Syrian official and author, George Antonius; and the poet C. P. Cavafy. He also, in the course of 1917, began an affair with an Egyptian tram-conductor, Mohammed el Adl. Until this happened, he had not greatly taken to Egypt or the Egyptians, criticising them as a 'pseudo-Orient'. Nevertheless he produced sketches on Egyptian topics for local journals, some of these being reprinted in *Pharos and Pharillon* (1923). Eventually, too, he set to work on a *History and Guide* to Alexandria, which was published in 1922 after endless delays and vicissitudes.

On his return to England in January 1919, he considered taking a full-time job. His friend Sydney Waterlow secured for him the offer of a post in the Inter-Allied Commission in Germany, and another in the Foreign Office. Forster himself wrote to his old friend the Maharaja of Dewas, to take up an earlier suggestion that he might visit the Maharaja or even take some kind of employment with him. Meanwhile, still believing his career as a novelist to be finished, he devoted his energies to literary journalism, acting for a brief period in 1920 as literary editor of the *Daily Herald* and producing, in 1920 and 1921, something near a hundred reviews and articles. Egypt was still much on his mind, both because of the political disturbances there and because of the troubles and imprisonment of Mohammed el Adl, and the articles on Egyptian matters gained him a reputation as an authority. At this same time he was seeing a good deal of Siegfried Sassoon and became a member of the 1917 Club, in London's Soho. The club, founded in honour of the Russian revolution, was much frequented by the radical intelligentsia, including the Woolfs, Aldous Huxley, and the Sitwells.

In February 1921 he went for a holiday with Lowes Dickinson to Lyme Regis, and while there he received a cable from the Maharaja of Dewas, offering a six-months' post at the Dewas court, as temporary replacement for another Englishman. It seemed an answer to many problems, and he cabled his acceptance that day.

129   To Ottoline Morrell

Harnham, Monument Green, Weybridge
4 October 1913

Dear Lady Ottoline
My plans have been uncertain—hence my delay in answering, and now that they are certain I find I can't come: not yet, I mean: I want to come later in the month and shall suggest myself. A wash of visitors, light but adhesive, prevails all this week, and next week I go to see Dickinson at Cambridge—we haven't met since India. I hope that when I do write (i) you may be able to have me (ii) Mr Morrell may be at home too. It will be a great pleasure to come & see you again: except for 5 minutes at Drury Lane I haven't spoken to you for nearly two years.

I wonder how you are. I am so fit myself—blatant. Every one ought to go to India. There is a desert of purple stone and cold air in

Rajputana where I caught some germ that will stop me ever being ill again.

With best wishes, and looking forward to seeing you soon:

Yours sincerely
E. M. Forster.

ALS: HRC

130 To Forrest Reid

Beech Lodge, Esplanade, Harrogate[1]
5 October 1913

Dear Reid

It's a good little sketch I think, and shows you can do a catastrophe if you choose.[2] I never guessed he had murdered his wife, but my mother did. I have kept it longer than I ought, and not for any reason. The second time I read it, I enjoyed it more.

We are here till the 10th, so let *The Gentle Lover* come accordingly. It has been a dull month, but not boring. I have done a good deal of writing, and read a good deal of Samuel Butler, whose *Life and Habit* I have appreciated. (I have appreciated, mind, not recommended to you; after *Women of the Country* I recommend nothing!)[3] I ordered *Chanson de Billitis* from the L[ondon] L[ibrary] and it came as *Byblis* which smelt of the boudoir rather than the forest, but I liked it.[4]

No doubt you will take up *Spring Song* again when *The Three Women* is off your mind.[5] You are pretty safe in that direction and I think needn't worry. I don't disapprove of fixing the title: in my case it didn't act, that is all. Best remembrances to J[ames] R[utherford].[6]

—Yours ever
E.M.F.

ALS: Stephen Gilbert

[1] While staying at Harrogate with his mother, EMF went to see Edward Carpenter (1844–1929): see above, p. 205. EMF was supposed to be writing on Samuel Butler and was reading his works, such as *Life and Habit* (1878), but he had intended for a year or two to take up Dickinson's suggestion that he go to see Carpenter, and he seized this opportunity to do so.

[2] This sketch is unidentified.

[3] *Women of the Country* (1913), by Gertrude Helena Bone.

[4] *Les Chansons de Bilitis* (1894), poems of Sapphic love by the French novelist and poet Pierre Louÿs (1870–1925). Instead, EMF had received Louÿs' *Byblis changée en fontaine* (1898); he puns on Byblis, a maiden who became a fountain in Greek mythology, and byblis, a carnivorous plant.

[5] Reid, *The Spring Song* (1916). Netta Syrett, *Three Women* (1912).

[6] On the Rutherford brothers, see Letter 98.

131   To Lytton Strachey

Harnham, Monument Green, Weybridge
1 November 1913

Dear Strachey
    I remember a landscape with 'Encore' on the other side. 'Let us try to meet again' I thought.—Please publish another novel shortly?—I am in love?—
    Would you write a letter to me—? I considered The Lacket when at Salisbury last week, but went to see Henry Newbolt instead.[1] We discussed the conventions, how no one ever breaks them in the right place.
    I hope part of your card does not mean that you are ill. I am very well myself and teaching English to eleven policemen of extreme beauty. On the 11th Nov. I go for a week to Cambridge
    Do you know of a suitable book for a beginner on Prosody?
    I repeat—read Following Darkness by Forrest Reid. Sigh but hear me.

Yours ever
E. M. Forster.

ALS: KCC

[1] Sir Henry John Newbolt (1862–1938) was Professor of Poetry at Oxford, 1911–21. His principal claim to fame was as a poet on patriotic themes.

132   To S. R. Masood

Harnham, Monument Green, Weybridge
4 April 1914

Dearest SRM,
    Have at last understood why you never write to me. You want me to send you a present. I'm damned if I do. All is now over between us for ever. I take leave of you in excellent health. A fortnight in Ireland has set me up, and I have come back to find the painters and decorators out of the house, and my room looking très distingué.[1] I'll put in a piece of the new wall paper if I can remember. On a large surface it has a beautiful shimmering look, especially when the sun shines. I am having Post Impressionist curtains of purple and pale blue, and must also get a carpet. Have turned out most of the furniture and all the photographs—the latter will now be in my bedroom. Poor Venus remains—very beautiful she looks.[2] The paper of the bedroom is pale grey.
    I don't suppose the above will interest you, but what in Hell am I to write about? Am about to join an association for being hospitable to your countrymen.[3] Like to know that? Or that I have reviewed a book by a Parsee named Mr. Wadia?[4] Or that I've had a long talk

with Bevan of your college?[5] Or that a Mr. [blank in Tr], on whose roof at Delhi we witnessed a nautch, has written to me, and we are about to meet?[6] (Do you know him intimately, by the bye?) Or that—but I will conclude. They think you 2/3rds as good as an Englishman, do they? A very generous estimate.

Thine for ever,
Morgan.

TTr supplied by Akbar Masood

[1] He visited Meredith in Belfast, in late March.
[2] Venus: a statue; see Letter 85.
[3] This may have had a connection with the work of Frederick W. Thomas (1867–1956), India Office Librarian and Adviser to Indian Students in London.
[4] Forster, 'The Indian Mind', in *New Weekly*, 1 (1914), 55; review of Ardaser Sorabjee N. Wadia, *Reflections on the Problems of India* (1913).
[5] Edwyn Robert Bevan (1870–1943), archaeologist, author of works on Greece and India; author of *Indian Nationalism: An Independent Estimate* (1913).
[6] Even in 1912, EMF could not remember this name; he wrote in his diary (2 November 1912. KCC): 'The Nautch was close by in a friend's house. I forget his name; rather a tiresome young barrister, but it was a beautiful house.'

133   To Florence Barger

Harnham, Monument Green, Weybridge
16 May 1914

Dear Florence

What wretched news—it would have been miserable if it had lived, I suppose.[1]

———————   ———————

I was awfully glad to hear what you told me for several reasons, some queer ones.—In our previous conversation, I wasn't very clear: will try again sometime. There just is at present this vague suspicion that the human relation comes second to something else—not to the divine: don't fly into a stew—: or rather that it's not enough to go through life helping people and being helped by them. You see I'm transcendental to[o], a little, and feel that creative acts, such as producing books or children, have inexplicable values. The fire may perish, and also that which we produced by its help. Yet something has happened. Whereas tinkering and being tinkered strike me as cold jobs—perhaps because I have done so much of the former, and done it inefficiently, and so often made unselfishness an excuse for idleness.

———————   ———————

I will quote Clutton Brock more accurately:—[2]
"All discontented with actual experience. Three ways of escaping from it—morally by trying to change oneself: intellectually, by withdrawing from the stream of events, artistically, by painting, &[ct]. The discontent *not* with the thing we experience, but with our

experience of it. We want something fuller than the eye &ct. can give. Hence art."

Love, Morgan

ALS: KCC

[1] Perhaps a miscarriage, or a stillborn child.
[2] Arthur Clutton-Brock (1868–1924) was Literary Editor of *The Speaker*, 1904–6; then on *The Times*' staff, and its art critic, from 1908. He had been pouring out patriotic items: *Thoughts on the War* (1914) and *More Thoughts on the War* (1915), both running into multiple editions; *Are We to Punish Germany, If We Can?* (1915); and *The Ultimate Belief* (1916).

134   To Alice Clara Forster

Baywell [Duns, Berwickshire][1]
Wednesday [22 July 1914]

Dearest Mother

Thank you for your two sweet letters. How nice of you to go to Kingston. I am sure you did it to please Poppy, and he appreciates it. I got the news in the midst of rather an exhausting day—this is rather an enervating place,—much greenery and flies, and one is apt to sleep badly at night and heavily in the afternoon when the weather is not all it should be. Yesterday it was, and we had a delightful outing to lunch with a hermit cousin of the Lows who lives all alone in the heart of the Lammermoors—Abbey St Bathans is his estate. We went by motor, bathing on the way. The cousin reminded me of Uncle Willie, only queerer.[2] No one waited in the immense dining room, and if he wanted anything he rushed out shouting 'Jenny!' to the aged maid. Fine old family portraits and a fair collection of books. Scarcely any one ever enters the house—crossed in love, I believe: very sad, for he's a fine looking man and only about 50. He has made a travelling swing across the Whiteadder, which runs through his grounds, and Malcolm & I left by it—very typical. "Get on!" he said, without bidding farewell, and before I knew where I was, I was in mid air, being hauled away by some arrangement of an endless wire. The torrent roared below, the swing twisted and twirled, and shot me on the further bank. Malcolm followed: then came a padlock, with which we had to secure the apparatus at our end. Having seen all was safe, he disappeared.

We walked down a glorious valley for 1½ hours and came in time to our beloved bathing place. I really 'seem to swim' a little better than I did. Then we rejoined Lady Low & Josie in the car.

I shall be home Saturday; train reaches King's X at 6.0. something, & I will get on as soon as possible. We gave up our walk in the Border as it is difficult to reach, and hope to go for 2 days tomorrow through the Lammermoors to the sea at Fast Castle. We should have started to day, and I should then have been with Mummy Friday only today is Malcolm's wedding anniversary and he did not want to leave his beloved Josie. He gave her a pair of earrings—14 came from which she might choose, and she chose the pair we had picked out as suiting her the day before—long jade pendants of a gypsy type. She looks well in them.

Monday—the apathetic day—we dined with the Turners, and the apathy had certainly touched Mrs T., who was most languid and peevish.[3] She is pretty, and dressed in an outré gown of white, high on the shins, low in the back, and shimmering with rainbow hues round her 'milieu'. Hueffer, rather a fly blown man of letters, was in the house, and kept exclaiming how bored he was.[4] Wyndham Lewis, the Futurist youth who has behaved so shockingly to Fry, was expected later—'that sulky tinker' as Desmond calls him.[5] Altogether the atmosphere was unattractive—except for Turner, who ran through it like a mountain stream. I wonder what he thinks of it all. He was a most ardent missionary, and has given up all that his wife may have a literary & social career in England, and it is evident she cannot rise high in either. She is an American millionairess, who tries to buy her way. Her novel *The Mistress of Kingdoms* is rather good, and contains an unvarnished portrait of herself. She writes under the name of Bridget MacLagan.[6] My neighbour at dinner was a militant suffragette—quite pleasant till she got on to her subject.[7] The T.'s sent & fetched us in their motor.

We have marked the Tennis Court while Malcolm was out. What with John Jerry's naughtiness and Lady Low's blindness, I nearly went mad.[8] He pulled up the measuring pegs as fast as we put them in, and dragged the cord side ways when we ran the machine down it, and upset whitewash by the bucket onto the grass. She tripped & fell. Josie remained perfectly calm & pleasant through the nightmare. I am sure we have got it all cock eye and blurred, but such as it is the Turners will play on it next week, and perhaps the presence of county families will excuse its defects to them. Lady L. proves very nice—so energetic, intelligent & kind. She is devoted to the Malcolms.

Much love,
Poppy

ALS: KCC

[1] Home of Jessica Darling's parents, Lord and Lady Low, south of the Firth of Forth, in the Lothians.
[1] This was George Turnbull, of a very old family in the area.
[3] On the Turners, see Letter 110.
[4] Ford Madox Hueffer, afterward Ford Madox Ford (1873–1939), novelist, critic, and editor, was the grandson of the Pre-Raphaelite painter, Ford Madox Brown. For another glimpse of Ford through EMF's eyes, see Forster, 'The Hat-Case', a review of Ford's *The English Novel*, in *The Spectator*, 144 (1930), 1055.
[5] Percy Wyndham Lewis (1882–1957), painter and novelist, originator of the Vorticist

movement. He joined Roger Fry in his co-operative Omega Workshop, opened in 1913, and started a furious controversy over disbursement of funds to the participating artists. Fry's biographer, Frances Spalding, writes that 'Lewis's suspicion of Fry was not totally unwarranted,' for Fry's management was a 'haphazard open-ended approach' (*Roger Fry: Art and Life*, pp. 185–8). Desmond McCarthy (1877–1952), literary critic; editor of *Life and Letters*; chief book reviewer, *Sunday Times*, 1928–52.

⁶ McLagan, *The Mistress of Kingdoms; or Smoking Flax* (1912), a version of her experiences in India.

⁷ The suffragette is unidentified.

⁸ John Jerry: John Jermyn, the Darlings' son.

135 To Alice Clara Forster

Harnham, Monument Green, Weybridge
16 September 1914

Dearest Mother,

Glad of your letter, and that you have got hold of the address. I am afraid the weather is very bad—it is even raining a good deal here. Stokoe arrives this evening. I ate in solitude last night a 'beautiful' leg of mutton, which Ruth had cooked for him. She asks me to tell you that she has got thirteen pots of damson jam and a taste out of 9 pounds, and that she is pleased. Had a most interesting letter from Malcolm this morning—posted at Aden; I will send it on in a few days. A Mr—I forget his name—has just called from Sir Theodore [Morison] about war help registration, and I am to go down Thames Street &c, asking everyone what they will do; Mrs Warren is outside my beat mercifully.¹ I have also got two English classes at the W[orking] M[en's] C[ollege] on Friday nights.

As for the Prince—I heard a great shuffling among the other workers, and thought they were troubled by fleas or something like that, but looking up found ~~that~~ an incredibly small little boy standing drearily in the middle of the room, and pretending to read a letter to conceal his shyness. I rose too, whereupon he said harshly "sit down please," and went back to the first page. His attendant—Ponsonby I suppose, asked me whether the card index was up to date. I said I didn't know, adding that they had given up making a complete one, after which some less truthful person intervened; there was a pause and then the Prince without a word or a gesture turned on his heel and shot out of our vision like a magic lantern slide. Though so close, I could not see him well, as Ponsonby's fat form intervened, but he is very thin and brown with charming gold hair, not ordinary as I had expected, but distinguished and refined. He looked overwrought and miserable, and did not leave a good impression with the workers, who thought him haughty and not of strong character.²

Stokoe has arrived, and we have had a good dinner; he sends messages to you—I think he may stop some time. I shall go over to aunt Laura if she wants me, but I am not sure that she does. I have written, saying that she is to say.

The concert I went to was almost all German music, the Hall crowded, and the applause after the Beethoven Concerto immense. I think people in the thick are never as silly and venomous as the sit at homes. Hand on as much of this as you dare. Henry Wood, or rather his manager, published a nice manifesto, in which they said that they had only knocked off German music for a little because compelled to by the owners of the hall, and that the masterpieces of art are common property, above the passions and prejudices of the moment.[3]

I must stop, and post this. Stokoe appears to have a cold. Rosie writes that the little girl goes on well, and that it is just a question of time.

POPPY

TLTS: KCC

[1] That is, Upper and Lower Thames Streets, and not Chancery Lane, the 'beat' of Mrs Warren in G. B. Shaw's *Mrs Warren's Profession: Being the Third of Three Unpleasant Plays*. Cf. Letter 29.

[2] This Prince, visiting the National Gallery, must have been Prince John (1905–19), youngest son of King George V. Frederick Edward Grey Ponsonby, 1st Baron Sysonby (1867–1935), who in 1914 was Keeper of the Privy Purse and Extra Equerry to the King, was the second son of Sir Frederick Henry Ponsonby (1825–95), ubiquitous Equerry and Keeper of the Privy Purse to Queen Victoria.

[3] In 1895 Sir Henry Wood (1869–1944) inaugurated the Promenade Concerts in the Queen's Hall, Langham Place, which was bombed in 1941. His manager Robert Newman (1858–1926) issued the statement 'emphatically contradicting the statement that German music will be boycotted during the present season. The greatest examples of Music and Art are world possessions and unassailable even by the prejudices and passions of the hour.' Quoted in Reginald Pound, *Sir Henry Wood*, pp. 128–9.

136   To Malcolm Darling

National Gallery [London] 6 November 1914

Dearest Malcolm,

I can so far answer your letter in a proper spirit as to say that you are a blasted idiot if you chuck India for an interpretership in France. For God's sake stick to your ~~job~~ highly specialised and supremely important job, and leave interpreting to the Indian students over here, who are spoiling to be useful. Really it is childish to think good work can only be done within the sound of a gun, and if the Gov^t of India encourages you, my opinion of it will sink lower than before.

And I am not a Pro-German, even in any of the senses that ~~we~~ you were attaching to the word on Oct. 14th. I have read the White Paper, and Cramb, and some Bernhardi, and I am sure we could not have kept out of this war.[1] But beyond this, I am doubtful of giving you satisfaction. You will be out at me for an Intellectual if I go on—I

shall run into the bomb of some Eternal Verity, and get blown up.
Would that I could recall the Union of Democratic Control
Pamphlets that I had posted to you last week.[2]

Margaret is right.[3] I did think that we should send no men to
France, but support our Allies by the Navy only. Since then I
changed my mind. Since then, I have come round to my original
opinion again, for the chances of a German Raid have certainly
increased, and we should boot it out much quicker if we had
reserved plenty of trained troops for the purpose. The losses are
immense, Flanders a soup of Hell. Our wounded, when not talking
for effect, say that they do not want to go back, but go, which is to
my mind far finer than heroics. The newspapers still talk about glory
but the average man, thank God, has got rid of that illusion. It is a
damned bore, with a stale mate as the most probable outcome, but
one has to see it through, and see it through with the knowledge that
whichever side wins, civilisation in Europe will be pipped for the
next 30 years. Don't indulge in Romance here, Malcolm, or suppose
that an era of jolly little nationalities is dawning. We shall be much
too much occupied with pestilence and poverty to reconstruct.

You may pertinently ask what I am doing. Irene thought I ought
to enlist—perhaps I ought, but I am not going to, and it was a very
great pleasure and comfort to find that Josie agreed.[4] I don't feel that
I am of value either to my readers my mother or my friends in any
sense in which *any* average man is not of value to his surroundings: I
have no claim (beyond physical) to exemption—though Josie most
charmingly tried to make one out for me, saying I was a 'Healer'.
But I shan't enlist unless the Authorities make me, which I should
feel all right.

Just now I sit in the N. G. having studied a notice that instructs me
to 'attack' a petrol bomb with sand instead of water. How am I to
know whether it is a petrol bomb? But it will probably spare me the
fatigue of considering. We expect aeroplanes for certain, Zeppelins
possibly. I hope that people—myself included—won't get panicky.
These stray bombs only concern the folks they hit, and if war was
only death I shouldn't have much to say against it.

I have just had lunch with our Belgian guest—a nice creature,
except that he will play the piano.[5] He stops with us 2 months, and
perhaps more—can't talk any English, and I ought to ~~talk to~~ teach
him, but hitherto have jabbered French. This evening I have classes
at the W[orking] M[en's] C[ollege]. 'Fool's Paradise' you'll say, but
my dear Malcolm the entire planet's that as I tried to prove to you
when we walked from the Whiteadder to the railway line on our
way to Wolf's Crag.[6] This war's like the Bible—we're all going to
take out of it what we bring to it. I, who never saw much purpose in
the Universe, now see less, you, naturally hopeful, think it's the war
that'll end war, while Josie proclaimed blood and glory for ever,

with the oldest county families in the van.—I write frivolously: if you want definite assurance I've been suffering I can give it you—to prove I am not too queer a fish.

My mother has had bad cough, but is better, and entertained by the Belgian: says she wouldn't mind a Zeppelin coming if it would only get the piano. Love to all: write again about Josie's arrival, and oh! don't think of chucking your job. Do tell how India's taking the war—and Turkey's entry into it. Also more about Sirsa.[7]

Yours affect[ly]
Morgan.

ALS: HRC

[1] Reports on the war, in a penny edition published in 1914: see *General Index to . . . Reports and Papers presented by Command, 1900 to 1948–49*, p. 775; *Germany and England* (1914), by John Adam Cramb (1862–1913), Professor of Modern History at Queen's College, London, from 1893. General Friedrich Adam Julius von Bernhardi (1849–1930) poured out books such as *On War of Today* (1912–13), *Britain as Germany's Vassal*, and *Germany and the Next War* (1914). Darling's letter does not survive, but its contents upset EMF, who wrote in his diary (31 December 1914. KCC): 'Malcolm & Josie—will the war wreck that double cause? A letter from M., in which he yielded to a flood of patriotic hate, drew a smart reply, in which I said that [he] found in war what he put there—Josie "all blood and glory, with the best county families in the van", and now I hear that her brother has been killed. I never should have been intimate with that pair if they hadn't been so sound about sex, and it's only a chance that they are sound. Liking them so much, I trust we shall pull through, yet this war is to bring a severe sorting of one's private life.'

[2] The Union published four pamphlets in 1914: E. D. Morel *et al. The Morrow of the War*; Norman Angell, *Shall This War End German Militarism?*; Bertrand Russell, *War—The Offspring of Fear*; and H. N. Brailsford, *The Origins of the Great War*. The Union of Democratic Control was suggested on 5 August 1914 by Charles Philip Trevelyan (1870–1958), brother of G. M. and Robert Trevelyan, who was a Liberal MP, 1899–1918, 1922–31. He was joined by Edmond Dene Morel (1873–1924), journalist and reformer, who founded the Congo Reform Association in 1904. The Union of Democratic Control was most active from 1914 to 1924, but it survived until 9 June 1966, never having budged from its opposition to secret treaties and its demands for lasting agreements for peace.

[3] Margaret: Darling's sister.

[4] Irene: another sister of Darling.

[5] Jules Quillery, Belgian refugee; see *EMF*, II, 4.

[6] Places visited during EMF's fortnight's visit to the Darlings in Scotland in July 1914; see Letter 134.

[7] Town forty-seven miles northwest of Delhi.

137 To Syed Ross Masood

Harnham, Monument Green, Weybridge
5 December 1914

Dearest SRM

Are you going to give me a Xmas present? I meant to give you nothing, but have lately thought of 'Georgian Verse' which has made some stir over here, so shall send it to you, packed up with mother's book.[1] It will keep you in touch with latest developments, though you will scarcely care for them.

Dodo Morison is at present the sole authority for your latest—the

rest of us marvel and are silent. O many sided youth! I am very fit
and well—occasionally have wretched fits of longing to see you,
followed by days when I don't think about you at all. I expect that's
much what you feel about me. In the bottom of my heart I long to
see you always.

Masood, a young lady has fallen in love with me—at least so I
judge from her letters. Awkward is it not—awkward and
surprising.[2] You would be flattered and twirl your moustache, but I
am merely uncomfortable. I wish she would stop, as she is very nice,
and I enjoyed being friends. What an ill constructed world this is!
Love is always being given where it is not required.

I have just been to Oxford for a week end, but saw little; an Indian
to tea—Hindu, I forget his name. The Universities grow more &
more concerned about your compatriots; it is indeed a problem. We
have lost the art of digesting you that we had in your father's time. I
can hardly hear of any cases in which an Englishman & Indian have
become real friends.

ever thine
Morgan

TTr supplied by Akbar Masood

[1] *Georgian Poetry*, the series of anthologies edited by Edward Marsh and published by the
Poetry Bookshop at approximately two-year intervals from 1912.
[2] Unidentified.

138   To Goldsworthy Lowes Dickinson

Weybridge. 13 December 1914

Dear Dickinson

I enclose R. R.—also cheque for £5 for Ogden fund—I may give
more later, but am not sure.[1] Your letter pleased me very much, as
you may imagine. The Scudder part certainly is better, but I agree.[2] I
might have been wiser to let that also resolve into dust or mist, but
the temptation's overwhelming to grant to one's creations a
happiness actual life does not supply. "Why not?" I kept thinking[.]
"A little rearrangement, rather better luck"—but no doubt the
rearrangement's fundamental. It's the yearning for permanence that
leads a novelist into theories towards the end of each book. The only
permanence that's not a theory but a fact is death, and perhaps I
surfeited myself with that in *The Longest Journey*: at all events the
disinclination to kill increases.

Keep the M.S. till I let you know—Sheppard & Keynes will soon
be through it, I suppose. I hope your play did turn up safely.[3]

What's to occupy me for the rest of my life, I can't conceive. I am
very glad to have got this done though it exhibits the emptiness of all
literary achievement in rather an acute form. I remind myself that

even if it could be published, in 20 years all would be as it is today.
Really why *does* one write? and feel despite all that writing's
important?

I went to the inside of a very nice concert at the Omega last
Friday.[4] Things are much pleasanter here as regards the Belgian. My
mother is appreciating his good points, which are quite real. Where
are you through the Vac[ation]?

EMF

ALS: KCC

[1] R. R.: perhaps some publication by Romain Rolland. Ogden Fund: perhaps assistance for
Charles Kay Ogden (1889–1957), later to be known as originator of Basic English, to sustain
The Cambridge Magazine (1912–23), 'a penny paper for the internationally minded'. It
published reports on the war and on European politics not easily available in England.
[2] Scudder part: in *Maurice*, Alec Scudder, the gamekeeper.
[3] Dickinson, *Business*, a four-act play written under the name 'John Goldie', performed by
the Stage Society, 19–20 March 1911, at the Aldwych Theatre.
[4] At Roger Fry's Omega Workshops, 33 Fitzroy Square.

139 To Forrest Reid

[N. p.]   23 January 1915

Oh my dear Reid, I have been in the most awful gloom lately, and
who do you think finally raised me from it? You will be so
contemptuous of me. D. H. Lawrence. Not the novels, but their
author, a sandy haired passionate Nibelung, whom I met last
Thursday at a dinner party. He is really extraordinarily nice.[1]

I'm not going to write about him though, but about a pretty
serious matter which I have not had the spirit to tackle until now. I
would rather have talked about it to you than written, but my
chances of Ireland recede. I have written a novel which cannot be
published, and if you were willing to read it I could send it you. You
would, in some way, sympathise with it, but I know that in other
ways it might put a severe strain on our friendship, which terrifies
me. My attitude—I realise more fully than you can—is not yours. I
have heard you feel things I cannot, and draw distinctions that mean
nothing to me. ~~Whatever I were, I am~~ I should be very miserable
indeed if your feelings towards me altered as the result of reading
this book, even though I should think (as I do think) that they ought
not to alter, for I have not written one word of which I am ashamed.
I am taking quite a grave risk for two reasons—first one's ordinary
desire to be read and secondly my knowledge that you will be glad
to know I have written *something*, and am not as sterile as I am
obliged to pretend to the world.

Whatever your decision, you will not mention the book's
existence to anyone, I know.

Yours ever
E.M.F.

ALS: Stephen Gilbert

1 At a dinner-party at Lady Ottoline Morrell's on 21 January 1915. This is described as a 'lunch party' in *The Letters of D. H. Lawrence*, ed. George T. Zytaruk and James T. Boulton, II, 262.) On 24 January Lawrence wrote inviting EMF to stay, which he did eventually on 10–12 February.

140   To Florence Barger

c/o D. H. Lawrence, Greatham, Pulborough[1]
12 November 1915 [11 February 1915]

Dear Florence,

Thanks for letter—so sorry about George, also Gladys. "It is as if poor Florence has first one thing, then another." I should like to come when you can have me. Altoringan [Altounyan] stops till Monday.[2] To mother's scandal I have left him to come here, whence I thought you would like a line. We are in a cottage, or rather barn, belonging to Miss Viola Meynell, and of Mr and Mrs Meynell, who are now away, but have left Master Sebastian Meynell in residence. The M's are a curious ineffective race, I believe with creole blood in them: all catholicism and culture.[3] The Lawrences I like—especially him. We have had a two hours walk in the glorious country between here and Arundel, and he has told me all about his people—drunken father, sister who married a tailor, etc: most gay and friendly, with breaks to look at birds, catkins, etc. Last night we painted pill boxes—a fascinating employment, which I recommend to you and the children.[4] You can be as post-impressionist, or as virginal as you choose, and in any case all is over in an hour, and the design, if a failure, can be painted out in black, and recommenced. L is now finishing off his new novel, which he thinks is good.[5] I leave tomorrow, and must alas! catch the 8.20 after a five miles walk. I am timed to reach London a wreck. Here comes tea. A[ltounyan] and I enjoyed the Franck even more than we expected. The day after, we went to Judas Maccabaeus at Weybridge—not a bad performance, but both music and audience were dowdy and middle class, and we felt sad.[6] I am getting awfully revolutionary in my old age. Respectability kills so much more than I once supposed. Lawrence gets almost mad with rage against it—paroxysms—apart from his personal annoyance against Sir Jesse Boot, who has refused to supply *The Prussian Officer* to his subscribers, and when pressed sends it in a special binding with a note that this is the only copy in his library and that he sends it to show how disgusting it is.[7]

Morgan

TTr supplied by Mollie Barger

1 D. H. Lawrence (1885–1930) and his wife, Frieda Richtofen Lawrence (1879–1956), who had been married in 1914, were living in one of the homes belonging to the Meynell family, a compound of cottages and converted farm buildings.

² Ernest Haik Riddall Altounyan (1889–1962) was of Irish-Armenian parentage and came to England at the age of eight. He was a doctor and minor poet with whom EMF was friendly at this time.
³ Wilfred (1852–1948) and Alice Thompson Meynell (1847–1922) were poets and dedicated Catholic journalists. Together they founded and edited *Merry England* (1883–94) and are remembered for their rescue and rehabilitation of the poet Francis Thompson (1859–1907). The Meynells had eight children. Viola (1886–1956) became a novelist and biographer. Sebastian (1878–1961), the eldest son, showed promise, but various careers were hampered by nervous breakdowns.
⁴ Actually 'bee boxes', used for transporting live bees.
⁵ Lawrence, *The Rainbow*, published by Methuen in 1915 and fated to have famous censorship troubles.
⁶ The oratorio by George Frideric Handel, first performed in 1747, at Covent Garden.
⁷ Lawrence, *The Prussian Officer, and Other Stories* (1914). Sir Jesse Boot, 1st Baron Trent (1850–1931), expanded his Nottingham chemist's shop into the world's largest chain of retail chemists' stores, which included lending libraries.

141   To D. H. and Frieda Lawrence

National Gallery [London]. 12 February 1915[1]

Dear Lawrences,
    Until you think it worth while to ~~write~~ function separately, I'd better address you as one.[2] I have got book for Lady O[ttoline Morrell]—*The Romance of Words*. The Romance of Names is also out.[3] Now I must get on with N. G. Catalogue, which grows urgent. As for coming again to Greatham, I like Mʳˢ Lawrence, and I like the Lawrence who talks to Hilda and sees birds and is physically restful and wrote *The White Peacock*, he doesn't know why; but I do not like the deaf impercipient fanatic who has nosed over his own little sexual round until he believes that there is no other path for others to take, he sometimes interests & sometimes frightens & angers me, but in the end he will bore him merely, I know.[4] So I can't yet tell about coming down. I am sure you are both willing I should come, and I shall see. I would like to see either or both in London, where you should certainly meet Altounyan. I will forward the Woolf novel to morrow, and read & return *The Rainbow* quickly if it is lent to me.[5]

E. M. Forster

ALS: HRC

¹ EMF returned from Pulborough early in the morning of 12 February and wrote this letter the same day.
² By adding a postscript to a Lawrence letter of 28 January 1915 (KCC), Frieda had provoked reproaches from EMF, who said he refused to have 'dealings with a firm' (this letter does not survive). Frieda replied (5 February. KCC): 'As to the firm you *did* hit a little sore point with me—Poor author's wife, who does her little bit and everybody wishes her to Jericho—' Lawrence was conciliatory in an undated letter ([24? February 1915.] KCC): 'I have been cross with you. Some things you should not write in your letters. But I am tired of being cross, & feel very friendly again. / I hope you weren't angry with me for shouting about you to Lady Ottoline. She is too good to be affected wrongly.' On 8 June Lawrence wrote (KCC): 'According to my promise, I send you as much as is done of my philosophy—about one/fourth. I can trust you to take me seriously, & really to read. Because whatever I may be, you *do* listen.'

³ *The Romance of Words* (1912) and *The Romance of Names* (1914), by Frieda Lawrence's first husband, Ernest Weekley (1865–1954).
⁴ During the latter part of the second day's visit at Greatham, Lawrence, who had been determined to enlist EMF for his social revolution, delivered an hours'-long diatribe against EMF's way of life, which, although he had expected it, angered EMF by its violence. Lawrence's *The White Peacock* was published in 1911. 'Hilda' may have been the American Imagist poet Hilda Doolittle (1886–1961), whose pen name was 'H. D.', who was married to the English poet, novelist, and editor Richard Aldington (1892–1962); both belonged to the Lawrence circle.
⁵ *The Voyage Out*, Virginia Woolf's first novel, was published on 26 March 1915. EMF was reviewing it: 'A New Novelist', *The Daily News and Leader*, 8 April 1915, p. 7. Lawrence wrote to EMF ([24? February 1915]. KCC): that it was 'Interesting but not *very* good—nothing much behind it.'

142   To Hilton Young

Harnham, Monument Green, Weybridge
20 February 1915

Dear Hilton,

I have half written to you many times: was much pleased with your letter, everything in which was news. Going into shares with Mother Julian! Fancy!¹ Am trying to write on Samuel Butler myself—have liked him for many years but now a chill descends²
    4 March 1915
did not your second letter avert it. I am really shockingly cheerful and fit. Since I failed to come with you to the Scapa Flow I have ~~no~~ done nothing for Britain and now that my cup of shame is full have an increasing tendency to throw it in her face.³ Has Satan possessed me? 4 days a week I work at the National Gallery, settling whether the Cotignola was in the 1825 Rogers Sale or the 1822, the other three days there is Butler as aforesaid, and other literary schemes, and occasional reviews for the Daily News, and W[orking] M[en's] C[ollege], and—most important!—César Franck's Violin Sonata. Then there is D. H. Lawrence, the strong novelist, who, mit frau, has burst upon my astonied ken, and I go to stop with them, and he is violent, as always, and I am violent, as never, and we quarrel, with housesful of the Meynell family lying all around; and then the Lady Ottoline Morrell thinks it is dreadful that two such interesting writers should quarrel, and she mediates, moving to and fro with soothing but indecisive gestures, and sighs of 'I'm making it worse,' and L. & I make it up surreptitiously, and as soon as we get really friends, ~~we shall~~ he will be violent again. He said— —⁴

So you see London is not all newspapers, or rather that we do still scuttle about under them, earwig fashion. I will write again soon, and more fittingly. At present I am worried by the Iron Duke's having no address. However will the postman know?

Our Belgian has left, thank God, and a *v*. nice Armenian has been here for the last six weeks, recovering from a complexity of diseases.[5] I haven't heard from Malcolm for a long time. His last letter was rather bloody, and my reply may have sickened him.* I simply don't know where this war will leave us all. There's bound to be some queer regrouping.

Yours affectionately
Morgan

*As for Josie, she seems to have stolen a pair of Field Glasses and a silver sugar sifter.

ALS: Cambridge University Library

[1] Hilton Young was Labour MP for Norwich, 1915–26, and the anchoress Julian of Norwich (1342–died between 1416 and 1423) was a notable religious figure in the area. Thus they were to 'go shares' on the constituency.

[2] EMF's book on Butler, commissioned by Edward Arnold, was never completed; see Letter 130.

[3] Young entered the Naval Reserve in 1914 and was assigned to HMS *Iron Duke*, operating from Scapa Flow. Whether EMF refers to an actual invitation or to failure to enlist, is unclear. For an account of Young's war service, see his *By Sea and Land: Some Naval Doings* (1920). Its tone is highly romantic, as, for example (pp. 182–3): 'I said to myself, "It is a wonderful romance to be going about the North Sea in this beautiful and terrible creature as a small part of her living will; and there is more in it than mere romance—one can really feel truly and keenly here that one is doing something to prevent the world from being Prussianized."'

[4] For Ottoline Morrell on Lawrence, see *Memoirs of Lady Ottoline Morrell: A Study in Friendship, 1873–1915*, ed. Robert Gathorne-Hardy, pp. 273–8.

[5] Belgian: Jules Quillery. Armenian: Altounyan. Later, EMF found him 'a queer unsatisfactory emotionalist' (to Masood, 2 September 1923. TTr by T. R. Kidwai).

143   To Ottoline Morrell

Oxford and Cambridge Musical Club
6 Bedford Square, [London] W. C.
20 February 1915

Dear Lady Ottoline
    The rest must be left to boil itself clear, but it would be very kind to of you if you could convey to him that I do not despise him.[1] It's annoying enough that he should think this—it's worse he should think it's the contempt of the semi-detached villa for the cottage: I've looked up to the class that produced him for many years now

Yours very sincerely
E. M. Forster

ALS: HRC

[1] Pertains to the quarrel with D. H. Lawrence; see Letters 140, 141.

144   To Edward Joseph Dent

Weybridge.   6 March 1915

Dear Dent

Thanks awfully for both your letters. You can scarcely imagine the loneliness of such an effort as this—a year's work! how one longs for praise shamelessly! You have given me the greatest comfort and pleasure. I wrote it neither for my friends or the public—but because it was weighing on me; and my previous training made me write it as literature, though for a long time I meant to show it to no one at all. Translation is depressing and publication in English impossible, so there we are, but if I die (which I do not anticipate or desire) I should like it given to Spohr.[1]

Carpenter has read and liked it, but he's too unliterary to be helpful: he took to Alec, and thought him improbable but possible, and as that part was then bad and unfinished he might think him better now. You did not mention A. in your 2nd letter—some day I would like to ~~know~~ hear your criticism. About the epilogue, I quite agree, and it shall be altered, as shall the B. M. allusion. M. mentions the menstruation to C. in ignorance of what it is: he's as blind to those troubles as ordinary people are to his.[2]

Roger Fry & Sydney [Waterlow] have also read the book, and their opinions, being totally unbiassed, are interesting.[3] R. agrees with you that it is beautiful and the best work I have done. S. finds it moving, and persuasive to all but bigots, admirable as a sociological tract, full of good things, but he finds the characters weighed down by these, Clive and his decay difficult, Alec vague, Mrs Hills' lack of a bed-pan incredible; and, speaking generally, nothing in it better than what I have done already. I am much dependant on criticism, and now, backed by you and some others, do feel that I have created something absolutely new, even to the Greeks. Whitman nearly anticipated me but he didn't really know what he was after, or only half knew—shirked, even to himself, the statement.

I have not read Platen yet, and some day will get you to show me the best parts, as German's a labour. I liked Hölderlein's *Hyperion*—I wish someone would translate it.[4] Have you read *The White Peacock* by D. H. Lawrence? If not, do not, for you cannot, but read one chapter in it called A poem of friendship, which is most beautiful.[5] The whole book is the queerest product of subconsciousness that I have yet struck—he has not a glimmering from first to last of what he's up to.

I should like to see you some time—I am at the National Gallery Office Mondays and Fridays now, and often other days. Let me have another line, any how.

Yours

E. M. Forster.

ALS: KCC

1 I.e. *Maurice*. Spohr: Probably Wilhelm Spohr, German socialist editor, active in the folk-theatre movement and in opposition to the Kaiser.

2 Edward Carpenter wrote (23 August [1914]. KCC): 'I have read your "Maurice" after all, and I am very much pleased with it. I don't always like your rather hesitating tantalising impressionist style—though it has subtleties—but I think the story has many fine points. You succeed in giving the atmosphere round the various characters, and there are plenty of happenings wh. is a good thing. Maurice's love affairs are all interesting, and I have a mind to read them again, if I can find time—so I won't send the MS. back for a day or two. I am so glad you end up on a major chord. I was so afraid you were going to let Scudder go at the last—but you saved him & saved the story, because [of] the idea that improbable is not impossible & is the one bit of real romance—wh. those who understand will love.' In the deleted epilogue (TS/MS. KCC), Kitty, Maurice's sister, later encounters him and Alec in Yorkshire as woodmen.

3 These opinions, if written, do not survive.

4 August, Graf von Platen-Hollermunde (1796–1835), German poet and dramatist, of homosexual tendency, who turned increasingly to classical models and uncompromising opposition to romanticism. *Hyperion* (1797–9) is a long poem by the German poet Johann Christian Friedrich Hölderlin (1770–1843).

5 In Lawrence, *The White Peacock* (1911), Part II, Chapter 8: a farm pastorale.

145 To Florence Barger

National Gallery [London]
28 March 1915

Dear Florence

Would you care to read my novel?[1] I forgot to say that, if you would, I could have it sent you in a few days—otherwise some one else shall see it first. George, by the way, is most welcome to read it too if he cares, but I doubt it interesting him. To you it will reveal a new and painful world, into which you will hardly have occasion to glance again: a tiny world that is generally unknown to all who are not born in it. My only fear is that it may make me seem remote to you—not for one instant repellant, but remote.

Let me hear at N. G. when you'll read it.

I was awfully interested (and saddened) by your domestic breakup. Your mother will certainly become less intractable shortly—even condescending to old May, I hope.

I am reviewing Virginia Woolf's novel 'The Voyage Out'. Amazingly interesting, and very funny.[2]

Morgan

ALS: KCC

1 I.e. *Maurice*.
2 Cf. Letter 141.

146   To Leonard Woolf

Harnham, Monument Green, Weybridge
20 May 1915

Dear Woolf,

A friend of mine who has been mad and is now not believes, from what I have said, that he was in the same state as Virginia; also that he can help her; this he is anxious to do.[1]

He is willing to meet you, or any one, in London and be questioned and cross-questioned to any extent. I wish you or Vanessa would have a look at him. Send him a line at once.

E. Altounyan,
    3, Worsley Road,
      Hampstead,
        N. W.

Yours ever
E.M.F.

I have chicken pox—this shall be fumigated.

ALS: Berg

[1] Virginia Woolf had been ill, with intermittent recovery, since the summer of 1913. Virginia's sister Vanessa (1879–1961) married the critic Clive Bell (1881–1964) in 1907.

147   To Syed Ross Masood

55 Bryansburn Road, Bangor,
Co. Down Ireland[1]
29 July 1915

Dearest SRM,

I wrote you a pretty dry letter last time, didn't I? Still, it is better than the letters I get from you, because they don't exist. This is just a line to say that I hope all goes well, and that the child will be a boy. Give him—(or her) my love as soon as he (or she) enters this curious place, the world. I also write because I may be leaving England shortly for the front in an Ambulance Unit—it is going out to Italy and I have been asked to join. It'll upset my mother very much, and I'm a bit nervous of collapsing physically and mentally when I get to work, for the horror of modern battle is inconceivable. Nor have I any sympathy with the Italian govt.—it is simply out for plunder.[2] Still, I may go. All one can do in this world of maniacs is to pick up the poor tortured broken people and try to mend them, and the Italian Ambulance Unit would give me an opportunity to do this. It will be strange and sad to go back to those mountains of our youth, and find them drenched in blood. I will let you know whether I go or not—it will be decided this week.

I had a pleasant afternoon with Lady M[orison] last week. I tried to keep off the war knowing we should disagree—she is so romantic and sentimental about it: thinks everyone who has shouldered a rifle is transfigured for life. But it was impossible. We all talk, think, eat, and sleep war in these unfortunate British Isles. Ireland—where I now am—is better than England, and blessed of blessed is India, where none of you, since the Emden, think about it at all.[3]

Well, much love, dearest Boy, and my kindest wishes to Zohra, and my sincere respects to your mother.[4]

Morgan.

TTr supplied by Akbar Masood

[1] EMF is in Bangor with the Merediths.
[2] G. M. Trevelyan was organising an ambulance unit and had asked EMF to join it. Italy had entered the war on 23 May.
[3] German raiding cruiser that sank many merchant and naval vessels and was eventually sunk off the Cocos Islands by the Australian cruiser *Sydney*, on 9 November 1914.
[4] Zohra: Masood's first wife.

148   To Malcolm Darling

Harnham, Monument Green, Weybridge
2 August 1915

BEGIN on Page Sheet 2

Dear Malcolm,

I have sent you 3 books from T. & H., but scarcely anything is published now: Forrest Reid's admirable study of Yeats—actually bound up—is not to be risked on the market till September. Since ordering them I have thought of *The Great Society*, which is amusing & stimulating, and shall follow next mail.[1] Your letter was a great pleasure, but I was sorry about Josie's throat, and felt sure she would disobey you. You also gave me a *second* account of Bapu Sahib's visit to you, much more vivid and delightful than the *first* account, which I received many weeks ago! What am I to conclude from this? That distance, &c? I don't suppose so.

Such news as I have is trivial. Dickinson continues in his own words 'the Sisyphean task of rolling the stone of Reason up the hill of Passion.' Hilton *is* R. N. No doubt I did say R.N.R. by mistake—the two are as alike as A.S.C. and H.A.C or R.A.M.C. and Y.M.C.A. It's an age of initials.[2] But he really is R.N., and I play chess with him by correspondence, and learn quaint sailor oaths. My mother is remarkably well, but a bit upset as I am in the throes of deciding whether I shall go to the Italian front in an ambulance unit. Fancy helping Spitaly! But I do feel all wounded flesh equal in the sight of God, and all Governments almost equal in the sight of the devil, so my going or not going will depend upon other considerations. (By the way, if Josie gets too ~~obstreperous~~ triumphant over Spitaly's behaviour, you might let drop the remark that, had the government been papal, that country would have entered the war just the same—only on the other side! This ought to squash her. The Pope has been as pro German as he dared throughout: witness his coldness to Cardinal Mercier.[3]—I think that is the only unpleasant thing I want to say: except that if *your* (occasional) wish was granted, and England invaded, it would certainly have the effect of tickling up the women and children fine. The Bishop of London does not even wish it occasionally. It is his steady hope that every nursery may share in the Baptism of Fire; for he believes—and I understand rightly—that no home into which a bomb has once fallen will ever be quite the same again.[4] Close brackets, however)]} and put fairly nearer them that I will send you Romain Rolland's pamphlet to counterbalance, J'Accuse.[5]

Am just back from a week in Ireland (Belfast). There was a notable dearth of submarines; but one got an oil ship close to Dunwich (East Coast) just before the Bargers arrived there the other day. I am longing for them to get back—at the present everyone is being nervous on account of someone else—a wasteful arrangement. We in London receive terrified letters from the provinces about Zeppelins, but don't think of them ourselves.

BEGIN HERE

Dear Malcolm

Your letter describing Sirsa just arrived—so nice to get it though ~~all it~~ what it conveys is[6]

> Bungalow of
> 2 rooms only

Can this be right? I had meant to include servants snakes and Sikhs in the picture, but perhaps have started it upon wrong lines, for even the Richards' at Lahore, whose extreme poverty was proved by the presence of a front door bell instead of the absence of a chuprassi—even the Richards' possessed a third room.[7] Have you to come down to this? No wonder you grow a little tart about the Nation, poor dears. You can't be expected to let live unless you are let to live, and I quite understand your attitude towards the British Working Man, and now that he has let the C. W. overflow through our own cieling [*sic*] even share it.

I read (and sometimes write) the New Statesman myself, but you wouldn't like it any better; also the Morning Post, which you might like almost too much. I enclose from it this jolly letter of Balfour's: it seems to me distinctly on the spot. Reventlow's was too much of a bore to send.[8]

You ask about Rupert Brooke.[9] Considering we were on Christian name terms, I did not know him well, though enough to contradict the legend that the press are weaving round ~~his name~~ him. He was serene humourous intelligent and beautiful—as charming an acquaintance as one could desire—and latterly most friendly. But he was essentially hard; his hatred of slosh went rather too deep and affected the eternal water-springs, and I don't envy anyone who applied to him for sympathy. The sonnets, on which his reputation is evidently to be based, differ from all his previous work, which was rebellious and unorthodox. They were inspired by his romantic thoughts about war, not by his knowledge of it; that also, had he been spared to gain it, he was hoping to express, and, knowing his grim and grotesque realism, I feel sure that he would have expressed something besides the Holiness in which—to me so inappropriately—his work concludes. I don't know whether the above conveys anything to you. If it errs on the side of unkindness he himself wouldn't like it the less, for he was extraordinarily free of conceit and sincerely desired to be done by as he did. But he goes down to posterity as a sort of St Sebastian, haloed by the Dean of St Paul's, and hymned by the Morning Post as the Evangelist of anti-Germanism. As far as I dare speak for Rupert, how he would hate it, or rather laugh at it.[10]

Either give away the Poems I sent from T. & H. or return them: I should like a copy.[11] I am sending you *The Great Society* gratis!

It gets late, and I must post this. Mrs Woolf's work is, from the point from which you approach it, certainly inferior to mine. But I do think it fine in other ways—its feeling for adventure, its knowledge that adventure can only be undertaken alone. From the tropical forest to the end struck me as unique in English literature[.][12] I hope T. & H. sent you Devindranath Tagore: they struck me as stupid.[13] Do you want a new (1 vol.) edition of Sleeman's Rambles and Recollections?

Now you may read the first part of this letter. I nearly tore it up, thinking the epigrams about Governments too tiresome, but let it pass with a grain of salt on the ~~British~~ Potsdam eagle's tail. Spitaly is off or almost so, as it upsets my mother who adduces all sorts of reasons against it. If she didn't I might have begun adducing them myself, but as it is I feel depressed and unhappy the moment I sit still. Ambulance work, especially when dangerous, seems to me the one thing worth *my* doing in connection with this war, the one spot of light in this world horror; and though I should be afraid when I got out there I don't feel afraid now, and though I am inadequate to the horrors of the Front, so is everyone. I wish you had been in England. I think any opinion of yours would have not only decided

me but left me easy. I had no one to consult. One 'oughtn't to leave
one's mother when she has no one else' I know yet the question is
complicated when filial piety finds compensation in an arm chair
and four meals a day served regularly. Creation's best—if I was
writing properly I wouldn't worry about wounded flesh. But when
creation fails one starts thinking of Vishnu.[14]

Mother sends love messages something. So do I. Think of me this
weekend at Dover, which I always enjoy.

Morgan

ALS: HRC

[1] Truslove & Hanson, booksellers in Sloane Street, London. Forrest Reid, *W. B. Yeats: A Critical Study* (1915). Graham Wallas, *The Great Society: A Psychological Analysis* (1914).
[2] Hilton Young entered the Naval Reserve in 1914. RN: Royal Navy. RNR: Royal Naval Reserve. ASC: Army Service Corps. HAC: Honourable Artillery Company. RAMC: Royal Army Medical Corps. On Young's war service, see Letter 142.
[3] Cardinal (Désiré) Mercier (1851–1926) had been Archbishop of Malines and Cardinal since 1907.
[4] Rt Rev. and Rt Hon. Arthur Foley Winnington Ingram (1858–1946) was Bishop of London, 1901–39. He was a strong believer in the disciplinary values of wartime, and in visits to the front he found much to admire. The *DNB* finds his 'intellectual equipment solid, but dated'.
[5] Rolland, *Au dessus de la mêlée* (1915), translated as *Above the Battle* (1916) by C. K. Ogden. *J'Accuse* (1915) was published anonymously by Richard Grelling, and translated by Alexander Gray, as *I Accuse (J'Accuse!) by a German* (1915).
[6] Sirsa is northwest of Delhi, in the Punjab, and part of Darling's administrative district, which was now Haryana State.
[7] Philip Ernest Richards (1875–1920), former Unitarian minister, went to India in 1911 as Professor of English at Dyal Singh College, and at Islamic College, Lahore. His wife Norah (1876–19??) was active in the Punjabi theatre movement. After his death, she returned to England but settled permanently in India in 1924. For an account of their life in Lahore, see his *Indian Dust; being Letters from the Punjab* (1932).
[8] James Arthur Balfour, 1st Earl (1848–1930), Prime Minister, 1902–5; First Lord of the Admiralty, 1915–16; and Foreign Secretary, 1916–19. His letter, 'What Our Fleet Has Done' (*The Morning Post*, 2 August 1915, p. 4) replied to Count Ernst zu Reventlow (1869–1943), German political writer and war historian, who had argued ('A Year of Naval Warfare', *ibid.*) that the German fleet, although unprepared for war, had frustrated the plans of the stronger and long-prepared English fleet for blockading German ports.
[9] Rupert Brooke died of blood-poisoning on a French hospital-ship in Trebuki Bay, Skyros, on 23 April 1915, which provoked a great outburst of pious commemoration in the newspapers.
[10] The Very Rev. William Ralph Inge (1860–1954), Dean of St Paul's, 1911–34, was dubbed 'the Gloomy Dean' because of his pessimistic outlook. In his Easter Sunday sermon he read Brooke's poem, 'If I should die', and eulogised him as the spirit of heroism and self-sacrifice; see 'Dean Inge at St Paul's: Spirit of the Martyr-Patriot', *The Times*, 25 April 1915, p. 8.
[11] Poems: unidentified.
[12] In Woolf, *The Voyage Out*, Chapter 20 ff.
[13] Devendranath Tagore (1817–1905), philosopher and Brahmo Samaj leader; father of the poet Rabindranath Tagore. The book is probably *The Autobiography of Maharshi Devendranath Tagore*, trans. Satyendranath Tagore and Indira Devi (1914).
[14] Vishnu: the Preserver in the Hindu Trinity.

149   To Florence Barger

Weybridge.   10 August 1915

Dear Florence

So much seems happening—at least emotionally and talkatively—
that I had better post you up, though no one much values a letter
when holidaying, and mine will be rather a silly one. Italy is
off—mother was too much against it, and I think on her account and
not through cowardice I decided not to go.[1] I feel rather wretched in
consequence, and that I am leading the life of a little girl so long as I
am tied to home. It isn't even as if I make mother happy by
stopping—she is always wanting me to be 5 years old again, so
happiness is obviously impossible for her, and she never realises that
the cardinal fact in my life is my writing, and that at present I am not
writing. (She knows I am not writing, but she can't realise it is
serious for me).—Then we are both rather upset at Altounyan's
marrying: I a little, for it must mean a change, and I didn't want a
change: she a great deal "this is the end of him" &ᶜᵗ, and much else
that is absurd but trying.[2] I've also got to chronicle to you—not to
anyone else I think—that Hugh can't again be in my life what he has
been.[3] He was very jolly, very happy, and very well during my visit,
which I much enjoyed, but he just isn't interested in me or in anyone
except as passing amusements, and since seriousness must be
reciprocal I find it less and less possible to be serious about him.
Affection remains, but I can't ever now ask him for sympathy or
advice: I should fear his attention wandering before I had finished
the sentence. And no doubt he will have his bad times just as now he
is having his cheerful ones, and will appeal again for sympathy and
advice to me, and I shall give them; but never again with the old
gravity—when *his* sufferings used to seem more important than
most men's. All this is rather awful, but the fact is, being a writer,
with a writer's touchiness or whatever you like to call it,—I was very
badly hit by his utter indifference to Maurice and the pain has
opened my eyes little by little to his general indifference. To turn a
hero into a jolly old boy is a ghastly task, but it must be done, and I
think I am through with it; at least I had no inclination to tell him
anything about Italy though my mind was full of it.—There! Now
that I have shared my discomfort with you—i.e. given you 100 times
more than your share—I feel easier. I have never forgotten that you
like me to tell you things and it is the greatest relief. You mustn't
bear only discomforts;—I have just been stopping a week end at
Dover with Shuttleworth and enjoyed being with him, as I always
do, and am certain that he enjoyed being with me.[4] Saturday we
became involved in a ridiculous cricket match of 'officers v.
wounded', Sunday afternoon we fell asleep on the top of
Shakespeare's Cliff, and Sunday evening I became most agreeably

drunk and my talk brilliant and profound. He told me a lot about the army—in fact I know all there is to know. And he paid my hotel-bill.

Christabel was most friendly and nice, and—I seem to be whining on this point!—*interested* in all one said. We had long talks about the children. R. was sweet. S. not bad and 'may send me a tin of toffee, but is not sure'. Adam yelled like a steam engine most meals, for he suffered from teeth. It is funny to see Christabel feed him, and beam all over when he spatters her with Benger.[5] If his teeth didn't hurt, he was sweet. Miss Shane has greatly improved, and came to see me one evening in her night dress, which I thought friendly of her.[6] The new nurse seemed also very nice.

On goes the N[ational] G[allery] catalogue. Yet another Index has presented itself, and I have been at it this evening again. Must go to bed. This letter reads as if I didn't care what holiday you were having, and wasn't looking forward to seeing Harold: none of which is true. Don't let the first page of it depress you.

Morgan.

ALS: KCC

[1] 'Italy is off': that is, service with G. M. Trevelyan's Ambulance Unit.
[2] In 1915 Altounyan married Dora Collingwood, daughter of Ruskin's biographer and secretary whom he had met at Ruskin's erstwhile Lake Country home, Brantwood.
[3] Hugh: i.e. Hugh Meredith. EMF had visited him in Northern Ireland in July.
[4] Lawrence H. C. Shuttleworth (d. 1925), schoolmaster of sombre temperament whom EMF had met in India in 1912, at Bhopal, where he was stationed as a trooper. During the First World War he was stationed in Cairo, and after the war he was a master at Cheltenham College. In despair after his wife's death, he committed suicide.
[5] R. . . . S.: Ralph and Sidney Meredith, twins. Adam was born in 1913. Benger's: a patent food for the very young and the very old.
[6] Miss Shane: unidentified.

150   To Virginia Woolf

Holmleigh, Salisbury
18 September 1915

Dear Virginia

You are at present Lawrence the strong-novelist's lode star, and I am particularly to enclose the enclosed. He was unusually mad about your book.[1] I had him to lunch with Mr. Collins Baker of the National Gallery and they got on dreadfully, while I—so sensitive once—ate on at my nut meat pie.[2] Ever since Cambridge my little parties have gone wrong—the guests either quarrelling or ignoring me—but since the war I can cope with anyone. I move in society seldom but freely. Last week end at The Lacket was very pleasant—Lytton, whose hair I cut crooked, Philippa his sister, and Roger [Fry] who was interested in everything, especially in the

poems of Mallarmé.³ Many scabious, harebells and white rabbits
(the Souls of the Dead?) upon the downs.

Here, except for the white rabbits and the company, it is exactly
the same. The downs begin close behind the city and are covered
with flowers. I go to Plymouth on Tuesday with regret, then to
Dover. Next month I'd like to come and see you again if it suits
you.⁴ I will write to Leonard and find out.

Yours

E. M. Forster

ALS: Berg

¹ The unidentified 'enclosed', probably pertaining to *The Voyage Out*, initiated no literary
correspondence, and Lawrence and Mrs Woolf had not met.
² C. H. Collins Baker (1880–1959) was Keeper and Secretary, 1914–32, at the National
Gallery, and Surveyor of the King's Pictures, 1928–34. He and EMF met again in California in
1947, when Collins Baker was on the staff of the Huntington Library. In 1959 EMF recalled
his post at the Gallery as 'amateur watchman and amateur catalogue-compiler' (to *The Times*,
14 July 1959, p. 9).
³ Hilton Young had let The Lacket to Lytton Strachey. Philippa ('Pippa') Strachey
(1872–1968) was one of Lytton's elder sisters. Fry, a devoted admirer of Mallarmé's work,
translated his *Poems* (1936).
⁴ EMF saw the Woolfs, perhaps at Asheham, in August 1915; see Woolf, *Letters*, II, 63;
EMF, II, 18. At Plymouth he visited his great-aunt Eliza Fowler, and at Dover he saw
Shuttleworth. These were by way of farewell visits: he left for Alexandria, as a Red Cross
'searcher', about 10 November, via Paris.

151 To Sir Henry Newbolt

Harnham, Monument Green, Weybridge
7 November 1915

Dear Newbolt

D. H. Lawrence, whom I regard as a man of genius and a serious
writer, tells me that his novel *The Rainbow* (Methuen) has been
confiscated by the authorities. I haven't read the book nor shall I
have time to do so before leaving England; but I don't think that
either that or the fact that certain passages in it would probably
offend me, makes any difference to my indignation. I write in great
haste—which please excuse—and I am not sure what your attitude
over the matter will be. But I venture at all events to bring it to your
notice, remembering all your frankness and sympathy while we
walked on the downs. Some people would say "Oh but *this* isn't the
time to make a fuss"; I feel myself that the right to literary expression
is as great in war as it was ever in peace, and in far greater danger, and
I write on the chance of your being willing and able to protect it.¹

I am off to Egypt on Red Cross work. If all goes well I shall come
and see you next spring. With best wishes and remembrances:

Yours very sincerely
E. M. Forster

You'll probably dislike *The Rainbow*—I make no appeal on that ground. But it represents over a year's hard and sincere work, I know.

ALS: Ashley W. Olmstead

[1] On 3 November 1915 Scotland Yard seized more than a thousand copies of *The Rainbow*. The case came up in Bow Street Police Court on 13 November. Methuen, ordered to show cause why the book should be spared, said that Lawrence had made two deletions at their request, then refused to co-operate further. They regretted and apologised for the book. It transpired that, since they did not expect the case to appear in open court, they had neither notified Lawrence of the seizure nor prepared a defence. See Harry T. Moore, *The Priest of Love: A Life of D. H. Lawrence* (4th rev. ed.), pp. 239–42, 246.

152   To S. R. Masood

Red Cross, St. Mark's Buildings
Rue de L'ancienne Bourse, Alexandria, Egypt
29 December 1915

Dear SRM,

I have just got your letter dated Oct. 30. If you had wanted me to adopt the boy I think you would have insisted on him bearing my name, or would *at the least* have written to me when he was born.[1] You left me to find out about him by chance. I look forward to seeing him some day, but cannot feel that he is in any sense mine, and am greatly hurt.

To turn to more inspiriting topics.

I am liking my work out here. I am what is called a 'Red Cross Searcher':—that is to say I go round the Hospitals and question the wounded soldiers for news of their missing comrades. It is depressing in a way, for if one does get news about the missing it is generally bad news. But I am able to be of use to the wounded soldiers themselves in various unofficial ways—I lend them books, get their watches mended, write their letters, &ᶜᵗ. They are so pleasant and grateful, and some of them quite charming.

I live in a comfortable hotel here, and start out about 10.0., returning for lunch and finishing about 7.0. In the evening I write my reports which go—ultimately—to the relatives in England and to the War Office. The Red X is a semi-military organisation, so, though technically a civilian, I wear officer's uniform, and get various privileges and conveniences, of which ½ fares on the trams and trains is perhaps the most considerable. I have one or two friends here, and the regular and definite work has stopped me thinking about the war, which is a mercy, for in England I very nearly went mad. Why do you think good is 'bound to come' out of this war? You only mean you would like good to come, with which everyone agrees.

I don't know how long I shall be here but at present the above is my address if you care to write, as I hope you will. I do not like Egypt much—or rather, I do not see it, for Alexandria is cosmopolitan. But what I have seen seems vastly inferior to India, for which I am always longing in the most persistent way, and where I still hope to die. It is only at sunset that Egypt surpasses India—at all other hours it is flat, unromantic, unmysterious, and godless—the soil is mud, the inhabitants are of mud moving, and exasperating in the extreme: I feel as instinctively not at home among them as I feel instinctively at home among Indians.[2] The only non-English person of whom I see anything here is a Syrian—a very nice and amusing fellow.[3] I am dining with him tomorrow and—discarding my uniform—shall then plunge in his company into the Bazaar, to see whatever may be seen, but understand that is not much.

Well, as I said before, do write if you feel inclined: the address at the top of the letter will always find me. If ever I get back to England I will let you know, but it is useless to make plans when at any moment one may be submarined or conscripted. You are lucky to be comparatively out of things, and still to have a chance of pursuing your career. All that I cared for in civilisation has gone forever, and I am trying to live without either hopes or fears—not an easy job, but one keeps going some how.

Now I will learn a couple of Arabic words; then go to bed.

With love.
E. M. Forster.

TTr supplied by Akbar Masood

[1] Masood's first son, Anwar, born 1915.
[2] 'Mud moving': the phrase is repeated in *PI*, Chapter 1: 'The very wood seems made of mud, the inhabitants of mud moving.'
[3] George Antonius (1891–1942), orientalist; Secretary-General to the Arab delegation to the Palestine Conference, London, in 1939; author of *The Arab Awakening* (1938).

153   To Syed Ross Masood

Red Cross, St. Mark's Buildings
Rue de L'ancienne Bourse, Alexandria
10 February 1916

Dearest SRM

Your letter of Jan 26th just arrived. I am so glad you wrote in answer to mine. It was not that I so much mind you not calling the boy after me—I was greatly disappointed, but not *hurt* at that, for I knew there might be family difficulties. What hurt me was that you did not trouble to write to me for months after his birth, and let me learn not only his name but his *very existence* from others. It quite broke me that such a thing could happen, for it seemed to show that I had no longer any part in your life at all. Dearest boy, I love you

234 SELECTED LETTERS OF E. M. FORSTER

and know that you love me—so why, damn your eyes, do you go giving me so much pain? I will write again in a day or two. Meanwhile much love.

E.M.F.

TTr supplied by Akbar Masood

154 To Virginia Woolf

[Alexandria]   15 April 1916

Dear Virginia,

The enclosed comes irresistably [sic] to you for old sake's sake, but I was just about to write for my own.[1] I have two incompleted letters for Lytton by me. I can't send them. Bachelors under 40 are too awful to contemplate. Leonard will be all right I suppose until the Tribunals decide that no marriages are valid unless solemnised in the Church, you will be right for a little longer and I for quite a time for I have just got £20 out here unsubmarised and am teaching English for £4 a month to a well-pleased Greek.[2] Also I am entirely living on Furness. (He sits in the garden with me now, recovering from diarrhoea). Indeed, I feel capable of cheering you all up, and it is unlucky that I cannot do so without joining you. I imagine it is here that civilisation will expire. It is already dead in Cairo, which has war correspondents and 119 Generals and clubs of perturbed and earnest men. But in Alexandria it seems still possible to read books and bathe. It's true I talk about the war all day, but to people who can say 'we fought every inch as dirty as the Turks', and whose deepest wish is peace at once. The Flanders armies are no doubt different. Germany has made no impression here, either on the soldier or the civilian. Shops still boast that they have supplied the Crown Princess of Wurtenburg [sic], and 'Schutz für junge Mädchen' is advertised in the trams.[3] I think quite a lot about Alexander the Great too, and St. Athanasius, and the author of the Wisdom of Solomon, and Furness continues to translate the Anthologia Palatina. Sometimes there is a party at a rich Levantine's house.

How long will it last? Booh! bumble! Any mail, I may be summonsed before the Tribunal myself.

When you—or L[eonard]—replies I want news of e.g. Lytton, James [Strachey], Duncan [Grant], [Harry] Norton, [Saxon] Sydney Turner, [J. M.] Keynes, Sheppard; even Dent.[4] My address is Red X, St. Mark's Building, Rue de l'ancienne Bourse, Alex.

Morgan

ALS: Berg
[1] 'The enclosed': unidentified.
[2] That is, the war-service Tribunals. The Greek was Pericles Anastassiades, a businessman

and patron of the arts. He worked in the Censorship Department under Sir Robert Allason Furness (1883–1954), a Kingsman who had entered the Egyptian Civil Service in 1906, retired in 1923 but continued to serve in various Egyptian posts, in 1929 joining the staff of the High Commissioner for Egypt.'
³ 'Refuge [i.e. hostel] for young girls.'
⁴ James Strachey (1887–1967) was Lytton's younger brother; the painter Duncan Grant (1885–1978), his cousin. Harry Norton (1887–1936) and Saxon Sydney-Turner (1880–1962) were minor members of the Bloomsbury circle. All were conscientious objectors.

155 To Florence Barger

Cercle Mohammed Aly [Alexandria]
2 July 1916

Dearest Florence,

A line to say that the wretched business is over at last—I am only waiting for the results of the medical re examination, when I shall wire to you.[1] Mother has the later details, and you will gather from her that whatever happens I am likely to remain, and safely, in Egypt for the present. The most satisfactory point is that never, even at the worst, did I feel I should be crushed—it was probably the presence of these amazingly competent and sympathetic friends here that gave me the feeling: still it is a satisfactory one. I went on altogether satisfactorily till the 29ᵗʰ when Miss Grant Duff obscured the issue by introducing the question of *utility*—i.e. saying I was of such value to the work that if I ~~attested~~ could be allowed to ~~attest~~ stop on at it on condition I attested, it was my duty to sink conscience and attest.[2] I permitted her to make this suggestion to Sir Courtauld. Nothing came of it because (i) he said I must attest unconditionally (ii) he has now arranged that we all, unattested, attested, and unattestable, stop just as we were. And I don't think, when the point came, I *would* have sunk my conscience. Still I did listen to the suggestion, and so got muddled. Miss Grant Duff is a splendid creature, but she holds the Gospel of work which I don't and oughtn't to. I am an artist—after a week of stress like this one has the right to utter that discredited word—and the artist must (yes! I am actually going to say this too!) live his life, and it was my life not to attest. I ought to have seen that always.

Well the above is only an abortive episode, which I mention to you because I oughtn't to mother—there is no occasion for her to know of such subsidiary soul stirrings.

We are all preening our plumage after the storm. Antonius & I are probably going away for a few days. Miss Grant Duff has been to Abousir on a donkey. It fell down and she fell off. Furness is trying not to repatriate enemy aliens. Mʳˢ Borchgrevink is resting.[3] I talk to patients; with one of them—a sensitive and intelligent fellow—I have become real friends. I must tell you about him another time. He is, incongruously enough, a Ship's Steward, but he makes cider when at home, and is very refreshing on the subject of religion. He is absolutely independent, but not with the theoretical independence of the Socialist.[4] He devours masses of Dickinson, ~~Ibsen~~ and Shaw.—Another week I'll make some reference to all of you for a change. Love,

Morgan.

Medically exempt. Have just cabled.

ALS: KCC

[1] In June EMF had been involved in a dispute with the Red Cross authorities over military service. Three months earlier the British Government had introduced conscription, rescinding an earlier reserve enlistment scheme under which men of military age were invited to 'attest' for future service. The right to attest continued until late June, and EMF's Red Cross superior, Sir Courtauld Thomson (1865–1954), had instructed able-bodied members of the organisation, including EMF, to attest forthwith. EMF protested violently, since he considered this a disgraceful piece of bad faith, and was considerably 'thrown' by the incident—the more so that he was not in the strict sense a conscientious objector. Eventually however the whole affair blew over and he was able to retain his non-combatant status.

[2] Victoria Adelaide Alexandrine Grant Duff (1876–193?) was the daughter of Sir Mountstuart Elphinstone Grant Duff (1829–1906), statesman and author; Under-Secretary of State for India, 1868–74, and Governor of Madras, 1881–6. The Egyptian post was her first employment and responsible assignment, and it is possible that its complications were too much for her. As will be seen, she and EMF had a violent quarrel, which ended in her resignation. She died in poverty in the 1930s.

[3] Mrs Aïda Borchgrevink (d. 19??) was the widow of a Norwegian judge, American by birth and trained as an opera singer: hence the change from her given name of Ada. She lived in a fashionable suburb of Alexandria and took a great interest in EMF.

[4] EMF later inscribed this letter, 'Enter Frank Vicary'. Vicary (d. 1956) came from a farming family on the Welsh border. He served as a ship's steward during the early years of the war, and after the war he attempted to become a miner, but his health broke down. EMF continually helped him with money, but nothing prospered for him, and the tragic death of one of his children finally demoralised him.

156   To Goldsworthy Lowes Dickinson

[Montazah]   28 July 1916

Dear Dickinson

I hope you get on passably and have tolerable news. Shuttleworth, after some pleasantly mischievous letters from Salonica, has cabled 'Invalided home alright'—I think with malaria. I wish you might meet. I have had a great crisis—for details apply the Bargers: I'm too bored to describe it and it's anyhow over in its present form: the Red X tried to empty me into the army. After a week's perfect Hell all seems as before, but I expect life to increase in discomfort and ignobility.

I'm writing though because I wished you were with me at Montazah this morning. It is the country Palace of the ex-Khedive and has been turned into a Convalescent Hospital. Amongst its tamarisk groves and avenues of flowering oleander, on its reefs and fantastic promontories of rocks and sand, hundreds of young men are at play, fishing, riding donkeys, lying in hammocks, boating, dosing, swimming, listening to bands. They go about bare chested and bare legged, the blue of their linen shorts and the pale mauve of their shirts accenting the brown splendour of their bodies; and down by the sea ~~some~~ many of them spend half their days naked and unrebuked ~~and unashamed~~. It is so beautiful that I cannot believe it has not been planned, but can't think by whom nor for whom except me. It makes me very happy yet very sad—they came from the unspeakable, all these young gods, and in a fortnight at the latest return to it: the beauty of the crest of a wave. I wish I could convey special moments: one, when I came to the top of a wooded knoll at ~~twilight~~ sunset, and found a vast fairy ring of them crowning it, here empurpled by shadow, there flecked with orange; another moment at the same hour, when I was bathing myself on the deserted beach and a man gallopped up on a donkey, stripped, and tried to pull it into the water with him. The lines of a straining nude have always seemed academic to me up to now but hereafter I shall remember red light on them, and ripples like grey ostrich-feathers breaking on the sand. He didn't—to grow less serious—get the donkey to follow him, but I don't know that I want to grow less serious. I come away from that place each time thinking 'Why not more of this? Why not? What would it injure? Why not a world like this—its beauty of course impaired by death and old age and poverty and disease, but a world that should not torture itself by organised and artificial horrors?' It's evidently not to be in our day, nor while nationality lives, but I can't believe it Utopian, for each human being has in him the germs of such a world.

I still like my work and do the motherly to Tommies as you say, and I hope in one case the brotherly. I was leaving him as he had no information for me when to my amazement he said 'I'm awfully interested in ideas—I'm more interested in ideas than anything'— and blimey so he was, and amusing and charming too. I lent him books by you, and though he stuck in *The Meaning of Good* as 'unlikely to help', *John Chinaman* he liked so much as to read part of it aloud to the rest of the ward.[1] "They said What do you want to read that for? I said It's very interesting about the opium as showing what Europe's like. They said But what does it matter? Who cares?" He was very funny about his own early Xtianity—he grew up in respectable circles in the west of England who believed that all one's cut toe nails resurrected with one on the last day—whether in bags or attached his grandfather was not sure. He's gone to England, and having bad heart and neurasthenia will be left there I hope.

I only see people like this, the office lady, who is very nice, and Furness and his friends—quite a lot & quite a variety, but nothing of club land or drawingroomia.[2] In some ways I have never been so free—it's an odd backwater the war has scooped out for me, and I don't know whether I most dread or long for England. Whenever I open a paper things seem filthier.

How is Bob? I have never heard of him since I left. Did you go to the Dinner? Turner (H. H.) wrote me a pleasant line about it from which I gathered there was no fiasco.[3] I agree with your complaint about H.O.M. It is very tiresome of him to view men and things as a spectacle and yet be unhappy.

I hear praise of dear Searight from men of his Rgt. He is immensely popular—they all love him.[4]

Everard Feilding is here—a nice fellow, though a queer one.[5]

EMF.

MS: KCC

[1] This was Vicary. Dickinson, *The Meaning of Good* (1901) and *Letters from John Chinaman* (1901). The latter was first published anonymously in England, where many assumed that it was indeed missives from a Chinese gentleman; it was published in the United States as *Letters from a Chinese Official, being an Eastern View of Western Civilization* (1903).

[2] 'Office lady': Victoria Grant Duff. EMF first thought her 'so generous and energetic', but by 1917 he saw her as 'a mass of conscientiousness and nerves' (EMF to his mother, 18 May 1916; 2 June [1917]. KCC).

[3] Bob: i.e. Trevelyan. Dinner: annual Apostles' dinner. Herbert Hall Turner (1861–1930), graduate of Trinity College, Cambridge, became Savilian Professor of Astronomy at Oxford in 1893 and was Director of the University Observatory.

[4] Searight: the officer met on the 1912 voyage out to India and visited at Peshawar (Letter 106).

[5] The Hon. Francis Henry Everard Joseph Feilding (1867–1936), second son of the 9th Earl of Denbigh, entered the Naval Reserve in 1914 and was on the Intelligence Staff in Egypt and Palestine, 1915–16. He was an active member of the Society for Psychical Research.

157   To Malcolm Darling

Red X, Rue de l'ancien[ne] Bourse,
Alexandria, Egypt.   6 August 1916

Dearest Malcolm,

My line to Josie showed we can't hope for Dewas yet awhile. The Red X has been allowed to keep on all its workers so I am still here, and a medical re-examination thinks I'm *un*fit, though I've received no exemption certificate so far. I'm mainly writing to ask for another letter—I loved yours, and my idealisation, we won't say regrettable but ahemmable, of India, mounts and mounts and mounts. Egypt feeds it by contrast. I hate the place, or rather its inhabitants. This is interesting, isn't it, because I came inclined to be pleased and quite free from racial prejudices, but in 10 months I've acquired an instinctive dislike to the Arab voice, the Arab figure, the Arab way of looking or walking or pump shitting or eating or laughing or anythinging—exactly the emotion that I censured in the Anglo-Indian towards the native there. What does this mean? Am I old, or is it the war, or are these people intrinsically worse? Any how

I better understand the Anglo-Indian irritation though I'm glad to say I'm as far as ever from respecting it!! It's damnable and disgraceful, and it's in me.

Now and then I have a hideous fear. Will this sojourn in the spurious East put me against the true East—Dewas, Aurangabad, Jodhpur? The fear generally passes, leaving only the regret that I'm no better than any one else, and one does want to be better than other people, much better: I've we've no use for the philosophy that says 'Come let's all be two feet high together.' But to this extent I'm glad I can't get on to India straight, I want to come from England direct, unstained by the Nile.

This sounds theoretical and gassy, and if but if it didn't take too long I would describe my one—and disastrous—Egyptian acquaintance: he is considered the pick of the natives here, and he performed an act of pure mud. He is serenely conscious unconciousness [sic] that it was mud. Oh will it take too long after all? (Or did I tell it you last time?) He invited me to go to a Haschish den if he could find one. I've always wanted to go, he found one, and with great difficulty and many protestations that we were genuine visitors and would not breath[e] a word to the police we wormed ourselves in, and the Hashish people were very pleasant to us, and I sat chatting Italian to them for some time—the owner was Maltese. A few days after I heard from Furness that the owner had been arrested hauled up, and on mentioning this to my Egyptian friend was sickened to the vitals to find that *he* had gone straight to police and peached. He was dining with me at the time. I could only gape. "Oh yes"—smiling modestly. "It was my duty. I am private gentleman in the evening but a member of the administration ⟨he's in the Police himself⟩ by day. I keep the two apart." The particular dishonour or rather dishonours of such a mind seem to me dirtier than anything old Moses hit upon, and he knew these fellows too.

I saw from the Hospital Lists than an officer from Lovats Scouts was here, and went round at once to get news of Jermyn [Moorsom]. But he was still in England, an adjutant the officer thought "in which capacity he finds that dry manner useful." I had entertained such hopes of finding that 'dry manner' here. My only other link with our joint past is the Hot Stuff article in last month's English Review, which was provided by Mrs Turner. In fairness I must add that it contained more stuff than heat, stuff curiously disposed in metrical lengths. Quite three pages of the prose ran into the rhythm of Hiawatha. "There before us lay the village. Members of the état-major walked around Celestine's garret.' I cannot make out what she is up to, but then never could. Some sort of effect is evidently intended. I have often since the war broke out thought of her party at that coniferous grange.[1]

What about Vicky? Has anyone been found?[2] Josie's description of her duties amused but distressed me—it is rotten she should have been so left in the lurch and had to do so much. Please tell me how you all are and how India is—pretty trying at the present moment I fear. Love to all.

Morgan

ALS: HRC

[1] Bridget McLagan (i.e. Mary Borden Turner), 'Bombardment' and 'Rousbrugge', in 'War Vignettes', *The English Review*, 23 (1916), 14–20.
[2] Vicky: i.e. Vikramsinha, son of the Maharaja of Dewas. In May 1917 he went to live with Philip and Norah Richards at Lahore. The Darlings hoped to shield him from the court intrigues.

158   To Laura Mary Forster

Sultan Hussein Club, Alexandria, Egypt
25 August 1916

Dear Aunt Laura,

Your welcome letter to Darkest Africa has been followed by a 'real' Missionary magazine, which I have also enjoyed. Work here is quieter again, which leaves me time for reading, and while you were at H. J.'s *Portrait of a Lady* I was tackling his latter and tougher end in the person of *What Maisie Knew*. I haven't *quite* got through her yet, but I think I shall: she is my very limit—beyond her lies *The Golden Bowl*, *The Ambassadors* and similar impossibles. I don't think James could have helped his later manner—is a natural development, not a pose. All that one can understand of him seems so genuine, that what one can't understand is likely to be genuine also.

I feel boiling to-day—partly because, just as I was leaving for my work my landlady presented me with a hot sweet potato on a saucer, and I ate it to please her, on the top of my breakfast, running afterwards for the tram. One does not recover quickly from such a treat. As for the weather, it is not so bad, and the early morning bathing is delightful. I have had 4 days' holiday at Ras-el-Bar, but you will probably have heard that through Mother, so I won't repeat.

We live among rumours and gossip, as I suppose does everyone. Did you hear about Townsend and the Turkish General who was an old school friend of his?[1] Townsend, in Kut, was preparing some suspicious looking tubes, so the general sent a message saying: "I say—are those for gas? I hope you're not going to try any of those dirty German tricks on me." Townsend replied: "Keep your hair on—they're for soda water; would you like some?" I have talked to several men who were in the Kut hospitals when the Turks entered, and they say that they behaved admirably, even buying kit at a fair price when they could have taken it for nothing. It is a great problem what to do with a nation that is at its best in war and its worst in peace. Our men have become so fond of the Turks that the authorities have had to give them lectures on Armenian atrocities, etc. to cocker them up—meanwhile making a perfect prince of a camp for the Turkish prisoners close by! As for the Canal fighting, I hear little except that the official accounts are not accurate; over that April engagement the inaccuracy was so extreme as to merit a severer name. Lemberg has fallen in the local Italian paper, but not anywhere else.[2] This completes my military information! Now I must crawl to a nice cool little Italian restaurant and then tram on to the hospital, where a few witnesses remain from the last convoy.

I wonder what sort of August weather you are having—do trust that you have been able to get out a little. The cold summer must have been wretched.

With very much love,

Ever yours affectionately,
E. M. Forster.

Yes, I had heard of Aunt Hope's grievous loss.[3]

TTr made for LMF: KCC

[1] Major-General Sir Charles Townshend (1861–1924), who commanded the 6th Division and Force in Mesopotamia, surrendered at Kut in April 1916, with 10,000 men.
[2] There was an April engagement at Lvov (Lemberg).
[3] Hope Elizabeth Wedgwood (1844–1935) married her cousin, Godfrey Wedgwood, head of the family firm, in 1905. She was sister to Laura Forster's friends 'Effy' Wedgwood (Letter 1) and Frances Julia ('Snow') Wedgwood (1833–1915). Her loss: death in France of her stepson, Major Cecil Wedgwood (1863–1915).

159   To S. R. Masood

Red Cross, St. Mark's Buildings,
Rue d l'ancienne Bourse, Alexandria
28 September 1916

Dearest SRM,

Your letter to your sweetest Morgan was admirable in tone, though it might have contained more than five lines and told him something he didn't know already. Long may you direct education at Hyderabad and soon may I visit you there! Your salary, the amount of which I learnt from Shazad, is gratifying.[1] For God's sake, get rich! We shall none of us have a penny in England.

My handwriting does not imply senility, but that I am lying in bed waiting for my breakfast which I hear being bought at the Greek baker's next door. Generally I have a swim before breakfast, but feel slack—result of dinner and cinema last night. Life here goes on comfortably enough—pleasantly, if I were not parted from those I love. I often think of England and almost as often of India and have in my room a reproduction of a little Moghul figure that Shuttleworth gave me. I often look at it and it takes my thoughts away from the war and also from this pseudo-orientation of Egypt, which I greatly dislike. (By the way a long letter to you lies about somewhere, explaining why I dislike Egypt: it was never finished or posted).

Are you growing respectable? Oh do not. It is the unforgivable sin.

I am—to resume—stuck down here indefinitely, and even if I am moved my letters will be forwarded. So write here and don't pretend you can't. What is your home news? Has your mother moved with you to Hyderabad? How is she, and Zorah and the boy? My mother sounds well—so does my aunt, but there is plenty of trouble at home in other ways. Mrs. Aylward has been very ill and has let her house and come to Weybridge. Charlie—my cousin Herbert's wife—you much liked them both I remember—has had another attack of consumption and is not expected to live. And Gerry— another cousin—you do not know him—has conscientious objections to military service, and in spite of the clause in the Act that expressly provides for men of his principles, is being arrested and imprisoned (I hope by the way that the censor won't hold up this letter for the above remark.[2] If he does, I permit myself to inform him that he doesn't know his job and is also moreover a shit.) To resume again.

Tesserete has been vividly in my mind of late—I do not know why. I have thought of the journey out there—how we knelt in the corridor of the express looking at the stars, how the old woman in the carriage to Basle was so beastly to you when you asked to smoke:—how the young lady in the next carriage was much nicer, even corresponding with you afterwards: how Pino and family met us and I nearly fell out of the window with fatigue. I can even remember the time the hurdy gurdy played in the room below us and the whirr of the skates, which ceased thank God at 11.00 P. M. Then the thunderstorm—sweetest fellow, the thunderstorm! And the crayons we bought and so damnably messed with on the summit of Monte Generoso. And my temper when, instead of doing Law, you insisted on wasting your time over Italian that you might intrigue with a most mediocre waitress. All that is past, and why will it come back to me? There's some permanent and indestructible beauty in such things, I suppose. There certainly is in affection.— Well, goodnight, dearest chap. I expect the above will be rather queer to you, for there's no reason Tesserete should be in your mind as vividly as it is in mine for the minute.

Am very fit physically. The climate has suited me. I wish I could get away though.

Morgan.

I feel sure you want to give me a present. I will accept either scent or Bidar work.[3] There used to be exquisite specimens of either in the Hyderabad Bazaar. So buck up.

TTr supplied by Akbar Masood

[1] Shazad: unidentified.
[2] Charlotte, first wife of EMF's cousin Herbert Whichelo (1874–1931). Gerald Whichelo died in the late 1960s.
[3] EMF was particularly fond of this Indian handicraft, of metal engraved and inlaid with alloys of tin, copper, lead, and zinc. He kept a collection of Bidar work to the end of his life.

160 To Florence Barger

Sultan Hussein Club, [Alexandria] Egypt
16 October 1916

Dear Florence,

I am grieved about Christabel—you will be mentioning her every week of course. It depresses me unspeakably too that they should again be twins—I can't explain as there's a touch of the monstrous and non human in it.[1] Your news of mother on the other hand is most cheering—and came when I needed it most. I hear by same mail that your visit was a great pleasure to her. The accounts too of Gerry are better than they might be. How wonderful your sister has been. If I've disappointed G. in some ways I've anyhow let people in for him who don't. I am writing to Miss Fry.[2]

Yesterday, for the first time in my life I parted with respectability. I have felt the step would be taken for many months. I have tried to take it before. It has left me curiously sad. I realise in the first place that I am tethered to the life of the spirit—tethered by habit, not by free will or aspiration. (Why do people alw assume that only the flesh binds?) To put it in other words I realise that the step would *not* have left me with these feelings had I taken it at the usual age—though it might have left me with remorse instead. I've none of that.—Then again, in all the strangeness of the thing, I *didn't* get it human, as it might have been. There wasn't and couldn't have been any glamour but it wasn't (from my point of view) really squalid, and gave a foundation on which something might have been raised. It's as if (in the novel) A had been gone straight away, you see. ordered to come and then dismissed at once.[3]

Upshot. In this, as in every thing, one is really after intimacy, however little one realises it. Something more than physical hunger drives one.

Well, my dear, this is odd news for a Matron to receive, but you've got to receive it because you're the only person in the world I want to tell it to. I don't even want George to know. I don't even know if it's important news. You may worry—as you always have—about the conditions that produced the step, but not about the step. That it'll repel you I haven't the least fear.

I read this over a few hours later—I wonder whether it will get sent. You see there is this enormous torrent in me that never stops and of which the novel is only one splash side—I call it a torrent I suppose in apology hopes of diverting you from its recent behaviour: a torrent sounds dignified, primaeval!—Well I could control it if I liked, but am weary of controlling. The life of hopes fears fancies ideals memories—all the unsubstantial fry[?] of the spirit—I am weary of feeding on it, even if, as seems likely, I am too old to change to other food. It's not good enough because it isn't all. Perhaps—but I'm not hopeful—it may be better for the next generation, even for the men and women in it who are like me. My life has *not* been unhappy, but it has been too dam lop sided for words and physically dam lonely.

I expect you dear you would stand pages more of this, but the mosquitoes can't. They bite my ancles that, that I must go to bed.

ALU: KCC

[1] Christabel Meredith had just given birth to their second set of twins, Elizabeth and Christopher.

[2] Since Gerry was about to go to prison as a conscientious objector for two years' hard labour, this was most likely Roger Fry's sister, Sara Margery Fry (1874–1958), social worker and prison reformer. This letter is untraced.

[3] EMF writes here of a casual beach encounter with a soldier. 'A': Alec Scudder, in *Maurice*.

161   To Florence Barger

11 Rue Abbasides, Alex[andria]
8 November 1916

Dear Florence

I've not written to you for some time—fact is there was a long private (and cryptic) letter I began to you, and Providence lost it. Possibly rightly. If you write about that sort of thing you get it out of proportion—I'd rather tell you about it when we meet, if I still remember it, which I mayn't do. (You will have guessed the sort of thing it was the Maurice sort.) I only make this super-cryptic allusion now as wanting to let you know that it is at once of you that I think when anything touches me.[1]

I was too depressed about the twins to write to H. or C.[2] I must try. To think that they nearly killed her, too.

This will be a poor letter—I am out of bed from a cold and can't think consecutively—have got through it wonderfully quick thanks to the extreme comfort of this house—hot baths and 3 Arab servants to wait upon me. I only collapsed yesterday—quite the fashionable thing to do during a first visit. My host, a theosophist and a solicitor, is a nice chap.[3] He will persist that I too am "on the path," in fact ~~many~~ several who have read my books here persist in importing creeds into them—rather in the spirit of the Helleno-Christian city, if you come to think of it. e.g. the doctrine of the Incarnation has been found in Howards End. There is plenty of interest and of tolerance in the mixed communities out here but nothing remotely resembling what Cambridge knew as thought. Ingenious muddlements take its place, and the religiously minded are in their element consequently.

I never thought when I began that paragraph that I should want to go and read about S. Athanasius at its close.[4] Resisting the impulse I'll return to one of my original points which was how glad I was to get your verdict about mother. It is most satisfactory. Your visit was a great success though she is still ossing to entertain Margaret[5]

Then for Gerry—I feel you've done all that could possibly be done. Here again the relief's extreme. Yes, it would be no help if I was in prison too. My trouble is that I shouldn't have had the courage to go, perhaps. But mercifully I'm not addicted to self torture—just to do the next thing seems all that is possible. I talk about G's case to everyone I know here—they are generally quite understanding, and some think such protests will do good. It is very possible. This war—unlike others—*can't* be ended by military operations. If people still had minds that should be clear to them, and Gerry's martyrdom may make one little circle think.

Have never talked about your music. Was so glad to hear you are playing. Also—could George send me a sketch or two?

P.S. Your letter (re H.'s illness) is in.[6] Do hope you'll keep fit *and* quiet through the winter.

ALU: KCC

[1] See Letter 160.
[2] H. or C.: the Merediths; cf. Letter 160.
[3] This was Charles[?] Leveaux. The biographer Robert Sencourt (1890–1969), who was then named Robert Gordon George, was returning via Egypt from military service in India, met Leveaux, and through him met EMF in May 1918. Sencourt left an unpublished description of Leveaux (now owned by Donald Adamson): 'He is a spiritualist and calls himself a Christian Theosophist. His appearance is striking, even distinguished, and he practises at the Egyptian bar—an Englishman, though with a French name Leveaux. He has inundated me with little books—"Christ in You"—and relations from mediums as well as Christian Science, a weird jumble not as good or interesting as himself. He sends me to a friend who is doing Red Cross work here and who went to India before the war with letters from Sir Theodore Morison to Mrs Besant and to the official circles as well. I am taking rooms in the same flat as he in the Camp de César, a mile or two out' (Cairo, 12 May 1918).

⁴ St Athanasius (295–373) was Bishop of Alexandria, 328–73. As a theologian, he fought for orthodoxy against the Arian Trinitarian heresy, which arranged the Christian Trinity in a descending order from God at the head.
⁵ Margaret: Florence's daughter, born 1914.
⁶ H: Harold, Florence's son.

162   To Malcolm Darling

No. 19 G[eneral] H[ospital], Alexandria
1 December 1916

Dearest Malcolm

I write in the interval between realization and anticipation—your delightful letters to self and Faun—(or dare I write 'to E.M.F. and self'?) have arrived, while one from Josie is promised.¹ The interval is perhaps a little long. Surely her signature should not take long in appending. "And surely", you may retort, "Morgan on the other hand she might have replied more promptly." Not at all. Morgan knew what he was about. He has been in a state of most unappetising gloom for weeks, depressing his friends, mangling his work, boring the prostrate soldiery, until Pop! last Thursday evening his mouth flew open and he was sick. Though still far from attractive, Morgan became a centre of attraction now. His friends crowded up to him with simples, retiring it is true as soon as their offerings were made; while his landlady, enduring extremer proximity, brewed a tisane from herbs that she had picked when a girl on the mountains of Corfù. Morgan drank the tisane, but Pop! as on Thursday night so on Friday; indeed Pop Pop Pop, while gleams of primrose passed over his face, and his eyes glowed with celandines, and his ancles wobbled like two cuckoo flowers. Scant pride had Queen Blue Poppy in him then.² So he turned to Science. 'This can't go on' he said. (Chorus of friends 'No it can't, no') 'I will go and see Dʳ Webb Jones.' And he did, who at once exclaimed 'The inoffensive blossom has the jaundice!' and despatched it to a Military Hospital, where it is to repose for some three weeks. And I don't know why, but every thing has suddenly turned right, which mayn't be apparent in this letter but the reverse would have ~~been~~ appeared had I written before. I lie with other officers (Yes, I am as an officer) in a 2ⁿᵈ story balcony looking over Lake Margut, and so aimiable is my mind that during the orange dawn and the whiteness of trees succeeding, it sometimes pretends to me that I am in India and that Bapu Sahib (streams of bath water issuing from it) carries on in the square house on the left among those palms. I feel now quite well, but the theory is that if I got up I should again be a public burden besides contracting subsidiary illnesses, so I am in bed for at least a fortnight, and then I suppose a Convalescent Home. Without concealment I am glad to do no work—very much I liked it and it has made me friends one of whom may last—but a year of the same thing breeds ennui.

What shall I talk about, dear Malcolm? for I want to talk. Shall I say a few words about Keats? How slightly I esteem him! As a poet, not as a man. I think he would have become a great poet, but he wrote during the years when the sex impulse is naturally strong and the main source of inspiration, and unluckily with Keats sex chanced to be unaesthetic. This sounds vague, but read 'Bright star would I were steadfast as thou art', read 'Happy is England...' and note in either sonnet how the romantic opening falls to shoddy sensuousness at the close. Read—the fall is less obvious yet equally significant—'When I have fears...' or the 'Melancholy'. Always fatuity, vulgarity, as soon as human passion is touched.—Now I make another complaint, connected with my first though I can't work out the connection. Just as some poetry is of the eye (form, colour) and some of the ear, so Keats is of the palate. Not only has he constant reference to its pleasures, but the general sensation after reading him is one of *tasting*. 'What's the harm?' Well, taste for some reason or other can't carry one far into the world of beauty—that reason being perhaps that though you don't want comradeship there you do want the possibility of comradeship, and A cannot swallow B's mouthful by any possibility:....and this exclusiveness (to maunder on) also attaches to the physical side of sex though not the least to the spiritual. But to get back. *Miss Brawne*. Her unfortunate name sums up my whole argument, though frivolously, and in frivolous moments such as these I am tempted to call Keats' Muse the Muse of the Picnic Basket. This won't quite do though, even as a joke. There *is* that Hampstead Heathiness in him, which contemporary critics ascribed to his social origin; but there is also—I see it mainly in his letters: deep thought i.e. deep poetical thought, and I see it too in Hyperion. There, partly through Milton's fine influence, he leaves the palate for the eye and ear where alone poetry wins great triumphs and can achieve the august.

> And like a rose in vermeil tint and shape
> In fragrance soft, and coolness to the eye,
> That inlet to severe magnificence
> Stands full blown, for the God to enter in.

He didn't live to enter in: but 'severe magnificence'! it is the final phrase about that palace round whose door we all grope, and you find echoes of it in the sonnet on Homer—not the overpraised literary one but in 'Standing aloof in giant ignorance— —'[3]

Now get down your Keatsies, both of you. And reply.

Your letter's not with me. It made me very happy. Never mind the graver parts now, though my heart agreed with them. Let me think, and let you tell me again, of Vicky and J. J., and of the Great

Intrigue.[4] My extra amusement is that I know Luard—in India and afterwards. Much I liked him.[5] How did he pan out? The whole thing is prime.

I suppose, with these posts, Xmas love had better be included. Fancy if Xmas, and this letter, found you at Dewas. But I am writing separately to Bapu Sahib. Some day—I feel confident now as I haven't for weeks—I shall get out to him; penniless, toothless, witless, perhaps. But I shall get out to him and squat on the shady side of Devi.

卐 aun.[6]

My aunt and mother both well.

ALS: HRC

[1] Faun: apparently a joking reference to himself.
[2] Poppy: reference to his mother's pet name for him.
[3] Keats, 'To Homer' (1818).
[4] The Darlings looked after Vicky (Vikramsinha) themselves from 1918 to 1921.
[5] Lt-Col. Charles Eckford Luard (1869–1927) was a friend of G. L. Dickinson. He entered the Indian Army in 1892 and in 1898 moved to the Political Department, where he became an authority on the Central States. EMF described him as 'the authority on Central India—the only authority, and the only Political Agent who is liked and trusted by the chief chiefs. . . . Quiet and friendly; eminent archaeologist' (to J. R. Ackerley, 26 October 1923. HRC).
[6] The swastika is an ancient Aryan symbol of extreme antiquity. For ancient Persians, Indians, and American Indians it symbolised good luck if the arms turned counter-clockwise. If clockwise, as adopted by Hitler, it signifies night and evil.

163   To Laura Mary Forster

Red Cross, Alexandria
1 January 1917

Dear Aunt Laura,

This is just to send you a line of my birthday love. I think so especially of you on this day, and of West Hackhurst. I wonder whether little Holland got over, to enjoy some of it for me.[1] The New Year has entered very quietly here. Miss Grant Duff asked me to lunch, and then I tried to work but all the patients were out at the Sports! and out in such a dust storm, too, that I shrank from following them, and ended at Mrs. Borchgrevink's for tea. Dust turned to rain—not of a disagreeable sort, and I tramped a little in it, for I feel to be getting rather fat. Supper I had in my lodgings, to which after a month's absence I have to-day returned. The dear old landlady has been so pleasant that I almost forgot I am in exile. For the last hour I have occupied myself with copying extracts into my "War Anthology"—not that it has any more visible connections with the War than has the Poet Laureate's "Spirit of Man".[2] I have put in "your" Milton passage and next to it a passage from Pater—that in which he describes the longings of Marcus Aurelius for the Ideal City that lies even farther from *his* grasp than it had from Plato's, because (unlike Plato) A. conceived of it as including tenderness and pity; virtue, wisdom, and beauty, were not enough. (The passage is in *Marius the Epicurean*—at the end of the chapter called Urbs Beata).³ Next, I will put in a short dialogue from one of the Indian sacred books. (A King asks what gives light to man. The sage replies 'The sun'. The King asks then what happens at sunset, leading up to the final answer which is:—"When the sun is set and the moon is set and the fire has gone out, the soul is the light of man.")⁴ It is somehow very tranquillizing to copy out passages such as these, and the very labour of writing seems to bring one nearer to those who wrote them in the past.

It is very late now, so I will close this scrap as I began it, with very very much love dear Aunt Laura,

Ever your
E. M. Forster.

TTr made for LMF: KCC

¹ Little Holland: unidentified. On this date EMF became thirty-eight.
² His 'War Anthology': at King's College Library. Robert Bridges (1844–1930), Poet Laureate since 1913, prepared *The Spirit of Man: An Anthology in English & French from the Philosophers & Poets made by the Poet Laureate in 1915 & dedicated by gracious permission to His Majesty the King* (1916), calculated to bring faith and fortitude to King and country in time of war.
³ In Walter Pater's novel, Chapter 17.
⁴ From the Bṛihad-Āranyaka [First] Upanishad: 'The light of man is the soul', conversation between Yājñavalkya and Janaka, king of Videha; cf. *The Thirteen Principal Upanishads*, trans. Robert Ernest Hume (2nd ed., rev.), pp. 132–3.

164   To Wilson Plant¹

British Red Cross Hospital, (Sa'idia School),
Giza, Egypt.   14 February 1917

Dear Mᵣ Plant

I feel I shall never meet you—it is such a disappointment. The latest is that I am not to put this foot of mine to the ground for 10 days. Will you still be in No 15 then?² I wish you'll write a line to cheer me up. It's not the sort of thing a sprained ancle ought to ask from two smashed legs, I suppose! Still, if you do write address c/o J. M. Furness, Khedivieh School, Cairo—I hope to get there in a day or two, and come out here just for out patient treatment.³ It would give me much pleasure to hear from you.

I trust the patients in your hospital are more interesting than they are in mine. Or perhaps I have not the gift of stimulating them. Not many books here, either. I have been enjoying Bridges and sticking, as I always do, in a Zola.

Like you, I am a great admirer of D. H. Lawrence, especially of his early work, before he became so didactic and theoretical. I know him a bit—most alarming and explosive but I like him. The Rainbow

I picked up in a book shop during the brief period it was for sale and thought it looked dull. How I wish I had bought it now. He has tried to send me a copy but none can be found. Really he has written some gorgeous passages. There is one in *The White Peacock* which is no more than a catalogue of the names of flowers yet it brings the glory of summer nearer to me than could pages of elaborate poetry.[4] That (*The W. P.*) is altogether a remarkable product—so very absurd and incompetent as a novel, the narrator recounting conversations he could never have heard, and the characters changing not only their natures but their outward appearances at the author's whim. Yet how vivid the impression it leaves!

Frank Rutter I don't know—have been less than I should have liked in the north of England, always gravitating round London. George Merrill's cooking tasted fine though I must confess I was unwell after it! Perhaps I should have been ill in any case, and anyhow don't want him to learn of the disaster.[5]

I hope you're progressing. It's really exasperating that I'm laid up in Cairo like this. I never come here but something goes wrong.

Hope M[r] Britling got round to you.[6]

Miss Grant Duff tells me that she has seen you.

Yours sincerely

EMForster.

ALS: KCC

[1] Wilson Plant (1883–1954) was a friend of Edward Carpenter, who wrote that Plant was in the hospital, wounded near el Arish. Carpenter's letter does not survive.

[2] Perhaps No. 15 General Hospital.

[3] Brother of R. A. Furness.

[4] The catalogue of flower names in *The White Peacock*: Part 2, Chapter 1.

[5] Frank V. P. Rutter (1876–1937), journalist, critic, art historian; art critic, *The Sunday Times*, from 1903; Curator of the Leeds Art Gallery, 1912–17. He spent his life in London, except for the period in Leeds. George Merrill (d. 1928) was Edward Carpenter's housemate at Millthorpe, Derbyshire.

[6] EMF had sent Plant a copy of *Mr. Britling Sees It Through* (1916), by H. G. Wells.

165   To Goldsworthy Lowes Dickinson

[Alexandria] 5 May 1917

Dear Dickinson

As usual I agree almost monotonously with you. A nation is not a person. It cannot be taught a lesson by another nation. This seems obvious. Obvious too, that if your son has been killed you will ~~gain~~ procure him no satisfaction by sending mine to be killed too. Yet both these are popular beliefs, held passionately, and one could add to their number.

Notes. Human Nature under War Conditions:—

When a man makes a statement now, it seldom has any relation to

the ~~truth~~ facts or even to what he supposes to be the facts. He is
merely functioning, generally under the stimulus of fear or sorrow.
Realise this, and he will puzzle you less.

Most men are unhappy and restless without Faith, and, to cover
up the path that led them to it, give out that Faith is splendid and
arduous and only fully attained by the elect. They can most
agreeably believe in an enlarged and everlasting man. Hence 'God'
in the past and the 'Nation' now. Either is the reflection of man's
~~conceit and~~ weakness upon a cloud.

It is easier to personify an enemy-nation than one's own, owing to
one's greater ignorance of the items that compose it. Only by
believing in a Germany have we become patriotic, just as we
remained religious only so long as we could ~~remain in~~ believe in a
Devil. A menace essential to Faith.

Man in his public capacity a contemptible failure. Even when
there was food and clothing to go round he could not distribute
them, and he seems less likely than ever to learn now. Privately most
men attain to love and unselfishness and insight and a priori one
would expect them to display these qualities in their social life,
for they certainly bring earnestness of purpose to it. But some
psychological hitch takes place, whose nature is not easy to
determine (desire to command?): could it be removed we should be
freed from all evils except disease and death. An observer from
another planet who watched not only the earth's wars but its public
institutions would never infer what sweetness and nobility there can
be in intercourse between individuals. Gulf between 'private' and
'public' has in the last three years grown dizzying, and thanks to
scientific organisation more and more of men's energy is diverted to
the public side.

The obverse of love is not hatred but fear. Hatred is only one of
the forms fear takes, cowardice being another and efficiency a third.

To merge myself. To test myself. To do my bit. To suffer what
other soldiers suffer, that I may understand them. These—apart
from compulsion—are the motives that send men to fight.

About enough. Some of them have been in my mind some time,
probably during my last letter to you. I am anxious to turn out
more, provided I can resist the temptation to twist them into being
helpful. How lamentably Clutton Brock has gone to pot. 'Mutton
Broth' the little boy next door used to call him, with impish
premonition. I am also anxious to re-read a little history and see how
its solemn arrangement of 'movements', which, while they bored
me, used to impress, look now, in the light of actual experience. I
have only tried Gibbon, whom nothing can disintegrate, but expect
that everyone and everything else will shatter into dust. The

EMF in Alexandria c.1917. He did Red Cross work there between 1915 and 1918. *Above right* Florence Emily Barger, who married EMF's undergraduate friend, George Barger, in 1904. For many years she was EMF's closest woman friend and principal confidante. *Below* Goldsworthy Lowes Dickinson, whom EMF first knew at King's College, Cambridge. With Trevelyan, he accompanied EMF on his first visit to India.

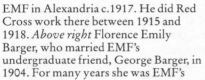

Hospitals here are full of such dust—boys calling out 'Oh Lord have mercy on me, Oh take this thing away', or even more terribly 'I'm in a fix, I'm in a fix.' One went sick at first, but gets used to it, and understands how the man in the next bed goes on with his Patience. It's more a wave of helpless indignation that still shakes me so that I look down the ward at the suffering and the efforts of the able doctors and nurses to alleviate it and wonder how long the waste must all go on. Occasionally one slams out and the reply is 'of course they suffer: why don't you take *your* turn and avenge them', or else 'our debt to gallant little Belgium is not yet discharged', or 'there are worse things than war.' Damn justice, damn honour. They were good enough trimmings for peace time, but the supreme need now is the preservation of life. Let us look after bodies that there may be a next generation which may have the right to look after the soul. Of course we must be materialists, but it must be and is a materialism in which love is far more precious than when it moved the stars.—And 'worse things than war.' Press the speaker, and if he doesn't mean artificial prevention it's either strikes or tango-teas—some little side slip at the most.

25 June 1917

And this has lain about over a month during which much has happened to me. Have actually at my age had 'adventures'. It is difficult to describe such gracefully. I had better just say that I have had one great piece of good luck—the sort of thing that comes to most men as a matter of course when they are 18 or 20.[1] It doesn't now, as it would have then, fill my life, but has made ~~my~~ me very happy, and the necessity for secrecy seems harmonious somehow. It is more like an affair of Searight's, than anything else I can indicate! This will convey to you age, race, rank, though not precisely relationship. Only I have hit on things of objective worth. Fierce independence for one, mental detachment for another; romantic curiosity seems on both sides to be passing into something more permanent. I don't know how it'll end. But how does anything end? One should act as if things last. That Plato of yours thought that they lasted, but elsewhere, and though I don't agree I think he was on sounder lines than people who expect life to be like a work of art or a play, with a crisis and a curtain, and reject as undesirable anything that might mar the general effect:—the lines, though he would not recognise them, of the average middle-class man.— Talking of whom I have a helpful tip for you. You can remain a patriot if you will become a snob. Realise that the lower class, not the middle, is the typical Englishman, and you can love our race without difficulty. Officers, stockbrokers, politicians, grocers— they run us, but they are not England numerically, and their selfrighteousness is not our national characteristic. Shuttleworth and I have decided to be snobs. We shrink, consciously, from such people, just as they shrink unconsciously from the lower class whom we love. We used to pretend we shrank from no one. But it's no good. Middle class people smell.

ALU: KCC

1 This was Mohammed el Adl.

166   To George Barger

[Alexandria]   16 May 1917

Dear George

Let me at all events begin to you a letter of censorable matter. It grows more and more on my mind to write one, for such English papers as I have seen yet, seem amazingly and genuinely in the dark.

On March 26th we got right round Gaza, some of our troops entering the town, and as you know a Turkish General and his staff was captured. Here was something tangible, and, according to my theory, without it our communiqués could not have ventured to raise this vast fabric of lies, and set the mandarins nodding. We retired from the encirclement—our reinforcements are said to have lost their way in the mist, while heavy Turkish reinforcements came up from Bir Sheba—and we took up a position on the Wadi to the South. Our second attack (April 19) was a big disaster, and men who have fought at Gallipoli say it was more terrible than anything they knew there. Having occupied some Turkish outposts—duly described as an 'advance'—we made a frontal charge, the distance being 2–3000 yds. over the flat. I know less of what happened to the Rgts. towards the sea. Those on the right of our line, going in 1000 strong, came back in some cases with 80. Our preliminary bombardment, though copious, seems to have failed, and the common expression is that the Turks had a 'Machine to a man': they had certainly done wonders in the way of defences since our first attack. Our tanks seem to have gone into action too soon. Some were destroyed, others captured. One man told me how he saw one in a Turkish trench all blown about and how the door in it opened and the men who had been working it reeled out, the last with his trousers in flames.

Every one in Egypt knows that we have been knocked, every one in belligerent and neutral countries knows it. The sole result of the censorship is to conceal what has happened from England. The men are disgusted. "It makes one wild, knowing what it was, to be told you've won a victory" is a common remark; and one chap put it to the parson that it wasn't much to the credit of Christianity that our communiqués should lie more than the Turks! Who laughed it off. I

Constantine Peter Cavafy, the
Greek poet, and *below*
Mohammed el Adl, both of
whom EMF met in Alexandria
in 1917.

would rather my hand should drop off—excuse melodrama: the times demand it—sooner than anything I wrote should imperil the life of a single soldier. But it can't. Even if I mentioned names of Regts. it couldn't.

I've no fear of an invasion of Egypt, but no hope of capturing Gaza. We haven't the troops. And why the hell should we want to capture it? Our job was to secure the Canal—admirably effected in the Jan. engagements. If the French want Syria let them go there and get it. Oh my God the mess—the suffering in the hospitals which here and everywhere are crammed, the decent young men all so free from nonsense and false pride, so calm about the enemy (though he has adopted Christian methods and shelled our First Aid Posts and Hospitals—this I hear from a friend at the front)—and over their heads solemn edifying bloody lies. War this end is almost devoid of hate. I don't know whether this makes it less or more terrible.

M.

Thank F. & the children for their letters. Also for writing to Sanger about Gerry.

ALS: Mollie Barger

167   To Florence Barger

[Alexandria]   29 May 1917

Dearest Florence

I have written so little lately—there are one or two reasons for this. I suppose, to put the most terrible first, I am getting rather out of touch with England. It is over eighteen months. Too long. The feeling—or rather the absence of feeling—did not come upon me until the completion of a year, and can't even now have come upon me as regards you, or I shouldn't tell you about it. I value your letters and *even more*!! the children's letters. Don't tell them this (or Harold that I never noticed he had signed Yours sincerely or Evert that I had never noticed he hadn't signed at all). And don't of course ever jog them up to write. When I say I value them I mean that children and the way they put things restore one's sense of reality in an extraordinary way. I am in an odd world at present—half work, half romance. The work dictated a recent letter to George.[1] The romance is only for you. I have plunged into an anxious but very beautiful affair. It seemed to me—and I proved right—that something precious was being offered me and that I was offering something that might be thought precious. And even if I proved wrong, I should have been right to take the plunge, because if you pass life by it's jolly well going to pass *you* by in the future. If you're frightened it's all right—that's no harm; fear is an emotion. But by some trick of the nerves I happened not to be frightened. It was merely the pressure of habit and social conventions trying to make me behave as *if* I was afraid. Which is corrupting. Do you know, I have often thought of your sister, and wondered whether her moods were at all like mine, and whether she, like me, suddenly found it impossible to behave other wise but in the most extraordinary way.[2] I long to tell you about it, but an outline would make me seem too silly and details (though they have convinced an anxious friend here who knows of the matter) are out of the question.

Well, all this blocks me from sensations of England. It's that I'm working round to. I shall jump up and tumble back some day. Till I do you'll have periodically this kind of letter.

Good night, dearest Florence
Morgan

[30 May 1917]

Good morning! Love to all. I am very glad to think of your Cornish holiday despite its expenses. Also, despite its fatigue, of your School Practise.[3] I think the latter provides (ahem!) a valuable change from domestic life and the ceaseless attacks of the Infanteria. Mademoiselle sounds a dear, though I still have no clear conception of her. Sad indeed that she won't come bobbing in her Trouville hat.

Mother's affairs, when I concentrate my mind on them, don't seem satisfactory. An exhausting time to and at Salisbury, followed by Aunt Eliza. I trust it won't knock her up. When will this damned war stop.

1 June 1917

Have received an absurd but welcome letter from you—absurd because it took since Ap[ril] 19 to come. A whole mail has been marooned somewhere. I have had letters from you of later date of course. It contained news of Gerry's arrest and Charlie Sanger's letter. My extreme calm on the subject is thus explained. I never heard of it while it was at its worst. It contains the languid cock and broody hen. A pleasing pair. It contains references to my M.S. &ct which are particular[ly] comforting to me at the present moment (See above).[4] I wish I could convey to you what I feel at this unique time—far far from the greatest time of my life, but for me quite new. It isn't happiness: it's rather—offensive phrase—that I first feel a grown up man. I felt the crisis coming just as I felt that very minor and grotesque episode coming last year.—This isn't a superstitious expression: it means that you feel faculties developing in you to grasp anything that comes. The practical difficulties—there is a big racial and social gulf—are great: but when you are offered affection, honesty, and intelligence with all that you can possibly want externals thrown in (including a delightful sense of humour), you surely have to take it or die spiritually.

> After all, I am running on,
> Love to you again dear.
> Morgan.

ALS: KCC

[1] Letter 166, on censorship.
[2] Florence's sister, Elsie Thomas.
[3] School Practice: Florence was perhaps helping to supervise the qualifications of student teachers.
[4] M.S.: *Maurice*.

168   To Florence Barger

[N. p. 17 June 1917]

Dearest Florence—That funny fool the mail has landed your letter of the 9th a week later than that of the 15th, so don't trouble to repeat your answer to my pencilled thing, because thank goodness I have it, and you do me even prouder than I expected. I like to think my present news will make you happy—before your 9th letter I hadn't so definitely realised it would. How or when it will end I don't know or want to know. I have never doubted that I was doing the right thing nor that there was anything else to do, and even if trouble or disillusion comes—and why should it?—I shall never repent. When the response came, though I told myself it never could come, I was not really surprised. It's a response I try not to exaggerate; based, for all its frankness, upon a gracious generosity rather than upon a nature exactly resembling mine.

Last night I went to the house of an acquaintance. His mistress was there, as was the mistress of one of his friends—an intelligent girl with whom I talked Dostoieffsky. I envied their security, but not their relationship. It was all coyness and flattery, and the basis commercial: which I find—not wrong but profoundly anti-aphrodisiac.

Owing to the hours of employment, it is only possible to meet alternate fortnights. How I wish I could present a less shadowy figure to you! Yet somehow I wouldn't even if it was prudent, describe full length. It must come by degrees. And the relationship itself has many degrees to go. But even if it goes no further I have been trusted and blessed and heard (an awful lie!!!) "Beautiful hair..", followed by 'I'm happy' which wasn't a lie. It's so off the accredited lines, Florence, with so much *cheerfulness* in it—none of the solemnity which Christianity has thought essential to Romance—, and which e.g. so puts me off the Vita Nuova. One's never afraid of doing the wrong thing. 'Love is a God and a terrible

God' and all that rot is dead.—[1] He's an illusion invented by people who would not look at each other. After all the Greeks and not Dante started him, but I grow very suspicious of the Greeks. It's the modern man, provided he doesn't shackle himself with science, who will really see beauty.

(No reference intended to George. Indeed, give my love to George.)

I want you to read E[dward] Carpenter's My Days & Dreams if you have not already done so.[2]

G's letter in—thank him for it.

                                                        Morgan.

ALS: KCC

[1] *Vita Nuova* (c. 1293) of Dante, detailing the events and stages of his love for Beatrice.
[2] Carpenter, *My Days and Dreams: Being Autobiographical Notes* (1916).

169   To Constantine Cavafy[1]

British Red Cross Convalescent Hospital N° 7,
Montazah, Alexandria
1 July 1917

Dear Cavaffy [*sic*],

Valassopoulo was over this afternoon and told me that since I saw you something occurred that has made you very unhappy; that you believed the artist must be depraved: and that you were willing he should tell the above to your friends.[2] It made me want to write to you at once, though I gathered nothing clear from him and consequently do not know what to say.

Of late I have been happier than usual myself, and have accepted my good luck with thankfulness and without reservation. But I suspect that at the bottom of one's soul one craves not happiness but peace. I seem to see this when the tide is flowing strongly neither way—I mean when I am disturbed by no great predominance of either joy or sorrow. I don't write this to console you—consolation is a very inferior article which can only be exchanged between people who are not being quite straight with one another. Only there does seem something fundamental in man that is unhappy perhaps, but not with these surface unhappinesses, and that finds its repose not in fruition but in creation. The peace that passeth all understanding is the peace at the heart of the storm. In other words—in extremely other words!—you will go on writing, I believe.

V. and I discussed depravity a little, but not to much effect. He seemed to connect it with passion, to which it is (for me) the absolute antithesis. I am not sure that I connect it with curiosity even, though if it exists at all it exists as something *cold*—and would consequently not be a particularly useful ingredient to the artist. That is the only thing I can tell you about depravity—its temperature. It has nothing to do with material. No action, no thought is per se depraved.

These two paragraphs are very muddle headed and I shall hardly clear them by telling you that in each I have thought of Dante: first of his remark that the Herald Angels promised not happiness but peace; secondly of the centre of his Hell, which was ice, not fire.[3]

I came here for a couple of days, but as there is work, and the Matron kindly urges me I am staying on.[4] I shall come and see you as soon as I return. This letter doesn't—then or now—expect an answer. It is only to remind you that among your many friends you have one on the edge of your life in me.

EMForster.

ALS: George P. Savidis

[1] Constantine Peter Cavafy (1863–1933), Greek poet, was the youngest son of a well-to-do Alexandrian exporter. He spent part of his boyhood in England, where his father's firm had a branch. When the firm collapsed in 1876 the family returned to Alexandria, and in 1889 Cavafy took a post under the British in the Irrigation Department, which he retained for more than 30 years. In 1907 he moved into a flat in the rue Lepsius in the old Greek quarter, shared it briefly with a brother, and thereafter occupied it alone. He began writing verse early and gradually acquired a coterie following in Alexandria and Athens, publishing his poems principally in periodicals. From 1911 onwards, his verse became more outspoken about homosexual love. EMF, who became friendly with him in 1917, introduced him to the English-speaking world in an influential essay, 'The Poetry of Cavafy', published in *The Athenaeum* (25 April 1919, pp. 247–8). He there evokes Cavafy as 'a Greek gentleman in a straw hat, standing absolutely motionless at a slight angle to the universe.'

[2] George Valassopoulo (1890–1972), Alexandrian lawyer who took a degree from King's in 1908, was Cavafy's friend and translator.

[3] The Last Circlet of Dante's Inferno is peopled by the betrayers, who are embedded in ice (Canto 32). EMF, in his 1908 paper on Dante, read to the Working Men's College, quoted from Dante's treatise, *De Monarchia* (1309), Chapter 4: 'When the shepherds watched their flocks by night, they heard not of riches, nor pleasure, nor honour, nor health, nor strength, nor beauty: but of peace; for the celestial soldiery proclaimed Glory to God in the highest, and on earth Peace and Goodwill towards men.' (Published in the *Working Men's College Journal*, 10 [1908], 285.)

[4] Matron: Lorna Beatrice Wood (1891–1944).

170   To Florence Barger

Alexandria.   4 July 1917

Private—at least partly so.

Dear Florence

I write in an odd isolated mood, not exactly depressed but—well you'll have enough of the mood before I stop. The incoming mail has gone down in sight of our shores and a fortnight's letters, which means two from you, are lost. Fortunately I have kept your old ones. Then man-hunting seems recommencing here. If they try to rope me I shall bolt—(if I can)—for England and my peep of you, then let the earth open. As for conscientiously objecting, I feel no longer to have the spirits, or to have any principles of any sort or any ideals. No! No!—this letter is going to be signed Morgan not Hugh, and life, damn its eyes, is as lovely as ever and people as loveable. But if I killed someone I did not know I should not worry afterwards, I fancy, whereas I do worry in a dumb way that others go to be killed, while I sit safe. In my present mood I would volunteer for stretcher work if it *was* voluntary, but once in the trap it closes and leaves you as it has left Shuttleworth.—Oh dear Florence I am so unhappy he did not answer your letter, because it means he is in a miserable state.[1] He has been like that with me. Once here it gave him so much pain to see me, that he asked me to keep away. He felt he had no right to inflict himself, and I know he was feeling he had no right to inflict himself on you. I love you more than ever for offering to go and see him, and your failure—apparent not real—somehow increases that love. I can't think how I should get on without you.

I enclose a letter from that ~~friend~~ fellow I spoke of in previous weeks to you—not a remarkable letter until you know that he is a tram-conductor, when it becomes both remarkable and charming.[2] I like 'Home of Misery'—his room. Let me have letter back. He has gone quietly on this line [several words inked out and illegible] as from the first, as if no other was conceivable. I did likewise, with the result that we have become friends. He is young in years, which would intimidate me but for the maturity of his mind. In his own words "I have always ate apart and lived apart and thought apart. Perhaps I am not my father's son." I can scarcely believe him the son of Egypt, for there is no Nile mud either in his body or mind. How misleading generalisations are, whether racial or social. I envy children their power of regarding each person as a new species.

This letter has been rigged in the eclipse—a total one of the moon.[3] I must try to write to Evert about it. Hélène, my landlady's daughter, was told that in order to see it she must look through a smoked glass! They have, in my absence, been moving houses, and having the strangest contretemps. When they arrived, the outside stair-case, which is the only route to their new apartments, had entirely disappeared. They stood gazing upward, like Moses and Elias wasn't it, while the cat struck an even deeper note of mystery by producing 3 kittens among their luggage. All is well now. The Scala Santa has flown back into position, one kitten died from the shock, another has been drowned, and the survivors are happily perched up on a balcony, trimming hats.[4]

Morgan.

ALS: KCC

[1] Shuttleworth, after being in the hospital in Alexandria, was invalided home.
[2] This was Mohammed el Adl. This letter is not among those from him that EMF copied out

many years later (KCC). However, a letter of 31 August 1917 conveys the quality of his personality: 'I told you before that I will let my photograph taken as soon as I make a new coat. Do you think that I am too proud to meet your friend whether he is a solider (Private) or a Captain. I want only to have no more friends. What I have are quite enough. / Be sure that your religious opinions do not put me off you as well as you respect mine as I do yours. I told you before that God knows what ~~has~~ happened, what happens, and is will be happened. He knew that some of the human beings will have evil thoughts therefore He created them, but did not order you to behave in them. God has created everything on and beneath the globe.'

3 Milton, *Lycidas*, ll. 100–1: 'It was that fated and perfidious Bark / Built in th' eclipse and rigg'd with curses dark, / . . . .'

4 EMF's landlady was an ebullient Italian-speaking Greek lady named Irene, a former maid of Mrs Borchgrevink's. Moses and Elias appeared at the Transfiguration of Christ (*St Mark*, 9, iv) and 'Scala Santa' (Holy Staircase) is a reference to the 'Casa Santa': the Holy House of the Virgin, reputedly transferred by angels in 1294, from the Holy Land to Loreto in Italy.

171   To Florence Barger

[Alexandria]   18 July 1917

Dearest Florence

Yours of 27.6.17 just in and yours and the children's (poems) which I thought and you thought were lost weren't I think and delighted me.—But I am glad we were acquainted before I left England. The medium for confidence is poor.

I am very very sorry about George's piles, but thankful the operation, if secondary, will be slight. It is wretched it should thus spoil your Cornish Holiday. I do hope you will enjoy it as much as may be. I think of you.

How glad I am that Shuttleworth in the end wrote. I believe he got your letter and has been lying. But I don't mind. I think you will like him. It is weeks since he wrote to me.

What would I not give to talk to you—mainly about myself—for ½ an hour. I must 'een write; taking a pen though!¹ I am glad all this affair doesn't seem unreal to you. It *must* seem odd. Yet it seems so far from odd on the spot. Its drawback is that it's an understanding rather than an agreement. Its strong point is that it's a very perfect understanding, such as may pass into agreement any moment, for the physical basis for an agreement does, on both sides, exist. If this should come I shall know perfection, if it doesn't I shall yet have been happy and acheived [*sic*] much intimacy. Have been 'acting rightly,'—always a bit of a bore—i.e. trying to get ~~el Adl my friend~~ that man a job in Cairo, where I shall never see him. He gets two bob a-day on his tram (I'm assuming my last letter reached you), and, what he minds more, no leisure "and I am continually in a temper which is bad for my health." So I sent him up with a letter to the lady who runs the Govt. Employment Bureau, and though no job was on she took his name and from what she has written thinks very highly of him, and will probably call him up soon to be a clerk (5 bob). I tell him that as his income increases so will his wants but he replies that to have wants is to understand life—an unsound reply yet, all things considered, a remarkable one. He is likely to understand more now, poor boy, for his mother to whom he is devoted, has died. I have not seen him since—a line came from his home, where he went for the funeral. He much dislikes his father and there is a second wife and duplicate families—materials for a bust up unknown in Christian England.—Also he has been struck on the leg by an officer's cane. The officer and a Sister were debating whether they should take "this tram or the next...shall we? shan't we...oh let's stop...no don't let's..", each with a foot on the step, so that he said firmly "will you please either stop sir or come." This, following though it does on a blow in the jaw from a drunken Sgt. Major, has not impaired his philosophy—'The English are good & bad.'

I wonder whether the above scraps convey anything to you my dear. Did I tell you how the first time I went to the 'Home of Misery' he suddenly opened the little trunk that contains the whole of his belongings and flung them out saying 'not much but all clean—now I have shown you all there is to show'? Well now and then he flings out his mind before me in the same way, and when he does I have a queer impersonal sense of triumph. It seems to me that to be trusted, and to be trusted across the barriers of income race and class, is the greatest reward a man can receive, and that even if the agreement is not attained, even if he goes to Cairo and forgets me, I shall not have failed; and that other people are winning similar victories elsewhere: you and I, too, are winning one.

The enclosed cheque looks like payment to the Matron, but it was coming even if you hadn't had to read the preceding. I seem to have money, and want you to buy yourself Russell's Principles of Social Reconstruction[2] if you haven't read it yet and other books with the surplus—poems—Carpenter's Autobiography—I don't know.[3] Now I had better go to work. The damp is great and so is often my depression about the war and all things, and this popular philosophy of 'one must keep going' no help. I am not a top, no more is the universe, though Dante thought otherwise.[4] I am an individual and the universe is not even balls[?]. Love from me._____[5]

ALU: KCC

[1] Here he shifts from pencil to pen.
[2] Bertrand Russell, The Principles of Social Reconstruction (1916), lectures written in 1915, delivered early in 1916.
[3] Edward Carpenter, My Days and Dreams: Being Autobiographical Notes (1916).
[4] Conceivably a reference to the last two lines of Dante's Paradiso, in which he describes the universe as rotated by Love.
[5] Signature and an apparent postscript have been torn off.

172   To Florence Barger

[Alexandria]   31 July 1917

Dearest Florence

I have not up to date heard how the operation went. What a Hell of a mix it all is. I am so anxious for news. Please repeat main facts on receipt of this. An Italian friend here has just had ops. for piles *and* double-rupture, and is in great pain, so I have a very visible reminder of what George goes through. Is it piles or anal fissure or both? He is bound to suffer greatly. How long did the operation take? Palli's were 1½ hour—½ hour after which he woke up without sickness or alarm, but to much agony. I saw him immediately after the operation and again today—two days after. He is better and there has never been danger, but he can still scarcely speak, the pain is so great. I took him a coloured Botticelli—Birth of Venus—very bad, but it pleased him, and he would not know it was bad.—I think the sight of so much preventable suffering has inured ~~one to~~ me against the sight of sufferings such as his and George's which, terrible as they are, are reasonable and salutary, and do honour to the sense of the men who had consented to endure them. Wounds, in nine cases out of ten, do no credit to the soldier. He was forced to enlist, forcibly trained, and led up to be shot.

I have thought so much about your spoilt holiday, too.

I wonder what of mine to you went down (mails leaving Port Said July 21 are officially sunk[)]. Perhaps my letter to Evert. Perhaps my cheque to you. I want you to buy for yourself Russell's Principles of Social Reconstruction if you haven't read it, and what you like with the surplus—poetry perhaps. I re-enclose cheque, ~~also a line~~ to Russell which please address.— ~~I think for one thing it's less likely to be opened if his envelope bears an English stamp. I don't know his address for another (Read line if you like)~~[1] Cheque's a <u>present</u>. (Some people are sometimes so dense)

And I wonder how much about that man was drowned. His profession (tram-conductor) perhaps.

Lubbock has written to me privately asking me to go to Salonika for a bit.[2] I refused—from personal and public reasons. There's no one to do the work here as it is: a foolish suggestion. He must send someone to S. from England. Private this.

I want to read *The Feet of the Young Men* by Herbert Tremaine (Daniel: for 2/– net) so make my cheque out for 1/– more than its predecessor. Please read it, then post.[3]

I had a very serious and very happy talk with my friend last night. He has told me what he thinks right and wrong—it is *most* curious to compare the inroads upon free thought and action made respectively by Christianity and Islam: Islam makes less mess ~~I am sure~~. I told you—many weeks back—we had parted with ℞

[Respectability]. Well, we hadn't entirely, and I wish to—it indeed seems right to me that we should, and I thought his objections trivial, and beat against them. He has made me see that I must not do this—they are profound if mistaken—but he has made me see it with so much tenderness and affection that I feel our friendship is only now beginning. I realised that he trusted me and that all he can possibly give me is mine. As soon as he can give more he will give it, and, conscious that in any case I have the one gift worth receiving, I must wait. His mother's death has thrown us closer together. He came back from the funeral very sad but, as always, very witty. There had been the expected family row, "in the midst of which father spoke very highly of the coffin, saying that the cover had been made of silk. He then produced a false bill for the vault and pretended he had paid twice as many sovereigns as the fact. All this I exposed."

I hadn't meant so much to intrude, but much has been lost I expect, and you know dear how full of it I must be, and will excuse. Am a bit bewildered for the moment—it is getting so very big, and before last night I felt in some need of help. That need has gone, for I realise he will help me. For all his foolery and charm, ~~he knows life~~ he isn't immature. Right at the beginning, for instance, when he called me by my surname without M^r, straightaway,—I put it down to delightful naivety in which perhaps there was a harmless touch of swank. I know now that it sprang from the right judgement of a sincere heart, and that he knew that unless we at once broke all social and financial barriers down we should never become friends.

To conclude, with love to the children and you both.

Morgan.
1.8.17

ALS: KCC

[1] Bertrand Russell went to prison in 1918 for publishing a pacifist article. EMF's 'line to Russell' (28 July 1917. McMaster University. Russell Papers): 'I was writing to Furness that you have really written—or rather already written—The Principles of Personal [*sic*] Reconstruction; and I think I will let you know this too. For a time I thought you would shake me out of my formula,—that though of course there is a connection between civilisation and our private desires and impulses and actions, it is a connnection as meaningless as that between a word and the letters that make it up. But the formula holds. The war will only end through exhaustion and nausea. All that is good in humanity must be sweated and vomited out together with what is bad. So far we may agree, but I [am] not with you who seem to think that personal decency now (and by personal decency we are both understanding the real article that may include martyrdom) will facilitate a more decent society in the future. We have got the letters to spell God with, and may even want to spell it, but the word is just as likely to come out as it has come—upside down—gdo—ogd—&^{ct} &^{ct}.' EMF's letter to Furness has not survived.
[2] Percy Lubbock was at the London headquarters of the Red Cross.
[3] Tremaine, *The Feet of the Young Men: A Domestic War Novel* (1917).

173   To Robert Trevelyan

Red Cross, St Mark's Buildings, Alexandria
6 August 1917

Dear Bob

Would you kindly post me a Selzer drome and anything else written lately that you think I should imbibe.[1] I should be so grateful. I enclose cheque for 10/-. I was asking Dickinson for news of ~~the~~ you the other week. How are you all. Please write to me.

I am composing a stinging paragraph on the Atonement, but it is not quite ready to be transcribed, and the Atonement is at present my only intellectual interest.[2] I am very well, and as an escape from the war Alexandria is matchless: or rather escapes: I went to see a Greek ~~friend~~ poet yesterday whose mind overflowed on the subject of a school at Volo.[3] This school has been the butt of mistakes or malignant criticisms, and a cause célèbre resulted which the Greeks of Alexandria, Smyrna, Jannina and the Tauric Chersonese have been following as best they may. The school triumphed, and its triumph is perpetuated in a very large expensive and red bound book, and in lectures delivered by Kyros Apostolopoulos and I know not whom else to crowded audiences.[4] But in triumphing it has expired. Its young ladies—for it was a female school—have returned unsmirched but unfinished to their homes.

There are other escapes—the Syrian, the Italian, the Bedouin &c—but I prefer the Greek, for the Greeks are the only community here that attempt to understand what they are talking about, and to be with them is to reenter, however imperfectly, the Academic world. They are the only important people east of Ventimiglia—: dirty, dishonest, unaristocratic, roving, and warped by Hellenic and Byzantine dreams—but they do effervesce intellectually, they do have creative desires, and one comes round to them in the end. I wonder if you will ever hear of the poet I have just mentioned—he is a great name in the Eastern Mediterranean and discussed in the little magazines that spring up and die without ceasing in its creeks. C. P. Cavaffy. He writes short things in Romaic: with much help I have read one or two and thought them beautiful.

The Syrians dance.

The Bedouins lay eggs.

The French give lectures on Kultur to the French.

The Italians build il nostro Consolato, nostro Consolato nuovo, ricco, grandioso, forte come il nostro Cadorna, profondo come il nostro mare, alto come il nostro cielo che muove l'altre stelle, e tutto vicino al terminus Ramleh Tramways.

The English have witnessed 'Candida' or 'Vice Detected'.

I send my love.

Morgan Smith.

ALS: TCC

¹ This is a rather opaque joking reference to Trevelyan's verse play, *The Pterodamozels: An Operatic Fable* (1916), in which a corps of mythological-prehistorical winged young ladies rescue air travellers down on a desert island. 'Drome' seems to have some connection with the aeronautical venue of the play, 'Selzer' (i.e. Seltzer water) with the oceanic aspect of this venue. EMF's signature *is* explainable, for the central character of the play is named Percival Smith. EMF wrote ([16 November 1917. TCC]): 'The Selzerdromes was of course a Pterodamozels. You grow very dull in Britain. I was almost ashamed to sign myself Morgan Smith—it so rammed the joke home. But ~~you~~ Britain retains ~~your~~ her old virtue of reaching the right conclusion by the wrong paths, and the play—which was my real reason for applying to you—came out all right.'
² Possibly for a talk to the Theosophical Society.
³ Volos: seaport of Thessaly in Greece.
⁴ Kyros Apostolopoulos (unidentified). The controversy involved Alexander Delmonzo (died 1956), a relation of Valassopoulo and an advocate of education in modern Greek. He is now regarded as a leader in modern education in Greece.

174 To Florence Barger

Alexandria, Egypt.   25 August 1917

Dearest Florence

A large and rather rending mail has come in. I will calm and strengthen myself by writing to you first. I am rent because thoughts of 'leave' in England are again in my mind. I don't know that I set great store on "seeing" Mrs Aylward again. But I shall not see her and mother is going to grieve that I haven't and now I don't much like the accounts of my Aunt Laura's health. Lubbock has enquired. He thinks—but doesn't guarantee—that I should not have to present myself for Classification on short leave. If I did, and was classed BI or over I should be dished; if below BI the Red X (who seem thoroughly pleased with me) could and would claim my services. I write not so much for advice as to let you know what is in my mind. Alexandrian civilisation seems to have passed its prime!—I mean by this that there is now no one here whom I am inclined to burden with my difficulties. Furness, Mrs Borchgrevink, and Antonius, are kind enough when applied to, but don't feel the passionate interest in my fate that they showed a year ago. As a romantic proposition I have outstayed my time. This sounds self centred and fastidious. Never mind! I will write of nicer things in a minute. Just now, my work here presents itself too clearly as a refuge—without pain but without joys. I know how, even if my leave in England ran smoothly, that [*sic*] it would be full of pain, yet sometimes an impulse seems pushing me towards it, much as it pushed me into love.

The half moon, with beautiful blue markings on its primrose, stands looking at the sunset. The sparrows—chattering as they never do in England—go to bed in the Square below. I am going to be chased off the verandah by dinner tables, so will get on.—It's the possibility of another child that I was thinking of as a nice subject, yet how I dread it for you if you dread it. I wonder whether you have a worse time than most women or whether it is only that you have told me more. I see the arguments in its favour. Your children are great successes and I cannot believe that by the time they grow up the beautiful materials of this world will be as ill arranged as they are now.—If you should produce another male, Morgan's his name I fancy.

Your long Cornish holiday has been a great delight to me. I see Evert's gatepost diorama, and Margaret emptying her pail on to the friendly child and you and Harold running to bathe from the cave. It does all sound so jolly, and so peaceful.

I am—except in one direction—restless and starved out here. Spending money cheers me up, but one gets very little for a lot in these days. Have bought Gibbon, which cheers me, and shall solemnly dedicate £1 to books. Then there are clothes—el-Adl says I must really do something. Taking me by the sleeve last night he said gently "You know, Forster, though I am poorer than you I would never be seen in such a coat. I am not blaming you—no, I praise—but I would never *be* seen, and your hat has a hole and your boot has a hole and your socks have a hole." I said I would try and dress better, to which he replied "Good clothes are an infectious disease—I had much better *not* care and look like *you*, and so perhaps I will, but only in Alexandria." He wants me to go to Mansourah (his native town) for the Bairam holidays, but it isn't feasible, of course; we have increased difficulty in meeting here, as his brother now shares the H[ome] of M[isery], and my landlady has got the wind up! (I have got it down and with complete success, but R[espectability] mustn't be further endangered.—What I so value in him is his realism and solidity. He has heaps of romance but no sentimentality consequently. Whenever I speak honestly he understands; and he despite his maxim—"I find a certain amount of lies necessary to life" is perfectly honest to me.—Does this read odd? It would read odder, indeed incredibly, to anyone who knew the country. Natives, especially of the lower city class, are dirty in body and mind, incapable of fineness, and only out for what they can get. That is the theory to which, after some reluctance, I had fully subscribed, and like all theories it has broken down. I will send you his photograph if I can get a decent one taken—he looks younger than his years and very very much younger than his mind, but the refinement of the mouth might come out. It is very sweet of you to think of us *both*—I feel so touched and happy: yet, considering the relation from outside, I imagine it is indeed worthy to be thought about; it is such a triumph over nonsense and artificial difficulties: it is a sample of the ~~endless~~ other triumphs that I am sure come off but of which we hear nothing through the brassy rattle of civilisation so called; triumphs varying greatly in form, but in spirit all the same. When I am with him, smoking or talking quietly ahead, or whatever it may be, I ~~feel~~ see, beyond my own happiness and intimacy, occasional glimpses of the happiness of 1000s of others whose names I shall never hear, and know that there is a great unrecorded history. I have never had anything like this in my life—much friendliness and tolerance, but never this—and not till now was I capable of having it, for I hadn't attained the complete contempt and indifference for civilisation that provides the necessary calm.

Against my leaving Egypt this, oddly enough, doesn't the least weigh. And by the way, if I *do* leave it can't be for many weeks, Miss G. D. having embarked on some slight but lengthy form of enteric which keeps her in hospital. And if I *do* leave—this is harder to face—I shall probably never come back, as there is dearth of searchers in France and Salonica.

Best best love and gratitude

M.

ALS: KCC

175 To S. R. Masood

Red Cross, Rue de L'ancienne Bourse, Alexandria
8 September 1917

Dearest Boy

Why don't I write? I who have so often been owed a letter by you now owe you one, and this makes me so sad, I don't know why. I have tried to write again and again, but something put me off though my love for you holds firm. It is the same with other friends—I can't write to the Darlings either. And the cause is the cause of all that is evil—i.e. this war which saps away one's spirit even when one's body's whole still. If we both live through it, I am coming to you, so plant a little tree on my jagir.[1] Alas, by the time I arrive it may be a big tree, and you and I, very old men, will sit in its shade. You will be a celebrated old man and I suppose rather a fat one. I shall be a thin bald old man extremely obscure, but we will sit together and your grandchildren shall wait on us.

I am fagged out with the weather and the work—not that either has been intense, but they do go on so long. I am weary beyond expression of Alexandria, its trams and its streets. One is as far from the East here as in London. All is so colourless and banal. But I oughtn't to grumble too much, for I have good friends here, and have lately got to know an Egyptian whom I greatly like and who sometimes reminds me of you. (On the whole I dislike the Egyptians).

Mother is well but our old friend Mrs. Aylward is dying and she is nursing her. My aunt is fairly well. Miss Hill has left her to go do War work now. I sometimes hear from Lady Morison, who has been very good to Mother in my absence. When I shall get home I don't know; write here. We still have Ruth and Agnes but Tizer has gone to a happier land and has a successor named Jellicoe.[2] Shuttleworth has been invalided here with malaria and now sounds unusually happy. I think that's all the news, dearest fellow. Now tell me yours. How's Shazad?[3] He does owe me a letter. Give him my love and tell him to write. Also give my love to Zorah and the boy. I wish you'ld send me a photograph of you here—I've none. Are you expecting any more children?

Love to you, I needn't add. We'll pull off the meeting some day, but these years of absence are awful, awful, and we are both growing older. Try not to forget me. On the surface I've altered, but not deep down, and our love springs from deep down. How long have we known each other now? It must be 10 years.

Morgan.

TTr supplied by Akbar Masood

[1] Urdu word: a grant of rent-free land.
[2] Tizer, Jellicoe: cats.
[3] Shazad: unidentified.

176   To Florence Barger

[Alexandria]   13 September 1917

Dearest Florence,

You enquire what A and I do. Talk mostly—you see our time together seldom averages over 2 hours a week. Occasionally chess but "I have learnt play but not learnt to think" he says.—Ways and means are an increasing difficulty. His ½ brother—"my brother and my enemy"—is still with him and squats blinking in the corner of the room that would otherwise be ours. While as for my room, my landlady has got the wind up:—I didn't—or hope I didn't—tell you this at the time, lest it worried you, and I tell you now because all is all right—she is calmed and has forgotten, being a simple soul. It didn't worry me the least, except as a practical problem: all my old awe of people's opinions has dried up, and A never had any. I told him why he couldn't come any more, and he nodded. Then we had 2 Sunday mornings together—one at Pompey's Pillar and the Catacombs, the other at Nouzha Gardens, and sometimes we meet of an evening in the Gardens in the middle of the town. We have laid down certain rules, and assume that so long as we keep them we are safe—that is the only sensible course, I think. We meet and part *at* the places—both in civilian costume—and never travel together on the trams. His other (third) suit—besides his uniform—is a long and rather unpleasing nightgown over which you button a sort of frock coat: bare feet in clogs. Thus attired he may walk with me in the neighbourhood of his room, but not elsewhere. He always wears a fez. He is unfortunately ~~rather~~ black—not as black as a child's face or ink, but blacker than Altounyan or Masood—so that our juxtaposition is noticeable. It was thoughtless of him to have been born that colour, and only the will of ~~God~~ Allah prevented his mother from tattooing little blue birds at the corners of his eyes. Blobs on his wrist have sufficed her.

Last night—perhaps the happiest of my life—has left me very solemn at least though not outwardly. All is far greater than I have yet realised. I tell you one thing not as wanting to confide it even to you, but because I want it to be known if ever I should die. We had by good luck his room to ourselves, and he said suddenly 'If we are to be friends for ever you must promise me something,' I asked if he ~~wanted~~ wished to be friends for ever. He said 'if you wish'. I said 'I do', and he went on:—'You must promise me at once to tell me when ~~if~~ I wrong you, so that we may make the place clean. One two three four wrongs may not matter, but if ~~more are left all turns~~ we leave more all will turn evil.'—That is all—. Then I told him about my work and he went to the heart of *that* with 'You stop the relations of those who are ~~missing~~ lost from having wrong ideas—thus you serve your King and Country better than by fighting, I think.' Then he went to the heart of my possible return to England—he knew nothing of it before. 'Give Mother money—not *enough* but *too* much—and do *not* go, for she will only be unhappy in case they make you a soldier.'————And apart from the joy of all this I feel, more deeply, its solemnity, and think of what you once said that the possibilities of human intercourse are only beginning. I hate faith as a creed—but when something happens that gives you faith you're very near heaven. I was resting my head on him all the time I'd like you to know, too: and his hands were stroking it. Then he said "But I *must* be independent—if I do not want to meet you, I must say 'I do not', if I am not sure, I must be able to say 'perhaps', you *must* respect me as I respect you."—No more now, dearest Florence.

ALU: KCC

177   To Florence Barger

Sultan Hussein Club, Alexandria, Egypt
30 September 1917

Dearest Florence—it is easier to write to you before I write to mother, and it was some how easier to hear of Mrs Aylward's death, as I did, from you before I heard it from her: your letter arrived the day previous. I don't know what to do, what. The English question must be decided in a day or two, when I shall wire. Every one would—and Miss G. D. and A. do—advise me not to go, but the strain never leaves my mind. I have grown out of touch with all the dead and living in England except you, and is this to go on as the war will, for ever? For the third time since I have been in Egypt my 'daimonion' seems whispering "do the bigger, the risky, thing." How it will end I don't know, and wouldn't worry you, were it not that my cable will anticipate this.

It is a relief that Mrs Aylward has died. Mother wrote calmly; but it is urgent she should be detached from the Miss Prestons as soon as possible—they are not her job and she shows a tendency to take them on "for Mrs Aylward's sake." I bless and trust you and your children.

Every thing seems breaking here—Furness going to Cairo. Miss Wood leaving Montazeh, and as a final blow I am almost certainly losing A. My own action—that is to say I have all but secured him a (safe) job in the Intelligence (Military) in a part of the country where I shall never go. Since the salary is 5 times as much as his present and since I was in this uncertainty myself, I could not hesitate, but the wrench will be mortal for us both. He will go to Mansurah first for a holiday, I hope: he was taking it in any case. And I propose to join him there for a weekend. If there is not room in his house we shall go to a hotel. Completely to part with R[espectability] he refuses "Never! Never!"—then with an indescribable mixture of detachment and tenderness turned my head away and said "I want to ask you a question. Do you never consider that your wish has led you to know a T= C=?[1] And do you not think that a pity for you and a disgrace?—While answering my questions you are not to look at me."—I have bungled the above and necessarily more than necessary, but the sensitiveness if nothing else will come through. Once before, with ~~infinite~~ proud sadness, he feared he was only externals for me. I said they had drawn me, it was true, and ~~it was the only way I~~ only they could have drawn me so close: but that if they vanished tomorrow I should remain where I was.—Oh dear[?]!

Thanks for *The Feet of the Young Men*, but I wish I hadn't docked 2/– from your £ for it: an undistinguished little book. I must read *Le Feu*—it is obtainable here.[2] Trevelyan has sent me '*A Portrait of the Artist as a Young Man*' by James Joyce: a very remarkable product. I enjoy books and such thoughts as proceed from them greatly, and am pleased to find I can understand a little of Spinoza and that he is every bit as fine as I had suspected. He holds my intellect at its utmost strain, and sets me wondering at what must lie beyond *its* reach—and the reach of the strongest intellects yet created on the earth. He is a corrective for the Platonism into which, when trying to think big, most of us, whether Christian or not, tend to slip. "Men find it far easier to imagine than to understand."—"Because men find order harmonious, or find that what is in order is easier to remember, they like to imagine that there is order in the universe[.]"[3] He conceives of the universe ⟨or, as he calls it, God⟩ as containing every *im*perfection conceivable to man as well as every perfection, it would not be infinite otherwise. And it also contains every *in*conceivable perfection and imperfection. ⟨Try the above on Sydney [Waterlow] next time he's over.[4] He will blow out his cheeks not half⟩.

Having been self centred and then self-decentralised, I will actually end by adding that I rejoice Mademoiselle is back safely from France. What a joy for you all.

I feel easier about Mother.

Morgan

ALS: KCC

[1] I.e. Tram Conductor.
[2] Henri Barbusse, *Le Feu: (journal d'une escouade)* (1916).
[3] Cf. Spinoza, *Ethics* (trans. W. H. White), Part I, 'Concerning God,' pp. 43-5.
[4] Sydney Waterlow plumed himself on his talent for philosophy.

178   To Florence Barger

[Alexandria]   8 October 1917

Dear Florence

I cable today I am not coming. The restlessness seems to have passed. I should not have come (if I had come) purely for mother. It would have been too much of a burden for her mind, that. My longing to see her was part of a general feeling that I had grown out of touch, useless, stale, and that life, whether in peace or war, can only be lived once, and that we are all two years older; and at the bottom of my mind is the belief that the war never *will* end and that to save oneself up against a better time is to save up a mummy. It has passed now, and instead of worrying about England I don't think about it. Those are the only alternatives.

When I said "I know what ~~you~~——your advice would be, so don't ~~ask it~~ trouble to give it" I only meant that I knew you would advise me not to come home, so didn't trouble to ask you! My grammar was ambiguous.

I have had letters from you with dates up to Sept. 20th. The latest news was the most satisfactory and I'm so glad it caught the mail. All the same I did not at all gather from the earlier correspondence that mother was the least annoyed with you or felt that you were intruding. How sorry I am you have had the extra worry of fearing this.

I am to have a longish holiday—Cairo I suppose. I want to get away from Alex. yet don't want to go any where else: sure sign a holiday is necessary, no doubt. The London Office has created me "Head Searcher for Egypt" whatever that means. I hope more liberty any how.

Your brief account of the M[eredith] household interested me. I like to think of H.O.M. blundering against your midnight couch!—Evert by the way wrote me such a sweet note. His mind apparently under the impression that he hadn't written for some time. As a matter of fact I owe both the boys a letter.—Yes, I will suggest their visits to mother. If she is *very* much cut up Margaret should perhaps lead the way, but that you will know.

I hope you go on with your music. The Orchestra here is not at all bad. Last Sunday it did the 7th Symphony: before that, Dvorak's 'New World', and the Coriolanus Overture.

Dearest Florence, R[espectability] has been parted with, and in the simplest most inevitable way, just as you hoped. I am so happy—not for the actual pleasure but because the last barrier has fallen; and no doubt it has much to do with my sudden placidness. Oct. 5[?]—H[ome] of M[isery]

A. has had his photograph taken, and if it's good and I can wheedle two you shall have one. He leaves in a day or two—to be a spy as he bluntly expresses it, but in safety and at over double his present pay. We didn't manage Mansurah—the stupid authorities didn't want him to have a holiday while his Pass was being prepared. No, he must sit near it in Alexandria. Holidays indeed! He is very good, very very good, at doing all I tell him. This not out of docility but because he has realised at last that it is not my particular vice to run people.

I wish I was writing the latter half of Maurice now. I now know so much more. It is awful to think of the thousands who go through youth without ever knowing. I have known in a way before, but never like this. My luck has been amazing.

M.

ALS: KCC

179 To Florence Barger

[Alexandria]   11 October 1917

A. went off this morning, and I write this to get him out of my letters to you—not that you have shown the least wish to have him out. But it felt like the fall of a curtain after an act when he slid out of the station calling 'Don't forget me, don't—'. Till we meet again my letters will be more ordinary. The previous evening we went to hear some native music—such bald bad stuff played on the aodh (a kind of guitar)—and a silly little drum. These people are most uninventive and puerile. Then we finished packing, and had next morning a hell of a time getting his heavy bag—which seemed made of tinfoil and brown paper—to the station. He should just be arriving now—on the Canal. There was a previous hell over his Police permit. I have never been through anything so Kiplingesque before. Do you think it beastly to have made him a spy? He and I think it rather beastly, but not very. Anyhow it's more interesting as well as more lucrative than his present work, and like all these people he has no ~~sense~~ feeling for truth except when he is dealing with a friend. It won't "harm" him in the least. And I, who have seen him battered and hustled and wearied in his present job have lost my high moral values and want him to have a little money and, through it, occasional leisure. I couldn't have borne the Canal 3 months ago, but by now our relationship is too deep and firm to fear separation. His photograph—the fly whisk once was mine—I sent you last week.[1] So much for A.

ALU: KCC

[1] On 10 November 1917, Mohammed wrote (ATr by EMF. KCC): 'I have mended our fly-whisk but not properly. You say that it is valuable but I think ivory is not yet included amongst the precious stones.'

180   To Norman Douglas[1]

Red Cross, St Mark's Buildings, Alexandria
10 November 1917

Dear Mr Douglas

South Wind has at last reached me, and I would like to thank you for it; down more agreeable approaches to crime I have never been led. It interests me particularly, because this place, where I have now been in exile for two years, rather resembles Nepenthe. Ideals and principles gently relax. Or take the case of an Italian musician here, with whom I yesterday lunched.[2] He was recently at a Bank and observed that one of the other customers had carelessly left on the counter notes to the value of several hundred pounds. Running after the man he returned them and was warmly thanked: then added "You are doubtless aware that I am *entitled* by section 193 to a remuneration of 10% on the sum." "I *am* aware of it," the careless customer replied, "but I respect your character and your artistic attainments too highly to put the law in motion." "I do not share your scruples," answered my friend, and he is bringing an action for the percentage, which may well be heard before Signor Malipizzo. Of course in one way we differ profoundly from Nepenthe: Alexandria provides, from no point of view, a precipice, so that if a lady when peevish with a gentleman should give him a push he can never fall further than fifteen feet and then upon sand.[3] But except for this—except that is to say that relaxation here never entails either danger courage or beauty—the resemblances are remarkable. I was hoping that you were coming to see them for yourself, that I should have the pleasure of seeing you, but Lomer (from whom I hear fairly often) now writes that you are returning to England.[4]

Yours truly
E. M. Forster

A footnote—in the manner of Mr Eames—on the subjects of Faithfulness and Tenderness.[5] Heavy words! And so—reasonably enough—there is no provision for either in the Mediterranean creed. They are 'not pretty' or not necessarily so. They are habitual rather than passionate. Are they to be dropped? The Count probably thinks so. But the trouble is that without them one becomes dreadfully like Goethe. Scenery, business, enemies, friends, all degenerate into opportunities for self developement, and better a little boredom, better a little self-sacrifice even than this, so it seems to me. I know that all Christianity lurks behind them (F. and T.) and is readily unless narrowly watched to slink in their wake, but there always must be a gap some where, always must be a crack through which some angel or devil is pestering to come in and make chaos of one's human order. And I almost think the gap had better be on this side.

ALS: Beinecke

[1] George Norman Douglas (1868–1952), novelist and essayist, was born in Scotland, served in the diplomatic corps in Russia, and finally settled in Capri, the model for his fictional island Nepenthe, in *South Wind* (1917).
[2] Presumably Enrico Terni (1879–1960), an Italian composer born in Alexandria, where he organised a cultural association. He wrote an atonal quartet published in 1925. His later years were spent in Italy.
[3] Precipice: allusion to a precarious 'Nepenthe' villa.
[4] Lomer is unidentified.
[5] In *South Wind*: Ernest Eames, BA and pedant; Count Caloveglia, Nepenthean aristocrat.

181 To Alice Clara Forster

Cercle Mohammed Aly   Alexandria
17 November 1917

Dearest Lily Forster—for thus you somewhat unexpectedly signed yourself. Your long and delightful letter (Oct. 22–24) has made me laugh so much. I cannot think how you can write like that in the midst of so much worry, not to say danger: I know I couldn't.

Having fidgeted to get you to Thompson, I am relieved to hear you are not going. The Zeppelins were terribly on my mind.[1] I am glad too that the work, though it sounds a dreadful business, isn't urgent, so that you can wait till conditions are safer. Yes, T. is very kind, and has done awfully well by me. This American here is clever and quick, but I always wonder both what he has done and what he is likely to do next. He is such a fly-round.

My most amusing news is that M[rs] Borchgrevink's kind heart has dictated me into a Police Court. We were walking through the big Square and I remarked in an evil moment "How funny those ducks look"—they were lying in a row on the pavement for sale, with their feet tied. It turned out this was illegal—they ought to have been in a comfortable cage—and being the leading light in the S.P.C.A. here off she rushed for a policeman, while I took charge of a growing crowd. She returned and gave the Arab who was selling them into custody—then found that she must at once meet her daughter at the oculist's, and couldn't see the thing through. So she asked me to go as far as the Station to see that the man was duly charged—the Police so often take money and let them go—and said I had only to mention her name and that of the S.P.C.A. I did, but the Police Officer only said "Oh you are quite sufficient, sir, let us keep a lady out of it, no need to drag in a lady," with the result that I have to attend as a witness next Sunday. My sympathy with the ducks was moderate only from the first: it did not strike me that they were incommoded gravely, and I am much sorrier for the ignorant Arab who had probably never heard of the new law whose defense at the Station was that he had never seen the ducks (they were at that moment seated in his lap). I long to say the same. The summons has come through the Red Cross, who of course don't prefer people in their uniform to appear in Native Courts. I explained what had happened to them.

As for our row, it drearily goes on. Granville has issued us the enclosed instructions, which as they (temporarily) give me my point, don't make Miss G[rant] D[uff] less frigid.[2] He has also shown us the copy of the letter he has written to Sir C[ourtauld] T[hompson], asking him to decide—he speaks very nicely of me in it. And Miss G. D. has shown me the letter she is writing Lubbock, in which she says that if London think my interpretation is right, she shall regard it as so severe an expression of want of confidence in her that she shall resign all connection with the W[ounded] and M[issing]. I have written to Lubbock too, but only to say that I'm happy to resign my new job and work under Miss G. D. as before. We shall see. If they want to get rid of her they will take her resignation, if they don't mine. I have stopped worrying about it now. I always knew it was coming. It is very sad she should have got into this condition.

I also enclose a first instalment of my Upper Egypt p[ost] c[ard]s.

Love   Poppy — or E. M. Forster.

ALS: KCC

[1] EMF was relieved that she was not going up to London to his dentist, David Thompson, during a raid.
[2] This row had to do with the conflict between EMF and Miss Grant Duff about expansion of his duties to include supervision of the Red Cross searchers in Alexandria and Cairo. Dr Granville was one of the Red Cross Commissioners.

182   To Alice Clara Forster

[Alexandria]   26 November 1917

Dearest Mother—Your sweet face (pronounced by Sir Bartle [Frere] yesterday to be a 'very fine photograph',) beams at me as I write, but a letter I haven't had for almost 3 weeks.[1] I expect that since the Italian disaster, they have stopped the mails coming by Taranto, which accounts for the delay.[2] I am very well, but pretty homesick, as you may guess. I feel getting so out of touch, and it has grown such an effort to write to most people, and it is this, not only the wish to see you, that made me nearly risk England two months ago. As Furness very rightly said, it would have been most wrong and unkind of me to have weighted you with the responsibility of my visit. If I had come it would have been on general grounds. But I know that you are relieved, that whether my grounds were general or particular, I didn't come!

Of course I am feeling the stupidity and deadness of my life here very much just now, partly because though there are these heaps of wounded to interview there are no results to be got; partly because of the office row. I forget where things, when I last wrote, were. D[r] Granville has given me—temporarily—the powers I claim, until we get an answer from London: but I am trying not to exercise them, to minimise friction. Miss G. D. has shown me the letter she is sending to Lubbock: she says that if he supports my view, it shows such a severe want of confidence in her that she begs to resign all connection with the W[ounded] and M[issing]. I expect they will accept her resignation. If they accept mine (of the Head Searchership) I shall ask Granville to work my transference to Cairo, as the strain here is trying for Miss G. D. and myself. We never speak.* Mrs Borchgrevink, who always disliked her, will be exultant, but hitherto no one knows about our upset.[3]

Heaven bless the ladies! I have just wasted the whole morning over those geese or ducks. I answered my summons by going to the wrong Police Court, and was sent on to the right one with an attendant. 'I shall be late' I remarked. The Police Officer said 'Oh no—this is Egypt—they say 9.0, they mean 10.0 or 11.0.' As they did. I was received with great distinction, and adhered to various plush chairs, and when at last I did enter the court the whole audience rose to their feet. On account of my importance our trial came first—indeed but for it I don't think the presiding Magistrate would yet have begun his day. There was a hitch, for he spoke neither English French or Italian nor could he read European writings, so the building had to be harried for an interpreter. I stated my name age and rank which were translated with infinite muddle into Arabic. The interpreter said "You speak true. You raise your hand to the God." I did so. I and the poor duck seller stood side by side before the magistrate and I related how I had seen him not steal the ducks (it was quite a job to ~~accomplish~~ convey this) but expose them for sale with their feet tied, instead of in a cage. I left —presumably he was fined. It was amusing, but odious—reminds me of the *Silver Box*—everything made easy for me because I had a position.[4]

I enclose some pleasanter samples of my activity. Perhaps you could make an 'Egypt' packet for the Post Cards: one to include the bigger photographs might be too big and clumsy, I suppose.[5] I wish the Egyptian Mail didn't print so badly: it pays properly and is businesslike and civil, so I have left the Gazette for it. I must try to write another article now. Did I send you the cinema one?[6] I also enclose some of my books that I should be very grateful for if you could find unconveniently. All are small.

Sir Bartle came here that I might beguile him into taking a room: if one isn't let, Irene may have to give up the house, so I make efforts for selfish reasons. Of course now that I want him to come, he won't—thinks that the sound of the sea would depress him and that he would miss the sight of the people walking across the hall at the Regina Hotel—as indeed he would, but I always understood they got on his nerves. He still likes me and a remark I made at dinner struck him as so witty that he made me write it out (rather a cooling process), and is posting it to his sister in Gloucestershire. This being so, I had better write it out to you. He got muddled between Henry James and his brother William the Psychologist. I said 'Oh they are quite different—William—you can understand what he writes but not what he means, while Henry you could understand what he meant if you understood what he wrote.' He is a funny old gentleman—has bought two hideous little marble fountains that are said to date from the 11th century. They are so coarse, so broken and botched, so devoid both of decoration and form, so physically and modernly dirty, that I made the unfortunate slip yesterday of asking him whether he had 'done anything to his fountains yet'—I thought at least he would give them a good scrub. He replied with gentle dignity "Done? There is nothing to do: my fountains are as they always will be." So I suppose they will always stand on his balcony at the Regina, resembling a pair of I can't say what, and not even holding water, for it seems to have been characteristic of 11th century fountains that they did not work. All are appalled by this purchase of the Baronet, which he gives us to understand he only accomplished through influence in High Quarters. One would have done nicely for the cat to sleep in, had he come here.

With sweetest love. I will write about other things when I hear from you. I have written to Lady Holroyd.[7]

Pop.

* I tried for about 10 days, but had to give up as she either snubbed me or did not reply.

ALS: KCC

[1] Sir Bartle Compton Arthur Frere (1854–1933), 2nd Baronet, had served in the Zulu War, 1879; in Bechuanaland, 1884–5; and in Burma, 1886–8.
[2] The Italian defeat at Caporetto, 24–5 October 1917.
[3] EMF's impression that she 'always disliked' Miss Grant Duff was not really correct. Mrs. Borchgrevink took an affectionate interest in her despite her eccentricities.
[4] John Galsworthy's play, The Silver Box (1919).
[5] Lily Forster made linen folders to hold picture postcards, with the name of the place embroidered on the front.
[6] Between 1917 and 1919 EMF published a number of articles in The Egyptian Mail, many of which are reprinted in Pharos and Pharillon (1923) and in Abinger Harvest; see Kirkpatrick, pp. 40–3, 55–8. The 'cinema one': 'Our Diversions: Diana's Dilemma', signed 'Pharos', in Egyptian Mail, 26 August 1917 p. 2.
[7] Sir Charles Holroyd (1861–1917), Keeper of the National Gallery of British Art (Tate Gallery), 1897–1906; and Director of the National Gallery, 1906–16. The Holroyds were Weybridge neighbours of the Forsters.

183   To Florence Barger

Alexandria.   6 January 1918

Dearest Florence,

I want to put a few things on record. Read this letter at your leisure for it is all old news, but news you haven't heard, I think, and pleasant news. My personal interest in it apart, I feel it oughtn't to be lost. It's a little the starved artist writing, in fact. I don't mean this to be an ordinary letter, except that it contains my love to you. Let me know if you get it. And keep it, for one forgets.

A and I came to Alexandria just about the same time and I remember noticing him while I was stopping with F[urness]—i.e. back in 1916: remarked to F he looked nice: noticed that he—almost alone of his clan—threaded his way between the passengers instead of treading on their feet. Then—that winter, and I think before I went to Cairo and sprained my ankle, I was sitting one cold night on the seat in which his coat was kept. He asked me to rise that he might get it. I had no idea he knew more English than their usual 3 words, but liked his manner, and he, he tells me, mine. For a little time afterwards he would half salute me at the Terminus if I happened to come along, but he isn't empressé and this died down. Each knew the other wasn't some one else, but no more was established. I told F., whom this sort of thing amuses.

March 1917 when I handed the coin he said quite unexpectedly 'You shall never pay.' It turns out that I had previously said 'Thank you' in a way that gave him pleasure—I have no memory of this. I said 'You speak English'—'A little. Practice makes perfect.'—'I wish I could talk Arabic.'—'Why?'—This disconcerted me—I had only said it because I wanted to say something. However I produced 'To read the 1001 Nights.'—He said 'Oh they were written by a philosopher.' Nothing to look back on, but surprising at the time. I waited next evening—not knowing there were fixed hours—carrying for him a copy of the well known humourous periodical, Punch. No go—and I may mix chronology—but soon after was a time when I offered him a cigarette and he replied 'I ~~never~~ seldom smoke—my Ministry of Finance does not permit me' [word deleted and illegible] humourously but misled me by thinking he wanted a tip. I administered it with poor success—insisted on paying—which had now become a regular dispute between us—and on him keeping the change. He closed up his fist and all the coins fell on the floor. Some were recovered—he pocketed them sulkily. I said 'Now you can buy an English book.' He retorted 'The sum is too small for a book' which I again misinterpreted. I can only say that all through I have been less stupid than most people.

Hitherto our meetings had been accidental (at least he supposed so—God knows how many hours I stood waiting that April and May). Then he lightened things by explaining—as far as he could—his hours. As I was going to the Hospital at the other end he said 'I want to ask you a question about Mohammedans, which please answer truly, sir.'—There wasn't time, so we agreed I should 'try' to catch the whatever it was back. The question was why did English people dislike M.s so. I said 'They don't.'—'They do, because I heard one soldier say to the other in the tram 'That's a Mosque for ——— (I beg your pardon) M.'s.'—'They were joking, I think.'—'You think—you are not sure.'—'No I am sure.—One of my greatest friends (i.e. Masood) was a Moham[?]. I went to India to see him.'—'That must have cost a great deal of money' said A. 'In what you spent seeing your friends you could have bought many friends in England. You can get friends if you have money': he added 'except one or two.' When I remembered that I enjoyed the travelling he replied 'You would have been better employed at home making some useful invention, I think. If I was rich I should build first an eye hospital then a Mosque the rest I should spend on myself. See England Scotland Ireland yes and Wales first, then go abroad.'

I have made notes on this conversation—it came very near the crisis, which I must now disentangle and which sprang from the reprehensible habit of joy rides. I never had a ticket and when the inspector came something was quickly said in Arabic—to the effect that it had blown away or that I had a Pass—any how something that wasn't true. 'I find a certain amount of lies necessary to life' was the calm reply when I protested. One day an Inspector who was told the Sta. Master had said I was to travel free telephoned back to verify. Answer in the Negative. No suspicion or blame attached to me—I was far too important a personage. After a terrific row the I. got off. A came and stood quietly by me and spoke of other matters. I insisted on knowing what had happened. At last he said 'I am to get the sack.'—I said 'This is too awful, too appalling' and he replied with a sort of regal detachment I shall never forget 'Why so? I have performed a good action.' ⟨as a matter of fact by 'the sack' he meant 'a fine'—he had got the phrase wrong. But his attitude would have been exactly the same had it been a real sack⟩ He added 'Please answer me a question when you went to India how many miles was it?'—'I don't know or care' I cried. 'Whenever shall I see you again?' He replied 'I might try to meet you one evening in my civil clothes perhaps.' Then I got off.

Early next morning I went to see F[urness], who was as always most sympathetic and helpful. By greatest luck he knew St[ation] manager, who was indeed under an obligation to him, and had to see him on other business that morning. By midday I got a message that all was well. Imagine the relief. F. then however got the wind up, in army parlance, and with the best intentions tried to put it up me. This is rather unlike me—I just went ahead, and it is the thing I am proudest of in all my life. I reflected that I was not yet afraid and must not take over other people's frights. F. was as enthusiastic over A's behaviour as myself, but now he began 'of course one knows nothing' &ct—and harped on about general conditions, onlookers &ct. I boarded A again—which F had advised me not to do for the present. He at once asked me if I had been to the Manager, since he had been let off. I said No. ⟨have told him since what happened, omitting F's name.⟩ Then I asked him if he would meet me. He replied vehemently 'Any time any place any hour', and the rest you know, dear Florence.[1]

F. of course knows no more, and thinks all has died down, [two words deleted and illegible] in Khartoum was, I ought to add, most helpful by letter.

I will write on other matters shortly.

Last letter from you was dated *Nov.*

Morgan

ALS: KCC

[1] EMF gives a more detailed account of these events in his 'letter' addressed posthumously to Mohammed, begun on 5 August 1922 and continued until 27 December 1929 (KCC).

184 To Robert Trevelyan

Cercle Mohammed Aly [Alexandria]
29 January 1918

My dear Bob,

I don't mind what books you send me so long as you describe them before hand, as you did for your letter arrived yesterday, and life has been one delicious dither. Far into the night, while rain dripped through the ceiling, Antonius and I discussed, first, what you said you were posting, secondly, what you had posted, and, thirdly, what would arrive. As regards the last, which alone I can yet answer, you have made two bricks. I am prejudiced beyond all explanation against the poetry, prose, personality, and papa of Edward Thomas, and Aunt Laura has sent me Years of Childhood Last time I wrote to you I nearly made a joke—Askanov—and if I had you would probably have taken warning and not have included any thing by him. It shows one can never be too funny. So I will return him for whichever of you minds him least, and in return please send me—Well I want *A Russian Schoolboy* but there is a risk that Aunt Laura, though she did not say, may send him too. She sent me *A Russian Gentleman*. He is magnificent, Askanov—they never grow up, those young Stracheys. Askanov is a very fine writer.[1]

I am already deep in *The Piddle Years*.[2] I never find Henry James difficult to understand, though it *is* difficult to throw off the interests of one's larger life, and flatten oneself—flat flatter flattest—to crawl down his slots. Intellectually the exertion is slight. Bring muscle or blood to bear, and you stick at once, and put down your failure to deficiency of brain.

God how this officer opposite sniffs. I shall have to go. I am glad you like my poem.[3] I do some journalism now—it is appreciated locally being over-facetious. I have been reading Racine and Claudel. Very glad of all your news.

I am going for a week to Furness at Cairo. Then I will read your letter to him and he shall guess what arrived, and then he shall read Edward Thomas to me, for everyone except me likes him. He once wrote a book called "Beautiful Wales", I methink and also an appreciation of "Richard Jefferies."[4]

I'd like your Lucretius.

With love to you both

Yours affectionately
EMForster

11 February 1918

Lucretius has come—I like him very much.[5] I haven't *The Principles of Social Reconstruction* if you remain in doubt about the new book.

Thanks so much for doing all this.

ALS: TCC

[1] Trevelyan was being tossed by conflicting literary currents. He wrote (22 December 1917. KCC): 'I could not remember how much you liked or disliked [Henry] James, but decided on one of his unfinished novels, which his admirers are rapturous over. However Virginia Woolf said I ought to send you his Memoir, The Loom of Youth [i.e. *The Middle Years*] which she had reviewed in the Times ['The Old Order', *TLS*, 18 October 1917, pp. 197–8] and liked far better than the novels. But then she is rather anti-James, and may be a bad judge. Well. I took her advice on that point. Then I ordered [Edward] Thomas's poems [*Last Poems* (1918)] and the New Georgian Poetry [1916–17 edition], which I also fortunately bought for myself, and very soon found to be very disappointing (there were some good things, but not enough for the money), so I countermanded that, and a novel [*The Loom of Youth* (1917)] by one [Alec] Waugh (which I had been recommended by the wrong people, and put right about by the right people[?], and instead went to lunch with Sanger who recommended a book translated from Russian by Duff (of Trinity), some sort of autobiography of a child, . . . But alas that evening I dined at our new 1917 Club opening dinner, and sat with James and Oliver Strachey and various young people, who both know Russian and what's what, and was horrified to hear the book was a bore.' Edward Thomas (1878–1917), Welsh journalist and nature poet, died in the battle of Arras. His father was Philip Henry Thomas (1854–1921). He was an independent Positivist preacher in London. Sergei Timofieevich Askanov (1791–1859) wrote *Years of Childhood* (1916), *A Russian Schoolboy* and *A Russian Gentleman* (both 1917), all translated by J. D. Duff. James Strachey and his wife Alix were to become translators and general editors of the Standard Edition of Freud's works (24 volumes, 1948–50). Oliver Strachey (1874–1960), another brother of Lytton, was a Civil Servant who gained renown in both World Wars as a code-breaker.

[2] I.e. James, *The Middle Years* (1917), uncompleted memoirs, published posthumously.

[3] Satirical elegy (1917. Berg) on the Duchess of Connaught, who died on 14 March. EMF's squib is perhaps a response to a special article in *The Times* (15 March 1917, p. 11), 'The Duchess of Connaught: A True Soldier's Wife: Share in the Work of Empire.'

[4] Thomas, *Beautiful Wales* (1905), paintings by Robert Fowler, described by Thomas; and *Richard Jefferies; His Life and Work* (1909).

[5] Trevelyan, *Translations from Lucretius* (1920), apparently sent in manuscript.

185   To Florence Barger

[Alexandria]   31 January 1918

Dear Florence,
    The Mail has tumbled in bottom upwards as usual. I am in a sea of letters and papers, all trying to neutralise each and make their senders seem unreal. From you I have had 4 or 5 letters—ranging from Dec. 19 to early January. What stands out is (i) your impulse—though it passed—to sacrifice yourself in the hope of getting justice done (ii) the extra £100. As to the second I feel great joy, as to the first some alarm lest it recur. But the children should—as you say—deter you from action. I can't face the *ethics* of the thing—my eyes are closing closing to ethics—I believe now that if everyone acted rightly the world might be quite as miserable as it actually is, and that the only use of holding 'principles' is that they bind together the character of the holder, and that it could be bound together by other means. Preservation is my cry, I worship Vishnu—and anything that in these days increases the sum of destruction, I abhor. You would argue that your destruction or risk of it might preserve others. Books say so, I know; but History

suggests that the blood of martyrs, when it does germinate, produces a Church they never anticipated. My attitude misses something, I know—Shuttleworth would be down on it—and it may be biassed by love. But self sacrifice to preserve a *particular individual* whom one knows (not a class, however closely it may generically express him) is to my present mood the only sacrifice worth making.

In another letter you said with great justice and acumen that E. C. had lived not by will but by vision. ⟨Digression: Do you know The Will as Vision—that touching chapter in Pater's Marius?⟩[1] It interested me that you should have used that semi-religious word, and I have been trying to define during the irritations of this morning what 'Vision' is and why I like it and do not like 'Ideals', nor, as afore stated, 'principles'. A vision isn't a distant gleam but a gleam that irradiates something under your nose, so that it belongs to you. That's as far as I get. Belongs to you not in the possessive sense of course—that would make visionaries of poor Miles [Matthews] & Edith [Meredith]—but in the sense that it becomes intellectually and spiritually yours, and that ~~you are frightened of~~ no one's power can take it from you, and no one's opinion frighten you away from it.[2] E. C. has looked at the whole of life thus, and I thus at scraps of it, and with great reward. Living by Will is all-fashionable in these days—to listen to clergymen and newspapers one would ~~gather~~ think there was no other means of rising from the beast. Its drawback is that you become discontented if you fail and unpleasant if you succeed, and in either case come into conflict with the wills of others whereas is there no such thing as a conflict of visions, vision belonging to another cosmogony.—Still, I mustn't belittle the Will, having so little of it!

So glad you liked E. C.'s book. I know G[eorge] M[errill]—he is uneducated and sentimental, yet one feels a great respect. Is amusing, too—but his celebrated cooking always made me unwell. I have been 3 or 4 times to their cottage. It is charming. Thanks for telling me about the food. What of coals?

I go on calmly when I do not think of conditions in England. It is impossible and perhaps unprofitable that they should be always in my mind, but I imagine pretty acutely at moments. I am so distressed at the Waterlow overturn—it is hideous.[3]

Any developments about Harold's education? Grandmother's crackers safely reached. So did the photographs—4. G very good. You less so, but I like it.

Morgan

Awfully touched about the Cel[estial] Om[nibus]. The Keats is a Sonnet on Homer—not of course the Chapman one.[4]

ALS: KCC

[1] Florence has read Edward Carpenter's *My Days and Dreams: Being Autobiographical Notes* (1916). In Pater's *Marius the Epicurean*, Marius flirts with the idea that certain beliefs are so humanly necessary that one must *will* oneself to hold them, and one of these is a possibility that there is a friendly and comradely presence just behind material phenomena.
[2] Hugh Meredith's sister married Myles Matthews in 1905.
[3] Unexplained.
[4] Keats, 'To Homer': Letter 162.

186   To Florence Barger

[Alexandria]   18 February 1918

Dearest Florence

[1] and [2] —latter describing raid—have come. I will try to ~~do~~ number likewise, but I may forget. My forte appears to be ~~purely~~ charm. This reminds me at once of H.O.M.—I could be more indignant over his behaviour if I had not appallingly forgot to send him the money this year—I have cabled to poor mother to put it right.[1]

I am glad Harcourt House or whatever it is clears out. I hated the thought of Harold being polished there. My solemn address to George—did it reach you?—falls flat. Never mind. Tell him to frame it all the same: 'Twas a fine piece of work.

I think as much of England as England of me, but have to resist a growing temptation to be content with thought—i.e. letter writing gets more and more difficult to me. It's not so much illness as the sense of the luxury here, the misery there. You will have seen from my little articles how cheerful and alert my Egyptian mind is, and how inapplicable to England. The other mind is also active, but in an increasing solitude. There is no one out here who has ever seen any of you, or to whom I can unburden. The food so depressed me that I have been refusing invitations to dinners—I could not bear the festal side of it, though the actual eating I keep on with as usual. It's a whim this—not a principle—and I shall go to dinner again as soon as it passes. I sit down to fish mayonnaise and two rissoles which I have bought at the cook shop on the way up: also bread and sour-milk cheese: the meal will cost a little over a shilling. Then I shall play the Piano.

You ask after dear A. I am sorry to say he is only to have 48 hours' holiday (after 3 months work) and most of it will be consumed travelling here and back. We expected 4 days at least and it is a great disappointment. The holiday has to be preceded by 5 days' quarantine which no doubt accounts for its shortness. He likes his job, so that's a comfort. But never to see him, or to see him only thus, is maddening. He writes every few days and so affectionately. It's a great misfortune about I.—otherwise I could perhaps have had him to stop. For she is in great need of money! Is it not all ironical and stupid. And I find that last night (I. and H. gave a party) I have been *accompanying the grocer's boy*: he sang (Iago's credo) and very splendidly he sang, though an insufferable youth: and this morning I chance to see him in shirt sleeves with a straw basket of groceries on his arm.² Did you ever! While A. now wields a pen, which is vastly more genteel. I. hasn't a leg to stand on.³ And she owes me £2. Enter the house A. really must. My solitude in regard to him is sometimes as worrying as my solitude in regard to England. What a blessing to me that a long series of previous confidences should have enabled me to tell you about him. It is certainly the most wonderful thing that's ever happened to me—has so outstripped my theories. The whole ending of Maurice and its handling of the social question now seems such timourous half hearted stuff. The question never occurs to me and to A. very rarely. Once while discussing my composition which he partially deplores he said shyly 'Do you not think that there is one disgraceful thing, that it should have caused you to know a T. C.?' As regards arrangements, precautions, his sweetness and good sense are extraordinary. I am ashamed, ashamed, to have to ask him to behave as I do. And I fear things will never be better, we shall never have an H[ome] of M[isery] again—though it did lead us to know and trust each other absolutely, and that can never pass.

You will like to know what I play. Beethoven, the Second Movement of the Waldstein. Schumann—Carnival. Franck—Prelude Aria & Finale. Chopin—Preludes 11, 17, 20, 22, and the first two Rondos. I accompanied the Verdi quite decently last night—the grocer's boy said it was 'pas mal pour la première fois.' also—on hearing me speak French and Italian he remarked 'Pour un Anglais—ça c'est très rare.' Greeks do not excel in tact.

Your raid experience makes curiously little impression on me, which was I suppose your aim!

I wrote to Evert and promised him that on Monday March 25 at 3.0 P.M. I would play the middle C and that he (having calculated the difference of time owing to longitude) was to do the same. I wonder whether it will come off. I shan't make such offers to Harold—he is too sensitive—it would likely as not get on his nerves.

Have been getting new uniforms. Am managing to make A. ask for my old clothes a little now, but it has been a job.

I think nothing posted to me in the last 3 or 4 months has gone down. All turns up in the end.

Love to all

Morgan

ALS: KCC

¹ The monthly allowance for Meredith.
² From Verdi's *Otello*. I., H.: his landlady, and daughter Hélène.

[3] On 19 January 1918, Mohammed wrote (ATr by EMF. KCC) that he could 'read all your letters easily I think that my English is greatly improved for I spend all my time going with the Englishmen. I want you to correct my mistakes but not to blame me. . . .'

187   To Florence Barger

[Alexandria]   23 March 1918

Dearest Florence,
 I am so depressed about A.—his last letter dated the 13 and he felt ill again and was probably returning to the awful hospital. I have not seen him for nearly five months and can see no end to it. That holiday together that you so sweetly wish us will hardly take place in this existance [sic]. I am sick with myself for having wrongfully accused him of untruthfulness—(I thought he had *had* his holiday at Mansurah, and wanting to save my feelings would not say so. He had been in hospital really.) He writes with that unfailing simplicity of his "What lies have you picked up from my letter? I remember that I did not tell you any in my letter. I think that this news annoyed me too much. Please write very soon." Nothing can go wrong with such a character as his—nothing internal I mean—of course like all we are at the mercy of circumstances, and of what circumstances! How I regret the old times—the H[ome] of M[isery] Yet we both laboured all we could to end them. Man is an odd creature. In these days if a friend takes even a little train journey he disappears forever. A. writes 'I feel as you do. We shall never meet again.' The shadow of tragedy seems very close now but thank heaven it will be tragedy and not squalor and perhaps it too may pass. If I don't hear from him on Monday I shall wire. The trouble is to get *at* these people—they are so insignificant, the army just shovels them about like dirt. If he is in hospital the wire will never be sent in to him. I have begun a long letter to you about him, continuing the account of our early meetings, but it must wait till I am in a more robust mood. I don't know what I should do without you to empty this on to. Here month after month passes and I can't so much as open my lips. I am so glad you wrote to E. C. when you sent the photograph, and that you feel as I do about the book. One can face bad luck and unhappiness. It is the prospect of Organisation and dehumanisation that is such a nightmare to me and that E. C.'s experience combats: and my own experience, in having had such friends as A. and you. Will the war leave nothing in the world but a card index?

23 March 1918
 To my relief I receive the enclosed this morning. He refers to my scheme—dashed like all—of being sent on business to Port Said. I

am writing to F[urness] to ask if he knows of a job—I hate doing so, but it is my only chance and will have nothing beyond my own sensibilities. I meant to write on other matters but this shall go.

Morgan

ALS: KCC

188   To Siegfried Sassoon[1]

Red X, Alexandria.   2 May 1918

Dear Sassoon

Damn you—I suppose for writing such a letter and for not being ill. I settled when I saw the Ras el Tin postmark that you were in the Hospital there and that I should come to see you. How one longs for people to be ill. It's a great disappointment to me that we shan't meet. I had read those 4 poems. I like possessing them. I am writing for more of you to England.

I began a short story about officers. It is called 'Inferior'. Two of them take cigarettes round their men in a Hospital, and come across a man whom one of them had shot at for "cowardice". But it was an inferior story. It's not that I'm off writing, but I can't any more put words between inverted commas and join them together with 'said' and an imaginary proper name. The atmosphere of the story, had it attained one, was exactly what your letter describes, though the officers only got their Rosaries and Cocktails as the curtain fell.[2] I have seen more officers than usual lately. What *is* it? What *is* it? I believe it's ~~power~~ the possession of power. Give a man power over the other men, and he deteriorates at once. The 'troops' are decent and charming, I believe, not because they suffer but because they are powerless.—And ~~they~~ the devil who rules this planet has contrived that those who are powerless shall suffer.

I expect to stop here until combed out. Two years—almost—ago they tried to empty us into the army. I ~~consciously~~ (can't spell it now) conscientiously objected and was starting for England, but the boat stuck or something in the Red Sea and before it arrived the whole Red X was exempted. Since then, what's happened. A profound belief that one's at war with the world—defensive warfare. Violent individualism. Conscious shirking. And the results not what W. B. Maxwell (it probably is) anticipates, but some glorious and inalienable gains.[3] There are things in these last two years that I can never be too gratified for, never. My work here is obscure and occasionally humiliating. Never mind. It's been worth my while. Petulant rather than puffy one steals ahead—the whole act of living seems one continuous theft now.

You talked about 'inflicting' things on me. How's this for an infliction? Anyhow, answer it. There's absolutely nothing I can do for you, except write, which I will do. How the Hell did you pick up Howards End? Oh dear what a pity you didn't get on shore. It could have been such a pleasure. Thanks for wishing me good luck—I appreciate it greatly.

Have just finished The Sense of the Past, and though it's so obscure—find it much nearer the work of other writers than is the rest of the later James.[4] He is really interested in his subject as well as in his treatment of it. And a topping subject. Perhaps I'll post you The Sense of the Past. I'll think. It's silly to suppose you'ld like it, because I get a letter from you the same day, but one does, owing to the unprecedented prolongation of the European crisis, suppose silly things.

So write again.

Yours
EMForster.

ALS: George Sassoon

[1] Some time during 1917 EMF received a letter from Siegfried Sassoon (1886–1967), poet and memoirist, and a member of the London banking family. It has not survived, but it was written out of his disgust with the war. He had hoped that his unit would go ashore at Alexandria so that he and EMF might meet, but this did not happen.

[2] The story 'Inferior' has been lost. Sassoon (1 May 1918. KCC) had written: 'I wish I had your power of reproducing conversations—A novel dealing with the bad side of the officer class in wartime would add something to the indictment against militarism. There are several generals & their staff on board;—fairly quiet; but most of them look like tailor's advertisements—One hears them talking in their superior, self-possessed voices— "I myself think".... "My own opinion is" . . . & so on... But 'red tabs' always 'get my goat' as the troops say. The troops! I wish you could see them asleep on the decks at night, with a few violet dim lights glowing overhead— . . . They are like a simple soul. Officers are merely nasty individuals who drink cocktails all day, & are touched by 'Because', 'The Rosary', & 'I hear you calling me', & read 'The Tatler' & 'The London Mail' & think of & put their own comfort before anything else... I suppose people are always nicer when they are having a rotten time.... And the prospect of France is not pleasant—I fear they'll do me in this time, or else send me off my chump.'

[3] William Babington Maxwell (1866–1938), novelist and journalist, had been writing patriotic articles.

[4] Henry James's novel about time-travel, published posthumously with other fragments in 1917.

189   To Florence Barger

Alex[andria]   16 July 1918

Dearest Florence

How I hope that this will reach you that you may share my happiness. I have just been to Mansurah for the week end, and it was even better than either of us hoped. Does one experience a *renewal* or a *deepening* of emotion each time? It feels so like the latter. Of course we have never before had perfect conditions—they have marked this meeting as one apart. I have told you of all his sorrow—death of father and, what is worse, death of brother by drowning. He has become—funny little fellow—a 'householder': or rather the family own 3 houses. They are situate in a lane near the station: nearly nearly a slum—ducks & chicks paddle, and O my dear the sanitation! only means ~to~ of washing is to strip in the passage under the stairs and pour little tins of water over each other which slither away into a far yet not far enough latrine. 'Perfect conditions!'—never before did I so bless my adaptability. Where would I be if I had gone in for 'requiring' things like Plugs and Plates. I don't know that the room was very clean either, but I seldom touched bottom, as on entering you crawled straight on to a sofa, and big bed, table, and wardrobe paved the rest. The rest of the house was let. Food—delicious and very lavish. Once we had a tray of roast mutton potatoes, tomatoes and onions as big as the top of a drum, and amazing good tea in the morning. They were brought in by a semi-slave from outside, who squatted in the passage while we ate and gave vent to her views on the world.

We emerged fairly smart from our lair, and saw the sights of Mansurah—pleasantly situated on the Nile with an esplanade (not too formal) and cafés. We drove, went in a boat. I saw some of his friends—they looked good stamp: some of them spoke both French & English: uncle of one of them a doctor, had been at London University. None of them know what *he* did at Alexandria, he says. Curious state of affairs! Our main topic was the possibility of his marrying his brother's wife. I am rather in favour of it. He likes her and has often seen her, she likes him and approves the scheme—which originates with his sister. She requires no dowry, and—being a widow—there will be no expense over her wedding. She wants him to protect the child—aged 2—of whom he is very fond. It wouldn't—as he agreed work in England, because he is not in love with her at all. But I see no disaster ahead in this country. They are so simple and the women simpler than the men. I wouldn't like him to miss a romantic marriage if it was possible, or if its romance was likely to outlast his curiosity. What do you feel for him about it?

He was awfully grave at first. The drowning was so inexplicable—cramp I think. He went to Tantah at once to see his sister in law and arrange business, but made no detailed enquiries about the death.[1] "What is the use? I shall only increase my sorrow? —. If only it had been the rest of my family instead." The second day of my visit he cheered up—I felt so proud & happy. He started ragging me in bed just as H[arold] or E[vert] might—'Morgan I will hurt you— Edward I will kill you' and we went on fooling till we fell asleep. To put the lid on, I travelled 3rd. Quite comfortably. I theorised to him, by the way, rather deeply against R[espectability]—how afterwards I found its absence even more important than at the time. He said very gently 'I quite understand'—so I have the happiness of knowing that things are sound even on an intellectual basis. He has given me for the time some nice gaiters and breeches, also consents to get measured for a suit a little too large for him which is to do for us both: advances towards communism we shouldn't have made a year ago. I don't see where things will end, so keep an open mind. Next month he should come to Alexandria to look for work. Reenlistment in the army he says is now *for duration*: this if true—and it's likely to be—renders it impossible. The net is falling on Egypt, though slowly. F[urness]'s failure to help me hurts very much. He has not mentioned the subject again. A. is so presentable and unscalliwaggy—I'm more and more certain that something could have been done, but have no one else to turn to. One mistake, A. points out, we have made. He ought from the first to have given me Arabic lessons in my rooms.

On I go—I meant to insert a sheet on other subjects but it's time for my stupid work. It has grown so tedious, but it's the basis of my existence out here. Much love and thanks. My life would have split beyond mending if it wasn't for you.

Morgan.

ALS: KCC

¹ Tantah: large town on the Alexandria–Cairo line.

190   To Siegfried Sassoon

[Alexandria]   3 August 1918

Dear Sassoon—I have a face but fear it has been locked up. We have moved for the summer and the more portentous objects have been left behind. I will see. I have also a Face—the face of a Thinker. It costs, even at the special rate, 2/11, and I do not think you would care about it greatly.¹ What about you? please. Re the poets you mention I have read some of them both. I liked Graves. Nichols not so much.²

This letter expects to be scrappy. I want something to go through. I was told that owing to its genteel behaviour the 74ᵗʰ had been allowed to visit England.³ It's the sort of thing one's told. I had made for myself one or two pictures of you there: conversing with Edward Carpenter in chief—I realised only lately that you knew him. However, this isn't. And I can't picture you or any individual at the front. I can see, geographically, scars across Europe and Asia, into which, from both sides all forms of life—men camels vegetables sugar—are being pushed by the respective governments. But to realise the individual—the individual camel even—there, passes my power. Even when (like ourselves) one's comparatively a dab at reconstruction, how feeble the power is really. Once round the corner, items get schematised. And to the average man I don't think that war so much as presents itself as the elimination of life. To M[r] Collins Baker, Secretary of the National Gallery, I once remarked that if all Albanians killed one another there would be no Albanians. While admitting that my statement contained an element of truth, he dismissed it as unbalanced. He could, he said, contemplate the extinction of an individual by force, but not of a nation. History taught otherwise. O History!—But never mind History nor M[r] Collins Baker, except that he was very kind to me. I want to drag this paragraph round to its main statement which is that when writing to you I think of you as situated more or less like myself.

I suppose I must have broken with Eddie, as with so many.[4] He did say a sort of good-bye. He has been so nice to me from first to last that I can't feel it is a break. One doesn't quite know who will be left. My demands grow more exacting, and much more so those of others. Authoritarians v. Libertarians—that is the chief split. Opinions scarcely mattered once. But war and the cosmogony of strife steal into one's inmost recesses. I suppose we had bitten off more toleration than we could chew. Now, quite inevitably, people become one's enemy! And what's tiresome, they become partly one's enemy. You get on with them in one direction and not in another. This, which usen't to signify, now does. They have to agree. Which is awful. In an age of destruction, unless people agree they cannot be friends.

Oh I feel so obscure. I don't seem to shave enough or even wash and the breast of my British Red Cross Tunic is covered with ink and jam. Please are you naturally dressy? You may be:—I admit dressy friends:—have in fact developed in theory a taste for toilette requisites. How ill tempered Tolstoy was over Nekhludov's dressing![5] He makes him pass through a long career of crime before breakfast. This was wrong. I live as economically as possible. Get a certain amount as Billeting, and make a little from journalism and lessons to Greeks. Very often I'm happy, and for good reasons. Ancient Alexandria—to mention one—is proving a most amusing companion. I'm constructing by archaeological and other reading an immense ghost city. How quite to fit into it Euclid, Plotinus, and Timothy the Cat I don't yet see, but they were all here, though not at the same moment.[6] Here Hypatia was slain and Cleopatra loved and died, please.[7] The latest is a prehistoric dock which theosophists attribute to the submerged continent of Atlantis. It debouches seaward—under the circumstances an unusual direction, but am told that they had occult powers.

It's lovely weather as usual. I'm so glad you were getting fine weather, rest, and good food. Yes I had heard of your 'Shell Shock' or of scraps of it.[8] I want to read Grey's pamphlet.[9] It's interesting that he should have got the wind up about civilisation. I have two hopes: one, very faint, of a league of nations, the other of general apathy and fatigue. All vigour is these days misdirected and must be for many years to come. The human race has gone more or less dotty, and the best it can do is to doze for a century in the sun.

Now I must go. Write again. You are sending me your new poems, I think I do hope so. If you ever get to England greet my friends for me.

EMF

Christian though he is, conversion is not important. (belongs to something else)[10]

ALS: George Sassoon

[1] Sassoon had written (30 June [1918]. KCC): 'It is a queer thing to write intimately to a man with no face! Could you send me a small photograph of your face (if you have one).'

[2] Robert Graves (1895–) and Robert Malise Bowyer Nichols (1893–1944): both served on the Western Front, Graves in Sassoon's regiment. Sassoon had written (ibid.): 'They are a queer couple, & quite extraordinary— . . . Nichols is rather mad & too much obsessed by his own sensations, but there is something about him, (apart from his burning genius for poetry), which draws me to him,—he is rather like Keats in appearance; . . . We Georgian Poets think such a lot of ourselves, just because Eddie Marsh has foisted 11,000 copies of our selected poems on to a crowd of people with a taste for verse.'

[3] 74th: Sassoon's and Graves's unit in the Royal Welsh Fusiliers.

[4] There had evidently been some dispute between EMF and Marsh, who worked for the Ministry of Munitions. They renewed communications after the war.

[5] In Tolstoy's *Resurrection* (Chapter 3), a detailed description of the seducer Prince Nekhludov getting up and dressing.

[6] See EMF's 'Timothy the Cat & Timothy Whitebonnet', in *Pharos and Pharillon*, pp. 42–5; see Kirkpatrick, pp. 41, 118, on other versions of the essay. It relates the story of the fifth-century contest between the followers of a Monophysite bishop ('Timothy the Cat') and those of a Nestorian ('Timothy Whitebonnet'). EMF is preparing to write *Alexandria: A History and a Guide* (1922).

[7] Hypatia (c. 370–415) was an Alexandrian Neo-Platonic philosopher and martyr.

[8] Sassoon had written (30 June [1918]. KCC): 'You may, or may not, have heard of my own futile protest last year which landed me for nearly 5 months in a shell-shock hospital. It was my feeling for the men which drove me back to the war. The publication of the "Secret Treaties" justified my action of 12 months ago: but the present situation is infernally awkward, with the damned Junker barricade between the world & German commonsense & kindliness. (This is only a surmise,—not an oracular statement).' The 'shell-shock hospital' was the Craiglockhart War Hospital, and the episode is described by Sassoon in *Sherston's Progress* (1936).

[9] Edward Grey, 1st Viscount of Fallodon, *The League of Nations* (1918).

[10] This encircled postscript is clearly legible in the letter and must have been an *aide-mémoire* in another context.

191   To Robert Trevelyan

[Alexandria]   23 August 1918

Dear Bob

I take up my pen in due haste for I should write to my friends all right—if I didn't first think of all the friends I hadn't written to and so fall to gazing at the blue Mediterranean. The amount you have sent me should invest you, in any mind but the Apostolic, with a prior claim to a reply, but we reject (do we not?) habitual standards; and I leave you to decide how far the enclosed cheque refers to the future and how far to the past. I am not sure that, in either case, it has a present.

I am writing two articles at once—one on Philo's Embassy to Caligula and the other on Army English—moving round the text "No persons will loiter within the vicinity of these steps."[1] Philo is connected with a graver work: a lecture on 'The Philosophers and Philosophies of Ancient Alexandria" to be delivered next week to the local theosophical society. Life here goes on as usual, though I grow increasingly irritable and increasingly unable to communicate that fact to others. Any bitterness of expression is, in this chivalrous war, an ~~unholy~~ amazing relief, and I think that's why one so appreciates Sassoon's poems.[2] No doubt truth was suppressed in previous wars, but there was not so copious a supply of the official substitutes. It's these that weigh one down like masses of decaying flesh, and drive one for cleanliness to fancy or the past.

I shall hear some time how you go. I had expected Dickinson would have mentioned it in his last. His general attitude was as usual. How is his health? Pretty good, is it not?

Thank you for your poem on Confuscius [sic].[3] It amused me very much. Perhaps some time I will send you a copy of my "Pericles in Paradise" but you do not know any of the people.

⟨Scene Heaven. A staircase stretching infinitely in either direction[.] Pericles [Anastassiades] is discovered standing in an attentive attitude upon one of the steps⟩

Pericles Someone must come along soon. Then I shall know which way to go. It's no use going up and having to come down or going down and having to come up. One assumes it will be up, but these places are very tricky ⟨nodding⟩ There must be some rule, some arrangement. I shall just stop still and see ⟨His face brightens at the sound of aged footsteps far below⟩ Hullo Sir Bartle! So you're following me!

Sir Bartle [Frere] ⟨ascending into the scene⟩ Bless me what a climb! Ah! ⟨he stops⟩ Hullo Pericles! What a delightful place what a perfectly delightful place

Pericles It's Heaven, eh, Sir Bartle.

Sir Bartle I should just think it was.

Pericles ⟨fidgety⟩ So shall we be getting on?

Sir Bartle But *isn't* it a delightful place.

Pericles ⟨genial⟩ One just wants a woman here and it would be perfect.

Sir Bartle And you shall sketch and sketch and sketch and sketch and sketch and sketch—

Pericles So shall we be[?] getting on?

Sir Bartle. And here comes our eminent friend Cavaffy. Oh better and better. *What* a delightful place! ⟨Cavaffy [*sic*] steps slowly into the scene, but from above⟩
Pericles ⟨laughing⟩ Hullo! why are you going the wrong way?
Cavaffy. A regrettable tendency, my dear Perry, a regrettable tendency.
Pericles But surely the show's upstair. You ought to go up with Sir Bartle & me, not down
Cavaffy Follow the Baronet, my dear Perry, follow the Baronet. Perhaps regrettably perhaps not regrettably I descend I descend ⟨he does so⟩
Pericles Now what's one to make of a chap like that? Now there's a chap of acknowledged talent, and yet he goes down. ⟨Sir B. repeating 'What a delightful place!' has resumed his climb⟩ Pon my word I believe Cavaffy would know. After all what's a title? Besides I'm an artist myself. I'll risk it. ⟨He runs down a few steps and collides with Terni⁴ who is ascending.⟩
Terni Accidente! zizift!
Pericles ⟨shrieking⟩ You call yourself an artist! Well, you ought to go down not up down not up! Why do

Love to all
                    Morgan liked Lytton & Desmond awfully

ALS, incomplete: TCC

¹ 'A Little Trip', probably published in the *Egyptian Mail*; see Kirkpatrick, pp. 11–12. 'Alexandrian Vignettes: Army English', signed 'Pharos,' in *Egyptian Mail*, 12 January 1919, p. 2.
² Siegfried Sassoon, *Counter-Attack and Other Poems* (1918), its grim tone set by the title poem, about a failed attack.
³ Not in Trevelyan's *Collected Works*. His spate of Chinese poems, inspired by Arthur Waley's translations, came much later.
⁴ Enrico Terni, Italian composer living in Alexandria.

192 To Florence Barger

[Alexandria.   November 1918]

Dearest Florence
    I have just received yours of Oct. 29 returning mine of A's. I was writing about him in any case, having been to Mansurah this week end. On the whole I am happier. He looked a little fatter. Indeed the first twelve hours of my visit were as perfect as I have known. Then there came a new anxiety, but I think not a grave one. He had the most awful itching—especially on stomach, arm pits, &ᵗᶜ. He had been having attacks for 20 days, but never so badly before. It came on worst at night when he was fatigued from his work—he had been in the cotton market 9 hours that day, so I didn't see much of him.—I massaged him which sent him to sleep, but he woke again,

THE FIRST WAR, 1913-20

and was nearly mad. His wife[1] got up and heated some water, which did bring relief, and he slept permanently. I think it is eczema, but have not yet heard the doctor's diagnosis. He was to go the morning I left. I am expecting a letter and will let you know.

His goodness in having me to stop is more than we can realise, as it is greatly against their customs to house a European. He has made more sacrifices for me than I ever have for him. When I stopped with him before we lived in a tiny room on the ground floor and ate out. The rest of the house—which he administers for the family—was let to a tenant. Since his marriage he has moved upstairs & brought the tenant down. Upstairs is much nicer—pleasant paved hall, 2 rooms, also kitchen & w. c. quite good according to local standards. His wife cooked such a nice dinner—roast duck, which A. previously slew, savoury soup, bamiehs (a good local vegetable) in gravy, boiled rice. For dessert we had dates. But you will want to know about her. I just had glimpses—very young, simple, and charming, and I loved hearing them laugh together. She is like some tame and pretty country animal, and he will be kind to her as to all, but the idea of companionship seems never to have entered his head. It is queer even to me, who know the East a little. Possibly she will develope character, and so touch his. At present he regards her alternately as a ~~play~~ comfort and a financial anxiety. I write to you rather nervously here. I am so anxious not to put you off him. He differs so from the northerner in being unsentimental, and in keeping his senses apart from his mind. Our own basis remains absolutely the same, but I find it very necessary to see him occasionally as absence raises chimeras. Once more for certain we shall meet. And then—? You will understand dear, and you alone, if I am not really in form when I'm in England

His business is buying cotton from the country people & selling it to the dealers. I lent him money for this (£70), and shall make it a gift when I leave. It will take the place of the 1/- a day I have been giving him since his illness for extra meat and milk. I have also acquired, by semi-legal means, some bottles of Horlick's Malted Milk—better than 'Clod Oil' as he calls it, in this climate.[2] His weight has gone up.

We talked endlessly, partly on Deportment, on which he holds the soundest views. "We have a book called 'Beware!' which if I read I lie awake laughing all night. It says 'Beware!—Shake hands with your host only, not with those who are with him.' I told him about Lady Grove, & 'Don't'.[3] These follies seem universal.—He is to get me some country pipes—if he can find them—for the children. He said "why do you not take them costlier gifts? Why not take them a pair of Egyptians?' (i.e. self & wife). I wish I could! I would like to get a libdah (a dung coloured skull cap such as the very poor wear) for Evert. It is hideous, but I see him strutting in it. What is his size? A. is altogether scandalised at the economy of my outlook.

Mansurah was looking pretty—the Nile in flood and the river front glowing in sunset. I insisted on being out when A. was, so spent much time at cafés.

A. worries about money, but not the least about his health. He eats because I want him to, but for no other reason.

It becomes necessary that I shall mention to mother that I have come to know a nice Eg. on account of letters.

ALU: KCC

[1] Mohammed's wife was named Gamila. He was married on 1 October 1918. He wrote to EMF (2 October, ATr by EMF. KCC): 'Yesterday was the first day of marriage—a happy day was it and I believe it was only two hours,—happy hours pass quickly.'

[2] I.e. cod-liver oil.

[3] Lady Agnes Geraldine (Fox Pitt-Rivers) Grove, *The Social Fetich* (1908), on social solecisms, and behaviour for travellers.

193   To Forrest Reid

[Cairo]   10 January 1919

Dear Reid

It is such a pleasure to get your book & letter in spite of much of your news. I so often think of you & so often nearly write, but never feel that absence has the least divided us. There are hopes of us meeting soon, for I am due to come home this month. I have stuck in Egypt all these years—happily on the whole and compared to most people very very happily. I had not heard about W. R. These deaths are so unreal to me—they were not at first, but insensibly one has dropped into the habit of thinking that a person who so much as goes out of the room in these days may not come back into it again. This is one way of putting it—the other way is yours—from the side of the dead—pointing out that they are 'sharing a secret glory.' I remember Ireland—once I read a paper on Butler and he was there.[1] I don't make it out at all. I wish I had your vision to see it as tragedy and not as a filthy horror. You and I have come through it—that is to say through its German phase; God knows what the next will be—and for my own part I've learnt nothing and feel that most people have likewise learnt nothing, despite the assurances of the newspapers to the contrary. I can't even feel that the dead have died in our defence. I didn't want W. R. to leave No 21.[2] It seemed to me no good and it still seems no good, and the knowledge that his end didn't seem meaningless to him doesn't fill it with meaning for me.

On the surface one keeps hopeful: and from the surface I am busy over a book on Alexandria—a superior sort of guide book with a good deal of history to it. It's a great resource and I'm very keen on the getting it lucid and dignified—the sense spirit of a procession is to inform it, if so I can contrive. Of course you will get a copy; the delays threaten to be eternal though.

One can't, as you say, write much in a letter. How I wish we could talk.

Some of your stories I have read before, but I am enjoying & admiring them all. 'Kenneth' made me laugh so nicely. The 'Trial of Witches'—the only one which my present work qualifies me to judge, for I'm no longer a novelist—seemed to me a most powerful invocation of the past.[3]

I hate to think of you alone in that house, but you do not let out to what extent it is bearable. What animals have you?

When I get back, will you send me a photograph of Kenneth to look at? I form no idea of him so far. How glad I am you have some one to look after and to look after you—they are the same thing.

I hear from Meredith sometimes and sometimes of him.

This concludes this set of notes.

With best wishes & with love.

Yours ever
EMForster

I am in Cairo for a week's leave—the first for over a year.[4] This afternoon we went up the Pyramid. I shall miss Egypt when it comes to the point—miss it dreadfully.

I could write about your book [novel?] in the 'Egyptian Mail'—but that's no good, I assume; and fear I shall be too late to do anything in England.[5]

ALS: Stephen Gilbert

[1] EMF read a paper on Samuel Butler to the Ulster Arts Club, on or about 28 March 1914, while on a visit to H. O. Meredith. The manuscript has not survived.
[2] Willie Rutherford died in France in 1916 or 1917. No 21: an address or an army assignment.
[3] Reid, 'Kenneth' and 'Trial of Witches', in his A Garden by the Sea: Stories and Sketches, pp. 39–46, 136–50. On Reid's friend Kenneth Hamilton (1904–27?), see Brian Taylor, The Green Avenue, pp. 88–104, Plates 14–20.
[4] EMF was visiting J. M. Furness (1868?–1944). At that time he was headmaster of the Khedive School in Cairo.
[5] Reid, Pirates of the Spring (1919).

194 To Florence Barger

[Alexandria.   January 1919].

I leave Egypt in comparative content. A. is far better than I could have dreamed—fatter, heavier, has not spat blood for many months, and no longer has the desolating feeling of fatigue. He says himself, he was just on the verge. We went a long walk in the fields yesterday morning. It was awfully like Cambridge—flat with ditches and in the distance misty farms and trees. Returned to a good dinner, cooked by the stunned Gamila. I gave G. an inlaid Indian Box (8/–) that I bought in Cairo for her. She said it was very pretty and that she supposed it cost 1/6. A. said "No—18/–" on which she exclaimed

"God help the man—he must be mad." I told A. it was his fault for lying. He replied 'If I had said 8/– she would have thought you were not mad but silly and madness is better.' I think it is all right about G.—their voices together are so nice. He acknowledges that he would have liked a companion, who would not refuse to go to the W. C. at night on the ground that there was an afreet in it.[1] But he is philosophic and gentle, and more inclined to make the best of people than to alter them, and he says that G. is intelligent in her country way.

What a relief all this is. I had expected to sail amid rending anxieties, and I leave him on his feet and don't deny myself the satisfaction of thinking that I helped to place him on them.

I have made a couple of sly references to Mohammed my Egyptian friend to Mother.

He comes to Alex. on the 20th in the chance of seeing me again, and will write once a fortnight. "If the letters cease it will only mean one thing—that I have died."

ALU: KCC

[1] Afreet: demon, in Muslim mythology.

195   To Siegfried Sassoon

Madeira Cottage, Lyme Regis[1]
28 March 1919

Dear Sassoon

I had got as far as 'Paddock Wood' and was hoping the latter had it when your note arrived.[2] Of course I shall write for you.[3] And crikey what pay. The trouble is that I am not sure what the Common People want. My past has, let me emphasise, been uniformly refined.—And (suddenly to turn heavy) isn't it awful how all the outward nonsense of England has been absolutely untouched by the war—still this unbroken front of dress-shirts and golf. I'm damned if I know what bucks one up.—So send books here, for I will review two—send them at once, that is to say: otherwise home. I know all about Egypt, Hellenistic History, religion, the Italian Renaissance, India and novels.

How are you?

As soon as I get to town we shall meet.

Yours
EMForster

ALS: George Sassoon

[1] EMF stayed at Lyme Regis for three weeks with G. L. Dickinson, who was recovering from influenza. EMF wrote that 'The world seemed settling down into its lost armchair for a moment's rest' (*GLD*, p. 146).
[2] Paddock Wood: town near Tonbridge in Kent.

[3] Sassoon had become literary editor of the *Daily Herald*, a Labour weekly during the war that became a daily paper in March 1919. The Labour leader George Lansbury was editor. The *Herald* called itself 'The Paper with its face towards the Future.' Sassoon paid three guineas per 1,000 words for reviews and commissioned a series of special articles at £10 each. EMF was substitute literary editor in 1920 when Sassoon went to the United States.

196   To Lorna B. Wood

Lyme Regis.   31 March 1919

Dear Matron

So glad to get your letter this morning and much look forward to seeing you soon and hearing about the spiritualism, and think and hope I shall not be stupid about it. It's a closed book to me, but a book whose binding always fascinates. Just now I am struggling at a great work on Pantheism (mainly Indian) in order to squash it into a 1000 words review, and attempting to master the difference between 'God is all' and 'all is God'[1] One can always explain away a creed by regarding it as an expression of human need, and I am fairly smart at such explanations. But the real, the supreme question, *Is it True?* isn't touched at all by such methods. Some people want the human to be the ultimate reality, others the non human. So much one can see, and from their wishes one can deduce their beliefs— Christianity in Europe, Buddhism, Brahmanism &ct in India. But it tells one nothing as to the *truth* of their beliefs—nothing about the ultimate constitution of the universe.—This last phrase sounds 'scientific', but do not damn it as such. Science will never explain the ultimate constitution, I am sure. It will get deeper and deeper in to the facts of life, and the *fact* of life will always elude it, like the retreating rainbow. Quite what this queer thing is which interpenetrates matter and animates in different degrees me, Sir Courtauld Thomson, the cats, the daffodils, and a grain of sand, we shall never know by science. We shan't know, either, by first deciding what we would *like* it to be. At least that's my present feeling.

Mother tells me the W. E. George has arrived.[2] She is keeping it against my return—i.e. for about a week. Thank you for it so much. I am having a good time here now that the weather has improved. It's the best—indeed the only nice—watering place I have ever seen. We are in an old thatched cottage, and look through the tiny panes of its curved bow window upon the sea, and upon nothing but the sea. The window itself is so pretty—fitted with a semicircular settee of bright chintz—and there is a kitten and two dogs and a hot bath and very good plain cooking. Expensive, naturally.

Yours very sincerely
EMForster

ALS: Hofstra University

[1] In Edmond Gore Alexander Holmes, *All Is One: A Plea for the Higher Pantheism* (p. 24):

'All is God because All is One. And All is One because All is God.' The Indian pantheism discussed by Holmes is principally Islamic.
² Perhaps the novel *Blind Alley* (1919), about the war and its aftermath, by Walter Lionel George (1882–1926).

197   To Siegfried Sassoon

[N. p.   Probably May or June 1919]

Dear Siegfried—here's the Daily News:—I meant to say, and had better write, that I like your poetry: I thought you knew I did—it is odd how things don't get through. ('Why Madam I spend my whole life defending you' Rogers remarked across the breakfast table when accused of slander.)¹

Abysmal depression all today. Mᵣ May Sinclair, I fancy, though no direct symptoms or conscious thoughts.² While trying to write my novel, I wanted to scream aloud like a maniac, and it is not in such a mood that one's noblest work is penned.³ Writing letters, on the other hand, relieves the tension a little, and that is why you get one. I feel dead tired but from irritability and sadness, for I have done nothing since we parted in Pall Mall. Part of the point of a general, surely, is to lead one into company where there might be escapades, but all that is finest in him recoils from this—I knew it when he drank only thin beer with his food, not even whiskey.⁴ I must really go to bed—it has been an awful day, and though others will be better I see no way out of this particular run. To get the £500 and then set out in sulky solitude southward—is that Elysium?⁵

I wonder what impression Vicary's letter will make on you. It occurred to me afterwards that it wasn't as amusing as most of them, and burdened by the pranks of myself. Typical of my mood that I have only just remembered what this letter was to be about. I can't now put it well, but it is to the effect that you ought to drop your Catholic. I think the objection is even greater than in the case of Colin. If *you* were involved, that's another matter, but it's merely your (too stupid to find right words)—inquisitiveness and so to speak vanity that was involved, while him you may get into a most frightful casuistic tangle. Not to have confessed the 'certain difficulties' is I suppose a sin, and anything that from our point of view would be better, would be infinitely worse.

EMF

ALS: George Sassoon

¹ EMF was doing many reviews at this time for the *Daily News*; which is referred to here is unclear. Samuel Rogers (1763–1855) was banker, conversationalist, and poet. The remark was to Lady Davy, who exclaimed across the dinner-table, '"Mr. Rogers, I am sure you are talking about me." "Lady Davy," answered Rogers, "I pass my life in defending you."' (P. W. Clayden, *Samuel Rogers and His Contemporaries*, II, 129.
² He was writing a review of *Mary Olivier: A Life*, by May Sinclair; see 'A Moving Document', *Daily Herald*, 30 July 1919, p. 8.

³ He was trying to get on with *A Passage to India*.
⁴ Sassoon must have taken him to lunch at the Reform Club, of which he was a member.
⁵ He was feeling very hard up financially.

198   To Siegfried Sassoon

[N. p.   c. June 1919]

Dear Sassoon

I had no idea you were not intellectual.[1] I used to think I was not. Now I think I am. It makes of course not the least difference to one's enjoyment or one's insight or anything else. I was very sorry we hadn't a longer talk, though it would have meant my missing the talk of two ladies in the train, one of whom said to the other, with extreme elegance of diction, that Chu-Chin-Chow was not much of a piss.[2] Now I sit—I never know whether in idleness or dignity, but anyhow alone, reading the Diaries of Blunt.[3] I doubt your ever coming here. They cannot be helped, these things, and you mustn't let them or kindred things worry you. Use society until you think it's using you, when drop it. As to satire, for God's sake only write it if it amuses you or if savage indignation impels you: the satirical *habit* means slow death of the most ignoble kind.[4] I should have ~~said~~ thought that, once out of the army, you would have lost interest in satire.

Thanks for the ticket. I expect I shall see you on Tuesday. But, except as a bit o' fun, I care decreasingly about mass-life. Even when serious things are said it remains trivial, and that's why it is so seamed with scandal and gossip: people are meeting one another in a wrong medium. So don't let the gossiping worry you. Bit of a sermon this letter—but I shall never forget the two letters you wrote me in Egypt and how they wound me up and set me going when I was running down. So best wishes, keep well, don't spend too much money, break your appointments, catch your trains, play bat and ball, &ᶜᵗ &ᶜᵗ &ᶜᵗ.

EMForster

ALS: George Sassoon

[1] See Sassoon, in *Siegfried's Journey*, p. 170: 'I can remember saying self-defensively to E. M. Forster, "You *must* realize that I am *not* an intellectual." No doubt he was already aware of it, and my anxiety that he shouldn't consider me clever evidently amused him. . . .'
[2] *Chu-Chin-Chow*: the enormously long-running (2,238 performances) pseudo-Chinese musical comedy, which opened at His Majesty's Theatre, 31 August 1916.
[3] Wilfred Scawen Blunt (1840–1922), poet and traveller; Arabist and translator; flamboyant encourager of Indian, Irish, and Egyptian nationalist movements; breeder of Arabian horses. EMF was preparing to review Blunt's *My Diaries, Being a Personal Narrative of Events, 1888–1900*; see Letter 201. For Sassoon on Blunt, see his *Siegfried's Journey*, pp. 224–38.
[4] 'Savage indignation': allusion to Jonathan Swift's epitaph, written by himself, in St Patrick's Cathedral, Dublin: 'Ubi saeva indignatio ulterius cor lacerare nequit.'

199   To Hugh Walpole

Bagot, Mannamead, Plymouth[1]
5 July 1919

My dear Walpole
   Damn those people—oh look here—in the first place I don't want to be introduced at all; in the second place I don't want you to introduce me, for the reason that you are natu minor and the veteran business does, just here, come in I find: in the third place this is the first intimation I receive that Knopf decides to handle me!—I don't know terms, not even his address. I wrote off to Curtis Brown (hence delay in replying to you) and they reply that they know nothing definite. K. really should have communicated through them instead of waving you and me to each other.[2]
   Thank you for writing and for the way you wrote: I appreciate both, very much, and only hope this doesn't read too grotesque as a reply. No acknowledgment necessary—but later on do let's meet in town. I came back from Egypt at the beginning of the year—was there three years, sometimes bored, sometimes not: not bad years on the whole: any how I learnt how to use the telephone and how to swim.

Yours very sincerely
E. M. Forster

TTr supplied by Rupert Hart-Davis

[1] Address of EMF's great-aunt Eliza Fowler.
[2] Walpole had just written that Knopf wanted him to write an Introduction to the first American edition (1920) of *Where Angels Fear to Tread*. Neither Walpole's letter nor EMF's to Knopf survives, and EMF did not usually employ the literary agent Curtis Brown. However, a letter (10 November 1919) to the Society of Authors, of which he was a member and whose advice he requested regularly, indicates that these negotiations ended with Knopf's publishing only that one of EMF's novels—with no Introduction.

200   To G. H. Ludolf[1]

[N. p.]   16 July 1919

Dear Ludolf
   I see where the trouble lies. In attempting to be ornamental I fail to decant. For weeks I have been intending to write you a good letter, so haven't even turned out a poor one. This, whatever it is, shall go. But I really can't begin with the thanking—the list appalls me: well I'll select two only—thank you and Mrs Ludolf for going to the Observatory, and thank you and the Post Office for the *magnificent* map of the Serapeum.[2] Now I'll go on. All you've sent has been embodied. So we'll leave it. Then where are all your letters? They should be before me as I write. Chaos answers 'Where?' Oh wait a sec—here is one: No: it's dated 26–iii–19, and I really have

answered that. I'll try again—26-6-19 is better: indeed it must be the last—the Cairo–Menasce stunt—the fine programme for which brave men and beautiful women waited, while others did see Mr Wu.[3] I ought to describe my last concert in return. It was of Old Instruments (I wrote the Athenaeum a note on it)—Sassoon gave me a ticket which cost £1-1-0, and the audience reeked of scent in consequence and little feathers dripped from the brims of their hats, so that when they wanted to see the performer they had to part them and peer through like monkeys in the jungle and we all sat upon exquisite gilt chairs that were placed too near together and Countesses impinged upon duchesses, which does not do. The door was guarded by a tall exquisite young man with a flowing tie and a retreating chin, and when during the music the countesses got hot they trilled '*Please* open the door' but the duchesses countered with *Shut that door Shut that door* so backwards and forwards it went.—That was a day.[4] For I went on to the meeting of the American Sub Committee of the League of Nations, of which I am grotesquely a member, and then to the Russian Ballet.[5] It—the Ballet—has a delightful item called La Boutique Fantaste [*sic*]—a doll shop where the dolls not only come alive (their universal tendency on the stage) but smack all the spoilt children and purse-proud parents who have been trying to buy them. The music (taken from Rossini) is pas fameux, but does nicely to dance to. The Ballet—and perhaps Abraham Lincoln—are the only two performances in London of any note: awful tosh for the most part.[6]

I sound frivolous—but don't feel so particularly. In fact I feel worried and cricked. The class to which you and I belong is sliding into the abyss. Dispassionately (and dispassionate judgments are easier to make than is supposed) I can't feel it much matters, but a certain amount of precious stuff, a certain tradition of behaviour and culture will perish. People here—Sir T[heodore] & Lady Morison—duly distressed, fling themselves into good works of a conciliatory tendency in the hope of persuading Labour not to vote Labour. And Vicary, the only homme du peuple I know (I really know him) is also appalled at the subsidence. At Cambridge scarcely any one takes Classics—it's all Science. Salaries of Professors and Readers remain stationary while those of boiler-makers, plate rollers go up, are reaching them, passing them. There's nothing to be done—and as a matter of fact I do record my unenthusiastic vote for Labour, because, for the wrong reasons, it wants some of the right things, and having attained the right things, it may possibly adopt the right reasons. But it's so puzzling and queer to feel that one's the last little flower of a vanishing civilisation, so exasperating to know that one doesn't understand what is happening, so chilling to realise that in the future people probably won't mind whether they understand or not, and that this attempt to apprehend the universe through the senses and the mind is a luxury the next generation won't be able to afford. If one has had a good time and good luck as I have, one wants others to have it too, and this not from Christian piety but because one wishes sensations so exquisite to be repeated. But one cannot have a good time, or even good luck, without preparation and I don't see how the boiler makers &ᶜᵗ are to be prepared. All they are capable of is pleasure, and that (hear! hear!) cloys very soon i. e. becomes a habit like the boiler-making itself.—Yes, it's this business of keeping one's faculties alert that's in danger: disinterested alertness as opposed to practical.

But now I'll go to bed—adding more tomorrow if I want to, but anyhow posting

I thought I had £62 at the Bank and it is £26

I wish you were here.

I will finish this letter another day.

E.M.F.

ALS: KCC

[1] G. H. Ludolf (untraced) was an official in the Alexandria Post Office. He was either wholly or partially German and thus had to be inconspicuous there in wartime. He was not a member of EMF's clubs there; they met because Ludolf was a part-time 'searcher' in the hospitals. He was self-doubting and often ill but, EMF wrote to Lily, 'elderly and beautiful in body and mind', and he had a 'hard, good managing wife' (30 March 1918. KCC). EMF dedicated the first edition of his *Alexandria* to him, in gratitude for his great helpfulness in pursuing information and in negotiating with the publishers after EMF returned to England.

[2] The Temple of Serapis, a syncretic divinity, was said to be second in magnificence only to the Capitol in Rome. It contained a library that rivalled (or may have been part of) the famous Alexandrian library. Until destroyed by order of Theodosius in AD 389, it was the centre of pagan worship. See *Alexandria*, pp. 157–63.

[3] These allusions are unexplained.

[4] See [Forster] 'A Concert of Old Instruments', *The Athenaeum*, 11 July 1919, p. 597. Violet (Gwynne) Gordon Woodhouse (1872–1948) was one of the leaders in revival of interest in earlier keyboard music. At Queen Anne's Gate on 1 July 1919 she played Scarlatti and Bach, of which EMF wrote: 'She proved . . . that the harpsichord is as versatile as the piano, though in another way, and opened a new region for our hearts and brains.'

[5] A letter to Lily ([c. 1 July 1919]. KCC) apparently refers to this Committee: 'The League of Nations Committee was even worse than the first. Only one sensible remark was made in 1½ hours, and that by me. It is too trivial to transcribe.'

[6] The Diaghilev ballet, *La Boutique fantasque*, with music by Rossini-Respighi, choreography by Massine, and décor by Derain; at the Alhambra Theatre on 5 June 1919, with Lopokova and Massine dancing. John Drinkwater, *Abraham Lincoln* (1918): it opened at the Lyric Theatre, Hammersmith, with Irish actor William Rea (1884–1932) as Lincoln.

201   To G. H. Ludolf

[N. p.]   10 October 1919

Dear Ludolf

I don't know whether this will be a long letter or a short one, so will begin by essentials. The first is your leave. I am so delighted at the thought of seeing you next year. I am sure that, if we exist at all, we shall be much nicer then than we are now: and if we do not exist you will of course not come.—Then: only I write too late, probably. Captain Altounyan, an Armenian friend, will be in Alexandria for a few days this month and desires to look you up.—[1] Then there is a job I want you to do in Room 12 of the Museum, but I'll send details thereon from Weybridge.—And then there is a conversation that I want you to have before long with Mr Mann and which will probably proceed upon the following lines:—[2]

G.H.L. Forster says you can print away at the M.S.

Mr Mann —It's not here. It['s] in my heavy luggage, and hasn't arrived.

G.H.L. As soon as it arrives. And he is even more anxious that you should get to work on the big Alexandria map.

Mr Mann. Now that map'll take some thought. I haven't gone into it yet. He wants it printed in several colours and I didn't allow for this in the original estimate.

G.H.L. Oh but I think you did.

Mr Mann H'm?

G.H.L. You did.

Mr Mann Oh did I?

G.H.L. Yes. And you also allowed for several illustrations. But the final arrangement is that the book is to have no illustrations. Consequently the money saved can be expended on the maps. Forster thinks it most important that the maps & plans should be got up attractively and if possible in colours—

Mr Mann Yes, yes, he said so.

G.H.L. —because the casual purchaser opens a book of this sort to see if it is full of pictures. It won't be, but if his eye is caught by an attractive coloured map—

Mr Mann I've no wish to stint the book, I want to do the book well. I'll go into the matter of the map, but not just yet.

G.H.L. And can you send him drawings of the maps to correct?

Mr Mann Probably not. I'll see. I'll see.

G.H.L. Or in any case proofs, *And soon.*

Mann and I met just before he sailed. I tied the M.S. on to a borrowed bike and tottered up to London on it—middle of the strike, and I had scarcely bicycled for 4 years. Quite thrilling. Mann was very pleasant and gave me the advanced cheque.[3] I thank you for it!

Your letter's not with me as I write. I liked your epigrams— especially 'buried hopes....'. The 'overstudy' one you had written out in a shorter form on the R. Rolland you gave me.[4]

As regards Snelling I don't mind his republishing if he acknowledges source.[5] Can't you persuade him to take in the Athenaeum on the chance of picking up Alexandria bits? (Which I don't think he will from me as I have probably exhausted my little vein—except that I have in mind two articles on the Pharos).—I do mainly dramatic criticism now, under signature of P. I don't know if you twigged my style.—I am so glad that the article on old Willcocks pleased you: what an attractive cove![6]

My immediate excitement is a visit to Wilfrid Blunt—also the result of a review: of his Diaries which I did for the Nation. I thought he wouldn't either read it or like it, but he seems to have done both and has asked me to lunch at New Buildings next Monday. I am exceedingly curious. I will write again after I have been, as it may be of interest to Mrs Ludolf and to you to hear how he gets on. How I wish I had tried to see Lady Anne! I daresay Mrs Ludolf would have been kind enough to give me an introduction if I had asked her.[7]

Much has been happening lately to me and to my surroundings, but as you say it is almost impossible to write a letter that's both sincere and respectable. The most dramatic event was an invitation from the Foreign Office to govern Germany at a salary of £600 a year; plus billeting allowance. Though I share your high opinion of my administrative capacity, I was a little surprised. The obstacle was my mother who would again, and for an indefinite period, be left alone, so I refused the offer after three wretched weeks of indecision. I think I have done wrong, but I thought so at the time too, so don't exactly suffer from regret. I should have gone to Coblenz—something secretarial in the Inter Allied Commission. Of course my friends whom I have consulted think I was mad to pass the offer. I am certainly sorry for the Germans' sake, for I should have governed them very well.—Don't mention this: offer wasn't official, being from a friend—but Sir Harold whatever his name was would have had me to a cert, because his wife had liked my novels. Thus are things done.—The money I regret greatly. My attitude to it isn't yours: no body could ever give me too much, *I* feel.

I have other things to say, but they must wait for the next letter. I wish—(say once in three weeks)—you would post me an Egyptian Gazette, as I should enjoy just occasionally seeing familiar news. Pick me out a spicy number if it isn't a bother.

My mother & I are stopping with an invalid aunt near Dorking. Then we go to see more old people in the Isle of Wight. Life is not very cheerful—nor has it been, for we were at home for 3 weeks without maids, cistern, or kitchen fire. Mrs Borchgrevink popped down for an afternoon call in the middle of it. Now maids are back—one had had an operation the other a holiday—but cistern and kitchen fire still wander in the illimitable inane. Here all is comfort: but I am back in that coat of yours, for every morning there's a white frost.

My Indian friend is over, which has been pleasant.[8]

I'll conclude these scraps.
Laughed so much at your account of the tram strike.

EMF.

ALS: KCC

¹ Ernest Altounyan was in the Royal Army Medical Corps; thus a visit to Alexandria, a hospital centre, was not improbable.
² Mann was editor of the Alexandrian branch of Whitehead, Morris, publisher of EMF's *Alexandria*.
³ That is, to the London headquarters of Whitehead, Morris.
⁴ This was Romain Rolland's *Musiciens d'aujourd'hui* (KCC), inscribed by Ludolf, 'To the Head Searcher / from G.H.L. / "Tout homme est une énigme, non / Seulement pour les autres, mais pour / lui" / Before two people have learnt to / understand each other, one of them is / usually suffering from over-study. G.H.L.' The French quotation, from Vincent D'Indy, is on p. 118.
⁵ Snelling is unidentified; he may have been the editor of an Alexandrian journal.
⁶ On the Pharos articles, see Letter 202. 'Article . . . Willcocks': EMF reviewed *The Nile Projects* (1919), by Sir William Willcocks (1852–1932), who had directed public works in India and Egypt since 1872; in 1898 he designed the Aswan Dam. This review, 'A Flood in the Office' (*The Athenaeum*, 8 August 1919, pp. 717–18), was to cause EMF enormous trouble. In his book, Sir William attacked not only the Nile-control plans but the integrity of another expert, Sir Murdoch MacDonald (1866–1957). EMF, commenting on charges of doctored designs, wrote, among other pointed comments, 'What led Sir Murdoch on this path of crime?' Sir Murdoch sued for libel when the review was reprinted in *Abinger Harvest* in 1936 (pp. 278–81). EMF made a financial and editorial settlement.
⁷ Blunt liked EMF's review of his *Diaries* (See Letter 198); see 'Gog and Magog', *The Nation*, 25 (1919), 479–80. Newbuildings Place was one of three Sussex estates in Blunt's family, and his final home. Lady Anne King-Noel Blunt, Baroness Wentworth (1837–1917), Byron's granddaughter, married Blunt in 1869. In later years they lived apart, and Lady Anne took up residence in Egypt, so that it is not unlikely that Mrs Ludolf had met her.
⁸ Masood was in England during the Peace Conference. On EMF's suggestion, Masood called on Blunt 'in search of wisdom and inspiration' (Elizabeth Longford, *A Pilgrimage of Passion: The Life of Wilfred Scawen Blunt*, p. 417).

202 To G. H. Ludolf

[N. p.   After 4 November 1919]

Dear Ludolf

I have so much to say and to answer, but as I write neither of your two welcome letters are before me. What's foremost in my mind is your health. I feel grateful to you for having written about it so freely. I won't detail fears—condolances [*sic*] still less—but I do beg you to follow doctor's orders as far as is practicable. I think the regularity of your life must be telling on you—it would on me and on any one who had not led a regular life from the first. It must be different for those who trooped quietly into an office when young. I know that holidays are more important to you than most men. It is distressing that you cannot have them in abundance and in all parts of the world. Have you still this funny illusion of not being 'worth' what you get?

E. Alt[ounyan]. I didn't write about him as soon as I said I did. However he is one who is his own herald—auto-angelistic, to coin another of the words that are giving a semi-scientific flavour to our modern prose. It was very good of you to ask him to tea. Fancy him launching out upon his novel! Europe, also, is bored to tears with the same. He has been flinging it at our heads for 4 years now until I am quite incapable of judging it critically. Good in some ways it undoubtedly is, but not the faultless transcendental masterpiece he asserts. I wish he'd get on with it more and talk about it less.

These long lines must be maddening for the eye. I will take stringent measures and shorten them. About Blunt.[1] Intervening influenza may have dimmed my literary graces, but I will tell you what I can—beginning with the strange cavalcade that met us in the woods as we drove from the station; a man leading a large brown horse which drew a sort of stretcher-perambulator attended by another man behind, by a lady assistant on the right, and by a little dog on the left. W.S.B., as you have already guessed, lay in the perambulator, and ordered it to emit a camp stool, on which I sat down and wondered what on earth I should say. We were now all motionless in the middle of a cold glade. I said something about the Wady Natrun, hoping to draw his reminiscences.[2] Didn't. But he began to talk about Francis Thompson instead, and was most pleasant and friendly.[3] I knew that I should find him impressive, but I also liked him, and more than I expected. He can walk now—weird sight to see him extend ~~his~~ feet shod in slippers of camel's hair and slowly ascend the steps of New Buildings (date 1685). We dined in a strange mixture of the baronial and the oriental. Along one side of the room was an ugly (I must say it!) Morris Tapestry of Botticelli's Spring, beneath which, on a long dais, lay some beautiful Persian and Arabic M.S.[4] The other side of the room was a copy, by himself, of a Tintoretto—so good that I thought it was an original. Our food was pheasants, baronial beef, and boiled potatoes which I caught the lady-assistant surreptitiously tapping, in order that she might get the best (the sort of thing I do see at great moments). We fared deliciously but poor Blunt had an attack, I think from the cold, and had to leave his chair by the fire and go to bed. It was there that I saw him last, more impressive than ever, in a huge carved bedstead, from whose canopy depended an ostrich egg and bunches of everlasting flowers. He was covered by some rare silk quilt. Pulling himself together he delivered a little speech about the happiness of men, destroyed by European industrialism—the speech of a vanishing age. Then he asked me to come and stop for a weekend next summer *if* he was alive: I do not think he minds death in the least. No doubt he is vain and intractable, but it is much to have staged oneself so perfectly. I made a little speech too, about the honour in which he is still held by the young generations of Indians and Egyptians—(I have been seeing something of orientals since I have been back.) The atmosphere seemed to demand speeches—indeed I made mine a second time to the lady-assistant downstairs. Then the carriage drove me away. I had only been for two hours at the house, but they were memorable ones. I don't gather that he has any Faith—he has wobbled so much over this all through his life, and I doubt, when one is so old, whether the absence or the presence of Faith can make any difference in oneself.

The newspapers you have sent are of the greatest interest and indeed value, for one scarcely hears anything about Egypt over here—I suppose because no one thinks it's news worth telling since I think there are now no censor restrictions. The latest in date that I have received are Nov. 4th—arrived this morning. I hope—in a way—that they will, in the future, never be so interesting: still if they are I shall be most grateful for an occasional specimen. ——Thank you, too, for so promptly interviewing Mann and for your hint as to his advertising schemes. I am writing diplomatically and pointing out that he cannot expect any English Publisher to disseminate my statements and those of Dr Garbola at the same time:[5] I mentioned my book to Arnold (my English publisher) and he at once asked "But will it be got up decently?"—I hope to enclose the Room 12 stuff—thank you so much about that too.[6]——As for my present work, I make efforts to start something 'real' but with no great success, and I don't know that I am justified in ~~blaming~~ laying my failure to the war. I have been under par some time—so damned nervous and cross—and for a period could do no writing at all, not even reviewing, but that is over. For the moment I am in bed, trying to get rid of a harmless ⟨doctor's verdict⟩ cough, the legacy of influenzinetta. I feel all right in myself and eat and drink tons. Next week I hope to go to Edinburgh and sit by a gas stove for a month—my great friends the Bargers have gone there, he as Professor.[7] Last week I was in London, stopping with Murry (editor of the Athenaeum) a very charming and intelligent young man. I am doing him 3 articles on Pharos.[8]—By the way, could you send me any addresses of people who are likely to subscribe to the Ath? If any occur to you, jot them down, and then Murry sends a dainty booklet and a specimen number that sometimes lands its fish.

Would you like me to lend you books ever—I could easily post them out. I don't know how much you are in their way now.

Best remembrances to Mrs Ludolf.

E.M.F.

White coat being renovated for Edinburgh. Pencil lost out of Pocket Book, but replaced successfully by one of a bright lemon hue.

ALS: KCC

[1] On EMF and Wilfrid Scawen Blunt, see Letters 198, 201.
[2] Wadi Natrun: a valley of lakes with four Coptic monasteries among them, in the Western

Desert between Cairo and Alexandria. Blunt visited them in 1893 and 1897, EMF in June 1918.
³ The English poet cared for, after he became a drug addict, by the Meynells; see Letter 140.
⁴ Two tapestries designed by Burne-Jones and made by the Morris firm—'Visit of the Magi' and 'Primavera'—still hang at Newbuildings Place.
⁵ Dr Garbola: unidentified.
⁶ Contents of (sculpture) Room 12 in the Greco-Roman museum in Alexandria.
⁷ George Barger had become Professor of Chemistry in Relation to Medicine, University of Edinburgh, a post he held until 1937.
⁸ John Middleton Murry (1889–1957), the critic, husband of Katherine Mansfield; editor of *The Athenaeum*, 1919–21. This greatest of the Victorian literary weeklies, which had become a monthly, under Murry again became a weekly. In February 1921 it merged with *The Nation*. EMF's articles, 'Pharos', appeared in issues of 28 November, 5 and 12 December, 1919, pp. 1250–1, 1282–3, 1330–1.

203   To Florence Barger

[N. p.]   6 November 1919

Dearest Florence,

I am certainly better and have turned out a column for the Daily News—first work for a month.¹ I think I will come to you about the 20ᵗʰ—that is the day Masood sails for India and I want to hang about while he is to be seen. He has been a dear. Just now I am full of excitement at the news from Egypt—or rather at The Times' attitude to it. Valentine Chirol—an old Anglo-Indian reactionary hack—is writing a series of articles saying that the Egyptians *must* ~~have~~ be given self-government.² Quite amazing. And Cameron—ex-consul at Alexandria—chips in with a revolutionary letter saying that we had better make Zaglorul Prime Minister. Evidently the powers that be have the wind up and it looks almost certain that the ill-omened Milner commission will not sail: the entire Egyptian Government has threatened to go on strike the moment it lands.³ I have been asked—via Woolf—to prepare a memorandum on Egypt for the Labour Party: he is particularly anxious I should, the alternative being Haden Guest!⁴ (I have not yet decided—so this is private still: the other public parts of my letter are not). Meanwhile I get the Egyptian Gazette of Oct. 27 containing terrific details of the then rioting at Alexandria, which has doubtless been exceeded by the rioting of the last two days.⁵ Woolf—like Masood with his knowledge of the East—thinks that the whole of Egypt is out of hand.

Old Furness keeps silence. Bennett, on the other hand has written a most affectionate and beautiful letter.⁶ I never dreamt he had so much in him or that if he had he would give it to me. He has been trying—during another brief visit to Cairo—to get to Mansurah, but failed since he could not leave his sister. He asks me to take the will for the deed, which assuredly I do. He says it is a pleasure to do any thing for me who have done so much for him, which moves me very deeply as I can't remember any thing I've done for him. I do think it's fine of him since owing to his Christianity and general etherialism he cannot entirely approve.—From M. a more cheerful letter, cursing me about Germany. "Not to go was silliness."[7]

I do not see the M[anchester] G[uardian]. Please send me a copy of your letter if it's published. I am glad the poor thing is dead and that in the face of so much difficulty, you paid that visit to her—I am delighted with the scraps about the children. I suppose their school is no stupider than most, but certainly education doesn't seem to have taken the strides since my day that it is supposed to have taken.

I slept last night at the Woolfs. Sidney Waterlow came to dinner, full of boyish delight at the various expeditions that he is making, in special trains, to all the capitals of Europe for the promotion of international amity. Woolf hissed 'Ridiculous' and poor Sidney collapsed—Virginia's novel is interesting.[8] I will lend it you. Mother wonders whether my clothes are good enough for Edinburgh. She seems to think I shall spend my visit closeted with Lady Ewing.[9]

I have heard from Hugh, much upset at the death of that unattractive R. T. Martin.[10] He is very nervous I think—easily touched by the sepulchral.

ALU: KCC

[1] Forster, 'The End of the Samovar', *Daily News*, 11 November 1919, p. 5. Review of Dostoievsky, *An Honest Thief and Other Stories*, trans. Constance Garnett.
[2] Valentine Chirol, 'The Egyptian Peril', eleven articles in *The Times*, 5 November–8 December 1919.
[3] Donald Andreas Cameron (1856–1936) was Consul-General at Port Said, 1905–9, and at Alexandria, 1901–9. His letter: 'Our Interests in Egypt', *The Times*, 6 November 1919, p. 11. Pasha Saad Zaghlul (c. 1860–1927), Egyptian statesman and patriot, led the Nationalist Party in the early 1900s. He came of peasant stock but obtained a law degree at the Muslim University of Al Azhar, Cairo, and became a judge in a native court of appeal. He held posts as Minister of Education and of Justice and in 1913 became Vice-President of a chamber set up under a new constitution, in which he counselled moderation during the war. After the Armistice, he asked for freedom for Egypt and an alliance with England, but he was refused permission in London, to travel to London to present the Egyptian case, since Lord Curzon remained implacably opposed to Egyptian self-determination. Zaghlul was deported to Malta in March 1919. The Commission under Lord Milner (1854–1925), Secretary of State for the Colonies from 1919–25, urged that Zaghlul have a hearing, but negotiations collapsed, and disorders broke out in Egypt.
[4] EMF contributed the historical section to *The Government of Egypt* (1921), published by the Labour Research Department of the Fabian Society. Leslie Haden Haden Guest, 1st Baron Haden-Guest (1877–1960), writer on political and social subjects, and a theosophist; physician and liberal MP.
[5] 'The Alexandria Riots', *The Egyptian Gazette*, 27 October 1919, p. 3: rioting lasted for two days, Government buildings were assaulted, and 60 cavalry and 250 infantry had to be sent in. The rioters seem to have been less than unified in motivation: some were protesting the Milner investigation, others, the presence of British troops.
[6] Edwin Keppel ('Francis') Bennett (1887–1958), as a student at the Working Men's College, met EMF there and went up to Cambridge on a fellowship endowed by G. M. Trevelyan. He became a Fellow of Caius and an expert on the German *Novelle*, and a friend of EMF's old age.
[7] This letter is not among those transcribed by EMF (KCC).
[8] Virginia Woolf, *Night and Day* (1919).

9 Lady Ellen Ewing, wife of Sir (James) Alfred Ewing (1885–1935), Principal and Vice-Chancellor of the University of Edinburgh, 1916–29.
10 R. T. Martin is unidentified: apparently a friend of Meredith.

204   To Robert Trevelyan

[N. p.]   23 February 1920

Dear Bob,

I am very glad to hear that you contemplate a novel. I was about to write and urge you up to it.[1] Your bothers distressed me the more because they were so like my own—though on the face of it the man who has never written a novel is in a better position than the novelist who can't write one. Did you read, and having read admire, Norman Douglas' *South Wind*? That, and Gide's *Les Caves du Vatican*, strike me as a possible line of development.[2] I see no end (in both senses of the word) to realistic stuff. All the same I advise you to try to be realistic.

I will send you and Bessie the unpublished thing when I get done, but I must ask you both first to promise that you will not mention it to anyone—except of course to Goldie. My reason for this solemnity [*sic*] request is purely practical. I do not want news to get into quarters where it may do me harm. As it is, it's known of where I would much rather it was not known.[3] I re-read it lately, with less approval than I expected. Parts are good, and I like the style, but there are grave faults some of which I may alter some day. I can't imagine it being useful to you! though I hope you may like it.

I had a funny day in London Friday—I forget whether I told you: I have written a memorandum on Egypt for the Labour Party. This entailed a pleasant tête-à-tête with Woolf and Shaw.[4]

The Agnews, who live at my aunt's feet, came to tea with us. I liked him. He evidently flies his Union Jack with a difference.[5]

Yesterday I had tea at the House of the Lord.[6]

It was so nice seeing you, but I forgot to say so much. I have been seeing Tovey *and* Miss W. at Edinburgh. Golly she is a proposition.[7]

Mother is reading 'The Arrow of Lead' as she calls it, and finds it very slow.[8]

Yours affectionately
Morgan

I go home tomorrow.

ALS: TCC

1 Trevelyan often though of writing prose, when he got stuck in a poem, but he never wrote a novel.
2 Douglas, *South Wind*: see Letter 180. André Gide, *Les caves du Vatican* (1914).
3 'Unpublished thing': *Maurice*. 'Quarters . . . harm': possibly Garsington Manor, with its

free-flowing gossip, and Lady Ottoline Morrell's impulsive manipulations of her friends' friendships.
⁴ *The Government of Egypt*: see Letter 203.
⁵ Neighbours of Laura Forster, thus also near neighbours of the Trevelyans.
⁶ Perhaps the House of Lords, in connection with a proposed Foreign Office job.
⁷ Sir Donald Francis Tovey (1875–1940), composer, pianist, musicologist; Reid Professor of Music at Edinburgh University, 1914–20; knighted in 1935. He and Trevelyan had been friends since 1905 and were at work on an opera, *The Bride of Dionysus*. Miss W: Sophie Weisse, the teacher who supervised Tovey's early musical education and involved herself in his career thereafter.
⁸ Lily's mischievous version of Joseph Conrad's *The Arrow of Gold: A Story between Two Notes* (1919).

205 To Florence Barger

[N. p.]   18 March 1920

Dearest Florence

Thank you so much for your letter—I've meant to write for so long and it's the more remiss of me because for the last month life has been more tolerable and my health more than tolerable—very good indeed: I haven't felt so fit for a long time. Now I will throw you some mean scraps of news. The Egyptian you will find enclosed—as you see it is very agreeable. I've also had a new photo of M. taken at Alexandria. He looks hideous and cheerful. The pamphlet has Bernard Shaw's corrections, which may interest you. He was very complimentary about it. It procured me a dam fine dinner too (oysters!) last night: dinner given by Langdon Davies to Zaglorul's secretary who made a pleasant little speech.¹ I have been away five days—a night with the Woolfs, then a week end at Cambridge with Maynard Keynes, then two more nights with the Woolfs, and have seen such a whirl of people and of their sorrows, joys, and plans, that I cannot begin to describe it to you. *But important point.* Sydney, point blank, has suggested that I should become a permanent official at the Foreign Office, where he has a post for me. I know no details yet. But would like your opinion. All the aesthetic push are against it, and so, a little to my surprise, is mother. It is, from the worldly aspect, a tremendous but a cavernous opening. I expect to see Sydney tomorrow and shall tell him I can't decide without hearing from you. If I was certain of writing more books I shouldn't consider it for an instant. I will tell you more when I know more. My immediate job is Literary Editorship of the Daily Herald. I have taken it on for a couple of months, until Sassoon returns. They give me £5 for 1½ days work (it works out thus) and seem polite and pleasant—Meynell, Gould, Ewer—that crowd.²—On I pour. I have lent, owing to his importunacy, *Maurice* to Bob Trevy and his wife, and have received from her a very fine and encouraging letter which has ~~encourage~~ inspirited me much. It's a comfort to feel one has done something, though it is (and ought to be) but a passing comfort.

Blackwood's have been so tiresome about the books. They are all here! that's the end of a long story. And twice too many of them, what's more!—24 copies in all instead of 12! I'm sending ½ back. You shall have yours when you come. For heaven's sake don't let them dump any on you, or I shall have to pay for them likewise.[3]

It was nice having your sister. But I won't begin on your affairs this time. I wanted to get these accumulations off my chest.

I go this week end to the Clutton Brock's.

It will be lovely seeing you.

Morgan

ALS: KCC

[1] G. B. Shaw wrote complimentary annotations in his copy of EMF's pamphlet.

On Zaghlul's negotiations with the British Government on behalf of Egypt, see Letter 202. In June 1920 Milner's group returned to England and Zaghlul was invited to come to London, but his efforts collapsed again; Lord Curzon tried to negotiate a settlement with the Egyptian Prime Minister, but it was evident that Zaghlul was the man with an Egyptian following.

[2] Francis Meynell (1881–1975) was the son of Wilfrid and Alice Meynell. He joined the staff of the *Daily Herald* in 1917, but his real interests were with the Pelican Press, which he started in 1916, and the very distinguished Nonesuch Press, which he established in 1923. He became Royal Designer for Industry, and Honorary Typographical Adviser to H. M. Stationery Office in 1945. He was knighted in 1946. Gerald Gould (1885–1936) was a miscellaneous writer and poet. William Norman Ewer (1855–19??), author of numerous books on international relations.

[3] Probably a delivery of the American edition of *Where Angels Fear to Tread*, published by Knopf and sent via Blackwood, the English publisher; cf. Letter 199.

206   To Siegfried Sassoon

Weybridge.   11 October 1920

Dear S— I re-read the story you returned, and found it better than I remembered, owing to your appro[bation] perhaps.[1] I am awfully glad you liked the latter part, as I was doubtful about it, and I wish I had asked you some more questions—e. g. at what moment, after first he appeared, did you get 'suspicious' of Alec; I meant him gradually to invade the scene, and it would be interesting to know at what moment he strikes the reader's consciousness. Also whether the crescendo-fortissimo of his arrival up the ladder, and the subsequent dialogue is well contrived. I took much trouble over these, frequently re-writing them. Nothing is more obdurate to artistic treatment than the carnal, but it has got to be got in I'm sure: everything has got to be got in. I can lend you some short stories one day, if you like: they are less reputable than what you have seen, also unlike it, but they purport to be literature.[2] I am glad I have got this stuff off my chest. It is done as well as I can do it, and I know nobody else who has done it, though possibly the real right thing, shaming our clumsy efforts, lies buried in a hundred drawers. I much hope you will finish what you have begun: it's among the few things I have cared for.

Disquisition on asceticism was to have concluded this letter. Point being that it can get things the other line of conduct can't, though it has to drop things as well. Which is 'better' is to my mind a most uninteresting question: what I want is a survey of the two respective fields. Science can't give it because she stumbles off into sublimations and repressions, and misses the quality and intensity of the emotion, which (however produced) is the real index of a man's merit. Asiatics live by emotion just as much as do their opponents.

Yours
EMF

ALS: George Sassoon

[1] I.e. *Maurice*.

[2] These are undoubtedly the stories he destroyed in 1922. He began writing them in 1911, then felt that they were getting in the way of his finishing *A Passage to India*. After it was completed, he began to rewrite some of the same stories and added one or two new ones. At the same time, he began to write some quite serious unpublishable stories on homosexual themes. In later years there were one or two further siftings of the 'indecent stories'.

207 To Florence Barger

[N. p.]   10 November 1920

Dearest Florence

What a pleasure to hear from you: the nicer side of Egypt was recalled by your handwriting. I have been meaning to write for some time to give you news more intimate than mother can transmit.

Not that I have any. Ludolf is a dear fellow, but so utterly uncomprehending that I could not tell him about M., nor could I see how to allude to M. as if he were an ordinary acquaintance, whom I sought to benefit. I don't think he could have done any thing, as a matter of fact, moreover my cowardice is palliated by somewhat better news from my beloved friend: he writes more cheerfully and is learning typing and shorthand. Furness' behaviour has perhaps rather shaken my nerve for asking favours. Not a line since I detailed the case in August. M⁰ˢ Borchgrevink asked me if I had heard from him on the matter (when I saw her in town last month): I replied I hadn't. She hadn't either.

Did I tell you (oh I can't have) that Antonius lost his hair over my Egyptian Pamphlet, said it was inaccurate and misleading and would do the Labour Party much harm! Ludolf entirely disagrees. But he regards Antonius as a serious and rather sinister figure who may raise the wind against me in Egypt. If the Milner negotiations come off it will do me no harm, but if they go away—and recent rumours are not favourable—and the British continue to camp in Egypt by force, Ludolf thinks it very likely that I should be refused a pass-port to the country.[1] I wrote the pamphlet for the sake of Mohammed and his sufferings and with my eyes open to such possibilities as this, so I do not feel that I have been tricked or done in. Antonius is very pleasant and clever, but a born intriguer, and fully aware that his job, whether as censor or any thing else, would disappear if the Milner report—let alone my Pamphlet!—was adopted. The Syrians in Egypt, like the Armenians there, only retain their footing as jackals to the British: when we go they will go, and with less dignity. Ludolf—who dislikes them and likes the Egyptians—was illuminating and copious on this point, which I had only apprehended dimly. He says that they live by making mischief and are greatly responsible for our unpopularity. And Antonius' remarks about the Egyptians to me were all part of an elaborate denigration, even when in isolation they seemed appreciative. It is bad that he is in with the Milner people, to whom—such is the trend of events!—one now looks in hope. If the Report passes Parliament he will be dumped back in to Syria, where he doesn't want to be for nuts. God damn those Oriental Christians! I understand why Turks cut their throats.

Mother's energy and good spirits are amazing. I think she may bring them on by an effort, but they seem sincere when brought on. I was going to London today, partly to lunch with E. V. Thompson and suggested at the last moment she should come too. Would you believe me, she jumped at it, had her hair done at Douglas', bought some blankets at Gamages, met us for the lunch and was all animation, and then went to a Pachmann Concert with me, and rushed up when the program was over to hear the encores that are habitual in these displays.[2] We sat close under Pachmann's nose and he seemed delighted to see us, nodding and making remarks in a variety of languages. His madness is not offensive—rather a dear old happy man I thought and his playing quite exquisite, the only defect being a lack of force which doubtless proceeds from age. I should hear him again if I got the chance. Life lately has been an orgy of concerts, the plums being the César Franck Symphony (conducted by Coates) Schumann's Kreisleriana (played by Fanny Davies) Bach's Chromatic Fantasia and some Preludes (Siloti), and a Rachmaninoff Piano Concerto (Cortot). Golly how bad the English composers are—such as we heard.[3] Elgar's Cockayne Overture was the worst; and a dry sour scrapy quartette by Ethel Smythe: and another overture by the aged Sir Villiers Stanford called 'The Travelling Companion' which is the title of some thing by Anstey so I based my hopes accordingly, but no, it was all that is drear, about some one who rose from the Tomb, and Stanford, when he came on for the applause, looked as if he had done the same.[4]

I want to finish this before turning in, so will pass to practical matters. I think I won't come north this year, the ~~more~~ less so as I shall have the happiness of seeing you in January. Do manage to tack on some holidays at the end of your work.

Christabel doesn't discredit education to me, but oh how she proves that 'education' is pernicious unless blended with sympathy and common sense! Those unhappy children—how they should wish that their mother had never heard of Froebel or whatever his name was! The Darling children, who have been brought up on no system whatsoever and by a mother of questionable morality, will have ten times their chance. What a mercy that Carol can still care to go to them.[5] She is the only visitor to the household; when I go I just see Hugh. You certainly shouldn't go, as I hope George agrees. Your own health and comfort apart, you can do far more good to them by occasionally enticing a twin over into your own family, and warming it in the happiness they generate. Oh what a scene! Old M[rs] Meredith within and Black & Tans without.[6] Mother wishes they would…I had better not detail what mother wishes.

I have never seen Coq d'Or.[7] What fun it must be! What an ass R. is—probably no more: mere ill breeding. Or does George still suspect the Two Bedsteads? M[r] W. (to pursue such themes) is a more serious nuisance. How glad I am that you have got into sane relationship with the T.s. How pleasant it all sounds.

I am putting this letter into an envelope that was once handled by your eldest offspring. Does he remember the circumstances? Give him and the others my love.

Dear me, there is much I haven't told you. I had such a delightful and instructive week end with Frank Vicary at Ramsgate. He was, as I expected, a perfect host, so gay and calm. We sat about in shirt sleeves and loafed at street corners talking to other miners, also went to a party where the host (a miner) played Scriabine, Grieg, &[ct]—with no great charm, but with thunderous execution. I liked the miners personally, but could not see that they were after anything but money of which (if you compare them with the other manual labourers and even make allowance for the special discomfort and risk) they have already their fair share, I think. Sentimentally I am on their side, but my intellect argues that clerks, university teachers &ct, are really the oppressed class today.

Well good night really now.

Morgan.

Young Indian artist (one Mukul Chandra Dey) comes this week end.[8] Monday mother restarts her gallivant, going for three days to M[rs] Mawe and seeing The Beggars Opera and I know not what else.

ALS: KCC

[1] On the Milner Commission, see Letters 203, 205.

2 Vladimir von Pachmann (1848–1933), Russian pianist known for his Chopin performances and for his eccentric behaviour.

3 Albert Coates (1882–1953), English composer and conductor. Fanny Davies (1861–1934), English pianist, one of the last in the 'Clara Schumann tradition', according to *Grove's Dictionary*. Alexander Il'ych Siloti (Ziloti) (1863–1945) was a Ukrainian pianist and conductor who emigrated first to England, then settled in New York in 1922 and began teaching at the Juilliard School in 1924, becoming one of its famous elders during his two decades there. Alfred Cortot (1877–1962), the well-known French pianist.

4 Dame Ethel Smyth (1858–1944), English composer whose String Quartette was composed between 1902 and 1912. *The Travelling Companion* (1919), by Sir Charles Villiers Stanford (1852–1924) is an opera with libretto by Henry Newbolt, after Hans Andersen. It had its first performance in Bristol in 1926; EMF was hearing an experimental performance of excerpts. Frederick Anstey (Thomas Anstey Guthrie, 1856–1934), humorous writer, published *The Travelling Companions: A Story in Scenes* (1892), reprinted from *Punch*.

5 Friedrich Froebel (1782–1852), German educationalist, founded the kindergarten movement, which spread rapidly in England after 1851. Caroline Cassandra Graveson (1874–1958) was Vice-Principal of Goldsmiths' College—'on the women's side'—from 1905 until 1934. She was at one time engaged to H. O. Meredith.

6 The Black and Tans were an auxiliary constabulary recruited in 1920 to combat the Irish Republican Army: so called because they wore army uniforms, with black berets.

7 Rimsky-Korsakoff's opera, *The Golden Cockerel* (1906), was first performed in 1909 in Moscow.

8 Mukul Chandra Dey (1895–) was in London as one of a group of Indian art students to be trained in mural-painting under William Rothenstein's direction at the Royal College of Art, the intention being a contribution toward Indian-ness in the decoration of the new Government buildings at New Delhi. Unfortunately, the plan fell foul of disagreements between the architects about the place of decoration with respect to architectural forms, and the students did only token work.

INDEX

Numbers in *italics* indicate a letter or letters from EMF
to the person concerned.

Adl, Mohammed *see* el Adl,
  Mohammed
Abbey Theatre Players 136
Abercrombie, Lascelles; work
  by 128
Abinger Hall 2, 14
Abinger Hammer 1
Abraham Lincoln (Drinkwater)
  305, 306
'Abt Vogler' (Browning) 96
Acton House 31, 32
*Adventures of Elizabeth in
  Rügen, The* (Arnim, E. von)
  81, 82
Aeneid of Virgil, The (ed. EMF)
  69, 72
Agarwalla 186, 201
Agnes: *see* Dowland, Agnes
Agra, described 161
Ajanta Caves 137
Akbar 145
Aksanov, S. T.; works by 283,
  284
Aldington, Richard 220
Alessandro Scarlatti (Dent) 47,
  48, 55
Alexandria, Alexandrian x-xi,
  205–6, 231; EMF in 232–
  300 *passim*; rioting in 312,
  313
Alexandria Museum 312
'Alexandria Riots, The' (news
  report) 313
Alford, Georgiana 11–12
Alford, Robert 11–12
Alford, Rosalie (Whichelo;
  EMF's aunt) 1, 3, 12, 18,
  82, 101, 102, 148, 213
Ali, Mohammed 144, 145, 152

Ali, Shaukat 145
Aligarh 88, 132, 137, 141–3, 145
Aligarh Anglo-Oriental College
  42, 88, 145
Aligarh Muslim University 88,
  137
Allahabad, described 174–5;
  'Bathing Fair' at 188–90
Allen, Hugh 49
Allen, Mrs 49
All Is One (Holmes) 301
Altounyan, Ernest 218, 219, 220,
  221, 224, 271, 307, 309–10;
  novel by 310
Ambassadors, The (H. James)
  240
Amritsar Massacre x, 98, 194
Anastassiades, Pericles 205,
  234–5, 295–6
Andersen, Hans Christian 320
Andes Mountains, described 128
Angelico, Fra 109
Ansari, M. A. 137, 141, 143,
  144, 145, 149
Ansell 4, 17
Anstey, Frederick (pseud. of
  Guthrie, T. A.); work by
  318, 320
Antiquary, The 26, 27
Antonius, George 205, 232, 233,
  235, 267, 317
Apostles (Society) 15–16, 64, 238
Apostololopoulos, Kyros 266,
  267
Apprentice to Power (Darling) 98
April Baby's Book of Tunes, The
  (von Arnim, E.) 73
Arab Awakening, The
  (Antonius) 233

Arabian Nights, The 121, 281
Archer, William 166, 167
Aristophanes 13, 92
Armenians, in Egypt 318
Armour, W. S. 175–6, 179
Arnim-Schlagentin, Beatrix von
    65, 66, 70
Arnim-Schlagentin, Elizabeth
    von (Countess) ix, 41–2, 65,
    67–8, 72, 73, 74–6; works
    by 42, 65–6, 70–71, 73, 81,
    82
Arnim-Schlagentin, Evi von 65,
    66, 67, 70
Arnim-Schlagentin, Felicitas von
    66
Arnim-Schlagentin, Henning
    von (Count) 65, 66, 72,
    74–6, 78
Arnim-Schlagintin, Henning
    Bernt von 66
Arnim-Schlagentin, Liebet von
    65, 66, 67, 68, 70, 72
Arnold, Edward (publisher) 106,
    221, 311
Arnold, Matthew viii, 89, 90,
    111, 112, 113, 116
Arnold, Thomas 89, 90
Arrow of Gold, The (Conrad)
    314, 315
Arya Samaj 156; College
    (Hardwar) 167
Asiatic Studies (Lyall) 120, 121
Asquith, H. H. 116
Aswan Dam 309
Athanasius, Saint 234, 245, 246
Athenaeum, The (London) 305,
    312
Atlantis 293
Au-dessus de la Melée (Rolland)
    226, 228
Augustus, Emperor 78
Austen, Jane 23, 24; works by
    24, 76, 78
Autobiographies, The (Gibbon)
    26, 27, 107, 268
Autobiography, The (Dickinson)
    157
Autobiography, The (D. Tagore)

227, 228
Ave (G. Moore) 128
Aylward, Mary Maria ('Maimie')
    1, *3–4*, 45–6, 59, 87–8, 115,
    122, 131, *141–3*, 148, 157,
    176, 184, 187, 242, 267, 270;
    death of 270, 271–2
Aylward, W. P. 3, 4

Bach, J. S. 306, 318
Backe, Fräulein 71, 72, 73, 75,
    76, 82
Baedeker xviii
Baillie, Mr 6
Balben, L. Auger de 65, 66, 67,
    70, 72, 73, 75
Baldeo 151, 155, 160, 162, 163,
    170, 174, 184, 196, 197, 202
Balfour, J. A. 226–7, 228; letter
    by 226, 228
Balkan War (1912) 143, 147, 152
Bamburgh Castle 31–2
Bangor (Ireland) 224
Bankipore 88, 137–8; described
    179–83
Bapu Sahib: *see* Dewas Senior,
    Maharaja of
Barabar Hills 138; described
    183–4
Barcroft, Joseph 43, 44
Barger, Evert 140, 147, 256, 261,
    264, 268, 274, 287, 291, 297
Barger, Florence xiv, *139–41*,
    145–8, 188, *209–10*, *218–19*,
    223, *229–30*, *235–6*, *243–6*,
    256–9, *260–5*, *267–9*, *270–5*,
    280–2, *284–9*, *290–2*, *296–8*,
    299–300, *312–14*, *315–16*,
    317–20
Barger, George 31, 40, 140, 218,
    223, 244, 245, *254–6*, 259,
    262, 264, 286, 312, 319, 320
Barger, Harold 140, 147, 176,
    179, 230, 245, 256, 268, 274,
    285, 287, 291
Barger, Margaret 140, 245, 268,
    274
Barrie, J. M. 52
Bashahr 110, 108–9, 114, 123

Basileon (*Basileona*, Cambridge) 15, 49
Baudelaire, Charles; work by 101
Baveno 106
Beaumont, Francis, and Fletcher, John; works by 61, 63
Beautiful Wales (Thomas) 283, 284
Beerbohm, Max; work by 128
Beethoven, Ludwig von; works by 16, 17, 28, 213, 274, 287
Begbie, E. F.; work by 17–18
Beggar's Opera, The (Gay) 319
Belfast xiv, 127–8, 129, 130–31, 134, 209, 226; Belfast, University of 129; *see* also Ulster
Belgium, in World War I 253
Bell, Clive 224
Bell, Vanessa (Stephen) 224
Bellini, Vincenzo 95
Belloc, Hilaire 41
Benares 137–8; described 177–8, 180
Benefactress, The (Arnim, E. von) 70–71
Bennett, Arnold 97, 124
Bennett, E. K. ('Francis') 313; personality of 312
Benson, A. C., 119; letter to EMF 119
Benson, E. W. 119
Benson, Mary S.; letter to A. C. Benson 119
Bernardino, Saint 157, 162
Bernhardi, F. A. J. von 213; works by 215
Besant, Annie 245
Bevan, Edwyn 208–9
Bhopal 172; Begum of 173
biography, nature of vii
Birds, The (Aristophanes) 92
Birket Foster's . . . English Landscape 79
Birth of Venus, The (Botticelli) 264
Black and Tans 319, 320
Blackwood (publisher) 42, 67,

68, 74, 78, 84, 316
Blackwood's (magazine) 67
Blake, William 110
Blind Alley (W. L. George) 302
Bloomsbury Group x, 15–16, 42, 63, 98, 235
Blunt, Lady Anne 308, 309
Blunt, W. S. 303, 308, 309, 311–12; entertains EMF 310–11; personality of 310
Böcklin, Arnold 57; works by 58
Boddh Gya 183; described 184–5
Boer War 38, 39, 40
'Bombardment' (Turner) 239, 240
'Boofie': *see* Darwin, Emma Nora; Darwin, Ruth
Boot, Jesse 218, 219
Borchegrevink, Aida 235, 236, 248, 262, 267, 277, 280, 308, 317
Boshtan Ballads (Begbie) 17, 18
Botticelli, Sandro 109; works by 264, 310, 312
Boutique fantasque La, (Rossini-Respighi) 305, 306
Bracknels, The (Reid) 126–7, 128, 136, 172, 173
Brahmanism 301
Brahmo Samaj 194, 228
Brahms, Johannes; work by 43
Braithwaite, R. B. 132
Branfoot, Arthur 139
Braun, Herr 74
Brawne, Fanny 247
Breaking Point, The (E. Garnett) 90–91
Bride of Dionysus, The (R. C. Trevelyan and Tovey) 315
Bridge, Frank 93
Bridges, Robert 248, 249
Brighstone (Isle of Wight) 3
Britain as Germany's Vassal (Bernhardi) 213, 215
British Dominion in India (Lyall) 120, 121
British Empire 180; *see also*

British Empire—contd
  EMF, attitudes and
  opinions, on English in
  India
British Museum 45, 109
Brooke, Rupert *126*, 227, 228;
  poetry of 227; works by
  126, 228
Brothers Karamazov, The
  (Dostoievsky) 105–6, 182
Brown, Curtis 304
Brown, Ford Madox 211
Browning, Oscar 15, 23, 24, 39,
  40, 44–5, 48, 49
Browning, Robert 106; works
  by 32, 96
Bryce, James 38
Brussels Exhibition 113, 114
Buddha, Buddhism 105, 123,
  164, 183, 184–5, 193, 204,
  301
Budget Crisis (1909) 103
Bulteau, Augustine; works by
  128, 134, 135
Burma 137
Burn, Richard 175, 179
Burne-Jones, Edward 312
Butler, Samuel 68, 207, 217, 220,
  298, 299
Byblis changée en fontaine
  (Louÿs) 207
Byron, Lord 309
By Sea and Land (Young) 221

Calcutta, 114, 181–2; transfer of
  Government from 186
*Calendar of the Letters of E. M.
  Forster* (ed. Lago) xvi, xi
'Caliban upon Setebos'
  (Browning) 32
Caligula 295, 296
Cambridge, Cambridge
  University ix, xv, 13, 21, 28,
  32, 35–6, 38–9, 43, 45, 46,
  47, 48, 55, 61, 64, 99, 108,
  121, 127, 206, 208, 216, 299,
  315; postwar salaries at 305
  see also: EMF, attitudes and
  opinions, on Cambridge;

King's College
'Cambridge and the Sirdar'
  (news report) 23
Cambridge Local Lectures
  Board 41, 92
Cambridge Magazine, The 217
Cambridge Platonists 13
Cambridge University Day
  Training College 45
Cameron, D. A. 312, 313
Candida (Shaw) 266
Candler, Edmund 138, 194
Canika, Raja of 182, 183
Carducci, Giosuè 110, 111
Carey, Clive 88, 91, 92
Carey, Hugh 49
Carlyle, Thomas 152
Carpenter, Edward x, 205, 207,
  222, 250, 285, 288, 292;
  letter to EMF 223; works
  by 259, 263, 285, 286, 288
Carpenter, Estlin 162
Carson, Edward 130, 131
Casa Santa (Loreto) 262
Cathédrale, La (Huysmans) 86
Cathleen ni Houlihan (Yeats)
  136
Cavafy, C. P. xi, xii, 205,
  259–60, 266, 295–96
Caves du Vatican, Les (Gide)
  314
'Celestial Omnibus, The' (EMF)
  93
Ceylon 107; Civil Service 64,
  135–6
Chalmers, George 23
Chamberlain, Joseph 105
'Chandrapore': *see* Bankipore
'Chanson d'Automne' (Verlaine)
  101
Chansons de Bilitis, Les (Louÿs)
  207
Chantecler (Rostand) 106;
  reviews of 106
Chartres 85
Chevrillon, André; work by 128
Chhatarpur 137, 161, 179, 195;
  described 162–3, 168–71
Chhatarpur, Maharaja of 137,

161, 162, 196–97; described
    168–71
Chhatarpur, Rani of 197
Chirol, Valentine 124, 312, 313
Chopin, Frederic; works by 287
Christianity 264, 301
Chu-Chin-Chow 303
Churchill, Clementine 130
Churchill, Winston 116, 128,
    129, 130–31
Cicero 28, 32, 33
Clapham, Clapham Sect 1, 3, 18
Clapham, J. H. 56
Clarke, Charles 28, 30
Clarke, W. L. 171, 172
Classical Society (Cambridge) 24
Claudel, Paul 283
Cleopatra 293
Clutton-Brock, Arthur 209–10,
    251; works by 210;
    entertains EMF 316
Coates, Albert 320
Cole, Arthur 68–9, 76–9
Coleridge, S. T. 89
Collected Works (Ibsen) 167
Collected Works (R. C.
    Trevelyan) 296
Collingham, D. H. 25, 28, 36,
    40, 49, 56
Collingwood, Dora 230
Collins Baker, C. H. 230, 231,
    293
Comrade, The (Delhi) 144, 145
Confederacy, The (Vanbrugh)
    62, 63
Connaught, Duchess of 284
Conrad, Joseph 124, 135, 136,
    187, 188, 314; works by
    187, 188, 314, 315
Contemporary Art Society 106
'Contemporary Novel, The'
    (Wells) 124
Contre Saint-Beuve (Proust) vii,
    xviii
Cooke, A. H. 22, 23
Coq d'Or (Rimsky-Korsakov)
    319, 320
Corelli, Marie 162
Cornford, Francis 96

Coronation (1911) 124
Cortina d'Ampezzo 55, 59
Cortot, Alfred 318, 320
Cotes, Everard 157, 159–60
Cotes, Jeannette Duncan 153,
    157, 159–60
Counter-Attack (Sassoon) 295,
    296
Counter-Reformation 85
Crace, Dorothy 49
Crace, J. F. 56, 57
Craft of Fiction, The (Lubbock)
    55
Craig, Edward Gordon 181, 182
Craiglockhart War Hospital 294
Cramb, J. A. 213, 215
Crewe, Lord 129
Crockett, S. R.; work by 17, 18
Croft (i.e. Crofton), Hugh 48,
    49
Cronje, P. A. 38
Cronwright-Schreiner, S. C. 38
Curzon, Lord 186, 313, 316

Daily Herald, The (London)
    206, 301, 315, 316
Daily News, The (London) 220,
    302, 312
Daniels, H. G. 49
Dans L'Inde (Chevrillon) 128
Dante 258–9, 263; works by
    258, 259, 260, 263
Darling, April 98
Darling, Colin 98
Darling family 99, 144, 145, 192,
    215, 240, 248, 269, 319
Darling, Irene 214, 215
Darling, Jessica 98, 111, 124–6,
    127–30, 133–4, 135, 150–51,
    152, 173, 191, 193, 210–11,
    212, 215, 221, 225–6, 238,
    239–40, 246; on World War
    I 214, 215
Darling, John Jermyn ('JJ') 98,
    110–11, 124, 127, 128, 133,
    151, 173–4, 190, 211, 247–8
Darling, Malcolm viii, 42,
    97–100, 102–5, 106–11,
    114–15, 122–4, 125, 128,

Darling, Malcolm—contd
129–30, *133–5*, 137, 148,
150–51, 160, 173, 178, 186,
191, 194, 195, 196, 199,
210–11, 212, *213–15*, 221,
225–8, 238–40; career of,
213, 228; letters to EMF
108, 129–30; letter to his
mother 109; on World War
I 215, 221
Darling, Margaret 214, 215
Darling, Mrs 99, 103
Darwin, Charles 14, 24, 96
Darwin, Emma Cecilia 13, 14
Darwin, Emma Nora ('Mrs
Boofie') 38, 43
Darwin, Erasmus 38
Darwin, Frances 96
Darwin, Francis 23, 24, 44, 96
Darwin, Henrietta Emma: *see*
Litchfield, H. E.
Darwin, Horace 13–14, 43, 44
Darwin, Ruth ('Boofie') 13–14,
24, 25, 28, 34, 35, 38, 43
Daulatabad, described 203
Davies, Fanny 318, 320
Davies, Langdon 315
Davies, T. L. 51, 52
Davy, Lady 302
'Dean Inge at St Paul's' (news
report) 228
*Decline and Fall of the Roman
Empire* (Gibbon) 108
de la Mare, Walter 127
Delhi 129–30, 137;described 144,
146–7, 149–51, 196–8; Fort
149
del Sarto, Andrea 95
Delusions and Discoveries
(Parry) 194
De Natura Deorum (Cicero) 32, 33
Denis Bracknel (Reid) 127
Dent, E. J. xiii, *46–9, 55–9*, 84,
85–6, 87–8, 91–3, 95–6,
222–3, 234; and A. Scarlatti
studies 47, 48, 55
Dent, J. M. (publisher) 69
De Officiis (Cicero) 28
Derain, André 306

Devi, Hill of (Dewas Senior) 248
Devises 121
Dewas Junior, State of, ix 98
Dewas Senior, Maharaja of ix,
42, 98, 103–4, 135, 138, 178,
206, 225, 240, 248
Dewas Senior, Maharani of 178
Dewas Senior, State of ix, 98,
99, 104, 137, 151, 162, 167,
173, 178, 191–5, 206, 238,
247–8
Dey, M. K. 319, 230
Diaghilev, Serge 306
Dickens, Charles; work by 115
Dickinson, G. L. xii, 15, 38, 39,
42, *51–3*, 60, 69, *84–5*, 98,
105, 106, 107, 108, 120, 206,
216–17, 225, *236–8*, 248,
250–4, 266, 295, 300, 314;
in India 137–204 *passim*; on
USA 98, 99, 107, 150; works
by 15, 84–5, 157,
217, 237
*Dictionary of National
Biography* 228
Digby, Everard 159, 162
Dimbleby, J. B. 30, 45
D'Indy, Vincent 309
Disraeli, Benjamin 85
Doolittle, Hilda 219, 220
Dostoievsky, Feodor 105–6, 258;
works by 182, 313
Douglas, Norman; work by
275–6
Dove Cottage 89
Dowland, Agnes 184, 270
Drury Lane Theatre 206
Dublin 130, 131, 136
Duet for Two Voices (Carey) 49,
92
Duff, J. D. 284
Duncan, Sara Jeannette: *see*
Cotes J. D.
Duns (Berwickshire), described
210
Durbar (1911) 124, 128, 129–30,
144, 149
Dvorak, Antonin; work by 28,
29, 274

East India Company 18
Economic Consequences of the Peace, The (Keynes) 64
Edinburgh, University of 311, 315
Edward VII, King of England 56
Edwardian Turn of Mind, The (Hynes) 91
Egyptian Gazette, The (Alexandria) 279, 308, 312
Egyptian Mail, The (Alexandria) 279, 280, 299
el Adl, Gamila 291, 297, 299–300
el Adl, Mohammed, x, 140, 205, 253, 254, 257–8, 261, 264–5, 268–9, 270–71; 272, 274, 280–82, 286–7, 288–9, 292, 296–8, 299–300, 313, 315, 317–18; home of, described 290–92, 297–8; leaves Alexandria 272, 275; letters to EMF 262, 275, 288; marriage of 291, 297–8, 300; on the English 262; personality of 262, 264–5, 268–9, 275, 292–2
Elephanta 202
Elgar, Edward; work by 318, 320
Eliot, George 4
Eliot, T. S.; work by xi
'Elizabeth': *see* Arnim-Schlagentin, Elizabeth von
Elizabeth and Her German Garden (E. von Arnim) 42, 65–6, 70, 71
Ellora Caves 137, 190, 201; described 203–4
Emblems of Love (Abercrombie) 128
Emden (German cruiser) 225
E. M. Forster: A Life (Furbank) xv, xix, 9, 44, 89, 130, 215, 231
'Emerson: A Literary Interview' (Anon.) 152
Emma (Austen) 76

England, the English: and India 165, 200, 216; and World War I 22; *see also* EMF, attitudes and opinions
English Novel, The (Ford) 211
English Review, The (London) 135–6, 239
English Soul, The (Foemina, pseud. of Bulteau, A.) 134, 135
Englishman Looks at His World, An (Wells) 124
Erewhon (Butler) 68
Escombe, Edith; work by 81
Essays Offered to G. H. Luce 139
Ethan Frome (Wharton) 128
Euclid 293
Euripide (?) 69
Ewer, W. N. 315, 316
Ewing, Ellen 313; 314

Fabian Society 126, 313
Farmer, Mrs 70, 71
Farrer, Thomas C. F., 2nd Lord 2
Farrer, Thomas H. F., 1st Lord 1, 2, 14
Farrer, Lady Katherine 2, 43, 44, 241
Feet of the Young Men, The (Tremaine) 264, 265, 272, 273
Feilding, Everard 238
Feu, Le (Barbusse) 272, 273
Feud, The (E. Garnett) 93
Fiction of E. M. Forster, The (Thomson) xix
Flaubert, Gustave viii
Flowers and Elephants (C. Sitwell) 194
Foemina (pseud.): *see* Bulteau, Augustine
Following Darkness (Reid) 127, 172–3, 187, 208; review of 187, 188
Forbes, B. C. 179
Ford, Edward Onslow 86
Ford, Ford Madox; work by 211

Foreign Office xiv, 206, 308, 315

Forest Lovers, The (Hewlett) 21

Forster, Alice Clara ('Lily') ix–x, xii, 2, 3, 4, 6, 9–14, 16–24, 27, *34–7*, 41, 42, *43*, *45–6*, *53–4*, *58*, *59*, 60, 62, *64–8*, *70–71*, 71–6, *79–82*, 86, *114*, 122, *130–31*, 132–3, 134, 137, 143, 145, 147, 152, *179–80*, *188*, *192–8*, *201–4*, *210–12*, *212–13*, 217, 218, 225, 228, 229, 235, 242, 243, 245, 248, 257, 270, 271, 274, 276–80, 286, 287, 300, 301, 308, 313, 314, 318, 319, 426, 465; relations with EMF ix, x; travels in Italy 108, 153, 162 *see also* EMF, relations with mother

Forster, Charles (EMF's grandfather) 1, 81

Forster, Charles T. (EMF's uncle) 23, 44

FORSTER, EDWARD MORGAN:

personal:
  business affairs xii, 309
  careers and career plans 25, 26–7, 200, 216–17; as cataloguer 205, 212, 214, 222; as government official 206, 308, 313, 315; as journalist 220, 279, 280, 283, 300, 302, 315; as lecturer 41, 62, 63–4, 82, 86, 91–2, 98, 126, 135, 220, 298; as private secretary ix, 206, 223; as teacher 65–82, 92, 208
  childhood 1–28
  health 26, 120, 121, 243, 246–7, 315
  personality vii–viii, xi–xii, 10–12, 78, 85, 243–4, 258–60, 268–9, 292–3, 303
  relations with mother 2, 11, 10, 126, 134, 167–8, 229, 273

travels and travel plans, Austria 59, 162; Egypt x, xv, 205–6, 231, 232–300; France 85–6, 99, 103; Germany ix, xv, 41–2, 57–8, 65–82; Greece 51, 52; India ix–x, xv, 41–2, 88, 103, 118, 120, 128, 134, 137–204, 238–9, 304; Ireland 127–32, 208, 209, 224–5, 226, 228, 230; Italy 41, 46–57, 59, 85–6, 95–6, 105, 106–8, 122, 124, 125, 137, 157, 162; Romania xv; Spain 128; South Africa xv; USA xv

war service 205, 206, 221, 224, 227–8, 229–30, 231, 232–300 *passim*, 305–6

literary: as writer viii–xiv, 41–2, 51, 83–4, 114, 200, 216–17, 298; and writer's block 187–8, 205, 206, 217, 289, 302, 314, 315–16; as writer of letters xi–xviii, 145, 286, 302; on novels, novelists vii, 136, 171, 216, 235; on other writers: M. Arnold viii, 111; Askanov 283; R. Bridges 248–9; R. Brooke 227; R. Browning 106; E. Carpenter 285; J. Conrad 135; Dante 258–9, 260; Dostoievsky 105–6; N. Douglas 275–6; Gibbon 107–8; R. Graves 292; T. Hardy 125; H. James 106, 240, 279, 283, 290; W. James 279; J. Joyce 272; Keats 246–7; Kipling 123, 135; D. H. Lawrence 231–2, 249–50; G. Meredith 106; R. Nichols 292; Pater viii, 248–9; F. Reid 126–7, 136, 172, 187–8; S. Sassoon 289, 295, 302; Spinoza 272–3; Swinburne 106; J. A. Symonds 52, 53; M. Symonds 52, 53; Tolstoy 106; H. Tremaine 272; L.

Woolf 135; V. Woolf 223, 227; Zola 249
letters to: J. R. Ackerley 248 (extract); Mary Aylward 3–4, 141–43; Florence Barger xiv (extract), 139–41, 145–8, 209–10, 218–19, 223, 229–30, 235–6, 243–6, 256–9, 260–65, 267–9, 270–75, 280–82, 284–9, 290–92, 296–8, 299–300, 312–14, 315–16, 317–20; George Barger 31–2, 254–6; A. C. Benson 119; Rupert Brooke 126; C. P. Cavafy 259–60; Arthur Cole 68–9, 76–9; D. H. Collingham 40 (extract); Jessica Darling 111 (extract), 124–6, 127–30; Malcolm Darling viii (extract), 97–100, 102–5, 106–11, 114–15, 122–4, 133–5, 213–15, 225–8, 238–40, 246–8; E. J. Dent xiii, 46–9, 53–9, 84, 87–8, 91–3, 95–6, 222–3; G. L. Dickinson xii, 50–53, 84–5, 216–17, 236–8, 250–54; Norman Douglas 275–6; Alice Clara Forster 2, 5–14, 16–24, 25–6, 27–30, 34–7, 39–40, 43–4, 45–6, 64–8, 70–76, 79–82, 130–31, 148–72, 173–82, 183–7, 188–90, 192–8, 201–4, 210–13 (extract), 238, 276–80 (extract), 306; Laura Forster 5, 24–5, 26–7, 37–8, 144–5, 190–92, 198–200, 240–41, 248–9; Edward Garnett 90–91, 93, 117; D. H. Lawrence 219–20; Frieda Lawrence 219–20; G. H. Ludolf 304–12; S. R. Masood 88–9, 96–7, 100–102, 113–14, 118, 120–22, 131–3, 201, 208–9, 215–16, 224–5, 232–4, 241–3, 269–70; Edward Marsh 115–16; Charles Mauron 84 (extract); Ottoline Morrell 105–6, 206–7, 221; Henry Newbolt 231–2; Wilson Plant 249–50; William Plomer (extracts) xi, 140; Forrest Reid 126–7, 136, 172–3, 187–8, 200, 207, 217–18, 298–9; Alys Russell 86; Bertrand Russell 40; Siegfried Sassoon (extracts) vii, xi, 289–90, 292–4, 300, 302–3, 316–17; Lytton Strachey 208; Elizabeth Trevelyan viii (extract); Robert Trevelyan (extracts) viii, ix, xii, xiii, 59–63, 83–4, 89–90, 91, 112–13, 138–9, 182–3, 266–7, 283–4, 294–6, 314–15; Hugh Walpole 93–4, 304; Nathaniel Wedd 32–4, 44–5; Louisa Whichelo 2–3, 4–5; Leonard Woolf 63–4, 135–6, 224; Virginia Woolf 230–31, 234–5; Lorna Wood 301–2; Theodor de Wyzewa 116–17; Hilton Young 220–21

attitudes and opinions (general) on: asceticism xi, 316–17; art 57; authoritarianism 293; censorship 231, 254–6; civilisation 104, 233; depravity 259–60; education 319; faith, faithfulness 250–55, 276; friendship vii, xii, 100, 215–16, 243–4; godparents 114, 110–11; gossip 303; human relationships and values 209, 259–60, 288; libertarianism 293; middle classes 253–4; miners 319; missionaries 109, 165–6; music 6–9, 15, 218; nationalism 134, 237, 250–54; political outlook

FORSTER, EDWARD MORGAN
—contd
   103, 134, 205, 250–54, 289,
   305–6; pacifism 245;
   personal values in wartime
   265; respectability 218, 243,
   264–5, 268–9, 272, 274, 291;
   satire 303; science 301;
   sentiment 100; suburbia ix;
   war, x–xi, 100, 215–16;
   women 97;
attitudes and opinions (specific)
   on: Cambridge: 47, 55, 230,
   245; Egypt, Egyptians
   205–6, 239, 232–3, 245,
   268–9, 274–5, 276, 277,
   286–7, 288–9, 318; Egypt
   and India compared 238–9;
   England, the English x–xi,
   51–2, 57, 85, 97, 102, 104,
   107, 113, 125, 131–2, 133,
   140, 175, 180, 181, 182, 225,
   253–4, 257, 267, 286–7, 300,
   305–6; England and India
   140, 147, 156, 164, 165, 188,
   191–4, 195, 195–6, 199–200,
   203, 209, 215, 238–9; India,
   Indians 108–9, 120, 123,
   145, 156, 157, 190–91, 193,
   197, 206–7, 238–9; Indian
   art 147, 174; Indian dance
   147, 149–50; India superior
   to Egypt 233, 238–9, 242;
   Ireland 128–9, 130–31; Italy
   52–3; religions: Brahmanism
   301; Buddhism 193, 301;
   Christianity 109, 258; Islam
   174; mysticism 113;
   Pantheism 301; World War
   I x–xi, 213–14, 224, 227–8,
   234, 240–41, 245, 250–56,
   264, 268–9, 284–5, 289, 295,
   293, 298, 305–6
works:
   Abinger Harvest 87, 280, 309
   'Adrift in India' 187
   Alexandria 206, 293, 294, 298,
   304–9, 311
   'Alexandrian Vignettes' 296

'Arctic Summer' 42, 127, 187,
   188, 200
*Arctic Summer and Other
   Fiction* 52
'Art of Fiction, The'
   (interview) xviii–xix
'At Dinner Margaret'
   (fragment) 56, 57
'Celestial Omnibus, The' 92,
   93
*Celestial Omnibus and Other
   Stories, The* 42, 60, 112, 113,
   115, 116, 117, 187, 188, 285
'Concert of Old Instruments,
   A' 306
'Dante' (lecture) 260
diaries ix, xi, 79, 103, 124,
   126, 131, 145, 188, 198, 209,
   215
'Elegy' 283, 284
'End of the Samovar, The' 313
'Enjoyment of English
   Literature, The' (lecture)
   194
'Eternal Moment, The' 63,
   59–60
'Flood in the Office, A' 308,
   309
Foreword, to *Flowers and
   Elephants* (C. Sitwell) 194
'Gog and Magog' 309
Goldsworthy Lowes Dickinson
   52, 300
Government of Egypt, The
   312, 313, 314, 317
'Greek Feeling for Nature,
   The' 24
'Hat-Case, The' 211
'Helping Hand, The' 76
Hill of Devi, The xi, xii, 135,
   137, 178
Howards End ix, x, xviii, 42,
   106, 114, 117, 118, 119, 121,
   166, 187–8, 245, 290
'Indian Mind, The' 209
'Indian novel': see *Passage to
   India, A*
'Inferior' 289, 290
'Italy in the Autumn' 51, 52

'Legs to Mrs Wilcox, Le'
    (translation, *Howards End*)
    84
*Life to Come and Other
    Stories, The* 76
'Little Trip, A' 295, 296
Longest Journey, The 15,
    87–8, 91, 116–17, 216
'Machine Stops, The' 99, 100,
    105
Marianne Thornton 1, 23
['Matthew Arnold'] (lecture)
    116
Maurice x, 15, 205, 216, 222,
    223, 229, 243, 244, 257, 258,
    302
'Mr. Andrews' 116
'New Novelist, A' 220
'Nottingham Lace' 15, 52
'Novelists of the 19th
    Century, The' 37
'Other Boat, The' ix
'Our Diversions' 280
Passage to India, A x, 138,
    178, 194, 200, 233, 302, 303,
    317
'Pericles in Paradise' 295–6
Pharos and Pharillon 206, 280,
    294
'Pharos articles' 309, 311
'Philosophers and
    Philosophies of Ancient
    Alexandria' (lecture) 295
'Poems of Kipling, The'
    (lecture) 61
'Poetry of Cavafy, The' 260
'Purple Envelope, The' 62, 63
'Relation of Dryden to Milton
    and Pope' 21
'Road from Colonus, The' ix
Room with a View, A ix, xiii,
    xiv, 3, 41, 49, 60, 61, 91, 94,
    95, 96, 116, 124
['Samuel Butler'] (unfinished),
    220, 221
short stories (destroyed)
    316–17
'Some of Our Difficulties' xix
'Story of a Panic, The' viii, ix,
    41, 60
'Suppliant, The' 187
'Syed Ross Masood' 88
'T. S. Eliot' (revision of 'Some
    of Our Difficulties') xix
'Timothy the Cat and
    Timothy Whitebonnet' 293,
    294
Two Cheers for Democracy 88
'War Anthology'
    (unpublished) 248, 249
Where Angels Fear to Tread
    ix, 42, 64, 71, 79, 81, 188,
    304, 316
'West Hackhurst: A Surrey
    Ramble' (unpublished) 2
Forster, Laura Mary (EMF's
    aunt) 1, 2, 3, 5, 10, 12, 13,
    22, *24–5*, *26–7*, 35, *37–8*, 39,
    45, 59, 60, 88, 112, 121–2,
    144–5, 157, 162, 180, *190–2*,
    198–200, 212–13, *240–41*,
    248–9, 267, 270, 283;
    described 2
Forster, Lucy (EMF's aunt) 13,
    14, 23
Forster, W. H. (EMF's uncle)
    25, 32, 84, 210)
Forster, Winifred (EMF's
    Cousin) 43, 44
Forster, Mr 22, 23
Fortnightly Review, The
    (London) 100
Foster, M. Birket; work by 78,
    79
Fowler, Eliza, (EMF's great-
    aunt) 4, 34–5, 35–6, 148,
    231, 257
Fowler, Frank 4, 34–5, 35–6
France, Anatole (pseud.); work
    by 78, 79
Franck, César 218; works by
    220, 287, 318
Franklyn, Frank 17, 18
Frere, Bartle 278, 279–80, 295–6
Freud, Sigmund; works by 284
Froebel, Friedrich 319, 320
Fry, Jack 4
Fry, Roger 112, 113, 129, 130,

Fry, Roger—contd
    134, 211, 212, 222; portrait
    of EMF by 129, 130, 134
Fry, Sara Margery 243, 244
Fulford, Francis 13, 16, 21, 24,
    37
Fulford, Mrs 18–21, 27–8, 34–5
Fulford, Phyllis 28
Fulford, W. H. 13, 17
Furbank, P. N. xv; EMF
    interviewed by xviii
Furness, R. M. 205, 234, 235,
    237–8, 239, 265, 267, 272,
    278, 281, 282, 283, 289, 292,
    299, 312
Furness, J. M. 249

Gale, Courtney 96
Galsworthy, John 123, 124, 200,
    280; works by 279, 280
Gamlen, R. L. 200
Ganges River, described 174–5
Garbola, Dr. 300
Garden by the Sea, A (Reid) 299
Gardner, Arthur 52
Gardner, E. A. 51, 52
Garnett, Constance 106
Garnett, Edward 42, 90–91, 93,
    106, 117; works by 90–91,
    93
Garsington Manor 314–15
Geisha, The (Jones) 16, 17
General Index (Command
    Papers) 213, 215; see also
    White Paper
Gentle Lover, The (Reid) 187–8,
    207
George V, King of England 124,
    129, 132, 149, 213
George, R. G: see Sencourt,
    Robert
George, W. L. 301, 302
Georgian Poetry (ed. Marsh) 60,
    116, 215, 284, 294
Germany and the Next War
    (Bernhardi) 213, 215
Ghirlandhaio, Domenico; work
    by 55, 56
Ghost Ship, The (Middleton) 136

Gibb, Roger 66
Gibbon, Edward; works by 26,
    27, 107, 108, 268
Gillett, Arthur 86, 159
Giotto; works by 51, 52
Godbole, Mr 194
Gitanjali (R. Tagore) 183
Goethe, Johann 125, 276
'Gog and Magog' (EMF) 309
Golden Bowl, The (H. James)
    240
Goldsmith, Oliver; work by 26,
    27
Goldsmith, Ruth 76, 78, 152,
    157, 168, 184, 212, 270
Goodall, Charles 135, 176, 182
Goodall, Mary 135, 152
Goyder, G. B. 195–6, 198,
    199–200
Graham, Catherine ('Tanty';
    EMF's great-aunt) 73
'The Grange' 2, 5, 9
Grant, Charles 18
Grant, Duncan 234, 235
Grant, Frank 18, 27
Granta (Cambridge) 18, 23
Grant Duff, Victoria 235, 236,
    237, 238, 248, 250, 269, 272,
    277, 278
Granville, Dr 277, 278
Grasmere 89
Graves, Robert 292, 294
Graveson, C. C. 319, 320
Greatham (Pulborough) 218
Great Society, The (Wallas) 225,
    228
Greek Tragedy (Sheppard) 128
Greenwood, Alice 4, 12
Greenwood, L. H. G. 86, 121
Greifswald 76–8, 79–81
[Grelling, Richard]; work by
    226, 228
Grey, Edward 96, 97, 132, 180;
    work by 293, 294
Grieg, Edvard 319
Grissel, H. de la G. 23, 24
Grove, Lady Agnes 297, 298
Gubbio 115
Guthrie, Thomas Anstey 318;

work by 320
Gya, described 184–5

Haden-Guest, Lord 312
Hamilton, Kenneth 299
Hamlet (Shakespeare) 140
Handel, G. F.; work by 218
Hardinge, Lord and Lady 186, 187
Hardy, Thomas 125
Harrogate 108, 114, 205, 207
Harnham: EMF and his mother move to 61
Hartley, A. F. 195, 198
Haskell, F. J. H.; EMF interviewed by xviii
Hasluck, F. W. 106, 110, 122–3, 195
Hatch, Mr 10, 11
Havell, E. B. 104, 105, 179
Haward, L. W. 32, 33, 34, 47, 92, 96
HD: *see* Doolittle, Hilda
Harris, Frank; work by 99, 100
Head, Mr 10
Headlam, W. H. 35
Heine, Elizabeth; work by 126
Heinemann, William (publisher) 67
Hélène 261, 262, 287
Henson 6, 9, 10, 12–13
Hell-fellows (L. Housman) 112, 113
Herringham, Christiana 5
Herringham, Christopher 5
Herringham, Wilmot 5
Hervey, Augustus 1, 9, 82
Hewlett, Maurice, work by 21
Hill, Miss 270
H. H.: *see* Dewas Senior, Maharaja of
Hindley, C. D. M. 185, 186, 187
Hindley, O. W. 187
Hindus, Hinduism 156, 157, 164–5, 170, 177, 181, 189–90, 198, 204; and Indian politics 179; 'Mystery Plays' 164, 165–6, 168, 171

History of British Policy in India (Seeley) 38
History of Italian Painting (Kugler) 24, 25
History of the Fairchild Family, The (Sherwood) 70, 71
Hodgkin, George 86
Hölderlin, J. C. F.; work by 222, 223
Holmes, E. G. A.; work by 301–2
Holroyd, Sir Charles, 280
Holroyd, Lady 280
Holy Roman Empire, The (Bryce) 38
H. O. M.: *see* Meredith, H. O.
Homer 78
Hort, F. J.A. 16, 17
Housman, A. E. xii
Housman, Laurence, work by 112, 113
Howley, J. H. E. 16, 17
Hsuan-Tsang 182, 183
Hubback, J. A. 180, 182, 185
Hueffer, F. M.: *see* Ford, F. M.
Humphrey, Laurence 34, 35
Hutchinson, C. P. 5, 9, 11, 12
Hutchinson, Hilton 12
Hutchinson, Tom 12
Huxley, Aldous 206
Huxley, Thomas 166
Huysmans, Joris-Karl 85, 86
Hyderabad, Nizam of 88, 120
'Hymne' (Baudelaire) 101
Hypatia 294
Hyperion (Hölderlin) 222, 223
Humayun 144, 145

I Accuse ([Grelling]) 226, 228; *see also J'Accuse*
Ibsen, Henrik 167, 236
Icknield Way, The (Thomas) 112
Idolatry (Perrin) 120
Imperfect Encounter (ed. Lago) 105, 162
Independent Review, The (London) 41, 63, 64
India: art of 104, 105; Civil Service 18, 42, 98, 182, 187,

India—contd
    192, 198; Educational
    Service 88, 183;
    Government of 98, 179,
    180, 193, 195; nationalism
    in 114, 192; philosophies of
    104; politics in 143, 215;
    role in World War I 215,
    216, 224; superior to Egypt
    238–9
India and the Future (Archer)
    167
India Museum (South
    Kensington): *see* Victoria
    and Albert Museum
Indian Dust (Richards) 228
Indian Mutiny (1857) 88, 194
Indian National Congress 143
Indian Sculpture (Havell) 104,
    105
Indian Summer (Irving) 129
Indian Unrest (Chirol) 124
Inferno (Dante) 260
Inge, W. R. 227, 228
In Praise of Krishna (trans.
    Dimock, Levertov) 167
Inter-Allied Commission (after
    World War I) 206, 308
Ireland 130–31, 208, 298; Home
    Rule in 320; role in World
    War I 224, 226
Irene (EMF's landlady,
    Alexandria) 262, 287
Iron Duke, H.M.S. 221
Ishaq, Mohammed 203, 204
Islam 87, 145, 147, 159–60, 180,
    264; history of 108, 144;
    nationalism in 137, 143,
    153, 159–60, 179
Islington, Lord 192
Italy, in World War I 224,
    225–6, 278

J'Accuse ([Grelling]) 226, 228;
    see also I Accuse
Jaipur, described 194–5
James, Henry xi, 31, 60, 92, 93,
    106, 240, 279, 283, 284, 290;
    works by 31, 60, 240, 283,
    284
James, M. R. 40
James William 62, 63, 128, 279;
    works by 63, 128
Japan-British Exhibition
    (London) 109; review of
    110
Jebb, R. C. 24, 25
Jehan, Shah 109, 192
Jenkinson, F. J. H. 43, 44
JJ: *see* Darling, John Jermyn
Jodhpur, described 195–6,
    190–200
Johnstone, J. W. D. 182, 183
Joyce, James xiv, 272; work by
    272
Judas Maccabeus (Handel) 218
Julian, Mother 220, 221
Juvenal 78

Keats, John viii, ix, 66, 247, 248,
    294; works by viii, 247,
    285–6
'Karain' (Conrad) 135, 136
Kennedy, J. M. 124
Kennet of the Dene, Lord: *see*
    Young, E. H.
'Kenneth' (Reid) 299
Kensit, Lord 25–6
Kent House 5–13 *passim*
Keynes, Maynard 15, 63, 216,
    315; work by 64
Khajraho Temples 162, 164, 168,
    170, 171
Khan, Sir S. A. 42, 88
Khan, N. H. 143
Khan, Raschid 89, 194, 197
Khedivieh School (Cairo) 249
Khyber Pass, described 153
King, Edward (Bishop of
    Lincoln) 43, 44
King Lear (Shakespeare) 97, 98
King, Willie 5
Kingdom of Twilight, The (Reid)
    127
King's College, Cambridge xv,
    xviii, 2, 15–43 *passim*, 92,
    107, 145; *see also*
    Cambridge University;

EMF, attitudes and opinions, on Cambridge King's College (Austen-Leigh) 38

Kingsley Temperance Hotel (London) 59

Kipling, Rudyard 135; work by 123, 124

Kitchener, Lord 22, 23

Knight of the Burning Pestle, The (Beaumont and Fletcher) 61

Knighton, E. W.; work by 191, 192

Knopf, Alfred (publisher) 304, 316

Kohlapur 178; Majaraja of 178

Krishna, Mr 156

Krishna 165–6, 171, 172

Kugler, F. T.; work by 24, 25

Labour Party 140, 312, 314, 317

Lacket, The (Wiltshire cottage) 97, 111, 113, 121, 122, 208

Lahore 98, 137, 150–51, 156, 191–2; Government College 194, 198

Lamb, Henry 136

L'Ame des Anglais (Foemina) 128, 134, 135

Landmarks in French Literature (G. L. Strachey) 128

Langdon-Davies, John 315

Lansbury, George 300

Last Poems (Thomas) 284

'Last Straw, The' (Kennedy) 124

Latimer, Hugh 131

Lawrence, D. H. x, 217, 218, 219–20, 230, 231–2, 249–50; letter to EMF 219; personality of 218, 220; on V. Woolf, The Voyage Out 220; works 218, 219–20, 222, 223, 231–2, 249–50

Lawrence, Frieda 218, 219–20; letter to EMF 219

Lawrence, T. E. xii

Leading Note, The (Murray) 123, 124

League of Nations 305, 306

League of Nations, The (Grey) 293–4

Lefroy, G. A., (Bishop of Lahore) 123, 124

Leith Hill Place (Vaughan Williams family home) 24, 63

Lewis, Wyndham 211–12

Leonardo da Vinci; works by 45, 61

Letters from a Chinese Official: see Letters from John Chinaman

Letters from John Chinaman (Dicksinson) 237

Letters of Virginia Woolf 231

Leveaux, Charles 245

Liebig, Baron Justus von 57, 58

Liesecke, Fräulein 57

Life and Habit (Butler) 207

Life and Works of Syed Ahmed Khan, The (Graham) 288

Life of Algernon Charles Swinburne (Gosse) 152

Lippi, Filippo 95

Liszt, Franz 72

Litchfield, R. B. 34, 35

Litchfield, Henrietta Emma 34, 35

Lloyd George, David 100, 107

Londonderry, Lord 130, 131

London Library 191, 207

London University 291

Loom of Youth, The (A. Waugh) 284

Lord Chamberlain 91, 132

Louÿs, Pierre; works by 98

Low, Lady (mother of Jessica Darling) 105, 134, 210–11

Low, Lord (father of Jessica Darling) 98, 129, 211

Luard, C. E. 248

Lubbock, Percy 49, 264, 267, 277; work by, 55

Luce, G. H. 137, 139

Ludolf, G. H. 304–12, 318; supervises printing of EMF's Alexandria 306–7

Lyall, Sir A. 120, 98
Lycidas (Milton), 262
Lyme Regis 206, 300, 301

Macaulay, T. B. 39
McCarthy, Desmond 211, 212, 296
MacDonald, Sir Murdoch 309
McLagan, Bridget (pseud.): *see* Turner, Mary Borden
MacMunn, H. F. 15, 16, 17, 27, 28
Magic Flute, The (Mozart) 58, 88
Mahler, Gustav vii
Mahmous 186–7
Mahoobia School for Girls (Hyderabad) 143
Maid's Tragedy, The (Beaumont and Fletcher) 62, 63
Mallarmé, Stéphane 117, 230–31; work by 230–31
Manchester Guardian, The 313
Manchester, University of 63–4
Mann, Mr 306, 311; *see also* Whitehead, Morris
Mansfield, Katherine 66, 312
Man Shakespeare, The (Harris) 99, 100
Mansurah, described 296–8
Manucci, Nicolo; work by 109, 110
Maradick at Forty (Walpole) 115, 116
Marius the Epicurean (Pater) 69, 249, 285, 286
Marsh, Edward *115–16*, 130, 216, 293, 294
Mary Olivier (Sinclair) 302
Mary, Queen 124, 129, 132, 149
Masood, Akbar (younger son of S. R. Masood) 81
Masood, Amtul (second wife of SRM) 89
Masood, Anwar (elder son of SRM) 88, 232, 233, 242, 270
Masood, Nadira (daughter of SRM) 88
Masood, S. R. 42, *88–9, 96–7,*

100–102, 113–14, 118, 120–22, 131–3, 141–3, 144–5, 146–7, 149–50, 152, 174, 180–81, 182, 183, 186, 190, 201, 208–9, 215–16, 224–5, 232–4, 269–70, 271, 281; at Bankipore 88, 137–8, 144; at Hyderabad 241–3; background of 42, 88; EMF's host in India 137, 179–82; letter to EMF 97; meets W. S. Blunt 308, 309; on missionaries 109; returns to India 131–3
Masood, Zohra (first wife of SRM) 88, 225, 242, 270
Masterman, C. F. G. 42
Matthews, Myles 285, 286
Martin, R. T. 313, 314
Mauron, Charles 84
Mawe, Cecilia, 18, 24, 66, 73, 76, 80, 81, 137, 148, 153, 162, 176, 319, 320
Mawe, Elaine 23, 24, 66
Maxwell, W. B. 289, 290
Mayor, J. B.; work by 30
Meaning of Good, The (Dickinson) 237
Melville, Ronald (Earl of Leven and Melville) 45, 46
Memoirs of Lady Ottoline Morrell (ed. Gathorne-Hardy) 221
Memories and Studies (W. James) 128, 135
Men and Memories (W. Rothenstein) 44, 179
Menasce, Jean de 305
Mercier, Cardinal 226, 228
Meredith, Adam (son of H. O. Meredith) 171, 230
Meredith, Christabel (wife of HOM) 140, 146, 171, 230, 319, 243, 244
Meredith, Christopher (son of HOM) 244
Meredith, Edith (Mrs Myles Matthews, sister of HOM) 285, 286

Meredith, Elizabeth (daughter of HOM) 244
Meredith, George 31, 38, 106
Meredith H. O. 15, 25, 26, 27-8, 32-3, 40, 61, 63-4, 75, 91, 106, 129, 130, 140, 148, 209, 229, 230, 244, 274, 286, 299, 319, 320; has financial help from EMF 168, 171, 176, 287; in Belfast 128; in Manchester 63, 90
Meredith, Ralph (son of HOM) 146, 148, 230
Meredith, Sidney 146, 148, 230
Merrill, George 205, 250, 285
Methuen (publisher) 67, 231, 232
Meynell, Alice 187, 188, 218, 219, 316
Meynell, Francis 315, 316
Meynell, Sebastian 218, 219
Meynell, Viola 218, 219
Meynell, Wilfred 218, 219, 316
Michelangelo vii, xviii, 49
Middle Years, The (H. James) 283, 284
Middleton, R. B.; work by 136
Millthorpe (Derbyshire) 205
Milner Commission (on Egypt) 312, 313, 316, 317-18
Milton, John; work by 262
Mir 192-3, 194
Miracle, The (Reinhardt) 128, 129
Mirza, Abu Saeed 120, 138, 175, 190, 201, 202, 204
Mirza, Ahmed 120, 174, 175, 190, 201
Mirza, Mohammed Aziz 120, 175
Mirza, Sajjad 120
Mistress of Kingdoms, The (McLagan) 211, 212
Mitter, Krishna 113-14
Modern Symposium, A (Dickinson) 85
Molière, Jean; work by 121
Mollison, W. M. 16, 17, 21, 22, 26, 36, 40, 56
Montazah, described 236-7

Montesquieu, Charles 37
'Monteriano' (early title): see Where Angels Fear to Tread (EMF)
Mont St Michel 18
Monuments of Egypt, The (C. Forster) 79, 81
Moore, George, work by 128
Moore, George Edward 15
Moorsom, Jermyn 98, 239
More Thoughts on the War (Clutton-Brock) 210
Morel, E. D.; work by 215
Morgan, H. A. 21
Morison, Dorothea (Mrs Richard Braithwaite) 131, 132, 215-16
Morison, Lady Margaret 120, 131, 132, 133, 164, 175, 225, 270, 305
Morison, Sir Theodore 42, 88, 120, 132, 137, 161, 164, 212, 245, 305
'Morley-Minto Reforms' 175, 179, 183, 186
Morley College (London) 136
Morning Post, The (London) 226
Morrell, Lady Ottoline 105-6, 113, 206-7, 218, 219, 220, 221, 314
Morris, William 310, 312
Morrow of the War, The (Morel et al.) 215
Motta, Marie 92, 93
Mount of Olives (Beethoven) 28
Mr. Britling Sees It Through (Wells) 251
Mrs. Warren's Profession (Shaw) 212, 213
Much Maligned Monsters (Mitter) 111
Musiciens d'aujourdhui (Rolland) 307, 309
Muslim League 143; see also Islam
My Days and Dreams (Carpenter) 259
My Diaries (Blunt), reviewed by EMF 303, 308, 309

My Life: A Fragment (M. Ali)
152
Mozart, W. A. 47; work by 58,
87, 88
Mozart's Operas (Dent) 88

Nassenheide xv, 64–82 *passim*,
113; described 65–9
Nation, The (London) 132, 226,
308
National Gallery (London);
EMF at 205, 213, 214, 219,
222, 223, 230, 231, 280, 293
National Liberal Club (London)
138
National Service League 134
Nature Notes (London) 26, 27
Nautch (Indian classical) dance
149–50, 152, 171, 209; *see
also* EMF, attitudes and
opinions, on Indian dance
Nelli, Octaviano; work by 115,
116
Nevinson, H. W. 132
New Age, The (London) 123,
124
Newall, H. F. 43, 44
Newbolt, Henry 208, *231–2*, 320
Newbuildings Place (home of
W. S. Blunt) 309; described
310–12
New Delhi, as new capital 187,
320
New Era at Hand, The
(Dimbleby) 30
New Machiavelli, The (Wells)
123, 124
Newman, Robert 213
New Statesman, The (London)
226
Nicholas Nickleby (Dickens) 115
Nichols, Robert 292, 294
Night and Day (V. Woolf) 313
Nile Projects, The (Willcocks);
see also EMF, business
affairs
1917 Club (London) 206
Nixon, J. E. 15, 39, 40, 55, 99
Northanger Abbey (Austen) 78

Norton, Harry 234, 235
Nuremberg 57

OB, The: *see* Browning, Oscar
'L'Objet et le Développement
du Roman contemporain en
Angleterre' (Anon.) 124
Oedipus Rex (Reinhardt) 128,
129, 166
Ogden, C. K. 216, 217
Omega Workshop 212, 217
On the Edge of Paradise
(Newsome) 24, 55, 119
On War of Today (Bernhardi)
213, 215
Orage, A. R. 124
Origins of the Great War, The
(Brailsford) 215
Oscar Browning (Wortham) 24
Osmania University
(Hyderabad) 88
Other Side of the Lantern, The
(Treves) 144, 145, 198
Otto, Emil; work by 67, 68
'Our Interests in Egypt'
(Cameron, letter) 312–13
Oxford University 62, 86, 88,
120, 121, 135, 152, 216
*Oxford Dictionary of Nursery
Rhymes, The* 59
Oxford and Cambridge Musical
Club 102, 118, 221
Oxford and Cambridge Review
105

Pachmann, Vladimir 318, 320
Paddock Wood 300
Pankhurst, Christabel 128, 129,
134
Pankhurst, Emmeline 129
Pantheism 301, 302
Parry, Sir Hubert; work by 92
Pater, Walter viii, 69, 249; work
by 249, 285, 286
Patiala Government College 194
Patna College 182, 183
'Peer-Gynt' (pseud. of EMF) 21
Penshurst Place 35
Pensione Simi (Florence) 48, 49,
162

Period Piece (Raverat) 35
Perrin, Alice; work by 120
Persia, Shah of 132
Persuasion (Austen) 24
Perugia, described 51
Peshawar, described 140, 153–5
Peter Waring (Reid) 127
Pilgrimage of Passion, A
    (Longford) 309
Pindar viii
Pino 131, 242
Pioneer, The (Allahabad) 124
Pirates of the Spring (Reid) 299
Pius X (Pope) 226
Plant, Wilson 249–50
Platen-Hollermunde, August
    von; work by 222, 223
Plato 249, 253; Platonism 272–3
Playboy of the Western World,
    The (Synge) 136
Plays Pleasant and Unpleasant
    (Shaw) 35
Plomer, William xi, 140
Plotinus 293
Poems (Browning) 24
Poems (Mallarmé, trans. R. Fry)
    230–31
Poetry Bookshop 216
Pollock, Alice Isabella 92, 105
Pollock, Sir Frederick and Lady
    92, 105
Ponsonby, F. E. G. 212, 213
Port Said, described 139–40
Portrait of a Lady (H. James)
    31, 240
Portrait of the Artist as a Young
    Man (Joyce) 272
Post-Impressionism 113, 129
Poston, Charles 39, 40
Poston, Elizabeth 40
Poston, Clementine 40
'Pragmatic Method, The' (W.
    James) 63
Pragmatic Sanction (1713) 63–3
Pragmatism (W. James) 63
Pragmatism, Pragmatists 62–3,
    119
Preston, James Blair 3
Preston, Katherine (Kate) 1, 3

Preston, Margaret (Maggie) 1, 3
Priest of Love, The (H. Moore)
    232
Prince John (England) 212, 213
Principles of Social
    Reconstruction (B. Russell)
    263, 264, 284
Pritchard, Colonel 170, 172
Pro-Boers, The (ed. Koss) 38
Proust, Marcel vii, xviii
'Prussian Officer, The'
    (Lawrence) 218, 219
Pterodamozels, The (R. C.
    Trevelyan) 266, 267
Puar, Tukoji Rao: see Dewas
    Senior, Maharaja of
Puar, Vikramsinha 178, 239–40,
    247–8
Puck of Pook's Hill (Kipling)
    123–4
Putnam, G. P. (publisher) 118
Puvis de Chavannes, Pierre;
    works by 72, 73
Pythian Odes (Pindar) viii

Quillery, Jules 215, 217
Qutb Minar (Delhi), described
    144

Rachmaninoff, Serge; work by
    318
Racine, Jean Baptiste 283
Rainbow, The (D. H. Lawrence)
    219, 250; suppression of
    231–2
Rambles and Recollections
    (Sleeman) 191, 192, 227
Rampur Fair, 102–3, 123
Rashid: see Khan, M. A. R.
Raverat, Gwen; work by 35
Red Cross 205, 231; in Egypt
    232–300 *passim*
Reddaway, W. F. 43–4, 99
Reeves, Amber; work by 134–5
Reid, Forrest xii, 42, *126–7*, 128,
    129, *136*, *172–3*, *187–8*, 200,
    207, 208, *217–18*, 225, 228,
    298–9; letter to EMF 188;
    works by 127, 128, 136,

Reid, Forrest—contd
171, 172, 173, 187, 207, 208,
225, 228, 299
Reinhardt, Max; works by 128,
129, 166
'Religious Conformity' (G. M.
Trevelyan) 63, 64
Reni, Guido 95
Resurrection (Tolstoy) 293, 294
Reventlow, Ernst zu; letter by
227, 228
Reward of Virtue, The (Reeves)
134, 135
Richard Jefferies (Thomas) 283,
284
Richards, Norah 226, 228, 240
Richards, P. E. 226, 228, 240
Richardson, Samuel 86
Ridley, Nicholas 131
Rimsky-Korsakov, Nikolai;
work by 319
Ring of the Nibelungen
(Wagner) 68, 92
Roberts, Lord 199
Roger Fry (Spalding) 129, 212
Rogers, Samuel 302
Rolland, Romain; works by 100,
226, 228, 307, 309
'Roman Anglais, Le' (de
Wyzewa) 117
Romance of Names, The
(Weekley) 219, 220
Romance of Words, The
(Weekley) 219, 220
Rooksnest (EMF's first home)
1–4
Rostand, Edmund; work by 106
Rothenstein, William 44, 105,
162, 177, 179, 320
'Rousbrugge' (Turner) 239, 240
Royal Academy of Art 57, 110,
140
Royal Commission on Public
Services in India 92
Rubens, Peter Paul 101; work
by 57, 58
Rügen, described 81
Ruskin, John; work by 37
Russell, Alys 86

Russell, Bertrand 265; works by
215, 263, 264, 283, 284
Russian Ballet 122, 136, 165,
305, 306
Russian, Childhood, A
(Aksanov) 283, 284
Russian Gentleman, A.
(Aksanov) 283, 284
Ruth: see Goldsmith, Ruth
Rutherford, Andrew 127, 129
Rutherford, James 127, 129, 207
Rutherford, William 127, 129,
298, 299
Rutter, Frank 250

Sabbatini, Amilcare 62
Saint-Saëns, Camille; work by
70, 71
Saleh, S. I. I. S. 183
Samson et Dalila (Saint-Saëns)
70–71
Samuel Rogers and His
Contemporaries (Clayden)
302
Sanchi, described, 169–70
San Gennaro, Festival of
(Gubbio) 53, 54
Sanger, Charles 62, 63, 256, 257,
284
Sassoon, Siegfried vii, xi, 206,
289–90, 292–4, 295,
300–301, 302–3, 305, 315,
316–17; and World War I
292–3, 294; comments on
other writers 294, 303;
letters to EMF 290, 294;
works by 294, 295–6, 303
Scarlatti, Alessandro 47, 48, 55,
306
Scenes of Clerical Life (G. Eliot)
4
Schenk, Herr: see Steinweg, D. J.
Schiller, J. C. 74, 75
Schreiner, Olive; work by 38
Schumann, Robert; works by
287, 318
'Scope of the Novel, The'
(Wells) 124
Scriabine, Aleksandre; work by

319
Seager, J. C. 4, 5
Searight, Kenneth 137, 140, 141, 238, 153–5, 253
Seeley, J. R.; work by 38
'Seizure of Letters in Calcutta, The' (news report) 114
Sencourt, Robert 245; journal of 245
Sense of the Past, A (H. James) 290
Sewell, R. B. S. 24
Shadow of a Titan (Wedgwood) 124, 127, 199
Shakespeare, William, 37, 89, 90, 97, 99, 100, 125; works by 97, 98, 140
Shalimar Gardens, described 192
Shall This War End German Militarism? (Angell) 215
Sharma, Nrusinh 177, 179, 180
Shaw, G. B. 35, 100, *236, 314, 315, 316; works by 212, 213, 266*
Shazad 241, 243, 270
Shelley, P. B. 86
Shelley (White) 86
Sheppard, J. T. 63, 64, 216; work by 128
Sher Shah 185
Sherston's Progress (Sassoon) 294
Shiffolds, The 60, 61
Shuttleworth, L. H. C. 229–30, 231, 236, 242, 253–4, 261, 262, 270, 285
Sidgwick and Jackson (publishers) 42, 112, 115, 116, 117
Sidgwick, Henry 69, 85
Siegfried's Journey (Sassoon) 303
Siloti, A. I. 318, 320
Silver Box, The (Galsworthy) 279, 280
Simla, described 157–9
Sinclair, May; work by 302
Singh, Sir Pratap 195, 198, 199
Sir Henry Wood (Pound) 213
Sitwell, Constance; EMF entertained by 192; work

by 193
Sitwell, Edith 194, 206
Sitwell, Henry; EMF entertained by 192
Sitwell, Osbert 194, 206
Si-ku-yi (Hsuan-Tsang) 182, 183
Sketch of Ancient Philosophy, A (Mayor) 30
Sketches in Italy and Greece (J. A. Symonds) 51, 52
Sleeman, W. H.; work by 191, 192, 227
Smith, R. B. 98, 138; EMF's host in India 174–5, 178, 186, 189–90
Smyth, Ethel; work by 318, 320
Social Fetich, The (Grove) 297, 298
Society, The: see Apostles
Society for Protection of Ancient Buildings 144, 145, 157
Sophocles 23
Sophocles (Jebb) 24, 25
South Kensington Museum: see Victoria and Albert Museum
South Wind (Douglas) 275–6, 314
Spartali, M. 195–6, 198, 199–200
Spencer, Herbert 162, 166
Spinoza, Benedict 272–3
Spirit of Man, The (Bridges) 248, 249
Spohr, Wilhelm 222, 223
Spring Song (Reid) 207
Sprott, W. J. H. ('Jack'; 'Sebastian') xii
Stallybrass, Oliver xviii
Stanford, Sir Charles; work by 318, 320
Steinweg, D. J. xv, 65, 66, 66–8, 73, 74, 75, 79, 80
Stephen, Caroline 43, 44
Stephen, Leslie 43, 44
Stephen, Thoby 43, 44
Stokoe, F. W. 112, 113, 212
Stones of Venice, The (Ruskin) 37

Storia do Mogor (Manucci) 109, 110

Story of an African Farm, The (Schreiner) 38

Strachey, Alix 284

Strachey, James 284

Strachey, Lytton 15, 63, 64, 98, 136, *208*, 230, 231, 234–5, 296; work by 128

Strachey, Oliver 284

Strachey, Philippa ('Pippa') 230, 231

Surprising Adventures of Sir Toady Lion, The (Crockett) 17, 18

Swift, Jonathan; epitaph of 303

Swinburne, Algernon 106, 152

Sydney-Turner, Saxon 234, 235

Sykes, Marianne 23

Symonds, J. A.; work by 51, 52

Symonds, Margaret; work by 51, 52

Synnot, Henrietta 115

Synnott, Inglis 3

Syrett, Netta; work by 207

Tabor, Mrs 39, 40

Tagore, Devendranath 195; work by 227, 228

Tagore, Rabindranath 179, 182, 183, 228; work by 183

Tennyson, Alfred, Lord 26, 27, 78

Terni, Enrico 276, *295–6*

Tesserete 124, *132–3*, 242

Thaïs (France) 78, 79

Theosophical Society 267, 295

Thomas, Edward 112, 283, 284; works by 283, 284

Thomas, P. H., 284

Thompson, E. V. 97–8, 105, 111, 113, 318

Thompson, Francis 219, 310, 312

Thomson, Sir Courtauld 235, 236, 301

Thomson, George H.; work by xviii–xix

Thornton, Henry, 1, 18

Thornton, Laura 1

Thornton, Marianne ('Monie'; EMF's great-aunt) 1, 3, 22, 41, 46

Thoughts on the War (Clutton-Brock) 207

Three Women (Syrett) 207

Times, The (London) 117, 124, 312

Tintoretto, Jacopo 310

'To Homer' (Keats) 248, 285, 286

'To Joanna' (Wordsworth) 90

Tolstoy, Leo 106; works by 108, 293, 294

Tonbridge School 2, 16, 25, 26, 29

Tovey, Donald 314, 315

Townsend, Sir Charles 240, 241

Tragedy of Nan (Masefield) 115, 116

Tragedy of Pompey (Masefield) 115, 116

Travelling Companion, The (Stanford) 318, 320

Travelling Companion, The (Anstey) 320

Trench, Herbert 98

Trevelyan, C. P. 215

Trevelyan, Elizabeth (Mrs R. C. Trevelyan) viii, 60, 61, 62, 314

Trevelyan, G. M. xvii, 38, 43, 60, 61, 160, 215, 230, 313; and Italian ambulance unit 225, 205; works by 39, 63, 64

Trevelyan, R. C. viii, ix, xii, xiii, 42, *59–63*, 215, 238, *266–7*, *272*, *283–4*, *294–6*, *314–15*, *315–16*; career of 60; in India *151–85 passim*; letter to V. Woolf 84; letters to EMF 84, 284; works by 266, 267, *314–15*, 283, 284, 295, 296

Treves, Sir Frederick; work by 144, 145, 198

'Trial of Witches' (Reid) 299

Turkey, in World War I 215,
254–5
Turner, George 150–51, 152,
156, 211
Turner, H. H. 238
Turner, Mary Borden (Mrs
George Turner) 152; work
by 211, 239, 240
Twixt Land & Sea Tales
(Conrad) 188

Ulster 42, 128, 131, 299; *see also*
Belfast
Ultimate Belief, The
(Clutton-Brock) 210
Union of Democratic Control
214, 215
Unwin, T. F. (publisher) 73–4
Upanishads 249
'Uses of History, The' (G. M.
Trevelyan) 36

Vaishnavism 167; *see also*
Hinduism, 'Mystery Plays'
Valassopoulo, George 259–60
Vanbrugh, Sir John; work by 63
Vaughan Williams, Margaret 62,
63
Vaughan Williams, Ralph 25, 63
Vedas 157, 194
Verdi, Giuseppe; works by 28,
59, 77
Verlaine, Paul; work by 101
Victoria University: *see*
Manchester, University of
Vicar of Wakefield (Goldsmith)
26, 27
Vicary, Frank 237–8, 302, 305,
319
Victoria, Queen 44, 107, 139,
213
Victoria and Albert Museum 45,
170
Vicky: *see* Puar, Vikramsinha
Vie de Michel Ange (Rolland)
100
'Villadom' (E. Garnett) 117
Village in the Jungle, The
(L. Woolf) 135–6
Virgil 13, 69, 72, 78

Vishnu 167, 184, 228, 284
Vita Nuova (Dante) 258, 259
Volos 266, 267
Vontade, Jacques (pseud.): *see*
Bulteau, A.
Vorticism 211–12
Voyage Out, The (V. Woolf)
219, 220, 223, 227, 228, 232

Wadia, A. S. N.; work by 208
Wagner, Richard; works by 59,
92–3
Waldstein, Charles 18
Walker, Thomas 177, 179
Walpole, Hugh 93–4, 115, 116,
304; works by 93–4
War and Peace (Tolstoy) 108
War Office 232
'War Vignettes' (Turner) 239,
240
War—The Offspring of Fear
(B. Russell) 215
War Service Tribunals 234
Ward, Mrs Humphry 160
Waterlow, Sydney 6, 28, 92–3,
105, 206, 222, 273, 313, 315
Wathen, Gerald 194, 198
Waugh, Alex; work by 298
W. B. Yeats (Reid) 225, 228
Wedd, Nathaniel 15, 25, 27, 28,
32–3, 39, 44–5
Wedgwood, Godfrey 241
Wedgwood, Hope 241
Wedgwood, Katherine
Euphemia ('Effy'): *see*
Farrer, Lady Katherine
Wellington (College) 199
Wells, H. G. 123, 124, 135, 200;
works by 123, 124, 251
West Hackhurst (home of Laura
Forster) xvii, 1, 2, 32–3, 60,
61, 248
Westminster Gazette, The
(London) 51, 52
Weston, G. B. 56
Weybridge: EMF and mother
move to 61
Weybridge Literary Society 61,
78, 113, 116

Wharton, Edith; work by 128
What Maisie Knew (H. James) 240
'What Our Fleet Has Done' (Balfour, letter) 228
Whichelo, Alice Clara: *see* Forster, Alice Clara
Whichelo, Charlotte ('Charlie') 242, 243
Whichelo, Georgiana ('Georgie' EMF's aunt) 1, 3, 176
Whichelo, Gerald (EMF's cousin) 242, 243, 244, 245, 256, 257
Whichelo, Harry (EMF's uncle) 4
Whichelo, Herbert (EMF's cousin) 242, 243
Whichelo, Henry Mayle (EMF's grandfather) 1, 3
Whichelo, Louisa (EMF's grandmother) 1, 2–3, 4–5, 6, 10, 13, 27, 40, 42, 44, 73, 75, 101, 116, 121; death of 42, 121
Whichelo, Mary Eleanor ('Nellie' EMF's aunt) 1, 3
Whichelo, Percy (EMF's cousin) 73, 74, 176, 177
Whichelo, Rosalie: *see* Alford Rosalie
White Peacock, The (Lawrence) 218, 219, 220, 222, 223, 250
Whitehead Morris (publishers) 307, 309
Whitman, Walt 222
Willcocks, Sir William; work by 308, 309
Wilhelm Tell (Schiller) 74, 75, 78
Wings of the Dove, The (H. James) 60
Winnington Ingram, A. F. (Bishop of London) 226, 228
Winston Churchill (R. Churchill) 131
Women of the Country (Bone) 207

Wonder That Was India, The (Basham) 105
Wood, Sir Henry 213
Wood, Joseph 25, 26
Wood, Lorna 260, 272, *301–2*
Wooden Horse, The (Walpole) *93–4*
Woodhouse, Violet Gordon 306
Woolley, L. H. G. 86
Woolf, Leonard *63–4*, *135–6*, 206, 224, 231, 234, 312, 313, 314, 315; work by 135–6
Woolf, Virginia x, 44, 64, 136, 206, 219, 223, 227, 228, *230–31*, *234–5*, 284, 313; comments on Henry James 284; health of 224; works by 219, 223, 220, 227, 228, 231, 284, 313
Wordsworth, William 89; work by 90
Working Men's Colleges (London) 41, 91–2, 157, 212, 214, 220
Worters, S. R. 15, 16, 17
Wyld, May 45, 46, 138, 143, 176, 179, 200; letter to PNF 143, 200; on *A Passage to India* 200
Wyzawa, Teodor de *116–17*

'Year of Naval Warfare, A' (zu Reventlow, letter) 228
Years of Childhood (Aksanov) 283
Yeats, W. B. 137; work by 136; F. Reid on 225, 226
Young, E. Hilton 98, 105, 111, 112, 113, 114, 121, 122, 225, 231; war service of 220–21, 225, 228
Young, Kathleen (Mrs Hilton Young) 98

Zaghlul, Saad, 312, 313, 315, 316
Ziloti: *see* Siloti, A. I.
Zola, Emile viii, 249
Zuleika Dobson (Beerbohm) 128